CULTURAL PLURALISM
AND MORAL KNOWLEDGE

CULTURAL PLURALISM AND MORAL KNOWLEDGE

Edited by

Ellen Frankel Paul, Fred D. Miller, Jr., and Jeffrey Paul

CAMBRIDGE
UNIVERSITY PRESS

Published by the Press Syndicate of the University of Cambridge
The Pitt Building, Trumpington Street, Cambridge CB2 1RP, England
40 West 20th Street, New York, NY 10011, USA
10 Stamford Road, Oakleigh, Melbourne, Victoria 3166, Australia

First published 1994

Printed in the United States of America

Library of Congress Cataloging-in-Publication Data

Cultural pluralism and moral knowledge / edited by Ellen Frankel Paul,
Fred D. Miller, Jr., and Jeffrey Paul.   p.   cm.
Includes bibliographical references and index.
ISBN 0-521-46614-8 (pbk.)
1. Pluralism (Social sciences) — Moral and ethical aspects.   2. Ethics.
I. Paul, Ellen Frankel.   II. Miller, Fred Dycus, 1944–
III. Paul, Jeffrey.
HM276.C85   1994
306–dc20   93-38126
CIP

ISBN 0-521-46614-8 paperback

The essays in this book have also been published,
without introduction and index, in the semiannual journal
Social Philosophy & Policy, Volume 11, Number 1,
which is available by subscription.

CONTENTS

INTRODUCTION

A distinctive view of value lies at the core of the cultural tradition of the West. Just as Western science has held that there are universal truths about the world, discoverable through reason and accessible in principle to people of all times and places, so Western philosophers such as Plato, Aristotle, and Kant have held that there are timeless moral truths, arising out of human nature and independent of the conventions of particular societies. This tradition acknowledges pluralism in the positive sense, but rejects it in the normative sense: it acknowledges the existence of a diversity of cultures and moral beliefs, but denies that the validity of beliefs and practices can vary across cultures.

A number of theorists have offered critiques of this ethical tradition,* while others have responded with vigorous defenses of universal truths. The philosophical issues underlying this controversy are the subject of the essays collected here. The discussions range from broad examinations of the relevance of cultural pluralism to morality, to studies of specific cultural practices. Some essays explore the relationship between pluralism and political theory; some contrast pluralism with relativism or distinguish it from reasonable disagreement. Others propose and defend a set of principles that apply to all societies, forming the foundation of a common moral system. Still others delve into questions of moral psychology, attempting to explain why people hold the values they do.

In the opening essay, "Explaining Moral Variety," Chandran Kukathas challenges the idea that differences in moral beliefs among various cultures cast serious doubts on the possibility of our gaining universal moral knowledge. The variety of beliefs and practices among different societies is taken as evidence that morality is to some extent shaped or determined by culture—with the implication that there may be severe limits to cross-cultural understanding and criticism. Kukathas argues that there is an alternative way of explaining moral variety and thus that the barriers to understanding among cultures may be less formidable than some have supposed. Drawing on Adam Smith's *Theory of Moral Sentiments*, he suggests that the role of sympathy in shaping people's beliefs can account for moral variety. The wellspring of morality is the human capacity to put oneself in the place of others, to take an interest in their interests. This natural sympathy leads us to want to be in harmony with those around

---

* Among them are Giambattista Vico, J. G. Hamann, J. G. von Herder, and other critics of the French Enlightenment; see Isaiah Berlin, "The Counter-Enlightenment," in his *Against the Current: Essays in the History of Ideas*, ed. Henry Hardy (New York: Viking Press, 1980).

us, to seek their approval and avoid their disapproval. This, in turn, leads us to converge on common standards of behavior, by which we judge our own actions and the actions of others. These standards arise in particular circumstances, and differences in the circumstances of different societies lead to the variety of moral beliefs and practices existing among cultures. Yet the fact that common standards arise out of the interactions of individuals suggests a way of overcoming cultural differences: as the members of different cultures interact, they may find that there are standards which they can all accept. Kukathas believes that this account reflects what we see going on as societies interact: cross-cultural criticism seldom leads to the wholesale abandonment of traditions, but it may well lead to their gradual modification over time.

Alan Gewirth defends a universal standard for cross-cultural criticism in his contribution to this volume, "Is Cultural Pluralism Relevant to Moral Knowledge?" He contends that there are certain fundamental rights to freedom and well-being that arise from the nature of human action itself and that therefore must be recognized in every culture. Gewirth's position is summed up in what he calls the Principle of Generic Consistency (PGC), which moves from each agent's recognition that he must have freedom and well-being if he is to act, to the generalization that all agents have rights to freedom and well-being. To deny this general claim would be inconsistent, Gewirth argues, since in effect one would be claiming both "I must have freedom and well-being" and "It is permissible that I not have freedom and well-being." The PGC, then, stands as a universal principle of human rights; and knowledge of the PGC counts as moral knowledge, accessible to all through a process of rational argument. Gewirth concludes by showing how the PGC can be applied to judge the beliefs and practices of various cultures, arguing that the principle imposes limits on how societies may treat individuals. In addition to prohibiting slavery and violence, the PGC calls for the institution of civil liberties, democratic processes, and certain forms of welfare provision.

Like Gewirth, John Kekes is interested in determining whether there are any values that bind people living under different cultures. As an advocate of moral pluralism, Kekes is committed to the thesis that there are many incommensurable, conflicting values, and that there is no single, authoritative standard for resolving value conflicts. Nevertheless, in his essay "Pluralism and the Value of Life," he contends that such conflicts may be reasonably resolved by appeal to the minimum requirements of human welfare. Like Gewirth's PGC, these requirements—the "primary values"—do not vary across cultures; they include physiological needs (e.g., for food and shelter), psychological needs (e.g., for companionship and hope), and social needs (e.g., for security and respect), all of which are necessary conditions for the pursuit of a good life. Any morally acceptable cultural tradition, Kekes argues, will include conventions which protect people in their pursuit of these primary values. Much of his essay is devoted to showing that these values should be conceived pluralistically, rather than along relativist or monist lines. The error of the relativist is his failure to recognize that the primary values provide a context-independent ground for resolving some conflicts among values. The error of the monist lies in his belief that primary values can provide an absolute, overriding standard. The primary values are of worth because they contribute to the realization of individual agents' conceptions of the good life; thus, if some agents judge that they have no hope of a good life, they may rightly reject the claims of primary values.

Charles Larmore agrees with Kekes that there is a plurality of fundamental values and conceptions of the good life, but Larmore's concern is to explore the connections between moral pluralism and political theory. His contribution to this volume, "Pluralism and Reasonable Disagreement," is an attempt to clarify pluralism's relationship to liberalism. Many theorists arrive at a liberal view after rejecting a monistic conception of value, under which society is organized to achieve a common goal or set of goals. Recognizing a plurality of incommensurable individual goals, such theorists regard pluralism as the ethical base of liberalism. Larmore rejects this view, arguing instead that the expectation of reasonable disagreement about values lies at the foundation of liberal political orders. Reasonable people tend to disagree about the nature of the good and about how they should conduct their lives, but liberalism seeks a minimal, core morality upon which all can agree. It seeks to outlaw certain kinds of harm and to accommodate disagreement by protecting the rights of individuals to make their own choices and pursue their own interests. Larmore concludes by distinguishing the acceptance of reasonable disagreement from a skeptical position, contending that failure to reach agreement need not compel us to suspend judgment on controversial moral issues.

Nicholas L. Sturgeon confronts the problem of disagreement from a slightly different perspective. In "Moral Disagreement and Moral Relativism," he asks whether widespread disagreements on moral questions that exist between cultures provide reasons for embracing moral relativism, the view that some disputes are unsettleable and that both sides in a dispute may in some sense be right. The moral relativist, Sturgeon argues, faces a dilemma. On the one hand, if he tries to reconcile opposing views to show that they do not really come into conflict, he winds up showing that the alleged disagreement was only apparent—thereby undermining the case for relativism. On the other hand, if he insists that both sides of a genuine disagreement can be right, he endorses a contradiction. To escape the contradiction, he is driven toward nihilism—that is, toward the view that the opposing positions are both mistaken, that on some issues there is no moral truth to be had. In the course of the essay, Sturgeon distinguishes several varieties of relativism and analyzes the positions of some contemporary theorists, examining how each handles the relativist's dilemma. He suggests, ultimately, that while relativism may be a reasonable response to cross-cultural differences in taste or aesthetic judgment, it is not a reasonable response to moral disagreement.

While Sturgeon considers relativism as a way of accounting for disagreement, Ernest Sosa considers it as a way of accounting for the tentative character of many of our moral judgments. In "Moral Relativism, Cognitivism, and Defeasible Rules," Sosa addresses a longstanding problem in moral theory: how to understand normative or evaluative claims made within a naturalistic framework. Naturalism denies that there is a fundamental normative realm; it holds that talk about what we ought to do must be understood without reference to special normative concepts or properties. Thus, notes Sosa, many theories have viewed moral language as prescriptive, with moral utterances playing the role of imperatives, or as emotive, with utterances expressing favor or opposition. But prescriptions fail to capture the prima facie character of some moral beliefs, and while emotivism fares better in this regard, it faces other problems. The emotivist confronts the problem of normative fallibility: since his judgments take the form of emotional responses rather than propositions, it is hard to see how he could entertain doubts about them or be led to revise them. Moral relativism, Sosa points out, offers a third way of understanding moral language. The relativist holds that to say an action is wrong is to say it is wrong according to a moral code, where moral codes may vary from society to society, as do legal systems or rules of etiquette. To capture the prima facie element of moral judgments, the relativist assumes that moral codes will contain weighted rules which may be taken as more forceful in some circumstances than in others. Yet Sosa questions whether any set of rules can be made flexible enough to handle the wide range of judgments and choices we must make every day, and he suggests that the relativist may need to revise his view along emotivist lines: conceiving of moral codes not in terms of rules but in terms of claims expressing tentative approval or disapproval.

Joseph Raz critiques relativism on different grounds, challenging the very idea that moral truth can be a function of the society one lives in. In "Moral Change and Social Relativism," Raz acknowledges the existence of a diversity of cultural traditions, but rejects the idea that these traditions determine what people ought to do or how they ought to live. The traditions and practices of a society may change radically over time, but morality itself, Raz contends, is not susceptible to radical change. His argument rests on the claim that, to be intelligible, a change in a moral truth must be one we can account for in terms of some moral principle — a principle which encompasses the new truth and explains why the old truth no longer holds. In such cases, we are forced, in effect, to apply some existing principle to changing circumstances (as when, for example, new medical technologies force us to expand or reinterpret a previously held principle of bioethics). But a truly radical moral change would be one which no formerly held principle would survive, and the possibility of such a change would make morality unintelligible. Since Raz believes morality is intelligible, he denies the possibility of moral change, and therefore denies that moral truths can be socially relative. Yet he maintains that morality is in some sense temporal, in that moral truths must be accessible to people at particular times and in particular circumstances.

While Raz and a number of other contributors discuss the possibility of changes in morality over time and from culture to culture, Wallace I. Matson focuses on changes in moral beliefs that have actually occurred in the modern period. His essay "The Expiration of Morality" traces the development of moral conduct from "coping" behaviors practiced by some animals through "low" and "high" stages of human morality. An animal copes, Matson writes, when it interacts with its environment in way that preserves its form. Some animals live in groups whose members develop cooperation as a way of coping, and such groups share some common characteristics. They are organized hierarchically; their members have "duties" to cooperate in nourishing their young and protecting the group from outside attack; and these members feel and manifest outrage against those who fail to fulfill these "duties." These characteristics of animal groups form the core of "low" morality in humans, and the development of language adds two new duties to the list: truth-telling and promise-keeping. Moreover, the faculty of imagination makes it possible for humans to conceive of gods, and with religion comes "high" morality, a set of additional duties, varying from culture to culture, thought to be owed to some higher power. The distinctive twist of the Western, Judeo-Christian tradition, Matson notes, is that it blurs the distinction between low and high morality by characterizing low-moral duties as commands of God, who punishes transgressors. The decline of belief in God in the West has led to the "expiration" Matson refers to in his title, as the precepts of low morality are eroded or abandoned along with religious high morality.

As the divine-command view of morality has declined in the modern period, secular theorists have proposed new ways of understanding the moral judgments we make. In "Common Sense and First Principles in Sidgwick's *Methods*," David O. Brink examines the work of one of these theorists, the British philosopher Henry Sidgwick (1838–1900). Sidgwick recognized a relationship of dependence between (1) our intuitive, common-sense moral judgments and (2) moral first principles (e.g., utilitarian principles) arrived at through dialectical argument. He believed that first principles could provide evidence to support common-sense judgments, but that the relation could not run the other way. But Brink argues that Sidgwick failed to distinguish between metaphysical and epistemic dependence. He agrees with Sidgwick on the metaphysical issue: that is, he agrees that particular moral truths are asymmetrically dependent on true first principles. However, he disagrees on the epistemic issue: he suggests that justification between first principles and particular beliefs can be bi-directional. Our justification for accepting a particular common-sense judgment consists in its being subsumed and explained by a suitable first principle, and what makes a first principle suitable is, in part, its ability to explain various particular moral judgments. Brink concludes by showing how Sidgwick's work can help explain why common-sense judgments are found to be generally reliable as guides for action.

Sidgwick thought we should evaluate moral judgments in terms of more general principles, but other theorists have offered different methods. David Hume (1711–1776) believed we could refine our judgments by taking a "general point of view," making allowances for limits in our knowledge and compensating for individual prejudices. Geoffrey Sayre-McCord explores Hume's position in his contribution to this volume, "On Why Hume's 'General Point of View' Isn't Ideal—and Shouldn't Be." The "general point of view" can be interpreted as the perspective of an ideal observer, one who is omniscient and impartially sympathetic to all people; but Sayre-McCord argues that this is not Hume's understanding. On Hume's view, we should judge an agent's character and actions based on the effects they tend to have on those who are associated with the agent. The focus on tendencies lends stability to our evaluations, since it allows us to pass consistent judgments on actions and character traits whose actual effects might vary considerably according to circumstance. The focus on those who are associated with the agent makes the "general point of view" accessible to people in the real world—people with imperfect knowledge and limited capacities for sympathy. Sayre-McCord defends his interpretation of Hume by addressing a number of arguments in favor of an ideal-observer view and by drawing an analogy between Hume's accounts of moral and aesthetic judgments.

In addition to justifying our evaluations, Hume's theory attempts to provide a psychological account of why we make the judgments we do; this question and related issues in moral psychology are the focus of Gilbert Harman's essay "Explaining Value." Harman surveys attempts at explaining people's values, beginning with Hume's and Adam Smith's discussions of sympathy, and moving to more recent philosophical discussions. He offers a lengthy treatment of contemporary examples involving the sacrifice of one person to save the lives of many others, noting that people's reactions to such cases vary. A number of theories seek to explain why such sacrifice is permissible in some cases but not in others, and Harman looks at each of these in turn. The principle of double effect distinguishes between harms that are intended and those that are merely foreseen as side effects of an action; the theory of positive and negative duties recognizes a difference in strength between the two, allowing for the violation of weaker positive duties in some instances; the deflection principle allows that, where harm is unavoidable, it may be deflected from a larger to a smaller number of people. Harman suggests that each of these theories can provide insight into people's moral evaluations, and he maintains that philosophers have much to contribute to empirical investigations into moral attitudes—investigations which could also draw on the resources of psychology, sociobiology, economic legal theory, sociology, and history.

The final essay, Bernard Boxill's "The Culture of Poverty," looks at attempts to explain the values of a specific group—America's urban poor—and the impact those values may have on people's economic situation. Boxill assesses the theory that some people stay poor because their culture—the "slum culture" or "culture of poverty"—keeps them poor. The theory holds that the culture of poverty emerges within a larger society which stresses the accumulation of wealth, and that the frustrations many poor people experience in such a society lead them to develop a distinctive set of attitudes and values, including feelings of helplessness and resignation, and an inability to control impulses and defer gratification. Attempts to eliminate the culture of poverty by providing opportunities to the poor are, on this view, bound to fail, since the culture itself discourages attempts to take advantage of opportunities. Critics of the culture-of-poverty theory object that the values of the poor are merely adaptations of the values of mainstream society, and that programs to reduce or eliminate poverty by providing opportunities may therefore achieve some success. Boxill examines these criticisms, suggesting that the culture of poverty may involve abandoning, rather than adapting, mainstream institutions such as traditional family life and the pursuit of careers. He concludes that the culture of poverty comprises an uneasy mix of both mainstream and nonmainstream values, and that the prospects for its elimination, while far from promising, are not as bleak as some theorists have believed.

As societies become more pluralistic, and as cultural issues become increasingly divisive, moral philosophy needs to take account of the diversity of cultural traditions. These twelve essays offer fresh insights into pluralism and its implications for our understanding of human values and institutions.

ACKNOWLEDGMENTS

This volume could not have been produced without the help of a number of individuals at the Social Philosophy and Policy Center, Bowling Green State University. Among them are Mary Dilsaver, Terrie Weaver, Maureen Kelley, and Carrie-Ann Lynch.

The editors would like to extend special thanks to Executive Manager Kory Swanson, for offering invaluable administrative support; to Publication Specialist Tamara Sharp, for attending to innumerable day-to-day details of the book's preparation; and to Managing Editor Harry Dolan, for providing dedicated assistance throughout the editorial and production process.

CONTRIBUTORS

Chandran Kukathas is Senior Lecturer in Politics at University College of the University of New South Wales. He is the author of *Hayek and Modern Liberalism* (1989) and coauthor of *Rawls: A Theory of Justice and Its Critics* (with Philip Pettit, 1990). He is coeditor of the recently founded *Journal of Political Philosophy*.

Alan Gewirth is E. C. Waller Distinguished Service Professor of Philosophy at the University of Chicago. He is a fellow of the American Academy of Arts and Sciences and a past president of the American Philosophical Association and the American Society for Political and Legal Philosophy. He has held two Rockefeller Foundation fellowships, two National Endowment for the Humanities fellowships, and a Guggenheim fellowship. His books include *Marsilius of Padua and Medieval Political Philosophy* (1951), *Reason and Morality* (1978), and *Human Rights: Essays on Justification and Applications* (1982). He is currently working on a sequel to *Reason and Morality* titled *The Community of Rights*.

John Kekes is Professor of Philosophy and Public Policy at the State University of New York at Albany. He is the author of *A Justification of Rationality* (1976), *The Nature of Philosophy* (1980), *The Examined Life* (1988), *Moral Tradition and Individuality* (1989), *Facing Evil* (1990), and *The Morality of Pluralism* (1993).

Charles Larmore is Professor of Philosophy and Chairman of the Philosophy Department at Columbia University. He is the author of *Patterns of Moral Complexity* (1987) and *Modernité et morale* (1993), and an editor of the *Journal of Philosophy*. In addition to his work in political theory and in seventeenth-century philosophy (focusing on skepticism), he is now engaged in writing a book on the philosophical contributions of Romanticism.

Nicholas L. Sturgeon is Professor of Philosophy and currently Chair of the Sage School of Philosophy at Cornell University. He has published a number of articles on moral realism and on related metaphysical and epistemological issues in ethics. He is also interested in the history of British moral philosophy in the seventeenth and eighteenth centuries, and has written on Butler and on Hume.

Ernest Sosa is Romeo Elton Professor in the Philosophy Department of Brown University. He has been editor of *Philosophy and Phenomenological*

Research since 1983 and of *Cambridge Studies in Philosophy* since 1990. He has published papers in epistemology and metaphysics and is author of the collection *Knowledge and Perspective* (1991).

Joseph Raz is Professor of the Philosophy of Law at Oxford University and Fellow of Balliol College, Oxford. He is a fellow of the British Academy and an honorary foreign member of the American Academy of Arts and Sciences. His books include *The Authority of Law* (1979), *The Concept of a Legal System* (1980), *The Morality of Freedom* (1986), and *Practical Reason and Norms* (1990).

Wallace I. Matson is Professor of Philosophy, Emeritus, at the University of California, Berkeley. He has written books and articles on the history of philosophy, philosophy of mind, philosophy of religion, Spinoza, and social philosophy.

David O. Brink is Associate Professor of Philosophy at the Massachusetts Institute of Technology. His research interests are in ethical theory, history of ethics, political philosophy, and legal theory. He is the author of *Moral Realism and the Foundation of Ethics* (1989).

Geoffrey Sayre-McCord is Associate Professor of Philosophy at the University of North Carolina at Chapel Hill. A coeditor of the journal *Noûs*, he has written on a number of topics related to moral realism, contractarian moral theory, and the history of ethics. His edited collection *Essays on Moral Realism* was published in 1988.

Gilbert Harman is Professor of Philosophy at Princeton University, where he has taught since 1963. He is the author of *Thought* (1973), *The Nature of Morality: An Introduction to Ethics* (1977), *Change in View: Principles of Reasoning* (1986), and numerous articles. He serves on the editorial boards of several journals, including *Behavioral and Brain Sciences*, *Philosophy and Phenomenological Research*, and *Social Philosophy & Policy*. He is co-director (with George Miller) of the Princeton University Cognitive Science Laboratory and is head of Princeton's Undergraduate Program in Cognitive Studies. His current research interests include explaining why people value what they value, moral objectivity, the nature of consciousness, the role of practical considerations in scientific reasoning, and the interpretation of probability.

Bernard Boxill is Professor of Philosophy at the University of North Carolina at Chapel Hill. A previous contributor to *Social Philosophy & Policy*, his essays have also appeared in *Philosophy & Public Affairs*, *Ethics*, *Social Theory and Practice*, *Philosophical Forum*, and other journals. A second edition of his book *Blacks and Social Justice* was published in 1992.

EXPLAINING MORAL VARIETY*

By Chandran Kukathas

What wide difference, therefore, in the sentiments of morals, must be found between civilized nations and Barbarians, or between nations whose characters have little in common? How shall we pretend to fix a standard for judgments of this nature?

David Hume, "A Dialogue"[1]

Reflection on the variety of forms of social life has long been a source of moral skepticism. The thought that there are many radically different social systems, each of which colors the way its members think about moral and political questions, has been thought by many moral philosophers to undermine confidence in our belief that our way of looking at— or even posing—these questions is the correct one.[2] The fact of cultural variety is held to reduce, if not eliminate altogether, the possibility of moral criticism of the practices of other societies. This thought is not a recent one; it is implicit, for example, in an observation made in David Hume's "A Dialogue," when he writes:

There are no manners so innocent or reasonable, but may be rendered odious or ridiculous, if measured by a standard, unknown to the persons; especially, if you employ a little art or eloquence, in aggravating some circumstances, and extenuating others, as best suits the purpose of your discourse.[3]

Moreover, he adds that "[a]ll these artifices may easily be retorted on you,"[4] suggesting that cross-cultural criticism is a risky enterprise.

* I would like to thank Brian Beddie, William Maley, Ellen Paul, Philip Pettit, and John Tomasi for their detailed and helpful comments on an earlier draft of this essay.

[1] David Hume, "A Dialogue," in Hume, *Enquiries concerning Human Understanding and concerning the Principles of Morals*, ed. L. A. Selby-Bigge, rev. P. H. Nidditch (Oxford: Clarendon Press, 1975), p. 333.

[2] This thought is raised directly by the philosopher David McNaughton in his *Moral Vision: An Introduction to Ethics* (Oxford: Blackwell, 1988), p. 147. The most influential philosophical treatment of this topic in recent years is probably John Mackie's *Ethics: Inventing Right and Wrong* (Harmondsworth: Penguin, 1978).

[3] Hume, "A Dialogue," p. 330.

[4] *Ibid.* Whether or not this reflects a thoroughgoing moral skepticism in Hume's thinking is, of course, another question. My own inclination is to accept David Norton's account

So even when not tempted down the path to moral skepticism, philosophers struck by the fact of cultural diversity have been induced to take great pains to stress the importance of toleration of cultural differences. Thus, Charles Taylor, for example, suggests that we accept a "presumption of equal worth" of cultures as an appropriate opening moral stance.[5] And many others have reflected on the difficulties that must be confronted when practicing cultural toleration means condoning intolerable practices.[6]

Cultural variety may be thought, then, to pose serious problems for moral theory, since it has thrown into question the possibility of moral criticism, and indeed the possibility of any sort of universal moral rationality. If moral systems are culturally shaped or determined, it may not even be possible to compare moral values. This thought appears to be implicit in the recent development of John Rawls's political philosophy insofar as he has abandoned his search for universal moral principles and recast his theory of justice as an attempt to articulate the principles of political justice appropriate only for modern democratic societies such as the United States.[7]

The purpose of this essay is to argue that cultural diversity is not the problem it is often taken to be.[8] It does not preclude the possibility of moral criticism or of developing universal moral standards. Nor does it make it impossible to compare moral values or to acquire moral knowledge. Central to this argument are an account of the meaning of culture and an account of the nature of moral variety. The case I wish to put is that once the nature of cultural diversity or pluralism is properly understood, it will not appear to be the problem for moral theory it is sometimes made out to be. This will become clearer if we can find an explanation for moral variety which shows why it arises and indicates why this need not issue in moral isolationism. I will suggest that such an account is available in Adam Smith's moral theory.

---

of Hume as a common-sense moralist. See Norton, *David Hume: Common-Sense Moralist, Sceptical Metaphysician* (Princeton: Princeton University Press, 1982).

[5] Charles Taylor, *Multiculturalism and "The Politics of Recognition,"* with commentary by Amy Gutmann, Steven C. Rockefeller, Michael Walzer, and Susan Wolf (Princeton: Princeton University Press, 1992), p. 72.

[6] One of the most important recent works addressing this problem is Will Kymlicka's *Liberalism, Community, and Culture* (Oxford: Clarendon Press, 1989).

[7] On the development of Rawls's thought and the move away from universalism, see Richard Arneson, "Introduction [to a Symposium on Rawlsian Theory of Justice: Recent Developments]," *Ethics*, vol. 99, no. 4 (July 1989), pp. 695–710.

[8] Some writers in the so-called "realist school" have also tried to defend this line over the last ten years or so. See, for example, David Wiggins, "Truth, Invention, and the Meaning of Life," in Geoffrey Sayre-McCord, ed., *Essays on Moral Realism* (Ithaca and London: Cornell University Press, 1988), pp. 127–65, where it is argued that the element of "invention" noncognitivists have identified in morality is something which can be accommodated by a realist moral theory.

The argument is offered here in three sections. In the first, I look at the question of the nature of culture as it bears on morality and suggest that there is not as much *cultural* conflict as might appear. Here I draw on the writings of T. S. Eliot on culture, and take issue with Alasdair MacIntyre's arguments concerning the incommensurability of rival cultural traditions. In the second, I turn to the problem of explaining moral variety and try to show what Smith has to offer. And in the final section, I attempt to explain why the nature of culture and the nature of moral variety should leave us optimistic about the possibility of cross-cultural moral criticism, and of developing some universal moral standards.

I. THE NATURE OF CULTURE

In how many circumstances would an Athenian and a French man of merit certainly resemble each other? Good sense, knowledge, wit, eloquence, humanity, fidelity, truth, justice, courage, temperance, constancy, dignity of mind: These you have all omitted; in order to insist only on the points, in which they may, by accident, differ.[9]

Much recent writing in moral and political philosophy has emphasized the significance of cultural diversity as a feature of the modern world. We might consider three examples. The first is a paper by the British political scientist Bhiku Parekh, reflecting upon the Rushdie affair. Soon after its publication in 1989, Salman Rushdie's novel *The Satanic Verses* was condemned as a work deeply offensive to Islam. The Ayatollah Khomeini issued a death sentence for Rushdie and, in Britain, a ban on the book was proposed by certain Muslim groups. Parekh reads the conflict, between the supporters of Rushdie and the Muslims who criticize and want to punish him, as representative of a wider conflict between different ways: "Rushdie thus stands at the centre of such large battles as those between Christianity and Islam, secularism and fundamentalism, Europe and its ex-colonies, the host society and its immigrants, the post and premodernists, art and religion, and between scepticism and faith."[10] The whole affair raises questions about "how to forge common values out of a welter of conflicting moral systems, how much diversity a society can accommodate without losing its cohesion," and so on.[11]

The second example comes from the work of the American philosopher Iris Marion Young in her book *Justice and the Politics of Difference*. Out of the Enlightenment, Young argues, came a revolutionary conception of

---

[9] Hume, "A Dialogue," pp. 333–34.

[10] Bhiku Parekh, "The Rushdie Affair: Research Agenda for Political Philosophy," *Political Studies*, vol. 38, no. 4 (December 1990), pp. 695–709, at p. 696.

[11] *Ibid.*, pp. 708–9.

humanity and society which regarded all people as equal. Its ideals of liberty and equality inspired movements against oppression and domination, and swept away norms defining rights and obligations on the basis of group membership (of different races, classes, religions, or sexes). Yet while this is all very well, the ideal of "liberation as the elimination of group difference" has become questionable: "The very success of political movements against differential privilege and political equality has generated movements of group specificity and cultural pride."[12] Young's book, indeed, offers a sustained critique of the moral ideal of justice, which she sees as resting on an ideal of assimilation.

The third example is the argument of Will Kymlicka that cultural communities, such as those of "indigenous peoples," ought to be accorded special protections by the law, so that their culture is not undermined. If a "cultural structure" is weakened by external influences, this may be severely damaging to the individuals who live within it, since their capacity to make meaningful choices may be diminished. The task for liberals, "in every country," is to find a way "to liberalize a cultural community without destroying it."[13]

These examples illustrate two kinds of concern about cultural diversity which are prevalent in contemporary discussions. The first is a concern about the existence of fundamental differences — and of moral conflicts — of a very deep kind in modern societies. The differences between Islam and Christianity provide a prime example of this conflict; the differences between the practices of the more remote and isolated or *traditional* Aboriginal societies in Australia and those of the European mainstream provide another. The second is a concern about the existence of conflicts between the values of different groups within society seeking to differentiate or distinguish themselves from the mainstream. Hispanics and ethnic immigrant minorities within the United States are examples of such groups, which share with the wider society a certain cultural inheritance but which nonetheless want to see themselves as culturally distinct.

It would be mistaken to think that there are not some real — and difficult — issues here. Where cultural differences prevail, moral conflicts, it seems, tend to arise. Yet it is worth asking at this point what it means to say that *cultural* differences exist, and how far differences do exist. We should begin by asking: What is (a) culture?[14]

Bernard Williams suggests that a culture is a "social world," and in recognizing that human beings cannot live without a culture, and that there

---

[12] Iris Marion Young, *Justice and the Politics of Difference* (Princeton: Princeton University Press, 1990), p. 157.

[13] Kymlicka, *Liberalism, Community, and Culture*, p. 170.

[14] There is, of course, a considerable sociological and anthropological literature on culture. Some of this is discussed in Michael Carrithers, *Why Humans Have Cultures: Explaining Anthropology and Social Diversity* (Oxford and New York: Oxford University Press, 1992).

are many cultures, we must see that there are many social worlds in which human beings must find their way around.[15] Kymlicka, however, offers a more substantial account, suggesting that culture should be defined "in terms of the existence of a viable community of individuals with a shared heritage (language, history, etc.)"[16] Yet we come closer still to understanding what a culture is if we recognize T. S. Eliot's contention that a culture is a "way of life."[17] Eliot's point is that culture is "not merely the sum of several activities."[18] To be sure, in every culture there are distinctive activities: all cultures produce art, display customs and habits, and practice some religion. But there is more to culture than that:

> [C]ulture is made visible in their [i.e., a people's] arts, in their social system, in their habits and customs, in their religion. But these things added together do not constitute the culture, though we often speak for convenience as if they did. These things are simply the parts into which a culture can be anatomised, as a human body can. But just as a man is something more than an assemblage of the various constituent parts of his body, so a culture is more than the assemblage of its arts, customs, and religious beliefs.[19]

Yet if it is true that the different parts of a culture cannot exist in isolation, it is no less true that the culture itself cannot do so. Indeed, while we may be able to distinguish different cultures in a general way, this does not mean that we can point to where one culture begins and another ends. We can, as Eliot suggests, speak, for example, of "European culture," but its boundaries cannot be fixed: "European culture has an area, but no definite frontiers: and you cannot build Chinese walls."[20] It would be a mistake to "consider the culture of Europe simply as the sum of a number of unrelated cultures in the same area"; it would be no less a mistake to "separate the world into quite unrelated cultural groups."[21] There is no absolute line that can be drawn between East and West, between Europe and Asia.

This is not to deny the existence of cultural variety, or indeed the depth of the differences between some ways of life. Muslim communities in urban Malaysia are very different from communities in rural Bowling Green, Ohio. But it would be a mistake to think they have nothing in common. This is not because they might share superficial things in com-

---

[15] Bernard Williams, *Ethics and the Limits of Philosophy* (London: Fontana/Collins, 1985), p. 150.

[16] Kymlicka, *Liberalism, Community, and Culture*, p. 168.

[17] T. S. Eliot, *Notes towards the Definition of Culture* (London: Faber, 1948), p. 41.

[18] *Ibid.*

[19] *Ibid.*, p. 120.

[20] *Ibid.*, p. 62.

[21] *Ibid.*, p. 121.

mon (like access to U.S. television sitcoms). It is rather that, at a deeper
level, they would share some common influences. For example, insofar
as Christianity and Islam share a certain heritage, these two communities
would have in common religious conceptions whose similarities neither
may be aware of. This is not to suggest that the two cultures are closely
related, though they have in common with each other more than either
shares with, say, the culture of the aboriginal people of New Zealand, the
Maori. The crucial point, however, is that they are not entirely unrelated.
And, arguably, many cultures have come to have more in common as
they have come into contact with one another. For example, Maori culture is held to be very strongly nonindividualist, with groups and their
welfare regarded as the prime values and individuals finding their identity in the group whose ends they exist to serve. Yet the advent of European settlers, by making the option of leaving the group real, brought
about a significant move away from the collective orientation of the
Maori — even before the influences of European religion and custom were
felt.[22]

A certain unity of culture is always to be found among people who
live together and speak the same language, "because speaking the same
language means thinking, and feeling, and having emotions rather differently from people who use a different language."[23] Yet, as Eliot suggests, "the cultures of different peoples do affect each other"; and "in the
world of the future it looks as if every part of the world would affect every other part."[24] The fact that we can distinguish separate cultures does
not mean that we can isolate them. The idea of an *uncontaminated* culture
existing in a single village or a *self-contained* national culture is absurd insofar as it implies that a culture can exist other than in relation to others.[25]

Cultures must be seen, then, as distinguishable ways of life which are
the product of the interaction of individuals within cultures and among
cultures. Because they are the product of interaction, and are subject to
numerous influences, cultures are also mutable. And changes over the
years may be profound: the members of a cultural community may grow
to have more in common with the culture of their neighbors than with
that of distant ancestors. A "fully individuable culture," as Williams puts
it, is at best a rare thing: "cultures, subcultures, fragments of cultures,
constantly meet one another and exchange and modify practices and attitudes."[26]

[22] See Richard Mulgan, *Maori, Pakeha, and Democracy* (Auckland: Oxford University
Press, 1989), p. 64.

[23] Eliot, *Notes towards the Definition of Culture*, pp. 120–21.

[24] *Ibid.*, p. 121.

[25] For an anthropologist's view rejecting the possibility of cultural isolation, see Carrithers, *Why Humans Have Cultures*, esp. ch. 2 and pp. 24 and 118.

[26] Williams, *Ethics and the Limits of Philosophy*, p. 158.

These points about the nature of culture are worth making because it has been argued that there are severe problems of communication across cultures. There are problems of translatability of concepts or notions, as well as problems of commensurability of standards or values. These problems, in turn, create serious obstacles to the development of any kind of universal rational moral discourse. This argument has been put most vigorously by Alasdair MacIntyre, and it is worth examining because it plays an important role in his critique of modernity and of modern moral theory.

The view MacIntyre wishes to reject, in the first instance, is the view most commonly associated with Donald Davidson, who asserts that there are no insuperable problems of interpretation and translation between languages or "conceptual schemes." Conceptual schemes cannot turn out to be wholly or radically incommensurable. Davidson's argument is an important one, not least because moral philosophers like David McNaughton have appealed to it to try to show that the commensurability of all conceptual schemes implies that different moral schemes cannot be incommensurable.[27] MacIntyre, however, is unimpressed by Davidson's argument, largely because it only denies the possibility of "radical" incommensurability. MacIntyre is quite prepared to concede this point on the grounds that anyone would accept that "there will always be something in common between any two languages or any two sets of thoughts."[28] But any stronger claim is less tenable.

For MacIntyre, the intimate connection between language and communal belief creates serious obstacles to translation. This is because cultures can be very different—so much so that they cannot be adequately characterized, let alone understood, without actually living in them for a length of time.[29] To understand their languages requires total immersion. But to go further, to translate a language's statements into another language, is to bring down further problems. Implicit in the terms of reference and classification of a linguistic community are substantive criteria of evaluation or standards of truth and rationality. To translate into the language of a very different tradition of beliefs poses enormous difficulties because the substantive import of a name or a term of classification may be lost in the move from one tradition-laden language to another. A different, but no less disturbing, difficulty emerges, MacIntyre argues, in attempts to translate from a "language-in-use" (or the language of a particular moral community) into one of the "international languages of modernity" (such as that of contemporary Western *intellectual* discourse).

[27] McNaughton, *Moral Vision*, pp. 152–54.

[28] Alasdair MacIntyre, *Whose Justice? Which Rationality?* (Notre Dame: University of Notre Dame Press, 1988), p. 371.

[29] *Ibid.*, p. 374.

Because the languages of late-twentieth-century modernity make only "minimal presuppositions in respect of possibly rival belief systems," and truth is "assimilated, so far as possible, to warranted assertibility, and reasonableness, so far as possible, is relativized to social content," when texts are translated from traditions with substantive criteria of truth and rationality, they are presented in a way which neutralizes the conceptions of truth and rationality and the historical context.[30] Translation in this case would produce a text which would not be recognized by the audience for whom the original was intended.

This argument is the basis of MacIntyre's contention that rival traditions and cultures are much less accessible to our understanding than we think. The "belief in its ability to understand everything from human culture and history, no matter how alien," he argues, "is itself one of the defining beliefs of the culture of modernity."[31] But the translations generated by modern discourse have, in his view, generally presented misunderstandings of tradition. The fact modern discourse has not been able to grasp is that "there may be traditional modes of social, cultural and intellectual life which are as such inaccessible to it and to its translators."[32]

MacIntyre's argument is important because he uses his claims about the problems of understanding between rival traditions or cultures to support his contention that rival moral traditions are also essentially incomparable. It is simply not true, according to MacIntyre, that there are standards of rationality adequate for the evaluation of rival answers to moral questions:

> [W]hat those problems are, how they are to be formulated and addressed, and how, if at all, they may be resolved will vary not only with the historical, social, and cultural situation of the persons whose problems these are but also with the history of belief and attitude of each particular person up to the point at which he or she finds these problems inescapable.[33]

The answer will depend on who you are and how you understand yourself. But there are no "tradition-independent standards of argument" to which an appeal might be made.[34]

The basis of this contention may, however, turn out to be very weak if we examine MacIntyre's arguments about culture and comparability more closely, particularly in the light of Eliot's understanding of the na-

---

[30] Ibid., p. 384.
[31] Ibid., p. 385.
[32] Ibid., p. 387.
[33] Ibid., p. 393.
[34] Ibid., p. 403.

ture of culture. If we begin with the criticism of Davidson, we can see that MacIntyre has a point: the fact that "radical" incommensurability between cultures or conceptual schemes may be ruled out does not pose any serious problem to someone who concedes minimal or trivial comparability. The question MacIntyre has asked is, How comparable are rival cultural traditions? — and his answer is, Not very. Yet we can question whether or not he is right on this point, if we consider the extent to which cultures are interrelated. Many rival cultural traditions, while superficially different, share common ancestries or origins. If we look to the rival cultures of Europe, for example, the Christian heritage provides a considerable source of cultural unity. It is not merely a matter of shared religious faith; as Eliot put it, through Christianity

> we trace the evolution of our arts, through it we have our conception of Roman Law which has done so much to shape the Western World, through it we have our conceptions of private and public morality. And through it we have our common standards of literature, in the literatures of Greece and Rome. The Western world has its unity in this heritage, in Christianity and in the ancient civilisations of Greece, Rome and Israel, from which, owing to two thousand years of Christianity, we trace our descent.[35]

To the extent that Christianity has spread beyond Europe, we can say that this inheritance has been embraced by a diversity of peoples, from black South Africa to the Philippines, who now hold in common some very fundamental ideas and beliefs. A similar point could be made about the impact of Islam, which finds adherents in regions as diverse as Egypt, Bosnia, and Indonesia.

Even when cultural traditions have their roots in rival religious conceptions, the extent of incomparability of their different ideas is reduced by the extent to which there has been a history of interaction of religious traditions. Again, the cases of Islam and Christianity come to mind, since these rival traditions at once define themselves in opposition to one another and yet share a common philosophical inheritance. If one looks at the matter through the history of Islam, for example, it becomes clear that Muslim contact through conquest and expansion with diverse cultures resulted in Muslim appropriation and development of different intellectual heritages. The integration of the philosophical legacies of Greece, India, and Iran contributed to the cosmopolitan character of Islamic civilization. And, as Azim Nanji explains, Christian and Jewish scholars, familiar with these legacies, "played a crucial mediating role as 'translators', particularly since they were also aware that the moral disposition of Muslims, like theirs, was shaped by common monotheistic

---

[35] Eliot, *Notes towards the Definition of Culture*, pp. 122–23.

conceptions based on divine command and revelation."[36] Indeed, when comparing cultural traditions, one is struck as much by the similarities as by the differences.

Now MacIntyre might well agree with much of this, conceding that there are large areas of common ground between many rival cultures or traditions. Nonetheless, he could maintain, there does come a point when the different cultures become inaccessible to one another because the substantive criteria of rationality underpinning the different systems make translation impossible. Translating Horace's *Odes* from Latin into the Hebrew of the first-century B.C. Jewish community in Palestine poses insuperable problems because of differing conceptions of god and of idolatry.[37] Yet even if this is so, its significance is doubtful. The most it establishes is that in some instances there are insurmountable difficulties of translation or understanding across cultures. It does not show that there is a general problem of cross-cultural comparability. While Davidson may have established very little in showing that there is *no* "radical" incommensurability between conceptual schemes, MacIntyre has established equally little by showing that there is *some* incomparability.

Several other considerations suggest that the extent of incommensurability between cultural traditions is not as great as is sometimes suggested. Conflict between traditions or cultures may, for example, be reflective not of fundamental disagreement or differences of value but of inadequate understanding of the traditions by rivals, and by practitioners themselves. For example, Muslims may insist on the subordinate position of women as a fundamental tenet of Islamic practice. Yet the Quran's strictures on the family display a concern to ameliorate the status of women by abolishing pre-Islamic practices such as female infanticide, and according women rights of divorce, property ownership, and inheritance. Arguably, many practices which weakened women's status were the result of local customs which were often antithetical to the spirit of emancipation envisaged in the Quran.[38] Conflict between differing cultural standards on such issues might be best explained, then, not by appealing to incommensurability of values or fundamental cultural incomparabilities, but by pointing to the fact that not only outsiders but also insiders often misunderstand the traditions. Cultural traditions may also be weakened from within not only by the swamping of deeper religious and philosophical traditions by local customs, but also by the overcoming of

---

[36] Azim Nanji, "Islamic Ethics," in Peter Singer, ed., *A Companion to Ethics* (Oxford: Blackwell, 1991), pp. 106–18, at p. 110.

[37] MacIntyre, *Whose Justice? Which Rationality?*, p. 380.

[38] See Nanji, "Islamic Ethics," p. 109. See also, for example, the essays of the Muslim writer Chandra Muzaffar, "Female Attire: Morality and Reform," and "Women, Religion, and Humanity," in his *Challenges and Choices in Malaysian Politics and Society* (Penang: Aliran, 1989), pp. 392–412.

traditional commitments by powerful interests—which may have the power to distort moral discourse. These factors may lead different cultural communities down separate paths, despite their shared cultural inheritance.

What this suggests is that there may be many cultures which exhibit superficial differences even though they share more fundamental commitments. This may be true of many of the groups Iris Young has in mind—groups which wish to differentiate themselves from one another and to celebrate their differences. To some extent, it may even be true of the communities Bhiku Parekh depicts as representative of wider conflicts between different ways. Yet, while it is conflict between them that tends to bring our minds into focus, it is of their shared presuppositions, which make coexistence generally possible, that we need to be reminded.

There is certainly plenty of cultural variety in the world; but, on an adequate understanding of the nature of culture, there is not as much *deep* variety—or difference—as is often asserted. And this suggests that the prospect of establishing cross-cultural moral standards may not be as remote as many suppose.

There is, however, an objection that needs to be considered.[39] Even if there is a deep level at which different cultural understandings converge—since different cultures have more in common than is often supposed—divergent substantive moral beliefs may still be defended or justified by appeal to divergent cultural understandings which are less fundamental. Even if a Muslim and a Christian come to see that they share the same cultural base on some deep level (e.g., a commitment to monotheism), they may retain their cultural disagreements that lie one level up (e.g., regarding the place of women in society). Those (less fundamental) cultural differences can thus serve as a justification for divergent substantive positions still one more level up (e.g., on whether women have certain rights). Deep convergence, it might therefore be argued, does not help us to understand substantive disagreements, since the divergence at the intermediate level has not been shown to be affected (much less dissolved) by the recognition of convergence at the deepest level.

This objection is well-taken insofar as it observes, correctly in my view, that moral conflict often takes place not at the level of deepest philosophical assumptions but rather at the intermediate level. However, there is no suggestion here that shared deep beliefs in themselves will ensure agreement on intermediate moral principles or on moral practice. The argument being advanced here is that the existence of shared fundamental ideas enhances the possibility of reaching moral agreement and establishing moral standards. In part, at least, this is because the existence of

---

[39] This was put to me by John Tomasi.

some shared premises makes moral dialogue possible. And this, I wish to suggest, will improve — though not guarantee — the prospects of establishing cross-cultural moral standards.

II. MORAL VARIETY AND MORAL THEORY

Yet the question will be asked: How, then, are we to account for the considerable moral diversity and moral conflict we observe? If cultural differences are not always as deep as is commonly supposed, why is there so much moral variety? After all, it cannot be denied that there are many competing and conflicting moral systems in operation, and that no universal moral standards have been settled upon. The most obvious explanation for moral variety seems to be that morality is a cultural product and cultural variety produces moral variety.

To show, then, that there is some prospect of discovering cross-cultural moral standards, it is not enough to argue that cultural differences are not always as deep as suggested. The existence of moral variety simply poses a challenge to that argument. What is needed is an account of morality which offers a plausible explanation of moral diversity as well as an explanation of how universal standards may be attainable. Such an account is, I think, available in the moral theory developed by Adam Smith in his *Theory of Moral Sentiments*. What follows in this section is an account of Smith's theory, and an explanation of its importance.

It was not Smith's intention to produce an explanation of moral variety; his concern rather was to produce a more general account of the nature of morality as something which arose out of the nature of human beings. Yet the account which emerges is capable not only of accounting for moral variety but also of suggesting what are the prospects of more general moral principles gaining currency.

Smith's explanation of the emergence of morality begins with an account of the capacity for sympathy with their fellows as the most important characteristic of human beings. We have a natural tendency to place ourselves in the situations of others, to take an interest in their interests, to desire that they take an interest in ours. When the mob gaze at the dancer on the slack rope, they "naturally writhe and twist and balance their own bodies as they see him do";[40] we cannot help but react to the sorrow of others; we sympathize even with the dead.[41] Yet there is an even stronger inclination in our nature: the desire to be in accord with our fellows.

> The great pleasure of conversation and society . . . arises from a certain correspondence of sentiments and opinions, from a certain har-

---

[40] Adam Smith, *The Theory of Moral Sentiments* (Indianapolis: Liberty Press, 1976), p. 48.
[41] *Ibid.*, p. 52.

mony of minds, which, like so many musical instruments, coincide and keep time with one another. But this most delightful harmony cannot be obtained unless there is a free communication of sentiments and opinions. We all desire, upon this account, to feel how each other is affected, to penetrate into each other's bosoms, and to observe the sentiments and affections which really subsist there.[42]

On the one hand, the "desire of being believed, the desire of persuading, of leading, and directing other people" Smith sees as "one of the strongest of all our natural desires" (and perhaps the one upon which is founded the characteristic human faculty of speech).[43] On the other hand, there is an equally strong desire not to be out of step, which inclines men to be led by others. For Smith, as Knud Haakonssen suggests, "it is basically this continuous exchange that underlies all human culture."[44]

The capacity for sympathy is the basis of all expressions of approval and disapproval, which, in Smith's account, is where moral judgment begins. Like Hume before him, Smith sees approval and disapproval as essentially emotions or passions. Our natural inclination is to express approval or disapproval as sympathy dictates; and of course, to seek approval. The important point here, however, is that the mutuality of human sympathy does not only lead men to observe others and to express approval or disapproval; it also leads them to an awareness that they too are being observed and judged. This in turn inclines each individual to try to see himself as others would see him by taking up the position of an imaginary spectator. In this process he further distances himself from his own original motives and sentiments in an effort to see and judge them from the standpoint of this spectator, who looks impartially at his behavior and that of others and expresses approval or disapproval accordingly. In such a process we come to judge our own behavior by the standards with which we judge that of others.

Others, then, are crucial for the development of standards of moral self-evaluation. But more than this, it is the process of self-evaluation by reflecting on the likely judgments of others that leads to the development of common moral standards. Once again, mutual sympathy and the desire to be in harmony with the sensibilities of others are crucially important. The individual agent longs for "the entire concord of the affections of the spectators with his own" feelings. But to achieve this he must also consider what would be felt reasonable by those others, and adjust his emotions accordingly, "lowering his passion to that pitch in which the spectators are capable of going along with him," and flattening "the

---

[42] *Ibid.*, p. 531.
[43] *Ibid.*, p. 530.
[44] Knud Haakonssen, *The Science of a Legislator: The Natural Jurisprudence of David Hume and Adam Smith* (Cambridge: Cambridge University Press, 1981), p. 49.

sharpness of its natural tone, in order to reduce it to harmony and concord with the emotions of those who are about him."[45]

What Smith offers here is an account of how common social standards can emerge without anyone's intending it. But it is not only social standards but also independent moral standards which come out of this process. Men in society learn to judge themselves by the same standard by which they judge others: a standard of propriety. Yet having asked whether others would regard their behavior as proper, they are led to wonder whether their behavior is *in fact* proper. They begin to ask not simply how their conduct would be regarded by other spectators but how it would be regarded by a third person: an impartial spectator. In the end, individuals want not merely the approval of others; they want to be worthy of approval. Nature has endowed them "not only with a desire of being approved of, but with a desire of being what ought to be approved of; of being what [they approve] of in other men."[46]

The striking thing about Smith's account of the emergence of moral standards in this way is that it relies solely on individual sympathy and capacity for expressing approval and disapproval. Utility and interest do not come into it. It is the search for approval coupled with a desire to be worthy of approval that creates intersubjective standards which exercise an independent hold on society's members. As Haakonssen puts it, the "general rules of morality are thus the unintended outcome of a multitude of individual instances of natural moral evaluation, but once they are in existence they are quite capable of directing our moral evaluations."[47]

Yet this account also suggests why we might find such moral variety as we do across different societies. Moral standards, like social standards generally, arise out of the interaction of individuals in particular circumstances or contexts. But as circumstances differ, so will the objects of approval and disapproval; thus, the standards of propriety which emerge in various contexts will differ. More importantly, they will differ because it is the sense of propriety rather than anything else (such as perceptions of utility) which inclines individuals to feel approval or disapproval. And the sense of propriety is, to some extent, highly subjective, since it is likely to be affected by perceptions of the beauty or deformity of an act or a character. (There is a tendency to find beauty in things which are useful and not hurtful, but Smith takes the view that in making assessments of propriety, usefulness tends to be an afterthought: it is the beauty or deformity of a form of behavior which first animates us.)[48] So the standards of propriety which emerge in various societies might vary

---

[45] Smith, *Theory of Moral Sentiments*, p. 67.
[46] *Ibid.*, p. 212.
[47] Haakonssen, *Science of a Legislator*, p. 61.
[48] Smith, *Theory of Moral Sentiments*, p. 310.

considerably, since they have their origins in the mutual sympathy of particular groups of people, with their own subjective perceptions of beauty and deformity. Since social standards are an unintended outcome of numerous individual acts of evaluation, it is not surprising that small differences in individual judgment can lead to significant differences between contrasting social systems. It must be remembered, however, that although Smith gives great weight to the subjectivity of evaluation at the initial stage, he is no simple emotivist. Moral standards emerge out of the process of interaction and mutual adjustment among individuals who have a strong capacity for sympathy with the joys and sorrows of others, but have an equally strong desire that those judged be genuinely worthy of approval or disapproval. Morality may have its origins in emotion; but it quickly acquires an independent standing which exercises a strong hold on individuals.

This last point is important because it indicates that, in Smith's theory, moral standards emerge which are more than mere reflections of popular opinion. Once standards are apparent, individuals do not merely accept them as givens, but rather embrace the idea of moral conduct, and become ready to criticize extant standards on the basis of their own interpretations of what morality demands. At the same time, however, this tendency is tempered by the desire not to be out of step with the community. In this process, in which individuals lead and look to be led, more refined standards of moral conduct are developed.

Different social standards will develop insofar as different judgments of propriety will be made in different contexts. But the moral standards that emerge will be more than mere conventions, insofar as the desire to be moral rather than merely conformist will subject social standards to disinterested evaluation and criticism. This is why Smith suggests that, although custom will always have a strong influence on a society's moral sentiments, it will not be wholly responsible for its moral development. While men are swayed by fashion and ideas about what is socially customary, this does not distract them entirely from the general search for "the natural propriety of action."[49]

What Smith offers, in one sense, is a descriptive science of morals, which explains the relation between human behavior and social (and moral) rules. Certain behaviors are repeatedly selected through sympathy as proper, others as improper. "By and by this recurrent pattern will stand out clearly and men . . . [will] read it off as rules or guidelines for their behaviour."[50] Yet at the same time, while he is offering an account of morality as something which is developed in social contexts, there is no suggestion in Smith that morality is *merely* a form of human behavior

[49] Haakonssen, *Science of a Legislator*, p. 60.
[50] *Ibid.*, p. 61.

"invented" by human beings. On the contrary, it is in their nature to seek to *be* moral; and it is within their capacity, aided by reflective interaction with others, to *become* moral.[51]

The importance of Smith's moral theory for our concerns is that it offers an explanation of moral variety without denying the possibility of there being universal moral standards. The crucial dimension of his theory in this respect is the suggestion that morality is *discovered* in a process of *convergence* upon moral standards. Within a particular social context, patterns of behavior are settled upon, but one of the motivating forces in operation is the *search* for standards of propriety. In this process modes of conduct may be settled upon as morally acceptable in that context; at the same time, whether or not they are morally worthy is kept open, since further reflection and criticism may in fact lead us to different conclusions. What is also kept open is the source of further reflective insight and criticism: it need not come from within the same society or cultural tradition.

Smith's account of morality as something which is discovered in a process of convergence in the course of the interaction of moral evaluations suggests, in fact, that further moral development might be possible through the greater interaction of moral agents from different moral systems. Morality, in Smith's theory, is not simply a cultural product; morality emerges in societies, and moral standards are to some extent shaped by cultural norms. But morality *develops*, as we reflect upon the moral standards which have come to be expected and criticize them; as we reflect upon our criticisms and ask whether they demand too much of our fellows; and as we listen and react to the criticisms of others. And the fact that it develops in this way suggests that it can change when the moral ideas of different cultures come into contact. Typically, cultural differences are seen as the source of moral conflict; on Smith's theory, the interaction of different cultures might turn out to be a source of moral insight.

This, however, raises the question of *how* cultural interaction might produce moral development, particularly since there may be cause for skepticism about the claim that cross-cultural moral disagreement can prove beneficial. One important objection runs as follows. Smith's argu-

---

[51] It is tempting to suggest that Smith might be categorized as a moral realist. My only reservation about doing so is the controversy which surrounds the term, but I am inclined to go along with Thomas Nagel, who writes:

> Normative realism is the view that propositions about what gives us reasons for action can be true or false independently of how things appear to us, and that we can hope to discover the truth by transcending the appearances and subjecting them to critical assessment. What we aim to discover by this method is not a new aspect of the external world, called value, but rather just the truth about what we and others should do and want.

See Nagel, *The View from Nowhere* (Oxford: Oxford University Press, 1986), p. 139.

ment suggests that we care about how others judge us and that this guides our moral reflection through the impartial spectator; and this is fine insofar as it tells us that the moral standards we establish reflect (indirectly) the judgments of our peers. But why think that the judgments of outsiders would have the same effect, or contribute to our moral reflection? Perhaps the mechanism in question only works locally.[52] This objection might be extended further: it seems clear that the shape and direction of sympathy in individuals is determined by their family, group, class, church, sect, and so on. Indeed, as Smith himself recognized, social pluralism necessarily entails a certain amount of competition and antagonism. To the extent that this is true, it would follow that the sympathies engendered within an individual toward certain of his fellows would entail antipathies or aversions toward certain others. My case seems to assume that pluralism entails merely moral differences when, in fact, pluralism also entails competition and antagonism.[53]

To some extent the objections are well-founded: there has been — and will continue to be — a certain tendency for people to reject the judgments of outsiders as irrelevant to moral discussion. On the other hand, this should not be exaggerated. For one thing, it is clear that, despite our tendency to favor those who are closer to us — members of our own family, or church, or local community — we have, nonetheless, acquired moral sentiments and developed moral standards which range more widely. We have developed the capacity to recognize injustice even when it is perpetrated by "one of our own" to the disadvantage of "strangers" from other families, or towns, or states, or sects. And while there is a tendency to dismiss outside moral traditions, there is also sometimes a tendency to romanticize them.[54]

There is, however, a more important argument to be made for thinking that Smith's mechanism is not one which works only locally. The crucial point here is Smith's observation that people are not entirely distracted by fashion and custom from the general search for "the natural propriety of action." This is because, in the course of moral development, they embrace not merely particular moral standards but, more importantly, the idea of moral conduct. People become, to at least some degree, interested not only in whether conduct conforms to existing moral standards but also in whether those standards meet the demands of morality. Morality comes to have a life of its own. But this enhances the

---

[52] This objection was put to me by John Tomasi.

[53] This objection was put to me by Brian Beddie.

[54] See, for example, the television series *Millenium*, hosted and narrated by Harvard anthropologist David Maybury-Lewis, which contrasts tribal societies — with their harmonious relations and profound wisdom about people and their place in the world — with modern societies, which are characterized by loneliness, greed, and environmental pillage. Less savory aspects of tribal societies are ignored; on this point, see Ron Brunton, "Millenium: Getting Tribal Rites Wrong," *IPA Review*, vol. 45, no. 4 (1992), pp. 51–52.

possibility of moral interaction and moral criticism. Once morality is less—or no longer—tied to custom, it is open to others, including outsiders, to appeal to it. For example, many Muslims in England who called for Salmon Rushdie's book to be banned appealed not to Islamic strictures but to the English blasphemy laws which favored Christian sensibilities. Muslims argued that consistency required the extension of the laws to other religions as well. This raised the possibility of moral standards being revised in either of two ways: first, by extension of the blasphemy laws, or, second, by their abandonment.

The point here is not to argue that moral standards are always revised peacefully and rationally, or that partiality and conflict have disappeared. It is simply to suggest that even when there is antagonism and competition, moral criticism and moral development are possible.

III. Cultural Pluralism and Moral Knowledge

Cultural pluralism is often taken to preclude the possibility of establishing cross-cultural or universal moral standards, or indeed of acquiring moral knowledge. In looking to reject this claim, I have tried, first, to show why cultural differences do not pose a problem: the reason is that there is already a good deal of convergence among cultural traditions. Although there are many differences of custom and moral practice, there is also a good deal that is shared which makes for the possibility of cross-cultural dialogue. Secondly, I have tried to show that there is a moral theory which can account for the existence of moral variety, and also to show how moral convergence might be possible. This is the moral theory developed by Adam Smith. My concern now is to try to draw out the conclusions of the essay, and to offer some final observations about the obstacles to, as well as the possibility of, moral knowledge.

The development of universal moral standards is not improbable, because convergence upon such standards can be regarded as a serious possibility. Cultural pluralism can be regarded as an obstacle to such a development only if there is no possibility of communicating across cultures and there exist no mechanisms through which moral differences might be mediated. But it is not true that communication is impossible; and differences are mediated—through dialogue, through informal associations, and sometimes through courts of law. So if there are any serious obstacles to the establishment of universal standards, cultural pluralism is not among them. The fact that cultural traditions in fact have much in common supports this contention.

There is an objection which can be raised at this point, however, which needs to be considered. It comes from MacIntyre, who denies the significance of the fact that competing traditions share much in common:

> It is not then that competing traditions do not share some standards. All the traditions with which we have been concerned agree in

according a certain authority to logic both in their theory and in their practice. Were it not so, their adherents would be unable to disagree in the way in which they do. But that upon which they agree is insufficient to resolve those disagreements. It may therefore seem to be the case that we are confronted with the rival and competing claims of a number of traditions to our allegiance in respect of our understanding of practical rationality and justice, among which we can have no good reason to decide in favor of any one rather than of the others.[55]

Here a couple of points need to be made. First, it may in fact be impossible to resolve disagreements between competing traditions by putting them up against one another. But if so, it may be because to approach matters in this way is simply asking too much. It is much more likely that disagreements will be resolved by traditions becoming modified in the course of communication between them. This seems much more like the way in which moral disputes generally are resolved; very seldom does one party accept the other's alleged "knock-down" argument: but on occasion moral debate sees one party reassessing his beliefs over time to accommodate, and perhaps concede to, moral criticism.

The second point is that MacIntyre may be adopting the assumption that the resolution of moral disagreements has to take place at the level of philosophical discourse. Yet once again this seems to be asking too much. For example, he writes:

Consider what is involved in the attempt to evaluate rival claims about practical reasoning by comparing each with what are taken to be the basic facts about practical reasoning. Hume, for example, claims that reason can be nothing but the servant of the passions. Aristotle and Aquinas claim that reason can direct the passions. Should we then proceed by considering as wide a range as we can of examples of human action, in which both reasoning and passion are present and play some part in generating action, and in the light of those examples decide between the two rival claims? The problem is: how to describe the relevant examples.[56]

But while there may be such difficulties if abstract assumptions confront each other, it is not clear that two individuals from different traditions attempting to resolve a moral disagreement must turn away because they have different basic beliefs. History is full of examples of different ways of life coexisting; and many traditions, such as the Islamic, have developed conventions for the fair treatment of "nonbelievers." The fact of successful interaction between different traditions, and the fact that traditions

---

[55] MacIntyre, *Whose Justice? Which Rationality?*, p. 351.
[56] *Ibid.*, p. 332.

have been modified by others, suggests that conflicts of basic assumptions identified by philosophers should not be seen as insurmountable obstacles to communication between cultures. It may well be that, in this matter, theory lags behind practice. This point is well made in a slightly different context by Michael Smith in confronting arguments about moral relativism. It is often argued, he notes, that if there is a fundamental relativity in our reasons then it follows that any convergence we find in our moral beliefs must be entirely contingent. Yet why not look at it the other way around? "Why not think, instead, that if such a convergence emerged in moral practice then that would itself suggest that these particular moral beliefs, and the corresponding desires, *do* enjoy a privileged rational status?"[57]

To the extent that theory *is* capable of describing how conflicts between traditions can be resolved in practice, I suggest that Adam Smith's theory provides us with the appropriate model. If Smith's account is right, then it is possible that universal moral norms can emerge out of the sympathetic interaction of moral agents, who act guided by a mixture of concern to be in accord with their fellows and desire to be moral and to be morally worthy. To the extent that this is the way in which morality develops, there is reason to think that there is also a possibility of moral convergence as different cultural traditions interact.

If one were to take the most optimistic view possible, one might even consider whether cultural pluralism, far from being an obstacle to the achievement of moral knowledge, might not turn out to enhance its prospects. If moral knowledge is acquired in a process of testing our moral evaluations in practice, and eliminating practices and standards as our sense of propriety is refined through moral criticism, then interaction among a large number of cultural traditions opens up the possibility of examining and comparing a wider range of moral hypotheses. If there is to be a convergence upon universal moral standards, the prospect of our finding such standards may be enhanced by a greater range of traditions to consider and to draw upon for moral insight.

Yet it may not do to be too optimistic. A number of difficulties stand in the way of our converging upon common moral standards. The first is that it may turn out that there is only a limited area over which universal standards can legitimately range. It may be that large areas of moral knowledge will remain local or contextual knowledge of practices which are appropriate only to particular forms of human interaction. Adam Smith thought this, and suggested that, in the end, it was only that part of morality which dealt with the rules of justice that was capable of universal application.

A second obstacle to the development of universal moral standards is that argument and persuasion are not the only forces operating in human

---

[57] Michael Smith, "Realism," in Singer, ed., *A Companion to Ethics*, pp. 399–410, at p. 408.

society. Interest is in many ways a more powerful force for social change, and it may be that interest will dominate over ideas in many circumstances, hampering moral development.

Thirdly, moral development or convergence may be held back by failures of moral insight. We may simply make mistakes in our reasoning when subjecting moral ideas to criticism.

Fourthly, moral development may be hindered by moral intransigence. People may refuse to consider alternative constructions and to subject their thinking to moral criticism. At worst, this may be exemplified in moral fanaticism, which would make moral interaction and moral development more difficult. This point is well worth pondering at a time when the demise of European Communism has led many prematurely to predict the triumphant march forward of the ideals of democracy and individual rights. On the one hand, there is no shortage of evidence that these ideals are held in high regard as the rulers and intelligentsia of the former Communist states appeal to human rights, freedom of religion, thought, and the press, and democracy in their daily debates and pronouncements. Yet on the other hand, we see in the same regions, from Georgia to Bosnia, ethnic animosity and moral atrocities which have their roots in conflicts based on religious antagonisms and reciprocal atrocities committed over centuries.

Generally, there may be enormous difficulties standing in the way of moral convergence and the acquisition of moral knowledge stemming simply from weaknesses in human character. These are more serious obstacles to moral progress and the development of universal standards than mere cultural variety.

> The fault, dear Brutus, lies not in our cultures,
> But in ourselves, that we are underlings.

Politics, University College, University of New South Wales

IS CULTURAL PLURALISM RELEVANT
TO MORAL KNOWLEDGE?

By Alan Gewirth

Cultural pluralism is both a fact and a norm. It is a fact that our world, and indeed our society, are marked by a large diversity of cultures delineated in terms of race, class, gender, ethnicity, religion, ideology, and other partly interpenetrating variables. This fact raises the normative question of whether, or to what extent, such diversities should be recognized or even encouraged in policies concerning government, law, education, employment, the family, immigration, and other important areas of social concern.

I shall argue here that moral knowledge can and should be invoked to help answer the normative question. But before I undertake this task, we must take account of two extreme, mutually opposed views about the relation of moral knowledge to cultural pluralism as fact. According to one extreme, the fact of cultural pluralism disproves the existence of moral knowledge. According to the other extreme, the existence of moral knowledge disproves the moral relevance of cultural pluralism. The position I shall defend in this essay is closer to the second extreme than to the first; but some important qualifications will also have to be acknowledged.

I. Some Preliminary Distinctions

To deal with these issues, we must first clarify the meanings of the constituent terms. First, as to 'moral', we must recognize a distinction between *positive* and *normative* conceptions of morality. In general, a morality is a set of rules or directives for actions and institutions, especially as these are held to support or uphold what are taken to be the most important values or interests of persons or recipients other than or in addition to the agent. The rules purport to be categorically obligatory in that compliance with them is held to be mandatory for persons regardless of their personal inclinations or their institutional affiliations that are not directly connected with the rules themselves.

Within this general characterization, the positive conception of morality consists in rules or directives that are in fact upheld as categorically obligatory; and this upholding, in turn, on the part of individuals or groups may be a matter of words alone, or of beliefs, or of actions, depending upon whether the rules or directives are those that persons *say* ought to be upheld, or *believe* ought to be upheld, or *do* in fact uphold in their own actions as being right or obligatory. In addition to such positive conceptions that incorporate the idea of 'ought', a positive morality may also be construed as existing independently of this incorporation, as consisting simply in mores, customary ways of thinking or acting with no reference to any ideas of what *ought* to be done. But without such a deontic component, mores are not moralities.

Contrasted with all such positive conceptions of morality is a normative conception. This consists in the moral precepts or rules or principles that are valid and thus ought to be upheld as categorically obligatory. The validity of morality in its normative conception, at least at the level of its fundamental principles, is independent of what persons or groups may contingently say or believe or do; this is the central difference between positive and normative morality. Some of the problems raised by this normative conception will be discussed below.

Given this initial distinction, we may contrast two different meanings of the phrase 'moral knowledge'. In one, moral knowledge is empirical knowledge about the various positive moralities. The positive conceptions of morality are appropriately studied by empirical disciplines like sociology, social psychology, anthropology, cultural history, and so forth. These disciplines investigate what positive moralities have been or are upheld in different times and places; they inquire both into the contents of the divergent positive moralities and into the causal and other conditions that underlie their various modes of acceptance, stabilization, and decline.

In contrast to such empirical modes of moral knowledge, the phrase 'moral knowledge' may also have a quite distinct normative import. In this sense, moral knowledge is rational knowledge of the normative conception of morality, i.e., of what truly is morally right or valid. Again, some of the problems raised by this normative conception will be addressed below.

Let us now turn to 'culture'. This is also used in both a normative and a positive sense. In the normative sense, 'culture' signifies a certain refined development of standards of excellence. In this sense, Matthew Arnold famously referred to culture as "a pursuit of our total perfection by means of getting to know, on all the matters which most concern us, the best which has been thought and said in the world."[1] This "humanist" sense of culture stands in contrast to a positive "anthropological" sense whereby 'culture' signifies a way of life as it is understood, symbolized, and evaluated by the group that lives it. In this positive sense, a culture is a set both of group practices and of related beliefs, and it includes both mores and positive moralities. Thus, in the positive sense,

---

[1] Matthew Arnold, *Culture and Anarchy* (Cambridge, UK: Cambridge University Press, 1960), p. 6.

cultures are plural and relativist, in that different societies uphold diverse values and have different sets of practices and beliefs.[2] Some anthropologists have indeed argued that there are "cultural universals," general sets of practices and beliefs that obtain in all cultures.[3] But this view has been criticized on the ground that the practices and beliefs thus delineated are excessively vague and indeterminate.[4] This point also suggests that there may be pluralism or diversity within as well as between positive cultures. How much diversity a positive culture may allow while being the "same" culture is a difficult question, some of whose ramifications will be discussed below.

The Arnoldian normative concept of humanistic culture has received the opposite criticism: that it is "ethnocentric" and "absolutist."[5] It is held to overlook the fact that there is a plurality of normative conceptions of humanistic culture, even within the same geographic area. The standards of being a person of culture in, say, Victorian England differed markedly from the standards accepted in post–World War II England, where awareness of sexual, racial, and class drives and differences features much more prominently in the intellectual and aesthetic spheres where "perfection" is cultivated. Nor, so far as has been shown — although this is, of course, a very large issue — are there rational criteria that could determine, in any definitive way, which among the various purportedly normative humanistic cultures comprise "the best which has been thought and said in the world."

An important question for the normative conception of morality presented above is whether it is also subject to such diversities. I shall advert below to some of the complex issues raised by this question. For the present, it must suffice to say that the normative conception as here envisaged holds that certain rational standards of moral rightness are universally valid. There are not alternative or mutually conflicting valid principles of what genuinely is morally right.

---

[2] On the transition from the "humanist" to the "anthropological" conception of culture, see George W. Stocking, Jr., "Matthew Arnold, E. B. Tylor, and the Uses of Invention," *American Anthropologist*, vol. 65, no. 4 (August 1963), pp. 783–99. See also Raymond Williams, *Culture and Society, 1780–1850* (New York: Doubleday and Co., 1959), pp. xiv–xv; and Ralph Linton, *The Cultural Basis of Personality* (London: Routledge and Kegan Paul, 1947), pp. 19–25.

[3] See, e.g., Bronislaw Malinowski, *A Scientific Theory of Culture and Other Essays* (Chapel Hill, NC: University of North Carolina Press, 1944), chs. 4, 8–10; and Clyde Kluckhohn, "Universal Categories of Culture," in *Anthropology Today*, ed. A. L. Kroeber (Chicago: University of Chicago Press, 1953), p. 516.

[4] See Clifford Geertz, *The Interpretation of Cultures* (New York: Basic Books, 1973), pp. 37–43; and A. L. Kroeber, *Anthropology: Culture Patterns and Processes* (San Diego, CA: Harcourt Brace Jovanovich, 1963), p. 120.

[5] A. L. Kroeber and Clyde Kluckhohn, *Culture: A Critical Review of Concepts and Definitions* (Cambridge, MA: Peabody Museum of American Archeology and Ethnology, Harvard University, 1952), p. 32. See also Williams, *Culture and Society*, pp. 126–39.

II. Is There Rational Knowledge of Normative Morality?

On the basis of these preliminary distinctions, let us now inquire into the relevance of cultural pluralism to moral knowledge. On the positive construals of both 'cultural' and 'moral', there are certain difficulties, but they are not insurmountable. The diversity of positive cultures as social facts provides the general subject-matter for the empirical knowledge of positive moralities. As I noted above, the anthropologist, the social psychologist, and other empirical social scientists find in the diversity of cultures the prime basis for their study of the contents and development of the various positive moralities. The conclusions they reach through careful empirical inquiry constitute 'moral knowledge' in the empirical, positivist sense.

There are, of course, well-recognized epistemological difficulties here. They include questions about what kind and degree of "objectivity" can be attained by observers who come from cultural backgrounds widely different from the cultures they study. For example, the moral or other predilections of some anthropologists may obtrude on the kinds of "reports" they file about sexual and other practices.[6] Such problems, however, can be surmounted by fuller and more resolute adherence to canons of empirical inquiry.

Much more serious problems arise, however, when we juxtapose the positive construal of cultural pluralism as fact and the normative conception of morality. The former is held to pose serious challenges to the latter. The main challenge is to the very concept of normative morality with its accompanying normative conception of moral knowledge as rational knowledge of what is universally morally right or valid. The opposed contention is that there is no such knowledge because there is no one universally valid set or system of what is morally right; on the contrary, what is morally right varies with, and is relative to, the diversity of cultures, the more general beliefs and practices of different societies. In other words, there are only positive moralities; there is no normative morality in the sense in which this has been contrasted with positive moralities. In this regard, then, the fact of cultural pluralism is held to disprove the existence of rational moral knowledge.

This issue can be approached on several different levels, including the question of how an array of empirical facts can disprove a normative thesis. I shall here confine myself to two of these levels. One level is conceptual. Here it is pointed out, in response to the allegation of "disproof,"

---

[6] See, e.g., Derek Freeman, *Margaret Mead and Samoa: The Making and Unmaking of an Anthropological Myth* (Cambridge, MA: Harvard University Press, 1983). This is a critique of Mead, *Coming of Age in Samoa* (New York: William Morrow and Co., 1928). See also Paul Rabinow and William M. Sullivan, eds., *Interpretive Social Science* (Berkeley: University of California Press, 1988).

that there is an important difference in the *concepts* of positive morality and normative morality. For one thing, the contents of the positive conceptions may conflict with one another, not only from one historical era or culture to another, but also within the same historical era, and not only from one contemporaneous but geographically distinct society to another, but also within the same society. An example of the conflicts between different historical eras is the ancients' and moderns' moral defenses of slavery and the more recent moral rejection of it. An example of these conflicts between different contemporaneous societies is Ayatollah Khomeini's threat of assassination, purportedly based on Islamic morality, against Salman Rushdie for having written a book traducing the Muslim religion, and Western countries' moral condemnation of this threat. Examples of these conflicts within the same society are the sharp moral disagreements in the United States today over such issues as abortion, affirmative action, and euthanasia.

These conflicts within the positive conceptions of morality insistently show the need for a different, normative conception. For the conflicts raise the normative question, which goes back at least to the Hebrew Bible and to Socrates: Which of these positive moralities, if any, is valid or justified, as against its various rivals? This question adduces a normative concept that is distinct from the positive concept, for it asks not, What is recognized, believed, or accepted? but rather, What is morally right or valid, so that it *ought* to be believed and accepted? Even without the consideration of such conflicts, this normative question of rightness or validity also insistently arises from the widespread conviction that many positive moralities, such as those of Nazis and Stalinists, are morally wrong, so that they are opposed, at least implicitly, to a normative criterion or principle of what is morally right.

This first, conceptual answer to the rejection of the distinction between the positive and the normative conceptions of morality is not conclusive. For, just as we noted above with regard to the humanist normative concept of culture, it may still be contended by the moral relativist that what I have been calling "normative" morality is simply one positive, ethnocentric morality as against others: it is only the positive morality of "our own" group or culture as against the positive moralities of "other" cultures. My use of normative language to differentiate normative from positive morality – my invocation of words like 'valid' and 'justified', as against 'recognized' or 'accepted' – does not succeed in distinguishing normative from positive morality, because every positive morality uses such normative language. Every, or nearly every, positive morality claims rightness or validity for itself: witness its use of crucial concepts like 'ought' and 'right'. Hence, the intended differentiation between normative and positive conceptions of morality has not yet been established.

This consideration shows that to justify the differentiation we must move to a second level: a level that is not simply conceptual but rather is theoretical and argumentative. The argument in question consists in showing that there is a supreme moral principle which is inherently rational, in that self-contradiction is incurred by any actual or prospective agent who rejects the principle. The system of morality based on this principle is normative, not positive, because even if it is not actually accepted in words, beliefs, or actions, it logically ought to be accepted as universally valid. This 'ought' is, in the first instance, rational: it signifies what is logically required by the most elemental and universal principle of reason, the principle of noncontradiction. Because of the connection of reason with knowledge and truth, the supreme principle in question is truly the valid and universal moral principle; it can be known to be so, and all actions and institutions rationally must adhere to it. And the argument that establishes this principle as normatively necessary, as well as the various arguments that apply the principle to human actions and institutions, constitutes genuine moral knowledge in the normative, rational sense indicated above.

I have presented the detailed argument for my strong claims about this supreme moral principle in many other places,[7] so I shall not give any extensive repetition of it here. The argument depends on the recognition that *action* is the universal and necessary context of all moralities and indeed of all practice. For all positive moralities and other practical precepts, amid their vast differences of specific contents, are concerned, directly or indirectly, with telling persons how they ought to act, especially toward one another. In addition, all persons are actual, prospective, or potential agents, and no person can reject for herself the whole context of agency, except, perhaps, by committing suicide; and even then the steps she takes to achieve this purpose would themselves be actions. The general context of action thus transcends the differences of the various positive cultures and moralities.

Taking off from this universal and morally neutral context, the argument for the supreme principle of morality undertakes to establish two main theses. The first is that every actual or prospective agent logically must accept that she has rights to freedom and well-being as the generic features and necessary conditions of her action and of generally successful action. If any agent rejects these features, then she rejects the necessary conditions that are proximately involved in her agency, so that she is caught in a contradiction. Freedom is the procedural generic feature of

[7] For a full statement of the argument, together with replies to objections, see Alan Gewirth, *Reason and Morality* (Chicago: University of Chicago Press, 1978), chs. 1–3. For briefer versions of the argument, see Gewirth, "The Basis and Content of Human Rights," in *Nomos XXIII: Human Rights*, ed. J. R. Pennock and J. W. Chapman (New York: New York University Press, 1981), pp. 119–47, reprinted in Gewirth, *Human Rights: Essays on Justification and Applications* (Chicago: University of Chicago Press, 1982), pp. 41–67; Gewirth, "The Epistemology of Human Rights," *Social Philosophy & Policy*, vol. 1, no. 2 (Spring 1984), pp. 1–24; and Gewirth, "The Justification of Morality," *Philosophical Studies*, vol. 53 (1988), pp. 245–62.

action; it consists in controlling one's behavior by one's unforced choice while having knowledge of relevant circumstances. Well-being is the substantive generic feature of action; it consists in having the general abilities and conditions needed for achieving one's purposes, ranging from life and health to self-esteem and education. The second main thesis of the argument is that the agent logically must also accept that all other actual or prospective agents likewise have rights to freedom and well-being. I also call them "generic rights" because they are rights to have the generic features of action characterize one's behavior. Although every agent necessarily has freedom and basic well-being while she acts, the claiming of rights to these necessary goods of action is not pointless, for two main reasons. Some agents may not have the abilities and conditions needed for generally successful action; moreover, since a person is not always an actual agent, she claims the generic rights not only as a present agent but also as a prospective agent, in which latter capacity she does not always have freedom and well-being.

Reduced to its barest essentials, the argument for the first main thesis is as follows. Freedom and well-being are necessary goods for each agent because they are the generic features and proximate necessary conditions of all his action and generally successful action, and hence are needed for whatever purpose-fulfillment he may seek to attain by acting. Hence, every agent has to accept (1) "I must have freedom and well-being." This 'must' is practical-prescriptive in that it signifies the agent's advocacy or endorsement of his having the necessary conditions of his agency. Now by virtue of accepting (1), the agent also has to accept (2) "I have rights to freedom and well-being." For, if he rejects (2), then, because of the correlativity of claim-rights and strict 'oughts', he also has to reject (3) "All other persons ought at least to refrain from removing or interfering with my freedom and well-being." By rejecting (3), he has to accept (4) "Other persons may (i.e., It is permissible that other persons) remove or interfere with my freedom and well-being." And by accepting (4), he has to accept (5) "I may not (i.e., It is permissible that I not) have freedom and well-being." But (5) contradicts (1). Since every agent must accept (1), he must reject (5). And since (5) follows from the denial of (2), every agent must reject that denial, so that he must accept (2) "I have rights to freedom and well-being."

I shall give an even briefer summary of the argument for the second main thesis. Since the necessary and sufficient reason for which the agent must hold that he has rights to freedom and well-being is that he is a prospective purposive agent, he logically must accept the generalization (6) "All prospective purposive agents have rights to freedom and well-being."

The supreme moral principle established by these two theses is thus a principle of universal human rights. I call it the Principle of Generic Consistency (PGC), because it combines the formal consideration of *consis-*

tency or avoidance of self-contradiction with the material consideration of the *generic* features and rights of action.[8]

If the above considerations are sound, they show that there is indeed an essential difference between the positive and the normative conceptions of morality, and that the reality of the latter is established by stringently rational argument. So there are moral principles and rules that are universally valid irrespective of positive conceptions of morality and the diversity of positive cultures, and we can know what these valid moral requirements are.

The PGC stands in contrast to kinds of ethical relativism which hold that moral requirements, if valid at all, can be so only in a partial and restricted way, by derivation from various particular cultural or other groups that accept them. On this view, a moral requirement R that is valid for group X may not be valid for group Y if the latter does not accept R. It makes no sense to say that R or any other moral requirement R_1, R_2, ... R_n is valid *simpliciter*.

Such a relativist view does indeed provide a sound diagnosis of many positive moralities. But when it is extended to the unrestricted position that there is no other sound way of construing morality, the view has crippling difficulties. It entails, for example, that a "convention or agreement" made by a group of Nazis that requires the killing of Jews is morally right "for" that group, and that all that can be said against it is that "we" ("our" group) disagree with this "convention." But our disagreement would reflect only our own "convention." On this view, there is no way to get beyond the relativism of some group's "convention or agreement."

What is especially damaging about this view, then, is not only that it could sanction the most monstrous violations of human rights, but also, more generally, that it makes it impossible to present rationally grounded moral criticisms, in a non-question-begging way, of the positive moralities of other cultures or societies. The inability of such relativism to ground criticism not only goes against the categorical obligatoriness of moral requirements, but also ignores the necessity and universality that can be achieved by rational argument as applied to the context of action and morality.[9]

---

[8] The argument for the PGC has received extensive discussion and criticism, to much of which I have replied. For an acute and thorough examination of just about every published objection (to July 1990) that has been brought against the argument, see Deryck Beyleveld, *The Dialectical Necessity of Morality: An Analysis and Defense of Alan Gewirth's Argument to the Principle of Generic Consistency* (Chicago: University of Chicago Press, 1991).

[9] For a statement and defense of the relativist view here criticized, see Gilbert Harman, "Moral Relativism Defended," *Philosophical Review*, vol. 84 (January 1975), pp. 3–22; Harman, "Relativistic Ethics: Morality as Politics," *Midwest Studies in Philosophy*, vol. 3 (1978), pp. 109–21; and Harman, "Justice and Moral Bargaining," *Social Philosophy & Policy*, vol. 1, no. 1 (Autumn 1983), pp. 114–31. Elsewhere, Harman says: "According to the moral relativist, the successful criminal may well have no reason at all not to harm his or her victims" (Harman, "Is There a Single True Morality?" in *Morality, Reason, and Truth*, ed. David Copp and David Zimmerman [Totowa, NJ: Rowman and Allanheld, 1985], p. 36).

It is true that the argument for the PGC also has a certain kind of relative status, in that its truth or correctness cannot be completely separated from, and so is relative to, the context of agency and of what agents logically must accept within that context. But this kind of relativism is not a limitation on the status of the PGC as a universal and necessary moral principle. For, as was noted above, action or agency is the universal and necessary context of all morality and practice. Since moral 'oughts' apply only or primarily to the context of action and hence to agents, to have shown that certain 'ought'-judgments and correlative rights-judgments logically must be accepted by all agents, on pain of contradiction, is to give the judgments an absolute status, since their validity is logically ineluctable within the whole context of their possible application. Such "absolutism" does not, of course, entail that there can be no valid exceptions to moral rules or precepts. But the exceptions must themselves be justifiable through the PGC. The universality and necessity of the PGC's agent-relativism thus stands in sharp contrast to the diverse particularity and contingency of the relativist thesis cited above.

III. The Epistemic Relevance of Cultural Pluralism to Rational Moral Knowledge

Let us now return to the issue of the relevance of cultural pluralism to rational normative moral knowledge. We may here distinguish two different modes of relevance: *epistemic* and *contentual*. Epistemic relevance concerns the mode of ascertaining the kind of knowledge that I have claimed for the rational normative knowledge of what is morally right. This bears on the question: Can we really know what is morally right in the stringently rational way upheld above, independently of the various positive moralities found in different positive cultures? Doesn't this variety at least suggest that the necessity and universality attributed to the PGC should be tempered or perhaps even entirely surrendered?

Some aspects of this latter question will be considered when I come to the contentual relevance of cultural pluralism to moral knowledge. But, to confine ourselves for the present to the epistemic relation as just interpreted, it yields the allegation that the fact of cultural pluralism disproves the existence of normative moral knowledge. This allegation, however, is incorrect, because the PGC can be known to be valid by purely rational means, and thus independently of the varieties of positive moralities that figure in cultural pluralism.

There is, however, a more extreme interpretation of epistemic relevance that attacks the alleged culture-independence of the cognitive powers of reason itself. According to this interpretation, conceptions of reason or rationality are themselves relative to the diversity of cultures. The 'rational' appeal to logical and empirical criteria of deduction and induction which is central to the argument outlined above for the PGC, and which is characteristic of Western culture, has as its counterpoise different conceptions of 'reason' that figure in the appeals of various Eastern and other non-European cultures to religious faith, myth, intuition, tradition, and other culturally based conditions as the sources of knowledge and truth. It is contended that there is no non-question-begging way of proving the superiority of one of these conceptions of 'reason' over the others.[10] Since these various sources or modes of "reason" are relative to diverse cultures, it is considered incorrect to hold that a rationally based moral knowledge that claims to be universally valid can evade the limitations set by cultural pluralism.

This contention raises many complex issues with which I cannot deal in any detail within the present limits of space. Although difficulties may be raised about the general justification of both deduction and induction,[11] it must suffice for now to note three points in reply. First, because they respectively achieve logical necessity and reflect what is empirically ineluctable, deduction and induction are the only sure ways of avoiding arbitrariness and attaining objectivity and hence a correctness or truth that reflects not personal whims or cultural influences but the requirements of the subject-matter—requirements that the other purportedly epistemic conceptions cited above also claim to satisfy. Second, concerning the various alleged rivals of deductive and inductive reason, such as religious faith or tradition, one may ask for their reasons in the sense of the justifications for upholding them; and any attempt at such justification must make use of reason in the sense of deduction or induction or both. But the reverse relation does not necessarily obtain. Third, although there have indeed been historical demands that deductive and inductive reason itself pass various justificatory tests set by religious faith, myth, tradition, and so forth, the very scrutiny to determine whether these tests are passed must itself make use of deductive or inductive reason. For

---

[10] See the essays collected in Bryan R. Wilson, ed., *Rationality* (Oxford: Basil Blackwell, 1970); Martin Hollis and Steven Lukes, eds., *Rationality and Relativism* (Oxford: Basil Blackwell, 1982); and Michael Krausz and Jack W. Meiland, eds., *Relativism: Cognitive and Moral* (Notre Dame, IN: University of Notre Dame Press, 1982). See also Ernest Gellner, *Reason and Culture* (Oxford: Blackwell, 1992).

[11] See, e.g., Karl Popper's claim that the "rationalist attitude," with its emphasis on "argument and experience," rests on an "irrational *faith in reason*," in Popper, *The Open Society and Its Enemies*, 2nd ed. (London: Routledge and Kegan Paul, 1952), vol. 2, pp. 230–31; emphasis in original. See also such critiques of deductive inference as Lewis Carroll, "What the Tortoise Said to Achilles," *Mind*, vol. 4 (1895), pp. 278–80; A. N. Prior, "The Runabout Inference Ticket," *Analysis*, vol. 21 (1960), pp. 38–39; and M. A. E. Dummett, "The Justification of Deduction," *Proceedings of the British Academy*, vol. 59 (1973). Cf. Ludwig Wittgenstein's remark that "the laws of inference can be said to compel us; in the same sense, that is to say, as other laws in human society," in Wittgenstein, *Remarks on the Foundations of Mathematics* (Oxford: Basil Blackwell, 1956), I, 116, p. 34. The appeal to contradiction in my argument for the PGC has been criticized by Michael Davis, "Gewirth and the Pain of Contradiction," *Philosophical Forum*, vol. 22, no. 3 (Spring 1991), pp. 211–27. I have replied in "Ethics and the Pain of Contradiction," *Philosophical Forum*, vol. 23, no. 4 (Summer 1992), pp. 259–77.

example, salient powers of such reason must be used in order to check whether the products of logical and empirical rationality are consistent with propositions upheld on the basis of religious faith, or whether the use of deductive and inductive reason is compatible with adherence to tradition, and so forth. Thus, any attack on deductive and inductive reason or any claim to supersede it by some other human power or criterion must rely on such reason to justify its claims.

It remains the case, then, that with regard to the epistemic relevance of cultural pluralism to normative moral knowledge, the former is irrelevant to the latter. The epistemic diversities of cultural pluralism do not disprove the existence of rational moral knowledge as depicted above. We can have rational knowledge of what is morally right in a way that is independent of the diversity of various positive cultures with their divergent positive moralities and positive conceptions of 'reason' and 'knowledge'.

This point about epistemic relevance can be pushed further. Not only is cultural pluralism irrelevant to judging the knowledge claims of rational moral knowledge; the latter knowledge, with its reliance on logical necessities and empirical ineluctableness, brings out the epistemic inadequacies of modes of cultural pluralism that rely on religious belief, myth, tradition, and other such sources as definitive bases of knowledge. For all of these can be shown to be arbitrary in ways that the rationality adduced above is not, at least so far as concerns their ability to attain veridical knowledge of subject-matters. So rational moral knowledge is epistemically relevant to cultural pluralism, but not conversely.

IV. The Contentual Relevance of Cultural Pluralism to Rational Moral Knowledge

Let us now turn to the contentual relevance of cultural pluralism to rational moral knowledge. This involves two interrelated questions: First, what bearing does cultural pluralism have on the contents of rational moral knowledge? Second, what bearing does rational moral knowledge have (especially in the way of requirements or permissions) on the contents of the various positive cultures, and thus of cultural pluralism?

On the first question, there is the widespread contention that various components of what I have called "rational normative moral knowledge" do not have the universality that such knowledge claims for them. This contention bears especially on the concept of human rights. It is held that this concept is "a Western construct with limited applicability," this limitation deriving not only from "ideological differences" but also from "cultural differences whereby the philosophic underpinnings defining human nature and the relationships of individuals to others and to society are markedly at variance with Western individualism."[12] A prime emphasis of this culture-based objection is that in different cultures the unit of society is not the individual (to whom human rights are ascribed) but rather the group: the family, the clan, the tribe, the kinship circle, the community, the state, and so forth. On this view, then, the proper conception of the self is provided by the communitarian thesis that individuals are constituted or defined by the various biological or cultural groups to which they belong. Hence, if rights are to be invoked at all, it is groups or communities, rather than the individuals of traditional rights theories, who can properly be said to have rights.[13] Thus, the cultural-pluralist contentual objection against the rational moral knowledge depicted above is that, far from having universal validity, it is ethnocentric in extrapolating from a specifically Western cultural conception to a doctrine of human rights as belonging to all individuals regardless of their different cultural contexts.

To this objection it is added that the very concept of a right is a relatively recent idea, stemming from fourteenth-century Europe, and not to be found in ancient times or in non-Western cultures.[14] So the charge of ethnocentrism is reinforced, and the pretension of rational moral knowledge to universal validity is rejected. More generally, the invocation of universal human rights is held to ignore or suppress the rich variety of norms and ways of life that obtain in diverse cultures.

I have dealt with these objections in considerable detail elsewhere.[15] Here I shall just note three points. First, the fact that the idea of human rights has not been accepted in various eras or cultures does not prove that the idea is invalid or that it has limited relevance. For the idea of human rights is a normative, not a positive or empirically descriptive conception; it provides a rationally grounded moral model for how persons and groups ought to be regarded and treated even if existing systems of interpersonal and political relations depart from it. Even if 'ought' implies

---

[12] Adamantia Pollis and Peter Schwab, *Human Rights and Cultural Perspectives* (New York: Praeger Publishers, 1979), p. 1. See also A. J. M. Milne, *Human Rights and Human Diversity* (Albany: State University of New York Press, 1986), pp. 2–4; and, for more general discussions, Alison Dundes Renteln, *International Human Rights: Universalism Versus Relativism* (Newbury Park, CA: Sage Publications, 1990), chs. 3, 4; and James W. Nickel, *Making Sense of Human Rights* (Berkeley: University of California Press, 1987), ch. 4.

[13] See Alasdair MacIntyre, *After Virtue* (Notre Dame, IN: University of Notre Dame Press, 1981), pp. 204ff.; Michael J. Sandel, *Liberalism and the Limits of Justice* (Cambridge, UK: Cambridge University Press, 1982), pp. 158ff., 179ff.; and Milne, *Human Rights and Human Diversity*, p. 4.

[14] See H. L. A. Hart, "Are There Any Natural Rights?" *Philosophical Review*, vol. 64 (1955), pp. 176–77, 182; Isaiah Berlin, *Four Essays on Liberty* (London: Oxford University Press, 1969), p. 129.

[15] See Gewirth, *Reason and Morality*, pp. 98–102; Gewirth, "Human Rights and Conceptions of the Self," *Philosophia* (Israel), vol. 18 (1988), pp. 139–49, and Gewirth, "Rights and Virtues," *Review of Metaphysics*, vol. 38 (1985), pp. 745–51.

'can', the obligations do not entirely lapse when existing social conditions render them difficult or impossible. For such impossibility is not ingrained in the nature of things if it derives not from unavoidable material conditions of life but from social practices, institutions, and traditions that can be changed by enlightened forms of individual and social action.

Second, it is false that the idea of human rights is exclusively a modern Western conception. As I have shown elsewhere,[16] even when the *words* 'a right' or equivalent expressions are not used, the *idea* of a right can be found in ancient and medieval sources as well as in non-Western cultures. This is not surprising, in view of the generic features of action, on which human rights are based. Thus, Aristotle's analysis of human action, which focuses on these features, is just as applicable today as it was in ancient Greece or in the late medieval period when Thomas Aquinas took it over with certain qualifications.[17] This does not mean, of course, that the idea of human rights, including the generic right-claims that logically must be accepted by every agent, had the same degree of positive support in all eras or climes; historical and nonrational factors strongly influenced the idea's acceptance.

Third, on the large issue of the purported "individualism" of the principle of human rights, I must here content myself with two brief replies. (Further considerations will be adduced below.) First, most moral and other practical precepts are addressed, directly or indirectly, to individuals. Since the argument for human rights proceeds in part from the assumptions common to all practical precepts, regardless of their divergent contents in different cultures, the fact that the precepts are addressed to individuals disproves the contention that the "individualism" of human rights is an ethnocentric limitation. Even when moral and other practical precepts are directly addressed to groups—as in the Marxist "Workers of the world, unite!"—and even if it is recognized that individuals are strongly influenced and perhaps even constituted to some degree by the communities to which they belong, this does not alter the fact that the precepts require actions and that, in the final analysis, it is individuals who act. Even in "social-role" moral precepts it is assumed that, within limits, action is under the control of the persons addressed by the precepts—that they can have knowledge of relevant circumstances and choose to act in one way rather than in another for purposes or reasons they accept. Thus, the generic features of action still apply in such cases.

[16] Gewirth, *Reason and Morality*, pp. 98–102. See also A. W. H. Adkins, *Moral Values and Political Behaviour in Ancient Greece* (London: Chatto and Windus, 1972), p. 104 and *passim*; Brian Tierney, "Tuck on Rights: Some Medieval Problems," *History of Political Thought*, vol. 4 (1983), pp. 429–41; and Tierney, "Origins of Natural Rights Language: Texts and Contexts, 1150–1250," *History of Political Thought*, vol. 10 (1989), pp. 615–46.

[17] Aristotle, *Nicomachean Ethics*, Book 3, chs. 1–5; Thomas Aquinas, *Summa Theologica*, 1.2, qus. 6–17. See Alan Donagan, "Thomas Aquinas on Human Action," in Norman Kretzmann et al., eds., *The Cambridge History of Later Medieval Philosophy* (Cambridge, UK: Cambridge University Press, 1982), pp. 642–54.

A second reply to the "individualism" charge is the normative emphasis that the primary point of human rights is to protect individuals from unjustified threats to their freedom and well-being on the part of communities or cultures to which they may belong. In opposition to a certain kind of "communitarian" thesis, whether or not the demands or obligations deriving from one's environing communities ought to be fulfilled depends upon their impact on the rationally grounded moral rights of individuals.

It may still be contended that the moral universalism I have attributed to the idea of human rights is contradicted by the fact that this idea is interpreted in conflicting ways, so that a drastic pluralism obtains within normative morality itself. Some upholders of human rights confine them to political and civil rights, while others extend them to social and economic rights, and a "third generation" of communal and cultural human rights has also been advocated; for some thinkers human rights are solely negative, consisting in "side constraints" that prohibit the transgression of personal "boundaries," while for other thinkers human rights are also affirmative, entailing duties to provide assistance to persons in dire need of help.[18] These diversities of interpretation, however, are also not insurmountable; they can be resolved by fuller analysis of the rational arguments for human rights.[19]

The contentual diversities of cultural pluralism, then, do not disprove the existence of rational moral knowledge.

V. The Contentual Relevance of Rational Moral Knowledge to Cultural Pluralism

Having rejected the contentual relevance of cultural pluralism to rational normative moral knowledge, we must now examine the reverse relevance. This concerns the question of how rational moral knowledge judges the rightness or wrongness, and thus the obligatoriness, permissibility, or impermissibility, of the various contents or components of cultural pluralism. The general point is that moral knowledge, as set forth in the PGC, can rationally adjudicate the moral status of the divergent positive cultures. In this relation, the PGC is applied to evaluate various cultural traditions and institutions.

Such applications involve a host of complex factors, of two main kinds. First, there must be adequate empirical knowledge of the cultural phe-

---

[18] In addition to texts cited below, in n. 28, see, e.g., Maurice Cranston, *What Are Human Rights?* (London: Bodley Head, 1973), pp. 66ff.; and Robert Nozick, *Anarchy, State, and Utopia* (New York: Basic Books, 1974), pp. 29–35.

[19] I have dealt with some of these issues in *Reason and Morality*, pp. 217–30, 312–27; "Human Rights and Conceptions of the Self"; "Economic Rights," *Philosophical Topics*, vol. 14 (1986), pp. 169–83; and "Private Philanthropy and Positive Rights," *Social Philosophy & Policy*, vol. 4, no. 2 (Spring 1987), pp. 55–78.

nomena that are to be morally judged, especially of the various positive moralities. Such knowledge must include analyses of the causal backgrounds, including beliefs and external conditions, that serve to generate and explain the contents of the divergent positive moralities. Second, there must be careful analysis of just how the PGC applies to these phenomena. The problems of such analysis are especially pressing for at least four reasons. (1) The PGC is a very *general* principle, so it raises the question of how its requirements become specified in relation to the various particular cultural phenomena with their diverse material and other circumstances. (2) The PGC is a principle of *rational* moral knowledge, so this raises the question of how it applies to cultural practices based on ignorance, superstition, and similar nonrational or irrational sources, where the practices diverge from the PGC's requirements. (3) The PGC is a *universalist* principle that requires the equal and impartial promotion or protection of all persons' most important goods or interests, so this raises the question of its relation to those particularist emphases, found in very many positive moralities, that require that special and preferential consideration be given to the members of one's own family, tribe, class, race, religion, community, state, or other restricted cultural group. (4) The PGC's content may also render difficult its various applications because of its own internal complexities and possible *conflicts*. These include its provisions for rights both to freedom and to well-being, and for each of these as pertaining both to each agent and to those upon whom she acts, as well as different levels of well-being and the diversities engendered by applications to individuals and to social rules and institutions.

I cannot deal with all these problems here.[20] In the present context I shall confine myself to two main kinds of normative applications of rational moral knowledge (as represented by the PGC) to the contents of cultural pluralism. The first kind is *mandatory* and *negative*: the PGC shows that many cultures, including their positive moralities, contain morally wrong practices and institutions, so that their contradictory opposites are morally right in the sense of required. The morally wrong positive moralities are epitomized in the twentieth century by the cultures of Nazism and Stalinism, with their monstrous violations of the human rights to both freedom and well-being. So there are drastic limits to 'cultural freedom', where this refers to the freedom of various cultures to treat some of their human members in drastically immoral ways.

Questions may be raised about whether Nazism and similar tyrannical regimes were indeed cultures. Some definitions of 'culture' seem (perhaps unwittingly) to incorporate apparently egalitarian answers to the

---

[20] I have dealt with the last two problems in some detail in the sections of *Reason and Morality* on "The Completeness of the Principle," pp. 327–38, and "Conflicts of Duties," pp. 338–54. See also my "Ethical Universalism and Particularism," *Journal of Philosophy*, vol. 85 (1988), pp. 283–302.

distributive question of whose needs and interests are given favorable consideration. For example, Bronislaw Malinowski wrote: "Culture is then essentially an instrumental reality which has come into existence to satisfy *the needs of man* in a manner far surpassing any direct adaptation to the environment."[21] Does this mean that every culture satisfies the "needs" of all humans equally, including slaves as well as masters, subjects as well as rulers? Insofar as the answer to this question is negative, the fact that cultures may provide for drastic modes of oppression and subjugation shows the relevance, and indeed the necessity, of their being judged by rational moral knowledge. In his last book, written during World War II, Malinowski recognized the differential and oppressive impacts of some cultures: "[C]ulture is based on the existence of rules, on their recognition, and their acceptance. Such rules by and large are the essential instruments of freedom. Certain of the rules, however, may be used for discrimination and oppression and thus become inimical to freedom, and at times annihilate it completely." And: "We see, therefore, that freedom can also be denied by culture."[22]

By virtue of prohibiting such morally wrong cultural practices and institutions, the mandatory normative application of rational moral knowledge also requires that cultures include certain basic protections of freedom and well-being for all the prospective purposive agents among their inhabitants. These protections include not only the prohibition of slavery and other basic harms but also the securing of civil liberties, certain democratic institutions, and provisions for welfare. Although the charge of ethnocentrism is especially brought against these political requirements, the avoidance of subservience and subjugation is needed for the securing of economic as well as political rights. I have discussed these applications in some detail elsewhere, so for reasons of space I shall omit the accompanying arguments.[23]

It is also in this context, however, that the difficulties of applying the PGC noted above become especially pressing. I shall here confine myself

[21] Bronislaw Malinowski, "Culture," in *Encyclopaedia of the Social Sciences*, eds. E. R. A. Seligman and A. Johnson (New York: The Macmillan Co., 1931), vol. 4, p. 645 (emphasis added).

[22] Bronislaw Malinowski, *Freedom and Civilization* (New York: Roy Publishers, 1944), pp. 172, 322. See *ibid.*, pp. 191, 201. See also the references to some cultures as upholding slavery and fostering "spiritual frustration," in Edward Sapir, "Culture, Genuine and Spurious," in Sapir, *Culture, Language, and Personality: Selected Essays* (Berkeley: University of California Press, 1964), pp. 90, 93. Anthropologists, fearing for their "scientific" objectivity, have generally been very reluctant to criticize other cultures in the name of human rights. Even in the face of the horrors of Nazi Germany revealed after World War II, the American Anthropological Association could produce only an intellectually ineffectual document which asserted that "no technique of qualitatively evaluating cultures has been discovered. . . . Standards and values are relative to the culture from which they derive" ("Statement on Human Rights," *American Anthropologist*, vol. 49 [October–December 1947], pp. 539–43).

[23] See my *Reason and Morality*, sections on "The Minimal State," pp. 280–304, "The Method of Consent," pp. 304–11, and "The Supportive State," pp. 312–27. See also Alan Gewirth, "Starvation and Human Rights," in *Human Rights: Essays on Justification and Applications*, pp. 197–217; and "Economic Rights."

to the first two kinds of difficulties. One kind arises from adverse particular material circumstances which render difficult or even impossible the PGC's general requirement of the equal and impartial fulfillment of the rights to freedom and well-being. As was suggested above, the difficulty rests in large part on an interpretation of the thesis that 'ought' implies 'can' (so that 'cannot' implies 'not-ought'): if material conditions in various cultures render impossible the equal protection of freedom and well-being for all persons, then it is not the case that such protection ought to be provided. An extensive statement of this point was given by Edward Westermarck:

> Hardships of life may lead to the killing of infants or abandoning of aged parents or eating of human bodies; and necessity and the force of habit may deprive these actions of the stigma which would otherwise be attached to them. Economic conditions have influenced moral ideas relating, for instance, to slavery, labour, and cleanliness; whilst the form of marriage and the opinions concerning it have largely been determined by such a factor as the numerical proportion between the sexes.[24]

With regard to practices like those just mentioned, however, it is vitally important to inquire whether the material conditions in question are really so insurmountable that no alternative modes of response are available. The general emphasis of the PGC is to invalidate such kinds of killing and oppression and to require that adverse material circumstances be responded to in ways that, so far as possible, do not violate persons' equal rights to freedom and well-being. At the very least, the PGC shows the need to reject the invidious comparisons whereby some persons are judged superior to others with regard to basic rights, so that the latter may be sacrificed for the sake of the former.

A second kind of difficulty of applying the PGC arises from the nonrational sources of many cultural practices, where 'rational' is defined by the canons of deductive and inductive logic with their norms concerning empirical inquiry. What does the PGC require when such infringements of human rights as the killing of innocent persons are justified on the basis of certain nonrational religious ideas? (This question also bears on the issue discussed above of the epistemic relevance of cultural pluralism to the criteria of rationality.) Consider, for example, the Hindu religious practice of suttee, where a widow was required to throw herself on her husband's funeral pyre. Concerning this practice it has been written:

> [S]uttee works, for those for whom it works, as a representation and confirmation through heroic action of some of the deepest properties

[24] Edward Westermarck, *The Origin and Development of the Moral Ideas* (London: Macmillan and Co., 1908), vol. 2, p. 742.

of Hinduism's moral world. In that world existence is imbued with divinity. The gods have descended to earth. . . . A shared cremation absolves sins and guarantees eternal union between husband and wife, linked to each other as god and goddess through the cycle of future rebirths.[25]

Even if one gives the most benign interpretation of the widow's willingness to commit suicide with this justification, there remains the question of whether her conduct is free or voluntary in the sense that she not only controls her behavior by her unforced choice but has knowledge of relevant circumstances, and is to this extent rational. If one views the religious beliefs in question as having been instilled through a long process of enculturation, with no opportunity provided for their critical (including empirical) assessment, then suttee and similar practices are egregious violations of the rights to freedom and well-being.

Let us now turn to a second kind of normative application of rational moral knowledge to cultural pluralism: an application which is *permissive* and *affirmative*. It is here that the tolerance sometimes invalidly attributed to "cultural relativism" finds a place. All those diverse cultural practices and institutions that do not violate the PGC's essential requirements are morally permitted, and indeed are largely encouraged, to exist. In this way a vast array of freedoms and modes of well-being, what J. S. Mill called "experiments of living,"[26] are shown to be morally legitimate. This tolerance is itself an application of the PGC to cultural pluralism: the differences between cultures are to be respected; one must not try to force all cultures into the mold of some dominant culture, for such forcing would violate the rights to freedom and well-being of the members of the various subcultures.

In this context, cultural pluralism is contentually relevant to rational moral knowledge. Detailed awareness of it, as provided especially by cultural anthropology, but also by other empirical disciplines, including history, shows the many different ways of life pursued in different cultures, including their divergent standards of what is permissible and impermissible. This awareness helps to loosen what might otherwise be unduly dogmatic restrictions on the freedom to follow alternative modes of belief and action. But the restrictions imposed by the human rights to freedom and well-being must remain in force.

The permissiveness here upheld may also be viewed as a form of moral relativism. It is relativist because it maintains that what is morally right is determined by the traditions or conventions of various cultural groups, and it may be morally right only for such groups. But this is a *restricted* relativism, in contrast to the unrestricted kind criticized above, in that the

---

[25] Richard A. Shweder, *Thinking Through Cultures* (Cambridge, MA: Harvard University Press, 1991), p. 16.
[26] See J. S. Mill, *On Liberty*, ch. 3, para. 1.

contents that it regards as morally right must be restricted by the requirements of the PGC. Such a restricted relativism does not incur the difficulties pointed out above for unrestricted moral relativism. Thus, many positive moralities may also be normatively moral, but only within the normative moral domain whose principle is the PGC.

It may not always be easy to draw the line between the PGC's mandatory-negative and permissive-affirmative applications to various cultural practices. As noted above, especially where the practices are controversial the applications require both detailed empirical scrutiny of the practices in question, including their causal backgrounds and effects, and careful analysis of how the PGC's contents bear on these practices. Examples of such controversial practices include various modes of sexual conduct, including premarital sex and polygamy, as well as diverse economic policies and institutions, ranging from entirely "free" markets to modes of governmental regulation. Less controversial, but still quite salient, are such phenomena as the "drug culture" and other practices that adversely affect the well-being of persons. The PGC upholds modes of life that respect the inherent dignity of human beings as having the capacities for rational agency, including the personal virtues that are reflective of such dignity. The PGC's applications to the economic sphere still await detailed scrutiny.

Certain affirmative applications of the PGC as rational moral knowledge to cultural pluralism bear so heavily on the rights to freedom and well-being that they are more mandatory than permissive. These applications deal not with the ways in which cultural groups may treat their individual members by violating their human rights, but rather with the ways in which diverse cultural groups may themselves be treated by the state or the society at large. What is at issue here is the well-founded contention that the members of various groups — including, within the United States, African Americans, Native Americans (American Indians), Hispanic Americans, women, and others — are markedly inferior to the members of other, dominant groups in their effective rights to freedom and well-being, power, wealth, and status. The members of such submerged groups are discriminated against by the dominant political, economic, educational, and other salient institutions of the wider society. As a result, the persons in question suffer from serious material disadvantages, but also from deep feelings of inferiority, envy, and injustice. What the PGC requires here is that cultural pluralism be affirmatively protected: the right to cultural pluralism is an affirmative as well as a negative right. The needs of the members of various subcultures within the dominant culture must be recognized and steps must be taken toward their fulfillment.[27]

---

[27] On this issue, which is, of course, the object of a vast literature, see, for a representative discussion, Marilyn Gittell, "Cultural Pluralism in Higher Education," *Social Policy*, vol. 5, no. 4 (November–December 1974), pp. 38–45.

This issue may be conceptualized in two different ways, with two different upshots for the moral protection of cultural pluralism. One way is to maintain the PGC's direct focus on individual rights. Insofar as the individual members of the submerged cultural groups suffer violations of their generic rights, action must be taken by the state to remove these violations. In this regard, the specific cultural affiliations of the individuals in question would receive no special consideration, except insofar as this was necessary to correct the violations.

Against this approach it has been argued, however, that the members of many submerged groups are so closely linked together by strong ties of group identity—whether in terms of language, history, religion, tradition, race, class, gender, or other variables—that to deal with them only as individuals apart from this identity would fail to respect an essential part of their personhood. On this view, what must be protected is not only individual rights as such but the rights of groups to maintain their own culture within the larger society. An important facet of this distinction bears on the controversial issue of whether, to receive the benefits of affirmative action policies, individuals must be able to show that they have personally been discriminated against, or whether it is sufficient to show that the individuals are members of various hitherto oppressed groups.

Even here, however, the concept of 'group rights' admits of at least two distinct interpretations. On one, more individualist interpretation, the basis of group rights is in their consequences for the rights of individuals: that individual members of a group achieve effective fulfillment of their rights to freedom and well-being requires that the group to which they belong be protected in maintaining its cultural heritage of language, customs, traditions, and so forth. Only so will the autonomy and dignity of the individual members of the group be respected. On another, more collectivist, communitarian, or even organicist interpretation, the group's maintenance of its cultural identity is intrinsically valuable, among other reasons because certain communal goods cannot be parceled out among the distinct individuals who compose the group, but can be had and enjoyed only collectively.

The questions of whether it makes sense to talk of 'group rights', whether they may be classed among human rights, and whether they are reducible to individual rights have been much debated.[28] It is not neces-

---

[28] See Vernon Van Dyke, "The Individual, the State, and Ethnic Communities in Political Theory," in *Human Rights and American Foreign Policy*, ed. D. P. Kommers and G. D. Loescher (Notre Dame, IN: University of Notre Dame Press, 1979), pp. 36–62; Jeremy Waldron, "Can Communal Goods Be Human Rights?" *Archives Européennes de Sociologie*, vol. 27 (1987), pp. 296–321; and Jack Donnelly, *Universal Human Rights in Theory and Practice* (Ithaca, NY: Cornell University Press, 1989), ch. 8. See also Joseph Raz, "Right-Based Moralities," in *Theories of Rights*, ed. Jeremy Waldron (Oxford: Oxford University Press, 1984), pp. 182–200. The question of the reducibility of "group rights" to individual rights also reflects the debates over "methodological individualism": whether and in what way the facts

sary, however, to take a position on these questions in order to note that the PGC requires emphatic recognition that individuals as members of various suppressed groups have equal rights to freedom and well-being. These rights include acceptance, toleration, and support for diverse cultures so long as these do not transgress the PGC's requirements.

It is also in this context that the movement for "multicultural education" must be accredited. The promotion of multicultural education is motivated both by directly intellectual concerns and by moral concerns. Knowledge of other cultures serves not only to increase students' awareness of alternative histories and ways of life but also to foster respect for other cultures and the human individuals and groups that comprise them. Such respect falls under the PGC's requirement of equal human rights to freedom and well-being.

There may be conflicts between the intellectual and the moral goals. The diverse epistemic criteria of various cultures discussed above raise questions about the intellectual excellence whose promotion must be a prime goal of education. Certain forms of the moral demand for equality may come into opposition with this goal.[29] This difficulty is not, however, insurmountable; but it points up the need for further evaluation of cultural pluralism in the light of rational moral knowledge.

From the above considerations, then, there emerge two general normative relations between cultural pluralism and the moral universalism established by rational argument. Negatively, moral universalism sets the outer limits of the legitimacy of the various practices of cultural pluralism. Affirmatively, within these limits moral universalism encourages and upholds the diverse practices of cultural pluralism, the differences between human beings with regard to values and ways of life.

VI. CONCLUSION

In brief summary: After distinguishing between positive and normative conceptions of morality, moral knowledge, and culture, I have argued for four main theses. First, there is rational moral knowledge of normative morality, as represented in the PGC, so that the essential distinction between the positive and the normative conceptions of morality and moral knowledge is valid. Second, cultural pluralism is not epistemically relevant to rational moral knowledge; the relevance goes rather in the reverse direction. Third, cultural pluralism is not contentually relevant to

---

about social wholes can be reduced to facts about their individual members. On this issue, see the essays collected in *Modes of Individualism and Collectivism*, ed. John O'Neill (London: Heinemann, 1973), parts 3 and 4.

[29] I have discussed some of these issues in "Human Rights and Academic Freedom," in *Morality, Responsibility, and the University: Studies in Academic Ethics*, ed. Steven M. Cahn (Philadelphia, PA: Temple University Press, 1990), pp. 8–31.

rational moral knowledge: the varieties of cultures do not disprove the universal validity of the PGC as the principle of human rights. Fourth, rational moral knowledge is contentually relevant to cultural pluralism, in that the PGC adjudicates what is required and what is permitted among the vast diverse contents of the various cultures.

Philosophy, University of Chicago

PLURALISM AND THE VALUE OF LIFE

By John Kekes

As an initial approximation, pluralism may be understood as the combination of four theses. First, there are many incommensurable values whose realization is required for living a good life. Second, these values often conflict with each other, and, as a result, the realization of some excludes the realization of others. Third, there is no authoritative standard that could be appealed to to resolve such conflicts, because there is also a plurality of standards; consequently, no single standard would be always acceptable to all fully informed and reasonable people. Fourth, there are, nevertheless, reasonable ways of resolving conflicts among incommensurable values.

The purpose of this essay is to defend pluralism by contrasting it with the less satisfactory alternatives of monism and relativism and by showing how it can handle conflicts involving the value of life. One reason for concentrating on the value of life is that it is particularly resistant to a pluralistic interpretation. It may be thought either that life takes precedence over all other values that may conflict with it, or that if not even life does that, then all conflict-resolutions are ultimately arbitrary. It seems, therefore, that either monism or relativism is correct, and there is therefore no room left for pluralism. What seems to be true, however, is not—or so it will be argued.

I. Pluralism Versus Monism and Relativism

Pluralism is that rare thing: a genuinely new approach to thinking about values. Its novelty, of course, does not preclude historical anticipations; various passages in the writings of Aristotle, Michel de Montaigne, David Hume, John Stuart Mill, and William James readily lend themselves to pluralistic interpretation. Yet there exists no authoritative formulation of pluralism, although Isaiah Berlin and Michael Oakeshott began to struggle with the task in the 1940s and 1950s. By now, pluralism has become a recognizable label; nevertheless, it remains less than clear why those who are usually included under its heading are included.[1] We may well doubt, however, whether at this early stage of development an

---

[1] Annette Baier, Richard Brandt, Stuart Hampshire, Thomas Nagel, David Norton, Martha Nussbaum, Edmund Pincoffs, John Rawls, Richard Rorty, Michael Stocker, Peter Strawson, Charles Taylor, Michael Walzer, and Bernard Williams are all pluralists in some sense or another, although many deep disagreements divide them.

authoritative formulation of pluralism is either possible or desirable. In any case, none will be attempted here. We shall begin by sketching one version of pluralism, but it must be emphasized that no claim to finality, general acceptance, or sufficient detail is made on its behalf. In the interest of brevity, it will be referred to as "pluralism," but it should be understood that there are other versions as well.

Pluralism, then, is a theory about values. The point of view from which pluralists approach values is that of human beings trying to live a good life. The central thesis of pluralism is that there are many reasonable conceptions of a good life and many reasonable values upon whose realization good lives depend. These conceptions and values are often so related, however, that the realization of one excludes the realization of another. Consequently, conflicts among reasonable conceptions of a good life and among reasonable values must be recognized as unavoidable features of an adequate understanding of morality and politics. Pluralists believe that living a good life must be essentially concerned with coping with these conflicts, but doing so is formidably difficult because the conflicts are often caused by the incompatibility and incommensurability of the values whose realization is regarded as essential.

The incompatibility of values is partly due to qualities intrinsic to the conflicting values. Because of these qualities, the realization of one value may totally or proportionally exclude the realization of the other. Habitual gourmandizing and asceticism are totally incompatible, while a lifelong commitment to both political activism and solitude are proportionally so. The incompatibility of values, therefore, derives at least in part from the nature of the values, rather than from our attitude toward them. For the favorable attitude of some people toward both of the incompatible values does not make them compatible. Their compatibility depends also on whether or not the intrinsic qualities of the values exclude each other. But the intrinsic qualities of some values are only partly responsible for their incompatibility. Another part is contributed by human nature. It is only for beings like us that the intrinsic qualities of some values are incompatible. If gourmandizing did not give us pleasure, it would not be incompatible with asceticism. And if split personalities were normal for us, then we could combine solitude and political activism.

It is worth noting, if only in passing, that the incompatibility of values, created by the conjunction of qualities intrinsic to them and qualities intrinsic to human nature, constitutes a further reason for regarding at least some values as objective. For their incompatibility shows that prizing them is not merely a matter of having a favorable attitude toward them, but that we prize them also because our favorable attitudes are toward qualities intrinsic to the values which it is reasonable or unreasonable for beings like us to prize.

The basic idea of incommensurability is that there are some things so unlike as to exclude any reasonable comparison between them. Square roots and insults, smells and puns, canasta and telescopes are utterly disparate, and they seem to exclude any common measure by which we could evaluate their respective merits or demerits. That this is so is not usually troublesome, because there is scarcely a need to compare them. It is otherwise, however, with values. It often happens that we want to realize incompatible values, and it becomes important to compare them so that we can choose among them in a reasonable manner. But if incompatible values are also incommensurable, then reasonable comparisons among them become problematic.

There are three main reasons why pluralists suppose that values are incommensurable. First, it does not seem to them that there exists a highest value, such as happiness, to which all other values could always be reasonably subordinated and with reference to which all other values could be authoritatively ranked. Second, they are also dubious about there being some medium, such as money, in terms of which all the different values could be expressed, quantified, and compared in a way that all reasonable people would accept. And third, they are similarly skeptical about claims made on behalf of some one or some few canonical principles, such as Kant's categorical imperative, which could be appealed to in resolving conflicts among values to the satisfaction of all reasonable people.

Incommensurability and incompatibility are logically distinct notions. Incommensurable values need not be incompatible, and if they are not, then they can, and often do, coexist in a life. Patriotism and spelunking are incommensurable, but not incompatible. If values were merely incommensurable, without being incompatible, it would not be hard to reconcile them, for we should only have to develop sufficiently capacious conceptions of a good life to include all the incommensurable values we want to realize. The reason why this strategy cannot work is that many values are not only incommensurable but also incompatible. Consequently, they cannot all be fully realized in even the most receptively rich conception of a good life. Moral conflicts of the relevant type occur precisely because we want to realize both incompatible and incommensurable values.

Nor need incompatible values be incommensurable. We often want to realize two readily comparable yet mutually exclusive values. If I wanted to be alone for a few days, I could go camping or visit a strange city, but not both; or, if I wanted to improve my finances, I could cautiously husband my resources or make risky but possibly lucrative investments, but the more I do of one, the less I could do of the other. Pluralists are committed to the conjunction of two claims: moral conflicts are frequent, and many of them are due to our wanting to realize incompatible and incommensurable values.

We may express the conclusion pluralists draw from the incommensurability and incompatibility of values positively, by saying that reasonable commitment to values should be conditional, as well as negatively, by saying that it is unreasonable to regard any value as being always overriding. The possibility that conditionality excludes and overridingness hinges on is that of resolving conflicts among values in a way that would *always* command the assent of *all* fully reasonable people. As it has been succinctly put: "There is no consideration of any kind that overrides all other considerations in all conceivable circumstances."[2]

Pluralists, of course, do not deny that many conflicts among values can be resolved by appealing to some reasonable ranking of the values in question. Such rankings are acknowledged by pluralists to be both possible and desirable. The point they insist on is that just as there is a plurality of equally reasonable conceptions of a good life and of values, so also there is a plurality of equally reasonable rankings of them. According to pluralists, reason does not require commitment to some one highest value, or to some medium for comparing values, or to some one or few authoritative principles. On the contrary, reason allows people to commit themselves to any one of a plurality of equally reasonable values, ranking schemes, or principles.

Pluralism is intended to occupy the middle ground between two other theories about the nature of values: monism and relativism. Monists are committed to there being some overriding value, but they need not suppose that it is a single value; their commitment may be to some small number of values, principles, or ranking schemes on the basis of which values could be compared in a way that all reasonable people would find compelling.

A value is overriding, then, if it meets two conditions: in conflicts it always defeats the claims of any other value, and the only justification for violating it on any particular occasion is that by the violation its realization would be generally served. For instance, if life were an overriding value, then in conflicts with freedom or justice life would always take precedence; furthermore, the only justification for taking a life would then be to preserve other lives.[3]

In contrast with overriding values, there are conditional values; their claims may be defeated by the conflicting claim of some other value. We may define "conditional" values as nonoverriding values. If life were a conditional value, then in conflicts with freedom (e.g., is life worth living under tyranny?) or justice (e.g., should lives be risked in resisting injustice?), the claims of life could be defeated by the claims of these other values.

---

[2] Stuart Hampshire, *Innocence and Experience* (Cambridge, MA: Harvard University Press, 1989), p. 172.

[3] The distinction between overriding and conditional values is not the same as the distinction between absolute and prima facie values. Overriding values may be prima facie because they may be justifiably violated in any particular case provided that that is the best way of protecting the value in general.

Pluralists are opposed to monism because they reject the idea of there being an overriding value. It makes no difference to this rejection whether the overriding value is thought to be single or a combination of a few values, whether it is a principle or principles, or whether it is a simple or a complex ranking scheme. It is the very idea of there being some evaluative consideration that should *always* take precedence over *all* other evaluative considerations that pluralists oppose.

Yet pluralists see, as well as monists do, that if values are incompatible and incommensurable, then they will conflict, and all conceptions of a good life require that there be some reasonable resolution of these conflicts. Pluralists and monists therefore agree about the need for reasonable conflict-resolution; their disagreement concerns the question of whether it can be based on some overriding value.[4]

The other theory about values that pluralists reject is relativism. Relativists agree with pluralists about there being no overriding values, about all values being conditional, about the plurality of incompatible and incommensurable values, about the like plurality of principles and organizing schemes, and about the need for conflict-resolution. But relativists go beyond pluralism and think that all conditional values are conventional in character. They regard all values merely as the products of the customs, practices, and beliefs which happened to have developed in a particular tradition, and they deny that any value can carry epistemological or moral authority outside of its traditional context. Relativists may concede that reason has a role to play in settling conflicts among values, but, according to them, reason is confined to play that role *within* particular traditions. There is no reasonable way of settling conflicts *between* values belonging to different traditions, because what counts as reasonable is itself a product of particular traditions.[5]

Pluralists disagree because they believe that there is a context-independent ground to which we can reasonably appeal in settling conflicts between incompatible and incommensurable values, even if the values are conditional and the conflicts occur in the context of different traditions. At the same time, pluralists and relativists may join in their opposition to the monistic commitment to an overriding value. Similarly, pluralists and monists may agree in opposing the relativistic denial of a context-independent ground for resolving conflicts, even as they disagree about basing an overriding value on that ground.

---

[4] Some classical versions of monism are those of Plato, Kant, and John Stuart Mill, among others; contemporary versions have been defended by Alan Donagan, Alan Gewirth, R. M. Hare, and others.

[5] Some classical versions of relativism are those of Protagoras, Montaigne, Giambattista Vico, and Johann Gottfried Herder, among others; contemporary versions have been defended by Clifford Geertz, Gilbert Harman, Joseph Margolis, Richard Rorty, Michael Walzer, and others.

The central idea that pluralists aim to develop and defend against both monists and relativists is that there is a context-independent ground for settling conflicts among conditional values that would be acceptable to all sufficiently informed and reasonable people. Relativists reject pluralism because they deny that there is a ground answering this description. And monists reject pluralism because, while they think that the ground pluralists appeal to exists, they also think that on its basis some values can be shown to be overriding, and not merely conditional. One consequence of this dispute is that pluralists must always argue on two fronts: against relativists, to whom they must show the existence of a context-independent ground for resolving conflicts among conditional values; and against monists, to whom they must show that only conditional and not overriding values can be based on this ground.

The context-independent ground required by the pluralistic thesis is constituted of the minimum requirements of human welfare. These requirements are set by universally human, historically constant, and culturally invariant needs created by human nature. Many of these needs are physiological: for food, shelter, rest, and so forth; other needs are psychological: for companionship, hope, the absence of horror and terror in one's life, and the like; yet other needs are social: for some order and predictability in one's society, for security, for some respect, and so on. Let us call the satisfaction of these basic human needs "primary values," in contrast with "secondary values." Secondary values derive from the satisfaction of needs that vary with traditions and conceptions of a good life. We can say, then, that the minimum requirements of human welfare are met by the realization of primary values. Let us call the rules, customs, and principles protecting people in their pursuit of primary values "deep conventions." It follows, then, that any morally acceptable tradition must protect people belonging to it by deep conventions.[6]

The pluralistic claim for the universality, constancy, and invariance of primary values concerns only the bare fact *that* human welfare requires their enjoyment. It is readily acknowledged by pluralists – indeed it is part of their thesis – that there are vast historical, cultural, and individual differences about *how* primary values are enjoyed. Correspondingly, the pluralistic claim is that any morally acceptable tradition must uphold deep conventions, although it is further acknowledged and insisted upon that the range of cases covered by particular deep conventions may vary from one tradition to another.

We can now state more sharply the dispute that pluralists have with relativists and monists. As pluralists see it, relativists fail to recognize that

---

[6] This distinction between primary and secondary values needs much more explanation than it is possible to provide here. For further explanation, see the author's *Moral Tradition and Individuality* (Princeton: Princeton University Press, 1989), ch. 1, and *Facing Evil* (Princeton University Press, 1990), ch. 3.

there are primary values and that they need to be protected by deep conventions. These values and conventions will command the assent of all sufficiently informed and reasonable people because they protect the minimum requirements of human welfare regardless of what conceptions of good life and what other values are recognized in any particular tradition. Primary values thus constitute a context-independent ground for settling some conflicts among some values.

There are two reasons why the existence of this context-independent ground does not support the monistic claim that we are entitled to regard primary values as overriding. First, primary values may conflict with each other. Even if the claims of primary values always overrode the conflicting claims of secondary values, this could not be true of the conflicting claims of primary values. Second, the claims of primary values are conditional on their contribution to the realization of the agents' conception of a good life. But agents may reasonably judge in adverse circumstances that they are prevented from realizing their conceptions, and so they may judge as well that they have no good reason to recognize the claims of primary values. If people have no hope of a good life, then they will not be convinced by the claims of a value based on its necessity to a good life. It is for these reasons that pluralists regard even primary values as conditional.

It should be remembered that this account is only of one version of pluralism and that it is no more than a sketchy description without supporting arguments. The full case for pluralism cannot be made in a single essay.[7] What will be done instead is to show how both monistic and relativistic arguments fail and the pluralistic argument succeeds about one value which has perhaps the strongest claim to being primary: the value of life.

II. LIFE AS A PRIMARY VALUE

There can be no serious doubt in anyone's mind that life is one of the most likely candidates for being a primary value. It is unclear, however, what precisely this claim implies.[8] There is much cant about the sanctity of life. Albert Schweitzer, for instance, tells us that "[t]he fundamental principle of ethics . . . is reverence for life. . . . [R]everence for life contains within itself . . . the commandment to love, and it calls for compas-

---

[7] Such a case is attempted in the author's *The Morality of Pluralism* (Princeton: Princeton University Press, 1993).

[8] For accounts of some of these controversies, see Jonathan Glover, *Causing Death and Saving Lives* (Harmondsworth: Penguin, 1977); Eike-Henner Kluge, *The Practice of Death* (New Haven: Yale University Press, 1975); Daniel H. Labby, ed., *Life or Death* (Seattle: University of Washington Press, 1968); and Bonnie Steinbock, ed., *Killing and Letting Die* (Englewood Cliffs, NJ: Prentice-Hall, 1980).

sion for all creature life."[9] Does this mean that without reverence, love, and compassion for AIDS viruses, bedbugs, and turnips, we cannot be ethical? But perhaps Schweitzer should restrict his claim to human lives. The question, then, is whether this reverence, love, and compassion for human lives commit one to oppose suicide, just wars, capital punishment, abortion, motorcycle racing, sunbathing, overeating, and rock climbing?

There *are* strong reasons for regarding life as a primary value. But these reasons do not commit us to accepting the indefensible claim that life is an overriding value. In some circumstances, it is reasonable to give or to take a life. The problem is to specify the circumstances. Formulating the problem in this way has considerable importance. We are no longer asking *whether* the deep convention protecting life can be reasonably violated; we want to know rather *when* its violation may be reasonable.

We may approach the problem of specifying the circumstances in which it may be reasonable to give or to take a life by reflecting on our actual situation. What we find around us is a glaring discrepancy between rousing declarations and actual practice. Everybody knows that many lives would be saved if we lowered the speed limit, destroyed tobacco crops, sent drug addicts to concentration camps, discouraged mining, outlawed parachute jumping and Himalayan expeditions, and instituted such lifesaving measures as forcing fat people to lose weight, over-achievers to slow down, and the sedentary to take exercise. Of course, we neither act on this knowledge nor advocate that others should do so; and if we tried either, a great howl would be heard throughout the land. The appropriate laws would be unenforceable, much as the lifesaving legislation establishing Prohibition in America was and the speed limit is. The reason for this is that although we value life, we also value other things. Freedom, justice, prosperity, adventure, privacy, free trade, civic harmony, and countless other values continually come into conflict with the value of life. As the examples just given show, the claims of these other values are routinely judged by a very large number of people to override the claims of life. If genuine moral commitments require corresponding action, then very few people indeed hold the commitment they avow to the sanctity of life, or to the right to life, or to life being inalienable, indefeasible, or imprescriptible.

The source of this discrepancy between avowed commitment and actual practice is not so much hypocrisy as lack of thought. People consult their conscience and passionately declare their attachment to something they regard as good, much as Schweitzer did. There is no reason to doubt the sincerity of many of these declarations. The trouble is that

---

[9] Albert Schweitzer, *The Teaching of Reverence for Life*, trans. R. and C. Winston (New York: Holt, Rineheart, and Winston, 1965), p. 26.

in the grip of moralistic fervor these people forget that they are also committed to other values, and that they cannot have all of them. The claims of conflicting values must be balanced against each other. As soon as this is realized, sincere commitment to some value must be supplemented by a reasoned account of how the conflicting claims of it and other values should be resolved. And that realization brings us to pluralism, the moral theory concerned with reasonable conflict-resolution among a plurality of values.

It may be objected to this description of our actual moral situation that, while it may be a correct account of how things are, the concern of moral theory is with how things ought to be. Our actual situation reflects our moral defects. But the lamentable aspects of our humanity no more tell against the merits of a moral theory than a prevalent form of sickness tells against the merits of a medical theory which proposes a treatment of it. It may be argued that the immorality, inconsistency, and confusion reflected by our actions not only fail as arguments against human life being an overriding value, but actually demonstrate the importance of reaffirming our commitment to it. The reasonable way to resolve the conflicting claims of life and other values is to recognize the overriding value of life. And that means the acceptance of some form of monism as opposed to pluralism.

In reply to this monistic argument, we need only to remember that what it is reasonable to value is not life itself, but a life with some duration and enjoyment, one that merits self-respect and some sense of accomplishment. It is a life that is judged to be at least acceptable by the person living it, rather than an intolerable burden. All of us can imagine circumstances in which we would not want to go on living. In doing so, we tacitly appeal to some values whose lack would make us lose the motivation to sustain our life. And this shows that the value we attribute to our own life is not always overriding. Furthermore, such judgments may reasonably be extended to lives other than our own: those involving, for instance, irreversible coma, excruciating pain and terminal illness, or gross indignities brought on by Alzheimer's disease.

It is important to add by way of necessary caution that the judgment that in some circumstances our own or someone else's life would not be worth living does not imply any particular action. What follows may be resignation, pity, self-deception, resentment, or religious conversion; or it may be suicide, euthanasia, or murder. The reasonableness of the judgment is one thing, the moral credentials of the response to the life reasonably judged not to be worth living is quite another. The pluralistic case appeals only to the possibility of the former.

If this is right, it follows from pluralism that in some contexts life may be reasonably taken or given up. And this begins to look suspiciously close to relativism. For relativists may agree that life is a primary value, but go on to insist that traditions may reasonably differ about the circumstances in which the deep convention protecting life may be defeated. Different traditions have different conventions about the appropriate ways of treating the old, infants, criminals, enemies, traitors, and so on. Each tradition may recognize life as a primary value, and yet legitimize widely different reasons for taking it. In the context of a tradition, the exposure of the old, infanticide, capital punishment, or death caused by torture or mutilation may be regarded as reasonable. As we move away from a monistic insistence on the overriding value of life, so we seem to move toward the relativistic view that any attitude toward life is reasonable in a given context, provided only that it is sanctioned by the prevailing tradition.

The problem for pluralists, therefore, is to arrest the movement that begins with the rejection of monism and ends with the acceptance of relativism. Or, to put the point in moral terms, the problem for pluralists is to show that if we give up the view that life is of overriding value, we still need not embrace the view that there is no reasonable prohibition against taking life that all traditions should recognize.

But it is useless to try to grapple with this problem in generalities. We shall consider, therefore, a concrete case which occurs in the context of a well-established tradition. It involves members of a society killing one of their own in a way that strikes our Western sensibility as exceptionally brutal. As we try to understand the tradition in the background, however, the killing will start to look less brutal. As a result, we shall find our attitude shifting back and forth between monistic moral imperialism and relativistic moral promiscuity. This will motivate us to seek a pluralistic position between them where it may be reasonable to rest our judgment.

III. THE MORALITY OF LIVE BURIAL

The case is a custom of the Dinka, a tribe of about a million people, living in Africa, in the southern Sudan. The custom no longer exists because the Sudanese authorities have outlawed it. The account of the custom and its significance for the Dinka comes from Godfrey Lienhardt, an ethnographer who lived with the Dinka; his book about them is widely regarded as an outstanding work.[10]

The custom is the live burial of the most important and respected religious and political leaders the Dinka have, the spear-masters. At the appropriate time, the Dinka dig a deep hole in the ground and, in the midst of various religious ceremonies, place the living spear-master into it. Then the assembled people throw cattle dung on the spear-master until it covers the hole in which he lies, except for a very narrow opening, and

[10] Godfrey Lienhardt, *Divinity and Experience: The Religion of the Dinka* (Oxford: Clarendon, 1961); page references to this book will be given in parentheses in the text below.

the spear-master slowly suffocates in the excrement which is piled on him (300–304). This seems to us a spectacularly gruesome form of murder, involving the illegitimate violation of a deep convention. But let us look further.

The appropriate time for the live burial is when the spear-master is quite old and feels the proximity of death. When that time comes is usually, although not invariably, announced by the spear-master himself. In most of the cases about which Lienhardt has information, the choice of the time, although never the method, of his death was left to the spear-master. He had known that he would die in this way ever since he became spear-master many years ago. The attitude of the Dinka toward the spear-master's death is also instructive. The "people should not mourn, but rather should be joyful. . . . For the . . . master's people . . . the human symbolic action involved in the 'artificial' burial must be seen to transform the experience of the leader's death into a concentrated public experience of vitality" (316–17). It should be noted as well that cattle dung is not a repulsive object for the Dinka. Their economy depends on cattle, and they believe that cattle dung has curative and restorative powers. The significance of throwing cattle dung on the spear-master is not that of heaping excrement on a moribund old man.

The heart of the matter, however, is the live burial itself. Why do the Dinka and the spear-masters themselves believe that spear-masters should not die a natural death? Lienhardt says: " 'Life', *wei*, is the same word in Dinka as that for breath. . . . *Wei* is something which living creatures have and which is the source of their animation, and more, the source of their vigorous animation. Life is therefore in creatures to a larger or smaller degree" (206). The reason why spear-masters are so important and respected is that they are "thought to have in them more life than is necessary to sustain them only, and thereby sustain the lives of their people and their cattle" (207). The Dinka believe that "[i]t is because the master of the fishing-spear's life is bound up with the vitality of his people that he must not . . . die as other men die, for this would be the diminution of the vitality of all" (208).

The significance of the ceremony of live burial of the spear-master is that "[i]f he 'dies' like ordinary men, the 'life' of his people which is in his keeping goes with him. . . . What they [the Dinka] represent in contriving the death which they give him is the conservation of 'life' which they themselves receive from him" (316). Through the narrow opening left in the cattle dung under which they bury him, the life, or breath — the *wei* — of the spear-master leaves him and passes on to his people so that they can continue with their lives. "In his death, then, the Dinka master of the fishing-spear is made to represent to his people the survival with which masters of the fishing-spear are associated. . . . Notions of individual immortality mean little to non-Christian Dinka, but the assertion of collective immortality means much, and it is this which they make in the funeral ceremonies of their religious leaders" (318–19).

If we come to appreciate how the Dinka themselves see the live burial of the spear-master, then the moral significance we attribute to this violation of a deep convention will change from the initial uninformed judgment of regarding it as gruesome murder to a more sophisticated response. Live burial is clearly a violation of one minimum requirement of human welfare. But the Dinka believe that it is morally justified because it is necessary for the transmission of life from the spear-master to his people. Live burial for them is like donating blood or a kidney is for us, except that for the Dinka one person is the donor for all of them, while we proceed on a one-to-one basis. It is true that both blood or kidney donors and spear-masters suffer various degrees of injury, but it is in a good cause, and both the altruistic victims and the beneficiaries see it as such. So the live burial of the spear-master should be seen both as a morally commendable sacrifice made by good people and as a possible case where there may be good reasons for violating the deep convention protecting life.

Moreover, if we abstract from the perspective of the Dinka and ask from a point of view outside of their context about the moral credentials of live burial, then the answer still remains that, provided the underlying beliefs are true, live burial itself is morally justified. Without it, the vitality of the Dinka would be sapped, as would be the vitality of those who would have to do without the blood or the kidney they need.

Relativists will conclude from this case that what counts as a morally acceptable form of killing partly depends on the beliefs that form the background of the relevant actions. Since the background beliefs vary from context to context, so also must vary reasonable judgments of what counts as permissible killing. The pluralistic attempt to provide reasons which would carry weight outside of the context cannot succeed, according to relativists, because what counts as an acceptable reason depends on the tradition which prevails in the context.

This relativistic argument, however, rests on a failure to distinguish between how background beliefs affect the moral status of particular *actions* and the moral status of the *agents* who perform the actions. If the Dinka's beliefs about the transmission of life from the spear-master to the tribe are false, then, by the actions involved in the live burial, they are violating one minimum requirement of human welfare. But since they are not doing it knowingly and intentionally, their moral status as agents is quite different from what it would be if their violations were deliberate. Just exactly what that status is depends on the balance of reasons available to them for the continuation of the practice. The position of the Dinka in this respect is analogous to what our position would be if future medical research were to reveal that blood transfusion and kidney transplants are harmful to the recipients. Since we have no reason to think that now, and we have good reasons to think the opposite, we, as agents — like the Dinka, as agents — should not be blamed if future developments force a shift in the present weight of reasons.

None of this, however, affects the question of whether our actions, or the Dinka's, adversely affect human welfare. If we distinguish between the question of the extent to which *agents*, whose actions violate deep conventions due to reasonably held yet false beliefs, are blameworthy and the question of whether or not particular *actions* violate deep conventions, then it is the relativistic argument rather than the pluralistic one that fails. We can subject various actions to a context-independent moral evaluation by asking how they affect human welfare, and we can answer without thereby necessarily committing ourselves to praising or blaming the agents of the relevant actions. We can reasonably claim from a moral point of view independent of any tradition that a tradition in which rightly respected leaders are allowed to die a natural death is, in that respect, morally better than one in which they are buried alive under cattle dung. And we can make the claim without prejudice to the moral status of the people who perpetuate either tradition.

IV. RELATIVISM REDUX?

Let us, however, go a little deeper. Suppose that a reflective Dinka or an ethnographer responds to doubts about the Dinka's belief that life passes from the spear-master to the tribe by saying that what matters is the symbolic, not the literal, truth of their belief. The fact is, it may be said, that as a result of the ceremony the tribe *is* revitalized. The members of the tribe reaffirm their identity, the continuity of their tradition, their solidarity, and their determination to face adversity together; and that is as good as if *wei* actually passed from the suffocating spear-master to the tribe. The significance of this for the issue between relativism and pluralism is that if this claim were acceptable, then there would be a new reason for thinking that what justifies the violation of the deep convention protecting life depends on the context. Live burial would be justified in the Dinka context because it would be a sustaining part of the tradition upon which the good lives of the Dinka depend, while in another context, such as ours, live burial remains morally impermissible. The moral status of live burial depends, therefore, on the tradition in which it plays a part. Given this symbolic interpretation, it is a mistake, it will be said, to attempt to evaluate actions from a perspective external to the larger context in which they occur.

The pluralistic response to this modified relativistic claim is that while it is true that the moral evaluation of actions must take into account their context, it is false that reasonable evaluations must appeal to considerations that carry weight only in the tradition which provides the context.

Contrary to the relativistic claim, the Dinka custom of live burial actually supports the pluralistic case.

To see why this is so, we need to focus on the nature of the relativistic argument. Relativists think that the reason why live burial is a justifiable violation of the deep convention protecting life is that for the Dinka it symbolically sustains life. By so thinking, relativists concede the fundamental point at issue, namely, that the Dinka think as we do about the value of life. It is precisely because they value life as highly as we do that they celebrate the spear-masters for sacrificing their lives. For the point of the sacrifices is to sustain the life of the tribe. The difference between our tradition and the Dinka's is not that the primary value we assign to life in our tradition is demoted to a secondary value in theirs. They and we agree about life being a primary value. What we disagree about is whether what they regard as a reasonable case for taking the lives of the spear-masters is indeed reasonable.

Nor is this disagreement closed to reasoned resolution. The relativistic argument concedes that the Dinka and we also agree about one good reason for taking a life, namely, that by taking it we protect many lives. If the Dinka were right in believing that the killing of the spear-master is the best way to sustain the life of the tribe, then we would have to agree with them about live burial being reasonable. Our disagreement with the Dinka is made possible only by the deeper agreement between them and us about the taking of a life being morally permissible if it is the best way of preventing the loss of many lives.

Reflection on the Dinka custom of live burial, which upon first encounter strikes us as a barbaric aberration, reveals two deeper levels on which the Dinka and we see eye to eye on moral matters. On the deepest level, the Dinka agree with us about the value of life. If they did not, they would not kill the spear-masters, since it is by killing them that they aim to protect life. On the next level, the Dinka also agree with us about one good reason for taking a life. If they did not, they would not celebrate the death of their respected leaders. Only on the third, morally much more superficial level do we have a disagreement with the Dinka. They think, and we do not, that live burial is a reasonable way of protecting life. But we should note, before turning to that disagreement, that it would be impossible to have it if we did not agree first on the two deeper levels, for the disagreement presupposes the agreements. We should note also that such plausibility as relativism has derives from its concentration on the more superficial disagreement, while ignoring the deeper agreement between us about the value of life and about one morally permissible reason for taking it.[11]

Let us now consider our disagreement. To begin with, if we interpret

---

[11] For a similar argument against relativism, see Renford Bambrough, *Moral Scepticism and Moral Knowledge* (London: Routledge, 1979).

the Dinka's belief literally rather than symbolically, then we must regard it as simply false. Life does not pass from the mouth of a dying person to members of his tribe. If the Dinka case for killing the spear-masters rests on the belief that it does, then it is a bad case. The symbolic interpretation, however, cannot be so easily dismissed. The tribe *is* sustained by its members' belief that life passes from the spear-masters to them. To be sure, they are not sustained by their belief as food sustains them. But — arguably — psychological sustenance may be as important as its physical analogue. Yet while it is true that the Dinka derive psychological sustenance from their tradition, their tradition is complex and the ceremonies connected with the live burial of the spear-masters are only a small, although important, part of it. If they were deprived of that source of sustenance, they might still receive sustenance in other ways.

We know that this is so because the Dinka tradition has remained strong even after Sudanese authorities have outlawed live burial. Indeed, Lienhardt's study was written after the desuetude of the custom. The symbolic interpretation of the Dinka case, therefore, also falls short of making it morally acceptable, since the killing of the spear-masters cannot be justified on the grounds that it was required for the survival of the tribe. And since that was the reason why the burial was thought to be a justified violation of the deep convention protecting life, the symbolically interpreted case for live burial also fails. We must conclude that the Sudanese authorities acted reasonably in outlawing live burial.

This still leaves two loose ends. The first is how the Dinka themselves should think about the matter and the other is the moral status of the agents who perpetuated the morally unjustifiable custom. We have no information about how the Dinka actually think about it, but it is not hard to reconstruct how they are likely to think. No doubt, some will perceive in the prohibition of live burial a serious threat to their tradition; others will say that one must move with the times; yet others will attend to their cattle and let the local pundits worry about the matter; and perhaps some will celebrate it as a step in the march of progress. The reason why this reconstruction is so plausible is that we can readily put ourselves in the Dinka's position as we reflect on *our* range of attitudes toward changes in *our* traditions regarding, for instance, homosexuality, the waning of religious belief, or the availability of life-sustaining medical technology.

The second loose end is the question of what moral evaluation would be reasonable of the Dinka *agents*, not of their actions, who took part in what we now see as the morally unjustifiable live burial of the spear-masters. Their moral situation was that they believed themselves to have good reasons for acting as they did, but they were mistaken. Our moral evaluation of them must depend on how we answer the question of whether their mistake was culpable. Given that the custom has persisted in their tradition since time immemorial, that critical reflection on prevailing practices has not been part of the Dinka tradition, and that both the victims and their authorities had agreed about the value of the custom, it would be wrong to hold the Dinka culpable for perpetuating their morally objectionable custom. The appropriate concrete reaction to the whole situation is just what the Sudanese did: outlaw it, enforce the prohibition, and let that be the end of the matter.

V. Conclusion

Reflection on the custom of live burial permits us to conclude that the form of relativism we have been considering is mistaken. The strength of relativism, as we have interpreted it, is its insistence on the richness and variety of human possibilities and its reluctance to condemn moral possibilities from a point of view alien to them. These are useful and needed correctives of moral dogmatism. But relativists go too far. There *are* human differences, but they are *human* differences. Traditions allow different possibilities, but there is a limit to the differences among them because they are allowing moral possibilities for human beings. The Dinka and we, radical feminists and ayatollahs, Tibetan lamas and stockbrokers are all human beings, and therefore they are — we are — united at a deep level of our being. The minimum requirements of our welfare are the same. These requirements create a case for meeting them, and that case will be found persuasive by all reasonable people who pause to reflect on it. The case is simply that if we can, we should want the human enterprise to go on as well as possible. This is what morality is about. Of course, beyond this elementary yet deep level, significant differences emerge about how different traditions interpret the human enterprise going well. But these differences all occur on that third level which is so close to the surface: the level on which we disagree with the Dinka about live burial.

What relativists miss is that moral disagreements are possible only if there are moral agreements in the background. *Moral* disagreements presuppose that the parties to it are committed to morality, which on any view of the matter involves commitment to human welfare, and that they are also committed to the shared procedure of settling some moral disagreements by evaluating some of the conflicting values on the basis of their contribution to human welfare. Of course, disagreements need not be moral, and of course many moral disagreements are not open to being settled in this way. The appeal to the minimum requirements of human welfare makes only some conflicts tractable, while it leaves many other conflicts unresolved. But the commitment to morality, and thus to human welfare, is sufficient to establish that at least one form of relativism is mistaken. For one consequence of that commitment is that, contrary to relativism, it is not the case that moral disagreements may affect *all* moral judgments made within the contexts of differing traditions. If traditions are healthy, then there must be *some* agreement in the moral judgments that can reasonably be made within them. It is this layer of agreement, derived from our common humanity, that transcends particular traditions and constitutes the context-independent ground of some moral judgments. Pluralism allows for it, relativism does not, indeed it cannot, and that is a reason for preferring pluralism to relativism.

The argument of this essay has been directed mainly against relativism. It should be noted, however, that the moral agreement reasonable people will share about primary values, which constitute the context-independent ground of judgment, cannot be used to support monism. Primary values remain conditional, and do not become overriding, as monists suppose, for the two reasons given earlier. First, they are conditional on the commitment to living good lives. Lives may be so bad, however, as to exclude the possibility of ever becoming good, and then the value of life, as of any other value, may be reasonably overridden. Second, any primary value may conflict with some other primary value, and it is not possible to decide a priori how such conflicts are to be resolved. Sometimes the claims of life reasonably override the claims of freedom or justice; sometimes reason points the other way. Since pluralists recognize this possibility, while monists cannot do so and remain consistent, we have reason to prefer pluralism to monism as well.[12]

Philosophy, State University of New York at Albany

---

[12] This essay draws on material from chapters 3 and 7 of the author's *The Morality of Pluralism*.

PLURALISM AND REASONABLE DISAGREEMENT*

By Charles Larmore

I. Political Liberalism

Liberalism is a distinctively modern political conception. Only in modern times do we find, as the object of both systematic reflection and widespread allegiance and institutionalization, the idea that the principles of political association, being coercive, should be justifiable to all whom they are to bind. And so only here do we find the idea that these principles should rest, so far as possible, on a core, minimal morality which reasonable people can share, given their expectably divergent religious convictions and conceptions of the meaning of life. No longer does it seem evident — as it did, let us say, before the seventeenth century — that the aim of political association must be to bring man into harmony with God's purposes or to serve some comprehensive vision of the good life.[1] The causes of this transformation are various, and not all of them lie at the level of moral principle. But a change in moral consciousness has certainly been one of the factors involved. As Hegel observed,[2] modern culture is inherently a *reflective* one: notions of principle are essential to our self-understanding and thus to the stability of the social forms in which we participate. Modern culture has no room for a dichotomy between "in principle" and "in practice." It is worth determining, then, what new moral conceptions have been responsible for the emergence of modern liberalism. Not only will we thereby better understand how we have become who we are, we will also have a surer grasp of the principles that sustain our political life.

A prevalent view about the moral sources of liberalism is that it arose out of the acceptance of value pluralism. Liberalism and pluralism are indeed often thought to be intimately connected ideas. Pluralism is often considered an essential part of the basis of liberal principles of political association. And a liberal political order is in turn often perceived as one that guarantees and fosters a pluralistic society.

* This essay was written while I was a *maître de recherche* at the Centre de recherche en épistémologie appliquée (Ecole polytechnique) in Paris, to which I am indebted for its hospitality and philosophical vitality.
[1] For this characterization of liberalism, see my "Political Liberalism," *Political Theory*, vol. 18, no. 13 (August 1990), pp. 339-60.
[2] G. W. F. Hegel, *Vorlesungen über die Ästhetik*, "Einleitung" (*Lectures on Aesthetics*, "Introduction"), in *Werke* (Frankfurt: Suhrkamp, 1970), vol. 13, pp. 24f.

I believe that this view is importantly mistaken. Liberalism does not draw its rationale from an acceptance of pluralism, nor must it seek to promote its virtues. But this is not because pluralism is a form of error from which liberalism would do best to free itself. On the contrary, I think that pluralism—once its content is carefully defined—is a truth we should accept. My point in this essay is instead that it is a truth without the special relevance to liberalism which many have believed it to have, and indeed, that it is a doctrine on whose truth or falsity liberalism need not pronounce. The mistaken association of liberalism and pluralism has arisen, I shall argue, because pluralism has not been properly distinguished from a very different idea, one which does lie at the heart of what should be the self-understanding of liberal thought. This idea is the recognition that reasonable people tend naturally to disagree about the comprehensive nature of the good life.

A recognition of the inevitability of reasonable disagreement about the good is indeed often described as the acceptance of pluralism. (That, I believe, is the reason why pluralism is then so closely tied to liberalism.) John Rawls, for example, identifies what he calls "reasonable pluralism" with the fact that "a modern democratic society is characterized by a pluralism of incompatible yet reasonable comprehensive [religious, philosophical, and moral] doctrines. No one of the doctrines is affirmed by citizens generally."[3] In such a society "a diversity of conflicting and irreconcilable—and what's more, reasonable—comprehensive doctrines will come about and persist if such diversity does not already obtain."[4] But if pluralism is meant also to be the outlook with which we are so familiar from the writings of Isaiah Berlin, if it is the conception that life affords "a plurality of values, equally genuine, equally ultimate, above all equally objective," that "there are many objective ends, ultimate values, some incompatible with others,"[5] then we are faced with a confusion. There have indeed been some who have equated explicitly Rawls's concern with Berlin's.[6] Yet the two cannot possibly be the same at all. What Rawls (like others) *calls* pluralism is the expectable inability of reasonable people to agree upon a comprehensive conception of the good. What Berlin has so memorably described as pluralism, however, is precisely a deep and certainly controversial account of the nature of the good, one according to which objective value is ultimately not of a single kind but of many

[3] John Rawls, *Political Liberalism* (New York: Columbia University Press, 1993), p. xvii.

[4] *Ibid.*, p. 36. See also Rawls, "Dewey Lectures," *Journal of Philosophy*, vol. 72, no. 9 (September 1980), p. 542.

[5] Isaiah Berlin, *The Crooked Timber of Humanity* (New York: Knopf, 1991), pp. 79–80.

[6] Despite his misleading use of the term "pluralism," Rawls himself does not do so. At one point, indeed, he seems close to acknowledging the difference between the two notions. See his "The Domain of the Political and Overlapping Consensus," *New York University Law Review*, vol. 64, no. 2 (May 1989), p. 237 n. 7.

kinds. Doctrine and reasonable disagreement about doctrine can hardly be the same thing.

Which of these two really deserves to be termed "pluralism" is in many regards an unimportant matter. There is nonetheless one good reason to reserve the term "pluralism" for the view that Berlin has advocated. Pluralism is naturally contrasted with monism, and then at least it is understood as one of two contrary doctrines about the nature of value: Are its ultimate sources one or many? And henceforth I shall mean by "pluralism" just such a doctrine.

What is really of significance, of course, is that we recognize the difference between pluralism and reasonable disagreement, whatever we may call them. The point is not simply one of conceptual clarity. In addition, reasonable disagreement bears an essential relation to the basis of political liberalism, which, as I have mentioned, pluralism does not really possess. Whether true or false, pluralism is an eminently controversial doctrine. It has been, as Berlin has emphasized, a peripheral view in the history of Western thought. It is incompatible with the religious orthodoxies which have sought in God the single, ultimately harmonious source of good. If political liberalism rested essentially on the acceptance of pluralism, it would itself amount to a very controversial doctrine. Yet liberalism's primary ambition, I believe, has been to find principles of political association, expressing certain fundamental moral values, which, to as great an extent as possible, reasonable people may accept, despite the different views about the good and about religious truth which divide them. Though we should not expect the principles of liberalism to stand above every element of controversy—for they are principles, however minimal, which we should regard as correct, and not just as widely shared—pluralism still seems to me too controversial a doctrine, far too exclusive of many views well represented in our culture, to have a rightful place among such principles. Indeed, these reflections show that what liberalism is essentially committed to accepting is the very different phenomenon of reasonable disagreement. Pluralism is itself the object of reasonable disagreement in our culture. So liberalism must aim to make its guiding principles independent of it.

II. THE NATURE OF PLURALISM

To understand fully this important point, we must look more closely at the distinctive features of pluralism and reasonable disagreement. Let us begin with pluralism. As I have said, a far from insignificant fact is that it is a doctrine, opposed to monism, about the ultimate nature of value. (From the standpoint of political liberalism, this is the most significant fact about it.) Yet what more precisely does pluralism assert?

A first observation is that pluralism may be an affirmation about the nature of morality, or an affirmation about the nature of human self-realization. Often it presents itself as both. Yet the two positions are logically independent. Morality is not the same thing as self-fulfillment or the good life. There are other things of value besides doing what we ought morally to do. It may not, of course, be possible to find, or wise to seek, a precise and permanent distinction between the two. Nonetheless, if we mean to spurn moralism, morality can figure as but one ingredient in the good life. More exactly, though some will dispute this, it should be understood as embodying, in its most fundamental requirements, the constraints we should observe in pursuing the other elements of the good life. One might, then, conceivably be a pluralist about morality, without being one about the other aspects of the good life, or vice versa. Kant, for example, seems to have been a pluralist about happiness, though obviously not about morality.[7]

What however does pluralism assert about morality or about the good life? In its broad form, it asserts that the kinds of moral claims upon us and the forms of self-realization we can admire are in the end not one, but many. It is, in other words, a doctrine about the *sources* of value. Moral pluralism, in one plausible version, is the view that our moral convictions cannot all be conceived in terms of the consequentialist principle of bringing about the most good overall. Some duties do fit this principle. But others are better understood as strict (deontological) demands that we respect people's inviolable rights, whatever other people may do as a result of what we do, and thus whether or not our action maximizes the total good of all affected. Still other duties (such as duties of friendship, or loyalties to particular cultural traditions) present themselves as ours only because we stand in particular bonds of affection to the people to whom we owe them.[8] Similarly, pluralism about the good life is the view that the value we find in different ways of life cannot be illuminatingly explained in terms of their all expressing or promoting a single kind of good, such as pleasure or freedom. These different forms of the good life call on the diverse concerns and interests which make up our malleable and complex nature, which constitute what Kant, and Berlin after him, called "the crooked timber of humanity."

It is in terms like these that Berlin characterizes his own position. Pluralism, he writes, may be best understood as the rejection of a Platonic ideal that has been at the heart of Western thought, the ideal that every genuine question must have but one true answer, there being a dependable path toward its discovery, and these true answers being themselves

---

[7] See, for example, Immanuel Kant, *Kritik der praktischen Vernunft* (*Critique of Practical Reason*), Akademieausgabe (Berlin: Preussische Akademie der Wissenschaften, 1900–1942), vol. 5, p. 25.

[8] For more details, see my *Patterns of Moral Complexity* (Cambridge, UK: Cambridge University Press, 1987), pp. 131–53.

compatible with one another.[9] The correct view, he claims, is that the genuine question of how we should live has more than one true answer. There is a plurality of objective, ultimate ends which reasonable people may pursue, and which indeed are in many cases not mutually realizable, but conflicting.[10] To the old Platonic problem of the one and the many, pluralism urges the opposite answer to the one which Plato and so many after him have given.

Pluralism is often linked, by Berlin and others, to an appreciation of the conflicts among our values and to the regretful recognition that not all good things can exist together in an individual life and in society as a whole. This is not wrong, but it can be a misleading view of pluralism. Monism, too, leaves room for value conflict and regret, as sophisticated utilitarians like R. M. Hare are eager to point out.[11] Once we consider pluralism as fundamentally a doctrine about the multiple sources of value, we can see that value conflict can have a special significance for the pluralist, not because of its prevalence, but because of its frequent difficulty, and this because of its ultimate explanation. Monism offers, in principle, an easy way with conflicts: the purportedly single source of value should be able to provide a common basis for determining the respective weights of the conflicting commitments. Pluralism harbors no such guarantee of solvability. In its lights, conflicting values can stem from different ultimate sources, and when this is so, there can be no assurance of a resolution. By that I do not mean that a reasonable settlement is impossible. On the contrary, sometimes we can find a solution to such a conflict, not by appealing to a common denominator of value, but simply by recognizing that one consideration carries more weight than the other. Value commitments may be, in other words, *comparable* without being *commensurable*, rankable without appeal to a common standard providing the reasons for the ranking. About this last distinction, which is evidently controversial, I shall have more to say shortly. For now we may agree that, if the distinction proves acceptable, pluralists will still have to admit that such resolutions of value conflict are likely to spark disagreement. They will also have to recognize that many conflicts among values of different sources cannot be reasonably settled by any means. In these two ways, value conflicts can display for the pluralist a difficulty they will not have for the monist.

Before I return to the proposed distinction between commensurability and comparability, it will be helpful to survey the different *kinds* of value consideration that may conflict. Here I follow Steven Lukes's discussion: [12]

---

[9] Berlin, *The Crooked Timber of Humanity*, pp. 5, 24, 209.
[10] *Ibid.*, pp. 11, 79.
[11] R. M. Hare, *Moral Thinking* (Oxford: Oxford University Press, 1981), pp. 25–49.
[12] Steven Lukes, *Moral Conflict and Politics* (Oxford: Oxford University Press, 1991), pp. 5f.

1. *Obligations* may conflict, as when we find that, having to keep an appointment and suddenly having to help someone in distress, we cannot do both things.

2. *Ideals* may conflict, as when it is said that one of the enduring problems of modern liberal democracies is how the ideals of liberty and equality often run contrary to one another.

3. Comprehensive *conceptions of the good*, views about the meaning of life, may conflict.

4. So, too, may *different moral frameworks*, such as the consequentialist view that right action consists in bringing about the most good overall, and the deontological conviction that, on the contrary, some things should never be done to others, even at the cost of not effecting the most good overall.

Because the distinctive feature of pluralism is what it asserts about the sources of value, conflicts of the third and fourth types are the ones on which the monist and the pluralist stand fundamentally opposed. For the monist, conflicting comprehensive conceptions of the good can at best prove to be opposing means to, or opposing specifications of, what is the one source of value in life; there cannot be ultimately divergent forms of the good life. So, too, for the monist about morality, there cannot prove to be conflicting moral frameworks, insofar as we understand by morality an ultimately authoritative form of practical evaluation. For the monist, conflicts between ultimately divergent conceptions of the good, as well as between different moral frameworks, can only be apparent. But for the pluralist they can be real. Such ultimate conflicts can then give rise in turn to conflicts of obligations and to conflicts of ideals that will be of a sort that the monist, unlike the pluralist, must refuse to acknowledge.

III. PLURALISM AND VALUE CONFLICT

It is also appropriate to look at the different *ways* values may conflict:

1. Some commitments may be logically incompatible, impossible ever to carry out together; in this case we should perhaps always revise them for the sake of coherence.

2. Some commitments may be logically compatible, yet offer incompatible directives in given (not in all) situations.

3. To some conflicts of this sort a solution may not be available, *either* because we do not yet have the information needed to resolve them (and so we should suspend judgment about what to believe is the best course of action, though we may still have to act),[13] *or* because we have good reason to think no new information will ever be uncovered about how to decide the issue. This second case is the truly irresolvable value conflict. To the extent we continue to believe we should act on the commitments

[13] Isaac Levi, *Hard Choices* (Cambridge, UK: Cambridge University Press, 1986), ch. 2.

in conflict (which is likely to be so, when they are of fundamental moral importance), we must see the world itself as deficient, as too narrow in its possibilities for us to do what we know we ought to do. However fascinating philosophically, this case is not one I shall pursue further here.[14]

4. To other conflicts between logically compatible commitments a solution may instead be available. By a solution I mean that we may reasonably rank one commitment above the others, in what it directs us to do either in the given situation or in a certain range of situations. (Of course, a solution may also consist in our ranking them as being of equal weight.)

Now on what basis can such a solution by ranking arise? One way is very familiar. If we regard the conflicting values as being of value because they promote or express some underlying value, and if we can describe this common value in terms which permit us to rank in importance what the conflicting values direct us to do in the given situation, or in a certain range of situations, then we have here one way of resolving the conflict. In this case, the values are certainly thought to be *comparable*, but in addition they are regarded as *commensurable*, rankable with respect to a common denominator of value. It is important to observe that such a ranking can be of different types. It may be a *cardinal* ranking, as when classical utilitarians asserted that different options are to be weighed in terms of precisely how much pleasure they produce. (In this case, pleasure is understood as the ultimate source of value.) It may instead be an *ordinal* ranking, as when one ranks different actions as more or less pleasurable, or ways of life as more or less saintly, without specifying by how much. Or, thirdly, the ranking may be, as I shall say, *imprecisely cardinal*, as when one deems, for example, one action "a lot more" pleasurable than another, without believing there is any more precise amount by which the two differ in pleasure.

That all values are thus commensurable (in one of these three forms, though not necessarily with respect to pleasure) is, of course, the conviction that distinguishes the monist from the pluralist. If commensuration were the only way values could be compared and their implications for action ranked, pluralism would not be wrong. But the pluralist would then have to admit that all conflicts between values deriving from different ultimate sources are rationally irresolvable. Should the pluralist accept this consequence of his views? Many believe he must. As we shall see, Isaiah Berlin himself seems to be one. But I do not share this conclusion, for I believe that values may be comparable without being commensurable.

Consider, for example, a situation in which, having made a rather unmomentous promise to one person, we discover that a friend of ours badly needs our advice on an important decision he must make, and that

---

[14] See my *Patterns of Moral Complexity*, pp. 149–50.

we can meet with him in time only if we do not keep the promise to the other individual. I will assume we agree that we should put helping our friend first and that indeed we ought morally to do so. The duties of friendship, when urgent and within certain moral bounds, take precedence over the (deontological) duty of promise-keeping, when the latter is not of great moment. The two values are thus comparable. But is there a common denominator of value with respect to which they are commensurable? What could it possibly be? It is not from a deontological perspective, focusing on the inviolable rights of others, that we judge that our friend's need comes first. For the duties of friendship are not deontological in character: they do not purport to be binding on us, whatever our own interests may happen to be, as deontological duties do, since we should do for our friends what friendship requires, only if we want to be friends with them. Nor do we weigh the two values as we do by aiming to bring about the most good overall. For, however the good is concretely specified, the consequentialist framework requires that we regard each individual involved as of equal weight ("each counting for one and only one"); yet what our friend expects of us, and what we express in putting our friendship for him first, is that we attach greater importance to him than to others.

This seems, then, a clear case in which values can prove comparable without being commensurable. Of course, in believing that we ought morally to put friendship first, we are supposing that there is a *common perspective* — the point of view of morality, in which the two values are being weighed against one another. Two things cannot be compared except from some point of view. But from this it does not follow that the framework of comparison must itself be a common denominator of value. It need not be describable in such a way as to show how the values being compared are more or less valuable depending on whether they promote or express that common denominator to a greater or lesser extent. It need not be a source of value that explains the value of what is being compared. It is in this sense that I mean that the two values, though comparable, need not be *commensurable*. The point may be easier to accept, if we observe that part of it must be granted by any pluralist, even by one holding that heterogeneous values cannot be compared. If it is to be claimed that the sources of moral value are not one, but many, these many sources must share enough to be grouped (though perhaps not compared) within the common perspective of morality — though they will not share so much as to be derivative in their value from some superior value.

Many pluralists have denied that heterogeneous values can be compared. (So, too, have many monists, to make their own opposing view appear all the more attractive.) The guiding assumption of these pluralists is that values can be compared, weighed against one another, only by determining how they may promote or express some superior value which is their source. As I have mentioned, Isaiah Berlin is one such pluralist. Pluralism, he has written, asks us to look upon life as affording a plurality of values, equally genuine, equally ultimate, above all equally objective; incapable, therefore, of being ordered in a timeless hierarchy, or judged in terms of some one absolute standard. . . . The fact that the values of one culture may be incompatible with those of another, or that they are in conflict within one culture or group or in a single human being at different times . . . does not entail relativism of values, only the notion of a plurality of values not structured hierarchically; which, of course, entails the permanent possibility of inescapable conflict between values. . . .[15]

Being equally ultimate, not derivable from a single form of good, plural values cannot, according to Berlin, be weighed and ranked, ordered hierarchically. This being so, there cannot be, as Berlin points out, universally valid principles for the evaluation of different cultures—in other words, values which should be ranked as being of paramount importance.[16]

I am not alone, however, in believing that pluralism need not take this form, that instead it can permit the ranking of heterogeneous values and thus encompass some universal standards of cultural evaluation. Oddly enough, J. G. Herder, who has been one of Berlin's inspirations, held just this sort of view. "*Ist nicht das Gute auf der Erde ausgestreut?*" ("Is not the good dispersed about the earth?") is the exclamation with which he announced his conviction that the good is ultimately various.[17] But he did not draw from it the conclusion that the forms of good are thus incomparable. On the contrary, in his *Briefe zur Beförderung der Humanität* (1793–97),[18] for example, Herder professed agreement with Kant that there exists an ethic of unconditional duties, binding on all. He was, to be sure, no Kantian in the sense that makes Kant's a monistic outlook: he did not believe that all moral value derives from the rational self-legislation of autonomous agents. So he was keen to point out the moral costs of this ethic, the other forms of good incompatible with it, such as the intense family loyalties of the heroic ethic. But he did not believe that the heterogeneity of these goods precluded their comparability. On this point I think we should follow Herder. Can we not in good conscience consider our own moral universalism as superior to earlier and very different tribal moralities, while acknowledging that thereby we have also lost the possibilities of good that they embodied? The weighing of heterogeneous goods is indeed unlikely to yield a cardinal ranking. But surely we can reasonably believe that some such goods are more important than others, and even a lot more important.

---

[15] Berlin, *The Crooked Timber of Humanity*, pp. 79–80.

[16] *Ibid.*, pp. 37, 224.

[17] J. G. Herder, *Auch eine Philosophie der Geschichte (Yet Another Philosophy of History)* (Frankfurt: Suhrkamp, 1967), p. 46.

[18] J. G. Herder, *Briefe zur Beförderung der Humanität (Letters for the Promotion of Humanity)*, Sechste Sammlung, section 79.

I suspect that many will regard these remarks about how incommensurable values may still be comparable as just so much assertion. If not by appeal to a common denominator of value, then *how*, they will ask, are the values weighed against one another? Now I admit that I have no fully satisfactory answer to this question, though I think recent accounts of "moral perception" might prove helpful.[19] Nonetheless, an inability to solve this problem is not, I believe, so damaging as it might seem. Sometimes we can legitimately claim to know something, without knowing how it is that we know it. This can be so, for example, when we make the claim directly, without having to go through any explicit reasoning. In this case, any account of the basis of the claim may be somewhat speculative, and less certain than the claim itself.[20] It seems to me that the example of ranking a friend's needs above an unmomentous promise is just like this: we know directly that the one should count for more than the other, without having any systematic account of why this is so — though we can exclude its resting on any common denominator of value.

IV. THE MODERN CHARACTER OF PLURALISM

So far our discussion has focused on the structure of pluralism. But another significant aspect is its historical character. Is pluralism about the right and the good a distinctively modern doctrine? Or, however much a minority view, has it also had distinguished exponents in premodern times? This question is clearly important for anyone who considers pluralism a central source of the distinctively modern outlook which is political liberalism. Now the customary association of pluralism with liberalism has been challenged, in effect, by some recent neo-Aristotelian thinkers. In general, the neo-Aristotelian revival has been devoted to showing that Aristotle's ethics, far from being so alien as sometimes supposed, serves to confirm and also to deepen many of our cherished ethical convictions. In particular, there have been a number of attempts to demonstrate that Aristotle himself was a pluralist at heart, though obviously he was no liberal.[21] Recall that Berlin presented his pluralism as the rejection of the Platonic view that all goods are ultimately one. The

---

[19] See David McNaughton, *Moral Vision* (Oxford: Blackwell, 1988).

[20] Cf. G. E. Moore, "Four Forms of Scepticism," in *Philosophical Papers* (New York: Macmillan, 1959), p. 222.

[21] See J. L. Ackrill, "Aristotle on Eudaimonia," in A. O. Rorty, ed., *Essays on Aristotle's Ethics* (Berkeley: University of California Press, 1980), pp. 15–33; Martha Nussbaum, *The Fragility of Goodness* (Cambridge, UK: Cambridge University Press, 1986), ch. 10, pp. 373–77, and *Love's Knowledge* (Oxford: Oxford University Press, 1990), pp. 56–66; J. O. Urmson, *Aristotle's Ethics* (Oxford: Blackwell, 1988), pp. 13ff., 119ff.; and Ronald Beiner, "The Moral Vocabulary of Liberalism," in *Nomos XXXIV: Virtue*, ed. John W. Chapman and William A. Galston (New York: New York University Press, 1992), pp. 145–84. Some of my remarks here are drawn from my essay "The Limits of Aristotelian Ethics," in *Nomos XXXIV: Virtue*, pp. 185–96.

neo-Aristotelian argument may be seen as claiming that a similar rejection lies already at the core of Aristotle's own critique of Platonic ethics (as expounded, for example, in *Nicomachean Ethics*, Book 1, chapter 6).

I, too, believe that the association of pluralism with liberalism is misconceived, yet not for this reason. On the contrary, not only does the pluralist interpretation fail really to fit Aristotle's thought, but pluralism is indeed a distinctively modern doctrine. It belongs to a disenchanted vision of the world, which sees itself as having abandoned the comfort of finding in the harmony of the cosmos or in God's providential ordering of the world the one ultimate source of value. There is good reason, then, to show that pluralism has no place in Aristotle's ethics, if only to understand better how it can be a modern phenomenon without being, as I also shall argue, a central source of political liberalism.

What makes the pluralist interpretation of Aristotle's ethics attractive is the apparently broad, "inclusivist" (as it is called) claim of Book 1 of the *Nicomachean Ethics* that our end is to unify our various strivings in a coherent conception of the good life (1097b14–20). This seems to acknowledge the heterogeneous character of the different activities reasonable people hold to be good. Yet the obvious obstacle to the interpretation is the clear assertion of Book 10, chapters 7 and 8, that the contemplative life of *theoria* is superior to the practical life of moral excellence. Perfect happiness, Aristotle wrote there, consists in contemplation (1177a17–19), and the life of moral excellence achieves happiness only in a secondary sense (1178a9). This perfect happiness is reserved for the gods (1177b26–27, 1178b21–22). But from this admission Aristotle did not draw the conclusion which the neo-Aristotelian pluralist would want him to draw, namely that the best human life consists in a reasonable mix of contemplation and action, a mix determined by *phronesis* (judgment).[22] Instead, Aristotle urged that our aim should be, as far as possible, to become like gods, leaving behind the human sphere and putting on immortality (*athanatizein*: 1177b33, 1178b23). Such views seem impossible to house within a pluralist conception of the good.

The pluralist interpretation of Aristotle's ethics has typically chosen to ignore these passages of Book 10, or else to banish them from the true core of Aristotle's thought. Martha Nussbaum, for example, has suggested that they may be either an interpolation or a residue of a Platonic ethics that elsewhere Aristotle had outgrown.[23] J. O. Urmson remarks that Aristotle's "enthusiasm" for his own scholarly life has momentarily gotten the better of him.[24] The fact, however, is that the aspiration to divinity is not confined to Book 10. It also stands in the background of

---

[22] Nussbaum, *The Fragility of Goodness*, p. 374; Beiner, "The Moral Vocabulary of Liberalism," pp. 161–62.

[23] Nussbaum, *The Fragility of Goodness*, pp. 373–77.

[24] Urmson, *Aristotle's Ethics*, p. 125.

Book 1, where Aristotle states that "the good for man is an activity of soul in accordance with virtue, or if there are more kinds of virtue than one, in accordance with the best and most complete kind" (1098a16–18). Nussbaum tries to yoke this passage to her pluralist interpretation of Aristotelian *eudaimonia* by arguing that "completeness" requires "the inclusion of everything with intrinsic value."[25] But since excellences or virtues are all of intrinsic value, this passage unmistakably rules out such an interpretation: it holds that the good will consist in one excellence or virtue among others, if one is the best.

The superiority of intellectual to moral virtue is, in fact, a theme that runs throughout Aristotle's ethical writings. It follows from his overarching metaphysics, in which it is obvious that there are many things of greater value than the human affairs with which morality is concerned. The idea that Aristotle assigned to *phronesis* the task of discerning the best life by devising a mix of contemplation and action is refuted by the clear *reductio ad absurdum* of Book 6, chapter 7 (1141a20–22): "It is extraordinary that anyone should regard political science or *phronesis* as most important unless man is the highest being in the world." Nor will it do to suggest, as Nussbaum does, that while proclaiming the superiority of contemplation to action, Aristotle still thought our true happiness should contain both.[26] It is true that, though X is better than Y, a life given fully to X may be less good than one devoted to some mix of X and Y (there can be too much of a good thing); but Nussbaum's main evidence that this is what Aristotle meant here is inadequate: at 1144a3f., Aristotle does say that *sophia* (wisdom) is, like *phronesis*, part of virtue, but this does not imply that each is part of complete happiness. "What is so hard for a modern reader to take seriously," observes Jonathan Lear—and this seems especially true of certain neo-Aristotelians—"is Aristotle's claim that man has a divine element in him. . . . Man is a composite, and yet he is *most truly* the highest element in his form. It is man's natural desire to understand . . . that propels him to transcend his nature."[27]

Now an important consequence of my earlier discussion of pluralism is that heterogeneous values may nonetheless be weighed against one another. So the fact that Aristotle did rank contemplation above action, and understood the best life as one devoted solely to contemplation, does not suffice to show that he did not have a pluralist conception of these values. We need to consider the sort of basis on which he made this ranking. Aristotle's fundamental thesis is that happiness consists in rational

[25] Nussbaum, *The Fragility of Goodness*, p. 376. Cf. also Ackrill, "Aristotle on Eudaimonia," p. 28.

[26] Nussbaum, *The Fragility of Goodness*, pp. 374f.

[27] Jonathan Lear, *Aristotle: The Desire to Understand* (New York: Cambridge University Press, 1988), p. 320. I also find very convincing the critique of the "inclusivist" interpretation of Aristotelian *eudaimonia* in Richard Kraut, *Aristotle on the Human Good* (Princeton: Princeton University Press, 1989).

activity and that things are good to the extent they contribute to or have a role in such activity (Book 1, chapter 7). The arguments of Book 10, chapter 7, in favor of the superiority of contemplation proceed by showing how contemplation is a more continuous, self-sufficient, self-directing form of rational activity. It thus expresses more purely the ideal of happiness, which is the exercise of our rational nature. Aristotle was, therefore, no pluralist. For him there was a single kind of value which the different forms of the good life exemplify to different degrees.

It is in these terms that we should understand the apparently pluralist-minded critique of Plato in Book 1, chapter 6. Plato was wrong, Aristotle there argued, to assert that all good things, or even just all intrinsic goods, share a single Form of the good. On the contrary, the different kinds of life devoted to honor, intelligence, and pleasure "have different and dissimilar accounts, precisely in so far as they are goods" (1096b23–25). This may sound like pluralism, but it is not. Aristotle assumed that a number of things can share a single Form (separable or not) only if they exemplify it equally—as a man and a monkey are equally animals. There can be, he believed, no Form for things related as "prior and posterior," which instead must be comprehended in terms of "focal meaning" (*aph'enos, pros hen*) or analogy.[28] Now as we have seen, Aristotle's argument for the superiority of contemplation consists in showing that it exemplifies rational activity more perfectly than does action. That is why he refused to consider the two forms of life as sharing a common Form of the good. But his argument is no less monistic for that, appealing as it does to a single supreme value, more or less fully realizable.

"Aristotle the pluralist" is too much like us to be much like Aristotle himself. Pluralism is a characteristically modern outlook. It is likely to appear attractive only against the background of metaphysical and religious disappointment. It recommends itself to those who continue to believe that value can be objective, something more than just the expression of our preferences, but who refuse to believe that it has its home in a harmonious cosmos (as Aristotle thought) or in God's plan. For example, the moral pluralism that accepts the mutual independence of deontological and consequentialist forms of deliberation appears only once it is recognized that theodicy, which generally sought to prove among other things that strict deontological rules are God's wise way of bringing about the most good overall, cannot succeed.[29] Now liberalism has distinguished itself from earlier political philosophies by its refusal, ever more pronounced, to base the principles of political association upon a vision of God's plan or of an ordered cosmos. It is perhaps natural, therefore,

[28] See the commentary in W. F. R. Hardie, *Aristotle's Ethical Theory* (Oxford: Oxford University Press, 1968), pp. 55–56, 63–65.

[29] See my *Patterns of Moral Complexity*, pp. 134ff., and also "Théodicée et rationalité morale chez Malebranche, Leibniz, et Bayle," in my *Modernité et morale* (Paris: Presses Universitaires de France, 1993).

that liberalism and pluralism should be regarded as closely allied. Indeed, they are both distinctively modern in that they have something to do with the metaphysical-religious disenchantment of the world. But their relations to this phenomenon are actually very different, and we are now in a good position to see why this is so.

V. The Nature of Reasonable Disagreement

Recall that pluralism is a doctrine about the nature of value. It asserts that the forms of moral concern, as well as the forms of self-realization, are in the end not one, but many. It stands, therefore, in opposition to religious and metaphysical conceptions of a single source of value. Liberalism, however, does not arise from an acceptance of pluralism. Instead, it seeks to found the principles of political association upon a core morality that reasonable people can accept, despite their natural tendency to disagree about comprehensive visions of the nature of value, and so in particular about the merits of pluralism and monism. This expectation of reasonable disagreement lies at a different, more reflective level than pluralism. It responds to the religious and metaphysical disenchantment of the world, not by affirming it, as pluralism seems to do, but rather by recognizing that like other deep conceptions of value this disenchantment is an idea about which reasonable people are likely to disagree, as indeed they do. Ours is a culture, after all, of which religious faith is still very much a part. This is why the expectation of reasonable disagreement, unlike pluralism, lies at the heart of political liberalism. We should therefore examine it more closely.

By "reasonableness" I mean thinking and conversing in good faith and applying, as best as one can, the general capacities of reason that belong to every domain of inquiry. The insight that has proven so significant for liberal thought is that reasonableness has ceased to seem a guarantee of ultimate agreement about deep questions concerning how we should live. In the early modern period, the expectation of reasonable disagreement arose primarily in the realm of religion; one learned to expect that reasonable people would differ about the correct path to salvation. But over the past four centuries the scope of this insight has broadened. It has become a salient feature of modern experience that on matters concerning the meaning of life, and also concerning certain deep aspects of morality, discussion among reasonable people tends naturally not toward consensus, but toward controversy. The more we talk about such things (sometimes even with ourselves!), the more we disagree.

In its full generality, the idea was embraced already by Michel de Montaigne, who was not so much the skeptic practicing suspension of judgment as the eager participant in the turmoil of thought. Thus he wrote:

En subdivisant ces subtilités, on apprend aux hommes d'accroître les doutes; on nous met en train d'étendre et diversifier les difficultés, on les allonge, on les disperse. En semant les questions et les retaillant, on fait fructifier et foisonner le monde en incertitude et en querelles, comme la terre se rend fertile plus elle est émiée et profondément remuée. *Difficultatem facit doctrina*. . . . Jamais deux hommes ne jugèrent pareillement de même chose, et est impossible de voir deux opinions semblables exactement, non seulement en divers hommes, mais en même homme à diverses heures.[30]

This expectation of reasonable disagreement about ultimate questions of value has not been an idea of solely political relevance. Having become a general feature of modern life, it has shaped many of the distinctive products of modern culture. The modern novel and its concern for the individuality of human lives is, for example, inconceivable without it. "The art of the novel," writes Milan Kundera, "came into the world as the echo of God's laughter. But why did God laugh at the sight of man thinking? . . . Because the more men think, the more one man's thought diverges from another's."[31]

Now an important and difficult question is *why* reasonable people should tend naturally to disagree about the meaning of life and about certain deep features of morality. After all, reasonable discussion about complicated issues does seem to lead to consensus in other areas, most notably in the sciences. The explanation cannot rest with prejudice and bias, since it is reasonable people who fail to secure agreement upon these matters. Nor can we be content to say, as Locke apparently was (*Essay concerning Human Understanding*, Book 4, chapter 16, section 4), that reasonable disagreement is only to be expected about opinions which can be but probable, never certain. For that would make incomprehensible the likelihood of agreement in the sciences. A more promising explana-

---

[30] Michel de Montaigne, *Essais*, III.13, in *Oeuvres complètes* (Paris: Gallimard, 1962), pp. 1043–44:

> By subdividing these subtleties they teach men to increase their doubts; they start us extending and diversifying the difficulties, they lengthen them, they scatter them. By sowing questions and cutting them up, they make the world fructify and teem with uncertainty and quarrels, as the earth is made more fertile the more it is crumbled and deeply plowed. *Learning makes difficulties*. . . . Never did two men judge alike about the same thing, and it is impossible to find two opinions exactly alike, not only in different men, but in the same man at different times.

(Translation by Donald Frame, *The Complete Essays of Montaigne* [Stanford: Stanford University Press, 1957], pp. 816–17.) Cf. also Thomas Paine, *The Rights of Man* (Harmondsworth: Penguin, 1984), II.5, p. 271: "I do not believe that any two men, on what are called doctrinal points, think alike who think at all. It is only those who have not thought that appear to agree."

[31] Milan Kundera, *The Art of the Novel* (New York: Harper and Row, 1988), p. 158.

tion has recently been proposed by John Rawls. He traces "the fact of pluralism," as he misleadingly calls the phenomenon of reasonable disagreement, back to "the burdens of reason":

(1) The empirical evidence may be conflicting and complex.

(2) Agreement about the kinds of considerations involved does not guarantee agreement about their weight.

(3) Key concepts may be vague and subject to hard cases.

(4) Our total experience, which shapes how we assess the evidence and weigh values, is likely in complex modern societies to be rather disparate from person to person.

(5) Different kinds of normative considerations may be involved on both sides of a question.

(6) Being forced to select among cherished values, we face great difficulties in setting priorities.[32]

Certainly, these factors play a role. Yet as Rawls himself observes, most of them are not peculiar to reasoning about values, and so fall short of the sort of explanation we seek. For my part, I believe that (4), the great variety of life-experiences created by modern society, with all its complex divisions of labor and its rich heritage of many different cultural traditions, provides the key to explaining the phenomenon.

But I also believe we will miss an important truth if we suppose, as we have done so far, that the peculiar fact requiring explanation is the likelihood of reasonable disagreement about complex questions of how we should live. It is perhaps a more peculiar fact, and the real departure from the ordinary course of things, that reasonable agreement should be so expectable in the sciences. This is not at all the way it has always been. Before the sixteenth and seventeenth centuries, reasonable disagreement was the norm in the study of the natural world. No two premodern physicists thought the same who thought at all. One of the distinctive features of modern science, which sets it off from the rest of the history of scientific thought, has been its remarkable ability to generate consensus. Reasonable disagreement in the handling of complex questions is perhaps just what we should expect (though our philosophical tradition has always preached that reason is what brings us together), and the extraordinary fact is that this has largely ceased to be so in the natural sciences. How should we explain *this* fact? The conventional answer, perhaps correct, is that in this domain of inquiry we have managed to get on the track of the truth. But we should also wonder whether such an explanation

[32] Rawls, "The Domain of the Political and Overlapping Consensus," pp. 236–37, and *Political Liberalism*, pp. 56–57.

does not reverse cause and effect, and whether "scientific truth" (as we now understand it) is not simply what a community of investigators will accept when they agree to subject their observation of nature to forms of reasoning designed to secure agreement.[33]

VI. Reasonable Disagreement and Skepticism

As I noted, explaining why reasonable people should tend naturally to disagree about fundamental questions of value is a difficult matter. I do not propose to solve the problem here. We do not need to have an explanation, in order to recognize the phenomenon. However, we do need to see how the expectation of reasonable disagreement differs from skepticism.

In a calm and careful discussion about the nature of the good life or about the precise role consequentialist and deontological considerations should play in moral reasoning, we would be foolish not to expect that our own views will meet with disagreement. From this expectation, though, we need not draw any skeptical conclusions. We need not suspend judgment about the correctness of our own views. We may still rightfully believe that, despite being controversial, they are better supported by experience and reflection than those of our opponents. This is because we can recognize that a view is reasonable, yet false: it may have been arrived at sincerely and in accord with generally accepted forms of reasoning, yet against the background of existing beliefs that our own viewpoint judges as false. When our background beliefs thus clash with those of someone else, this is not, I submit, a sufficient reason for us to suspend allegiance to these beliefs. To call them into doubt, we need some positive reason to think they may be false, one which we must be able to recognize as such by our own lights and which perhaps we may find in the opposing position, but one which must amount to more than just the existence of reasonable disagreement.

Some recent discussions fail to distinguish adequately the expectation of reasonable disagreement from skepticism. Thomas Nagel, for example, has suggested that reasonable disagreement of the sort I have been considering, toward which the liberal state aims to be neutral, occurs between views which fail to meet "a higher standard of objectivity"; such disagreement comes down finally to "a bare confrontation between incompatible personal points of view."[34] If this were the situation, then a skeptical suspension of judgment about such views would indeed seem the proper response, though Nagel denies it. But on the contrary, reason-

---

[33] See, on these lines, the fascinating study by Steven Shapin and Simon Shaffer, *Leviathan and the Airpump* (Princeton: Princeton University Press, 1985).

[34] Thomas Nagel, "Moral Conflict and Political Legitimacy," *Philosophy and Public Affairs*, vol. 16, no. 3 (Summer 1987), p. 232.

able disagreement can persist, even when we comply with the two conditions Nagel assigns to his "higher standard of objectivity": we may be
able to present others with the reasons for our view and even explain in
a detailed way what errors prevent them from agreeing with us. The
point is that when we do so, we are appealing to what we believe, to
what we have so far no reason to call into doubt, and these beliefs
amount to more than what reasonableness alone can guarantee. Different conceptions of the good life, and different conceptions of the weight
deontological and consequentialist considerations should have, generally
involve rather complex but different structures of purposes, significances,
and activities. It is on the basis of such structures that we can explain how
opposed views go wrong.

Thus, it is far from accurate to say, as Joshua Cohen has done, that in
affirming our own controversial view we are taking the "sectarian route"
of believing it "as a matter of faith," there being no further reason to take
our own view to be not only reasonable (about which there is no disagreement) but also true (about which there is).[35] On the contrary, we
may very well have reasons to hold our controversial view to be true. Our
allegiance to it may very well be more than a matter of faith. The point
is simply that our reasons lie outside what is the object of reasonable
agreement. Good faith and common reason are capacities we exercise
against the background of existing belief. It is, I believe, incorrect epistemology to suppose that they must suffice to decide between backgrounds
that conflict or that otherwise we must consider allegiance to such backgrounds as but a matter of faith. We examine the worth of any of our
beliefs (and so perhaps conclude it is but an article of faith) always in the
light of other things we already believe, if only because we could not otherwise establish the positive grounds for doubt that alone make it necessary to seek the justification of that belief.[36] We thus may have good
reason to believe more than what reasonable agreement with others can
determine. The expectation of reasonable disagreement should not lead
us to suspend allegiance to our controversial views or to regard them as
mere faith.

Thus, the idea that about matters of ultimate significance reasonable
people tend naturally to disagree, is distinct from both pluralism and
skepticism. It lies, moreover, unlike them, at the heart of a liberal political philosophy, which seeks to base the principles of political association
upon a core morality that reasonable people can accept despite the divergent conceptions of the good (and also of the right) that draw them apart.
If pluralism were an essential component of liberalism's self-understand-

---

[35] Joshua Cohen, "Moral Pluralism and Political Consensus," manuscript, pp. 18, 21,
forthcoming in David Copp and Jean Hampton, eds., *The Idea of Democracy* (Cambridge, UK:
Cambridge University Press, 1993).

[36] For more detail on the epistemology here, see my "Au-delà de la religion et des
Lumières," in *Modernité et morale*.

ing, then liberalism would fall significantly short of its ambition to build, as much as possible, upon common moral ground. For pluralism is itself an eminently controversial doctrine that many reasonable people, whether on religious or metaphysical grounds, do not accept; and even among themselves pluralists can achieve little agreement about what ultimate goods there are or what weight they should carry. A liberalism founded on pluralism would be too doctrinaire.

And if skepticism were an essential component of liberalism, it would be incomprehensible why the liberal project should be to look beyond the deep disagreements which divide reasonable people to the minimal principles on which they ought to unite. For if people were reasonable and skeptics about what they cannot agree upon, there would be nothing left to divide them, save at most personal acts of faith, but certainly not systematic visions of the good. A liberalism based on skepticism would be too irenic.

The natural tendency toward reasonable disagreement, duly distinguished from other notions with which it has been confused, belongs therefore at the center of liberal thought. Yet its significance, as I have observed, extends well beyond the political domain. Our intellectual tradition has been to a large and important extent *rationalist*, committed to the idea that *reason* leads naturally to *agreement*, that reason is what brings us together. The aspect of modern thought I have been examining challenges this preconception. We have yet, I believe, to take the measure of all that this challenge of modernity implies.

Philosophy, Columbia University

MORAL DISAGREEMENT AND MORAL RELATIVISM*

By Nicholas L. Sturgeon

In any society influenced by a plurality of cultures, there will be wide-spread, systematic differences about at least some important values, including moral values. Many of these differences look like deep disagree-ments, difficult to resolve objectively if that is possible at all. One com-mon response to the suspicion that these disagreements *are* unsettleable has always been moral relativism. In the flurry of sympathetic treatments of this doctrine in the last two decades, attention has understandably focused on the simpler case in which one fairly self-contained and cultur-ally homogeneous society confronts, at least in thought, the values of another; but most have taken relativism to have implications within a sin-gle pluralistic society as well.[1] I am not among the sympathizers. That is partly because I am more optimistic than many about how many moral disagreements can be settled, but I shall say little about that here. For, even on the assumption that many disputes are unsettleable, I continue to find relativism a theoretically puzzling reaction to the problem of moral disagreement, and a troubling one in practice, especially when the prac-tice involves regular interaction among those who disagree. This essay attempts to explain why.

The worries about practice I reserve to the end. Most of my discussion will explore two quite abstract difficulties about the relation of moral rel-ativism to moral disagreement. Neither is unfamiliar, but they seem to me related in ways not always noticed. One is that relativism seems in fact deeply ambivalent about how much moral disagreement we find in the world. There is a nice symptom of this problem in two recent survey arti-cles by David Wong, whose writings on this topic are frequently among the most helpful. One opens with a characterization of relativism as a

---

* I am indebted to the members of two graduate seminars on this topic at Cornell Uni-versity. I am also grateful for suggestions from the other contributors to this volume. I have benefited especially from discussions with David Phillips and Ki Jun Sung in the former cat-egory, and with David Brink, Gilbert Harman, and Geoffrey Sayre-McCord in the latter. Ter-ence Irwin also provided very helpful comments.

[1] Bernard Williams is an exception, by his own stipulation, in "The Truth in Relativism," in *Moral Luck* (Cambridge, UK: Cambridge University Press, 1981), pp. 137–38. He contin-ues to focus on differences between entire cultures in *Ethics and the Limits of Philosophy* (Cam-bridge, MA: Harvard University Press, 1985), pp. 156–67.

I do not mean to suggest, of course, that cultural differences are the only source of deep moral disagreements, or that there cannot be such disagreements in a culturally homoge-neous society. But cultural differences are one prominent source of such disagreements, and are often taken as central in defenses of moral relativism.

"common response to the deepest conflicts we face in our ethical lives," such as the "apparently intractable disagreement" over abortion; the other begins by describing the most interesting versions of relativism as doctrines that respond, *not* to conflicts or disagreements but merely to "differences in ethical belief," and do so by construing them "so that conflict or disagreement is either eliminated or mitigated."[2] The source of this tension is not far to seek. If relativism is the view that in these deep disagreements both sides are *right*, then on a couple of natural assumptions—that disagreement means holding beliefs inconsistent with one another, and that being right means believing something true—relativism threatens to endorse contradictions, not a promising line to take. The usual response by relativists, including Wong,[3] is to reconstrue the beliefs so that the inconsistency disappears. But then so does the disagreement. It is at least a superficial oddity in relativism about any topic, not just morality, that a view that typically begins by insisting on the intractability of disagreements that others might hope could be settled, should conclude that the disagreements were never real to begin with. I believe that this can become a serious problem for relativism, when pressed. I shall explain one philosophically interesting strategy for accommodating the oddity, a strategy that may help make relativism plausible about some topics. What I shall argue is that this strategy is not plausible for the moral case.

The second problem for relativism that I shall explore can be captured by the question "Why not nihilism?" One sometimes hears the apparently intractable disagreements among theistic religions offered as some evidence for atheism: that is, for the conclusion that all the competing views are mistaken, not that they are all somehow correct. It seems worth asking why moral relativists should not be content with a comparable con-

---

[2] David Wong, "Relativism," in Peter Singer, ed., *A Companion to Ethics* (Oxford: Basil Blackwell, 1991), p. 442; David B. Wong, "Moral Relativism," in Lawrence C. and Charlotte B. Becker, eds., *Encyclopedia of Ethics* (New York: Garland Publishing, Inc., 1992), p. 856.

A similar tension appears to shape Richard Brandt's presentation of relativism in "Ethical Relativism," in Paul Edwards, ed., *The Encyclopedia of Philosophy* (New York: MacMillan, 1967), vol. 3, p. 75. He defines "meta-ethical relativism" as the denial "that there is always one correct moral evaluation" on a given issue. But as written, that makes too many of us relativists: about a given action, one moral evaluation might be that it is right, another that it is good. (If the moral judgments they supply need not conflict, belief in more than one true morality is commonplace.) Am I being unfairly literal? Two sentences earlier Brandt speaks of "incompatible" evaluations, so perhaps that is supposed to be implicit in the definition of relativism. However, the examples he then gives of relativist views (E. A. Westermarck's, Ruth Benedict's) all insure that moral opinions which appear to conflict, don't really. Is it to be required, then, that the equally correct evaluations at least *appear* to conflict? He doesn't say. In an earlier definition in Brandt, *Ethical Theory* (Englewood Cliffs, NJ: Prentice-Hall, 1959), he requires that the conflict be genuine (p. 273); but relativism is there formulated as the view that conflicting moral opinions can be equally valid, where validity is clearly a kind of justifiability, not truth (p. 272). So no contradiction threatens. Thus, his formulations carefully steer clear of committing relativism to contradictions, but in consequence leave it unclear what it is committed to.

[3] David Wong, *Moral Relativity* (Berkeley: University of California Press, 1984).

clusion in response to apparently intractable moral disagreements. This seems to be J. L. Mackie's response, for example, since he takes the intractability of (especially) cross-cultural moral disagreements as evidence that *none* of the competing moral views is true.[4] Moral nihilism would have the advantage, on the first problem I mentioned, of preserving the apparent logical relations among the disputed views. Atheists can regard Trinitarians and Unitarians as really disagreeing. If they read the competing views as entailing the existence of a deity, they will see them as all false, and thus as logical contraries (statements of which at most one can be true, but which can all be false), not contradictories (of which at least one must be true). Another approach that might better capture the sense that theological disputes are "empty" if atheism is true, would treat most of the competing claims as merely presupposing theism, in something like P. F. Strawson's sense,[5] rather than entailing it, and so take them to lack truth values. On either of these variants of nihilism—I shall not attempt to choose between them in my discussion—the inconsistencies are where they appear to be, and the disagreements whose unsettleability creates problems for ethics are genuine.[6]

My suggestion is that a reasonable relativist ought to address both these problems by conceding (1) that at some level the disagreements *are* genuine, and that at that level nihilism is correct. What the relativist also needs to maintain, however, is (2) that it is still reasonable to keep the same *language* in which the disagreements were formulated, to express different but related pairs of propositions that do not conflict, and thus might both be true; and (3) to regard ourselves and others as having in some sense been getting at no more than these nonconflicting propositions all along. The primary challenge for a relativist, on my understanding, will be to explain and defend steps (2) and (3). They are not plausible steps in every case: none of the writers I am considering shows any temptation to relativism about religion, for example. I find Philippa Foot convincing when she claims that (2) and (3) *are* plausible for some judgments of taste: we show no discomfort in continuing to use the same objective-looking terminology in these judgments even as we realize that all we can reasonably be claiming (and should take ourselves to have been claiming) is something whose truth depends on our own community's reactions.

[4] J. L. Mackie, *Ethics* (Harmondsworth: Penguin Books, 1977), pp. 36–38.

[5] P. F. Strawson, *Introduction to Logical Theory* (London: Methuen, 1952), p. 175. Strawson takes a statement p to presuppose a statement q if q must be true in order for p to be *either* true or false.

[6] What I call "nihilism" could also be called "skepticism," and sometimes is. I prefer to reserve the latter term for an epistemological stance such as doubt or the view that we do not know which of the conflicting positions, including nihilism, is correct. But there is some precedent for applying the label "skeptic" to anyone who either "doubts of everything" *or* "who denies the reality and truth of things"; see George Berkeley, *First Dialogue*, in David M. Armstrong, ed., *Berkeley's Philosophical Writings* (London: Collier Books, 1965), p. 131.

I disagree, however, with her assertion that there is no principled barrier to our making the same relativistic adjustment in our moral language.[7]

I. Forms of Relativism

Before I go further I need to say what I understand by moral relativism, or at least which versions I propose to consider and why. A reader who looks to standard discussions will find uniformity neither in terminology nor in doctrines distinguished, though certain ideas recur.[8] The distinction I have found most helpful is one introduced by David Lyons between *agent* and *appraiser* versions of moral relativism.[9] Agent relativism takes the moral character of an agent or an agent's act (in my examples, always the rightness or wrongness of an act) to be determined by factors that include, essentially, some feature that can vary across agents. In Lyons's discussion, this feature is the set of norms accepted by the agent or the agent's social group; I ask below what else might count. Appraiser relativism, by contrast, sees the truth conditions for moral judgments made by a given appraiser as determined by factors essentially including a feature that can vary from appraiser to appraiser—such as, again, the appraiser's moral norms.

These two sorts of views—roughly, that we ought to judge others by their standards, and that we ought to judge them (and everything else) by ours—get conflated in popular and anthropological discussions but typically not in philosophical ones. Philippa Foot and David Wong defend forms of appraiser relativism, though Foot argues that this also implies a limited agent relativism.[10] The relativism defended by Gilbert Harman,

---

[7] Philippa Foot, "Moral Relativism," The Lindley Lecture, University of Kansas, 1978; reprinted in Michael Krausz and Jack W. Meiland, eds., *Relativism* (Notre Dame: University of Notre Dame Press, 1982); references are to the reprinted version.

[8] Compare just the four discussions by Wong and Brandt cited in note 2; also Gilbert Harman, "What is Moral Relativism?" in A. I. Goldman and J. Kim, eds., *Values and Morals* (Dordrecht: Reidel, 1978), pp. 143–61.

[9] David Lyons, "Ethical Relativism and the Problem of Incoherence," *Ethics*, vol. 86 (1976), pp. 107–21; reprinted in Krausz and Meiland, eds., *Relativism*; references are to the reprinted version. Lyons initially distinguishes agent's—from appraiser's—*group* relativism, but quickly generalizes to consider versions that focus on the individual's rather than the group's norms (pp. 211–13).

[10] To be precise: In "Morality and Art" (*Proceedings of the British Academy*, vol. 56 [1970]; all references are to the version reprinted in Ted Honderich and Myles Burnyeat, eds., *Philosophy As It Is* [Harmondsworth: Penguin, 1979], pp. 7–28), and in "Moral Relativism," Foot defends moral relativism against some common objections, and maintains that it might be true, not about all, but about a large number of moral issues, if they prove unsettleable. But at the conclusion of the latter article she explicitly declines to endorse it, because she thinks it premature to say how much is settleable. For brevity I shall sometimes refer to her as a relativist, always thereby alluding only to the portion of her argument in which she defends that view.

by contrast, is primarily an agent version that makes the wrongness of acts for an agent depend on requirements not to perform them that the agent accepts. His view also includes an appraiser element, in that a speaker is not normally to call an act wrong unless she endorses the agent's principles. But Harman allows that this normal implication of speaker endorsement can be canceled; and almost all of his *argument* is a defense of agent-relativity, rather than of this constraint on appraisers. (Also, no speaker endorsement is involved in *denying* that an act is wrong. Harman maintains, controversially, that because of his motivational makeup, it was not wrong of Hitler to order the Holocaust; but Harman does not take himself, in making this judgment, to be endorsing anything about Hitler's motives.)[11] Not all of the views that have been called relativist fit neatly into these two categories; I shall discuss below one proposal, Bernard Williams's "relativism of distance," that does not.[12] But, for reasons I shall explain in due course, I doubt that its failure to fit is a defect in the categories. In this essay, my main focus will be on appraiser relativism, for a reason I shall defend in my next section: namely, that it is appraiser relativism, not agent relativism, that is distinctively a response to the unsettleability of moral disagreements. Indeed, appraiser relativism is the doctrine I have so far just called "moral relativism." But I shall touch on some issues about agent relativism for comparison.

Since I mean to contrast relativism and nihilism, I find it a virtue of this classification that moral nihilism does not itself count as any kind of relativism. Both appraiser relativists and nihilists deny that there is a "single true morality,"[13] but nihilists do so because they think the correct number less than one (because it is zero), relativists because they think it greater. Here I break with some entrenched philosophical taxonomy, since the standard discussions do often count nihilism as a form of rela-

---

[11] For Harman's views, see his "Moral Relativism Defended," *Philosophical Review*, vol. 84 (1975), pp. 3–22; reprinted in Krausz and Meiland, eds., *Relativism*; references are to the reprinted version. See esp. pp. 192–95. See also Harman, "What is Moral Relativism?" and "Relativistic Ethics: Morality as Politics," in Peter A. French, Theodore E. Uehling, and Howard K. Wettstein, eds., *Midwest Studies in Philosophy*, vol. 3 (Minneapolis: University of Minnesota Press, 1980), pp. 109–21; and Harman, *The Nature of Morality* (New York: Oxford University Press, 1977), pp. 91–124.

[12] The view defined by Charles L. Stevenson — in "Relativism and Nonrelativism in the Theory of Value," in *Facts and Values* (New Haven: Yale University Press, 1963), pp. 71–93 — does not fit either category; but as Foot points out, in "Moral Relativism," p. 153, Stevenson's definition is decidedly strange, and he has not been followed by other writers. Another that does not fit is what David Wong, in "Relativism" and "Moral Relativism," calls "normative moral relativism." In Brandt, "Ethical Relativism," and Harman, "What is Moral Relativism?," this term names some kind of agent relativism, but Wong reserves it for a doctrine that condemns condemnation of those with irreconcilably different values and prescribes noninterference. I confess to not seeing what is relativistic about this view, as opposed to the agent- or appraiser-relative premises from which it is sometimes defended.

[13] David Wong's phrase, in *Moral Relativity*, p. 1.

tivism.[14] But I believe that intuition, at least, is on my side: recall, again, that no one thinks of atheism as a form of relativism about religion. For a similar reason, I confine my discussion to versions of relativism, especially appraiser relativism, that attribute truth values to moral opinions. Some discussions have formulated relativism in terms of 'validity' rather than 'truth', as the thesis that conflicting moral opinions can both be 'valid'. One reason has been to leave open the possibility that some noncognitivist views might be relativist, even though noncognitivists deny truth-values to moral opinions.[15] But precisely because it regards moral views as neither true nor false, I see noncognitivism as a version of nihilism: an important challenge, but one best addressed under that heading rather than in a discussion of relativism. Noncognitivism is a doctrine with well-known difficulties of its own, moreover; and many writers sympathetic to relativism (e.g., Foot and Wong) clearly see it as an attraction of their position that it offers an *alternative* response to failures of objectivity in ethics. So I put noncognitivist views to one side here.[16] Another reason for talking of validity appears to have been an interest in the question of whether competing moral views can ever be equally *justified*, in that it would be equally reasonable to believe either.[17] Here I confess to

[14] The four survey discussions by Brandt and Wong, cited in note 2, all count nihilism or near relatives as a kind of relativism. Brandt does note, in *Ethical Theory*, that the "methodological relativist" who denies that there are any "correct" ethical judgments, might better be called a skeptic than a relativist (p. 275); and Harman explicitly refrains from classifying such a skeptic as a relativist ("What is Moral Relativism?" p. 148).

[15] Lyons, "Ethical Relativism and the Problem of Incoherence," p. 211. Noncognitivism takes the primary function of moral language to be the expression of favorable and unfavorable attitudes toward the items evaluated, rather than the expression of beliefs capable of truth and falsity. (Some contemporary noncognitivists will regard my characterization of their view as misleading, on the grounds that they can in a principled way *mimic* everything a cognitivist might say about the truth-values of moral opinions. I doubt that they can. But if they can, then noncognitivist versions of relativism will after all fall under my definition, so long as the definition is expanded to cover mimic-truth as well as truth.)

[16] Of these two reasons for bracketing noncognitivism, the first is sufficient for ignoring it when saying how, on a relativist view, moral opinions can be *right*. Relativists should speak of truth. But I have already indicated my view that, at another level, a sophisticated relativist should be a nihilist. So might not noncognitivism serve at that level? It could promise an account of how disagreements can be in a way genuine (by being disagreements in attitude) without involving inconsistent beliefs. We might then have a position similar to A. J. Ayer's in the introduction to the second edition of *Language, Truth, and Logic* (New York: Dover, 1946), pp. 20–22: truth-values can be assigned to appraisers' moral judgments on the basis of their own basic moral principles; disagreements among appraisers with the same principles will thus involve genuinely inconsistent beliefs; but disagreements among those with different basic standards will be merely noncognitive. Here my second reason is needed: This is a possible solution, but one that, for good reasons, none of the writers I am focusing on wishes to adopt. Opposition to noncognitivism is a recurrent theme in Foot's writings. For Wong, see *Moral Relativity*, pp. 10–16; for Brandt, *Ethical Theory*, pp. 203–40. These latter two discussions, with Foot's "Moral Arguments" and "Moral Beliefs," both in her *Virtues and Vices* (Berkeley: University of California Press, 1978), provide a good introduction to difficulties with noncognitivism—though one should see in addition Peter Geach, "Assertion," *Philosophical Review*, vol. 74 (1965), pp. 449–65.

[17] Brandt, *Ethical Theory*, p. 272.

thinking that the answer is yes, but that this is not in any obvious way paradoxical. It will become paradoxical if one is thinking of ideal justification by the believer's standards, and thinks (as I do not) that this insures the truth of the belief; but in that case the doctrine again falls under appraiser relativism as I formulate it.

Agent and appraiser relativisms come in both social and individual versions. The relevant feature of an agent or appraiser might be, for example, either membership in a social group with certain standards, or individual commitment to those same standards. Many relativists have favored social versions, but most philosophers defending the view have thought that their arguments extended to the individual versions as well.[18] I shall take advantage of this latter concession by considering only individual versions except when I specify otherwise. I believe that everything I say applies with appropriate transformations to social versions also. On many points this will be obvious, on others it may not; but spelling out this extension for some of my arguments would impose a cost in length and complexity not compensated by anything new of philosophical interest.

A different question concerns what limits, if any, a definition of relativism should place on the "variable feature" of agents or appraisers that is said to determine the rightness of acts or the truth of judgments. We might decide to put no limit on this for appraiser relativism:[19] the proposal that altitude above sea level matters (you're right if you're over ten thousand feet, wrong otherwise) is a silly view without philosophical interest, but we might count it a silly, uninteresting version of *relativism*. With agent relativism, matters are more complex, however; for as is often noted, ethical doctrines no one would dream of calling relativist allow that features of an agent's circumstances (such as what promises he has made, or the options available to him and their consequences) can determine whether his act is right or wrong. Thus, we need to say what is distinctive about the features an agent relativist will appeal to. And the answer is, I think, more generally useful. For I believe that this same restriction is a good guide to the most characteristic and interesting versions of appraiser relativism, too, though not, as we shall see, to every doctrine that has been put forward under that name.

Harman seems to me to go wrong on this topic, in his attempt to define normative moral relativism (his term for one variety of what I am calling agent relativism).[20] He rejects Richard Brandt's definition, according to

---

[18] For example, Harman, *The Nature of Morality*, pp. 113–14; Foot, "Moral Relativism," p. 157; Brandt, *Ethical Theory*, pp. 279–80. On David Wong's view, see note 35 below.

[19] Except that we will not count relativism true because of the uncontroversially indexical features (tenses, overtly indexical terms) common to moral and other assertions.

[20] Harman, "What is Moral Relativism?" pp. 143–45. Only one variety, because he denies that what Brandt formulates is any kind of relativism, whereas I take it to be one version of agent relativism.

which what makes an action wrong is the agent's, or the agent's group's, *thinking* it wrong, and proposes a more abstract account instead.[21] Simplifying slightly,[22] Harman's proposal is that, according to normative moral relativism, agents can be subject to different fundamental moral demands. If we assume that it is morally wrong to violate fundamental moral demands one is subject to,[23] this gives us a definition of agent relativism, as the view that fundamental moral demands can vary from agent to agent, and that it is wrong for agents to violate them.

But this definition seems too broad. I agree that Harman's own version — according to which what demands one is subject to depends on which ones it is rational for one to accept, which depends in turn on which ones one already accepts — is relativist. But other stories about how basic moral demands can vary are not relativist. Consider a rule-utilitarian view like Brandt's,[24] according to which the moral demands on an agent are captured by the learnable rules that if recognized, etc., by her society, would maximize utility. It is understood that the demands may vary from society to society because of differences in circumstances. But isn't the rule-utilitarian principle itself a fundamental demand on all agents? No. It is a proposition about the correct rules, not a rule; and there is no guarantee that the corresponding rule ("Follow those learnable rules which if recognized by your society . . .") will be part of the ideal code for any society, much less for every society. Whether it is included will depend on whether that makes the code produce better consequences, and it may not. So fundamental demands on agents may differ. Or consider Hobbes's view in *Leviathan* that obligations (that is, moral demands) arise only from an agent's own acts. The acts Hobbes has in mind are such expressions of one's will as promises and covenants.[25] Samuel Clarke objected that on Hobbes's own view not *all* obligations could depend on human will in this way, for the general obligation to abide by one's promises and covenants cannot.[26] Clarke is right about one thing. Hobbes needs (and states) a general principle, that promises

---

[21] Brandt, "Ethical Relativism," p. 76.

[22] By assuming that in every set of moral demands some are fundamental.

[23] Harman will presumably not allow us to *say* that this is wrong, for a given agent, unless we also endorse the demands in question or else *explicitly* cancel the endorsement. See above.

[24] Richard Brandt, "Toward a Credible Form of Utilitarianism," in Hector-Neri Castañeda and George Nakhnikian, eds., *Morality and the Language of Conduct* (Detroit: Wayne State University Press, 1963), pp. 107–43. Brandt defines rule-utilitarian views as those "according to which the rightness of an act is not fixed by *its* . . . utility [relative to alternative acts], but by conformity with general rules or principles; the utilitarian feature of these theories consists in the fact that the correctness of these rules or principles is fixed in some way by the utility of their general acceptance" (p. 109).

[25] Thomas Hobbes, *Leviathan* [1651], ed. C. B. Macpherson (Harmondsworth: Penguin Books, 1968), pp. 191–93, 268.

[26] Samuel Clarke, *A Discourse of Natural Religion* [1705], in D. D. Raphael, ed., *British Moralists 1650–1800* (Oxford: Clarendon Press, 1969), vol. 1, pp. 194–95, 221–24.

and covenants create obligations, that he has not shown to depend for its truth on the agent's will. But Clarke is wrong about another point, for it does not follow that Hobbes must admit any obligations beyond those that agents voluntarily incur. He can deny that we have, in the normal case, a general obligation to keep promises and covenants.[27] There is the correct general principle, that promises create obligations, but normally no general obligation, only the specific obligations that promises create. So moral demands, including fundamental moral demands, will vary from agent to agent.

Hobbes's view is radically voluntarist and individualist. Other features of it, moreover, may be in some sense relativist. But there is nothing relativist about *this* fragment of it. Indeed, as I mentioned, that an act may be either right or wrong depending on what promises one has made is a standard example of the sort of dependence of morality on circumstances that no one thinks amounts to relativism.[28] Similarly for rule-utilitarianism, which is virtually never mentioned as a form of relativism.[29] So we need an explanation of why, although Harman's own view about the source of moral demands is certainly relativist, these other doctrines that would fall under his definition are not.

My suggestion is that the most characteristic versions of relativism are, in a sense I shall explain, forms of subjectivism. There are states and activities of appraisers (and of agents), of which the normal, preanalytic, perhaps naive view is that they function as *responses* to facts or reality of some sort—in the moral case, to moral facts or reality. This is clear about beliefs on almost any subject: their function is to respond to the world by representing the world correctly, though of course through malfunction they may misrepresent it. It is also a plausible view of moral (and many other) emotions: approval is supposed to be of what is good, admiration of what is admirable, resentment of what is wrong or unfair or unjust. On other topics, sensations or perceptions are thought of in this role: how things taste or look to us is supposed to reveal whether they are good-tasting or good-looking (and also, for example, what color they are),

---

[27] We will have it if, but only if, we have promised or covenanted to keep all our promises and covenants.

[28] And Harman clearly recognizes this; for in "Moral Relativism Defended," he insists that although the coordination in moral intentions that agents arrive at through implicit bargaining is a kind of "agreement," it is *not* an agreement "in the sense of a certain sort of ritual indicating that one agrees" (p. 199)—that is, not a promise or covenant. Similarly, when he describes the relevant sort of moral intention as the agent's accepting a moral demand "as a legitimate demand on him or herself" ("What is Moral Relativism?" p. 154), he cannot mean that this should be understood on the model of the agent's making a vow or promise, for the view that vows or promises can create obligations is hardly relativistic.

[29] Though, I should note, Brandt himself says that his view admits a "kind of relativism" in implying "that an act might be right in one society which would be wrong in another society"—a relativism, however, that "most philosophers" would view as "innocuous" ("Toward a Credible Form of Utilitarianism," p. 135). He is certainly right that it would be viewed as innocuous; I doubt that most would think it relativism.

though none of us trusts these indicators as perfectly reliable in fulfilling this function. To have a term, I shall call states (and activities) that are naturally, perhaps naively, viewed in this way *response-states*. And my proposal about relativism is this: Agent relativism is a view that takes one of these subjective response-states, understood to vary from agent to agent, to be what makes his actions right or wrong, what their rightness or wrongness consists in. And the most characteristic versions of appraiser relativism do the same for appraisers and their judgments, by promoting one of these apparently fallible subjective responses that varies from appraiser to appraiser to a status in which it sets the truth-conditions for their (differing) judgments.

This suggestion seems to fit the examples we have been considering. Rule-utilitarianism makes differing fundamental demands on different agents, but not at bottom because of any difference in their response-states;[30] and it does not seem relativist. Neither, for similar reasons, does the view that promises, and only promises, oblige. Here the differing demands arise from something closer to the agents, certain of their own acts, but still not from response-states. On a naive, preanalytic view there are, to be sure, promises we morally ought to make, but more typically we are (on that same view) morally free to promise or not, and the acts we promise to perform are understood to become obligatory only because of our promises. We are not malfunctioning as promisers when we promise to do something that would otherwise be morally optional, or fail to promise to do something that is obligatory anyway. The case seems quite otherwise, by contrast, with Harman's proposed source of varying moral demands, the agent's *accepting* a requirement "as a legitimate moral demand on him or herself,"[31] where this acceptance is not to be understood as making a vow or promise. The naive view is surely that, in accepting something *as* a legitimate moral demand, one should be sensitive to whether it really is one. Someone who accepts a moral requirement of lifelong chastity when there is no such requirement is malfunctioning as a moral-demand-accepter. And if there is a moral requirement not to do such things as ordering the Holocaust, and Hitler fails to accept it, then Hitler is malfunctioning. I should emphasize that Harman, like most sophisticated relativists, leaves room for a kind of malfunctioning here: anyone who corrected for ignorance and various uncontroversial mental defects, he believes, might accept different demands than she actually does. But he holds that the outcome of these corrections will vary depending on what demands people accept to start with. So his view still makes the demands they are subject to, depend on which ones they already accept; and on my definition that makes his view a version of relativism, as he intends.

---

[30] Any utilitarian view will of course attribute derivative importance to such differences insofar as they contribute to different consequences for actions or (in this case) moral codes.

[31] Harman, "What is Moral Relativism?" p. 154. See note 28.

My proposal also does a good job, I believe, in identifying the most characteristic versions of appraiser relativism. Taking as a model relativism about some judgments of taste, a doctrine she finds plausible, Foot suggests that relativism makes the truth of our judgments depend on our own or, more typically, our community's shared reactions: in these examples, on the way things look and taste to us.[32] She also says, in what appears to be meant as a more general and definitive formulation, that what is most characteristic of relativism is that it makes the truth of our judgments in an area a function of our standards for arriving at and evaluating such judgments.[33] This general formula strikes me as right: it seems to capture what relativists usually have in mind when applying their position outside ethics, for example.[34] On either characterization the appeal is clearly to response-states. The ways things taste and look to us are central examples of such states; and standards, on any ordinary understanding, are the sorts of things that are supposed to be correct but may fail to be so. This is clear when they are embodied in basic beliefs that we can formulate explicitly (for beliefs are paradigm response-states). But it seems equally true on the understanding Foot appears to favor, according to which the standards are implicit in our procedures for refining and criticizing our initial reactions. We certainly do have ways of challenging and refining not only our reactions of taste but also our more or less intuitive moral judgments, to arrive at a more reflective view. A relativist, according to Foot, will see the truth-conditions for our views as fixed by the most basic standards implicit in this practice. So her appraiser relativism fits my account nicely. So does David Wong's, for the same reason. Wong rephrases typical moral judgments into assertions about what an adequate moral system of norms would require; the view is relativist because it supposes that different appraisers accept different basic standards for the adequacy of such systems, and because these standards are said to fix the truth-conditions for their respective moral judgments.[35] I shall call any view of this sort a *relativism of standards*.

As nicely as it fits these central examples, however, my suggestion may be strained to accommodate another familiar kind of relativist proposal. These are views that can be developed out of an ideal-observer approach

---

[32] Foot, "Moral Relativism," p. 193.

[33] *Ibid.*, pp. 155, 157; Foot, "Morality and Art," p. 19.

[34] See, for example, the introduction to Krausz and Meiland, eds., *Relativism*, p. 3.

[35] Wong, *Moral Relativity*, pp. 40–73. Wong sometimes describes his relativism as a theory of "morality as social creation" (e.g., p. 61), but this is at least misleading. It is not obvious that there is anything in his view that actual systems of moral norms have evolved in response to human needs for resolving internal and interpersonal conflict that a nonrelativist need reject. What makes his view relativist is his skepticism about the possibility of settling disagreements about which possible systems are adequate, and his view that, in many of these (apparent) disagreements, both sides, appealing to different standards, are right. That is why, despite the talk of "social construction," his view can easily accommodate individual appraiser relativism.

to ethics. Ideal-observer theories propose that the truth about various moral issues should depend on what reaction an observer would have to the nonmoral facts of the case under specified, highly idealized conditions (full information, impartiality, dispassion, perhaps benevolence, etc.). But what if people differ in ways that would lead them, even under those idealized conditions, to react differently? One possibility is to say that the truth-value of any given appraiser's views on these issues then depends merely on what *her own* reaction would be under these ideal conditions. Proposals of this sort are certainly appraiser relativist, and they have found philosophical defenders.[36] Indeed, on questions of taste it would be possible to understand Foot's view as a relativism of this kind: that something is good-tasting or someone good-looking says something about how the appraisers would respond under modestly idealized conditions, even though under those conditions different communities respond differently.[37]

Whether I can fit these proposals under my suggested definition depends mainly on what sort of reaction by the ideal observer is supposed to matter. If the question is what the observer would resent or would morally approve of, for example, my proposal fits nicely, for these moral emotions are moral response-states.[38] So, as I have remarked, are the ways things taste and look, on questions of taste. But if all that is asked by a moral-ideal-observer test is what an observer would *desire* or *prefer*, then I face a problem. There will still be no difficulty if, in arriving at this desire or preference, an observer is supposed to rely on moral standards he cares about. For reasons I shall explain, however, it is typical of views of this sort to insist, not just that the observer need not, but that he *must* not, rely on his moral views. In that case, these proposals escape

[36] Roderick Firth proposes a nonrelativist theory in "Ethical Absolutism and the Ideal Observer," *Philosophy and Phenomenological Research*, vol. 12 (1952), pp. 317–45. Richard Brandt favors a relativist version in his subsequent discussion with Firth (*Philosophy and Phenomenological Research*, vol. 15 [1955], pp. 407–23) and is hospitable to a similar idea in his *Ethical Theory*, pp. 279–84, and (with a very different idealization) in *A Theory of the Good and the Right* (New York: Oxford University Press, 1979), p. 194. Harman also considers this sort of relativism in *The Nature of Morality*, pp. 44–46. Other alternatives if observers differ, of course, would be (a) to refine the idealization, or (b) to say that there is no (moral) truth about moral issues on which observers differ. Brandt mentions (a) in his discussion with Firth (p. 409); I explain below why this option will rarely be available to a relativist. I have been unable to find in this literature more than passing attention to (b) — that is, to my question, "Why not nihilism?" — though see Brandt, *Ethical Theory*, pp. 279–80.

[37] Foot denies emphatically that judgments of taste are "descriptions of reactions" ("Moral Relativism," p. 53); but her target in this remark is Stevenson, who has relativism equating value judgments with descriptions of "de facto approvals" ("Relativism and Nonrelativism in the Theory of Value," p. 82), something no *ideal*-observer theory does.

[38] Francis Hutcheson and David Hume, philosophical ancestors of this view, speak regularly of "approval," "approbation," and "a sense of virtue." In *Ethical Theory*, pp. 173, 248, 265–66, Brandt invokes emotions including indignation, and feelings of obligation, as well as mere preference, depending on the question being decided; in *A Theory of the Good and the Right*, he asks only about willingness to act in a certain way. Harman (*The Nature of Morality*, p. 43) suggests that we would need to know what an observer would approve of *morally*.

my definition. For although one can maintain that desire and preference are response-states to value in general (that is, that on an ordinary understanding desire is misdirected unless it is for something in some way already desirable), it is not plausible that as ordinarily understood they are supposed always to respond to *moral* value.[39]

Call the versions of appraiser relativism that fit my initial definition, both standards-relativism and some ideal-observer theories, *response theories*; and call the ones that elude it *reaction theories*. I return to consider the merits of all these views below, in Section V. Here I shall conclude this survey of alternatives by (1) noting how different in substance relativist reaction theories are likely to be from familiar ideal-observer theories, and (2) pointing out how different in motivation any ideal-observer theories, but especially the reaction theories, are from any relativism of standards.

1. In focusing on relativism as a response to unsettleable disagreements, we are probably safe in ignoring all but a very restricted range of possible ideal-observer theories, for the following reason. First, as is often noted, ideal-observer theories inevitably take certain moral standards for granted in the way they specify their idealization. For example, if the observer is required to be impartial among individuals, this amounts to assuming that everyone's interests count equally.[40] Second, the idealization in such a theory is supposed to tell us how to assess the truth of *anyone's* moral views, whether she shares our moral standards or not. Thus, an ideal-observer theorist must be careful to build into his proposed idealization only those moral assumptions that he regards as objectively correct.[41] If the ideal-observer theorist is a *relativist*, however, the class of assumptions he views in this way is likely to be quite small. It may not be empty, for the relativists I am considering do not all believe that there are no objective moral truths. But they think that there are none about issues that prove unsettleable, and they regard the number of unsettleable issues as large. This will limit the idealizations they can propose. To take an example, David Wong believes that there is no objective answer to the question whether, morally, everyone's interests count. Many of us would be inclined to reject as inadequate any moral system that ignored

[39] There are at least two readings of this latter view, a stronger and a weaker. The stronger would say that desire malfunctions whenever it is guided by anything but moral value, an absurd view. The weaker would say only that it is misdirected if it fails to accord appropriate weight to moral value. This may accord with *some* ordinary understandings, but I shall put no weight on it.

[40] I put this roughly. But even on Roderick Firth's careful (and thin) formulation ("Ethical Absolutism and the Ideal Observer," pp. 337–38) impartiality will preclude discounting someone's interests simply because she is "not one of us," and that is enough for my purpose.

[41] That is, if you are going to evaluate the truth of someone else's views by standards she would reject, you had better think that your standards are correct and hers not; you can hardly be thinking that yours are no closer to the truth than hers.

the interests of outsiders, but many *actual* moral systems have done this, and Wong thinks there is no way of settling a disagreement between their defenders and one of us.[42] No one who agrees with him could require an ideal observer to be impartial. And, in general, the idealizations available to a relativist will tend to lack many or all of the constraints present in familiar ideal-observer views, such as Roderick Firth's. Of course, as is often noted, these same familiar constraints are what make the idealizations look initially plausible as tests for *moral* judgments.[43]

2. The motivation behind these reaction theories contrasts strikingly with that behind any version of standards-relativism. As my term is meant to suggest, the idea behind these latter doctrines (for example, Foot's or Wong's) is that the truth-conditions of our judgments are set by our own basic standards. So, whether or not our basic standards can be defended objectively, we are to trust them. But these standards receive a very different welcome in any ideal-observer theory, especially the ones I am calling reaction theories. *Some* standards matter, of course, for the objective ones may be used in defining the appropriate ideal conditions under which an observer is supposed to respond. But the rest of our standards play no role at all. Indeed, *precisely because* they have no independent objective justification, the observer is instructed not to rely on them in any way.[44] Now, it is not clear that this is really possible if the observer is supposed to respond with a moral emotion such as moral approval or resentment, for these attitudes are sometimes thought to depend for their very identity on the appraiser's applying moral concepts.

---

[42] I believe he allows that an insider-morality will be (objectively) inadequate if the outsiders are in a position to make trouble about their exclusion; such a moral system will then not do a good job of resolving many interpersonal conflicts. But there is, he thinks, no objective way to fault a system of moral norms that ignores outsiders who cannot fight back. See Wong, *Moral Relativity*, pp. 55–57, and Wong, "On Moral Realism without Foundations," *Southern Journal of Philosophy*, vol. 24, Supplement (1986), pp. 107–11.

[43] See Brandt, *A Theory of the Good and the Right*, pp. 193–95, 225–28, for an idealization that abandons many of the familiar constraints, criticizing them partly for assuming things that are in dispute. For the suggestion that these constraints are part of what mark the idealization as a *moral* test, see Harman, *The Nature of Morality*, p. 43. For Firth's view, see references in note 36.

[44] When an ideal-observer theory is advanced as an analysis of the meaning of moral assertions, the attribution of moral beliefs to the observer can be rejected as making the analysis circular (Firth, "Ethical Absolutism and the Ideal Observer," pp. 326, 328; though this seems an objection only to requiring the observer to have such beliefs, not to allowing her to do so). But even those who do not take the proposal as an analysis commonly say that the observer will use no moral beliefs; see Harman, *The Nature of Morality*, p. 50. Brandt (*A Theory of the Good and the Right*, p. 203) makes explicit what I take to be the basic idea behind the restriction, that any reaction by the observer that is founded on a moral view "is based on what is at this stage a groundless belief": "at this stage" because, if every observer reacted the right way, the belief *could* turn out to be objectively justified.

Note that Brandt reserves the term "ideal-observer theory" for views like Firth's and does not apply it to his own, with its very different idealization; I am using the expression more broadly. Also, everyone realizes that *having had* various moral beliefs may influence how an observer reacts even when he no longer relies on them; but the hope appears to be to minimize this effect.

This is a recognized problem that I shall return to in Section V. Reaction theories clearly avoid this difficulty, however. They ask an observer to determine what she would want or prefer as the result of a process of deliberation from which her own standards and values are excluded, and to regard this fact about her motivational makeup as the truth-maker for her moral judgments. As a result we have, under the single label of appraiser relativism, two very different sorts of view. One, in the face of apparently irresolvable moral disagreements, instructs us to trust the basic standards we bring to these issues; the other, by contrast, tells us to distance ourselves from those standards as far as possible.

II. Disagreement

It is common to suggest that all versions of moral relativism owe their interest or motivation to the thesis that there are unsettleable moral disagreements.[45] But I believe that this is mistaken about agent relativism, for a couple of reasons. For one thing, whatever the interest and plausibility of such principles as that, when other guides are uncertain, one should be loyal to one's own deepest moral commitments, they do not depend on there being disagreements unsettleable in *principle*; they will have plenty of application so long as there are issues that are uncertain in practice. For another, agent relativism is itself a normative ethical theory,[46] and a highly controversial one. So if we cannot settle any controversial normative issues objectively, we cannot settle whether agent relativism is correct; and if we can determine, objectively, that agent relativism is correct, then we can also settle a great many other deep moral controversies on its basis. Thus, anyone attempting to establish agent relativism would be ill-advised to do so by appealing to the unsettleability of moral disagreements.

It is not surprising, therefore, that Harman, who does believe that his agent relativism can be established against alternative doctrines, nowhere defends it by such an appeal.[47] He offers two other arguments for it instead. In his earliest published defense, he calls it a "soberly logical thesis" and compares it to the view that judgments of largeness implicitly invoke a comparison class:[48] that is, to the sort of thing any competent

---

[45] See Brandt, "Ethical Relativism," pp. 74–75, and Wong, "Moral Relativism," pp. 856–57, where the suggestion, more precisely, is that versions of moral relativism will be uninteresting unless there are at least moral disagreements that would survive possession of complete nonmoral information. This weaker claim also seems wrong about agent relativism.

[46] And the term "normative relativism" is often reserved for some version of it; see note 12.

[47] He does appeal to *differences* in what people accept as moral demands. But these will involve no disagreement when agents accept these only as demands on themselves; and when appraisers disagree about what demands an agent is subject to, he regards the disagreement as resolvable.

[48] Harman, "Moral Relativism Defended," pp. 189–90.

speaker should be in position to recognize. In later presentations, he uses a different comparison and a different argument. The comparison is between moral relativism and the thesis that mass is relative to an inertial framework: [49] the latter is a substantial discovery, not a view accessible to just any speaker. The argument is that we have inherited a nonrelativist picture of morality which conjoins conditions that turn out, empirically, not be jointly satisfiable; and that his relativism, while of course not preserving everything in that picture, does a better job than various alternatives in holding onto its most central features.[50] It is the best fallback position. I am unconvinced, mainly because I think Harman underestimates the alternatives; but I regard this pattern of argument as entirely legitimate, and as far more promising than appeals to intuition about logical form.

My justification for focusing on appraiser relativism, then, and for turning to agent versions only for comparison, is that I am here exploring relativism as a response to disagreement: and defenses of appraiser relativism, by contrast with those of agent versions, do appeal centrally to the unsettleability of moral disagreements. Since my main interest is in a hypothetical question, moreover, of just how we are to get to relativism if some strong version of unsettleability is granted, I shall not balk at granting for the sake of argument that there are unsettleable moral issues, and that their unsettleability invites nihilism, the thesis that there is no moral truth about those issues, as one possible explanation. My question will then be how relativism might be plausible as a rival (or, I shall suggest, complementary) explanation for the same facts.

My concession is in one respect larger than it may look, because unsettleability in these debates is a very strong claim: not just that the issue cannot be settled with certainty, but that nothing could tip the scales, objectively, in one direction or the other. It is in another respect not very large, however, until we have said how many unsettleable issues there are and how central they are. These questions matter because writers like Foot and Wong think that some moral issues can be settled objectively even if others cannot, and that makes their position, abstractly, no different from any sensible version of moral realism. For realists must allow at a minimum, I think, that there are genuinely borderline cases about which there is no determinate objective moral truth.[51] The difference will presumably come over the extent and centrality of the indeterminacies,

[49] Harman, "What is Moral Relativism?" pp. 159–60.

[50] Harman, "Relativistic Ethics: Morality as Politics," pp. 113–14, 117–20.

[51] See Richard N. Boyd, "How to Be a Moral Realist," in Geoffrey Sayre-McCord, ed., *Essays on Moral Realism* (Ithaca: Cornell, 1988), pp. 212–13; Richard W. Miller, "Ways of Moral Learning," *Philosophical Review*, vol. 94 (1985), p. 509; and David O. Brink, *Moral Realism and the Foundations of Ethics* (Cambridge, UK: Cambridge University Press, 1989), p. 202. I understand moral realism to be the view that there are objective moral truths, independent of our beliefs and of our evidence for them, and that we have some knowledge of these truths. See Brink, ch. 2, for a discussion of problems in defining the position.

with relativists seeing them as more pervasive and as affecting more core issues than a moral realist would. Thus, for the sake of discussion I shall assume that relativists are right about this, too.

One might suppose that relativism could be right about the objectively indeterminate issues even if those issues were as few and peripheral as realists hope. But although that seems theoretically possible it is not a view with much intuitive pull. For when the unsettleable issues are nicely confined among clearly settleable ones, relativism does not seem a very plausible approach to them, compared just to the sort of local nihilism any moral realist might accept. Consider an example Foot and Wong both give of an unsettleable issue, that of the permissibility of abortion.[52] This would not be my example, since I regard the permissibility of at least early abortions as quite settleable; but since I do admit unsettleable questions, let me use their example for the sake of discussion. Suppose, then, that we have a standoff, objectively speaking, between the competing views, that at least some abortions are permissible and that none are; and assume that the neighboring issues are settleable, that there is nothing wrong with contraception, everything wrong with killing young children. On these assumptions I see no temptation whatever to say that both of the conflicting sides are *right*. Their views are understandable, no doubt, perhaps each right about some subsidiary issues, and equally justified; but on the main issue each thinks there is a determinate truth (and has a view about what it is) when, it seems more plausible to say, there isn't. Relativism has no obvious purchase on such cases.

The implausibility of relativism in such cases *might* just be a function of scale, however. For as the area of objective indeterminacy expands, a policy of simply ceasing to make the disputed claims will come closer and closer to ruling out moral thought and language altogether. On a view like Foot's or Wong's, it will never reach that limit; but the effect of this policy on one's moral judgments might be dramatic, even so, if one came to agree with Wong that it is objectively indeterminate not just whether one should accord moral standing of some sort to fetuses, but whether one should accord it even to competent adults outside one's own society.[53] One might then find attractive the idea that moral language could be enlisted for the sort of use the relativist has in mind, to express the implications of our own outlook even in the face of objective indeterminacy, rather than remain silent about so much. Of course, finding the idea attractive does not yet guarantee that it is plausible as a proposal for interpreting anyone's moral views. I return to this question below.

Even if relativism did look more plausible when applied to large-scale than to small-scale indeterminacies, however, it would still be in serious trouble if it had no counter to the accusation that it must construe dispu-

---

[52] Foot, "Morality and Art," pp. 14, 21; Wong, *Moral Relativity*, pp. 190–97.
[53] See note 42.

tants who are genuinely disagreeing as if they were merely talking past one another. To that central problem I now turn.

III. Genuine Disagreement

Recall the nature of the difficulty. Opponents of abortion say, "It's never permissible"; their opponents reply, "It's sometimes permissible"; and the relativist, who wishes to ascribe truth to both remarks but not to endorse inconsistencies, must say that the remarks do not contradict one another and that the disagreement is therefore not genuine.[54] Relativism thus requires us to understand different speakers who say, "It is permissible" (or who say things we would unhesitatingly translate with these words), as saying different things — as asserting only relativized or "local" propositions, I shall say, following Foot — since the remark may be true coming from one of their mouths but false from another's.

But that is at least counterintuitive, as relativists themselves seem prepared to concede. We would have one sort of philosophical debate if the parties simply divided into camps with conflicting intuitions, nonrelativists seeing as univocal disputes that do not strike relativists that way at all. Relativists might then regard this objection to their view as question-begging. Foot was once inclined to give this reply to the objection,[55] but in her subsequent, fuller exploration of moral relativism she drops this suggestion, and her discussion displays in clear, even surprising ways the force for her of her opponents' intuition (which I shall call "the univocality intuition"). Thus, in explaining the relativism about tastes and looks that she wishes to use as a model for moral relativism, she says that this view does face "a problem." What gives relativism purchase in this area are such facts as this: that although we apparently differ radically from the ancient Mexicans in our judgments about which faces are good-looking, we are inclined even in light of this knowledge to go on calling our own judgments true without disparaging theirs as false. The "problem" Foot sees is that, precisely because the standards employed on the two sides are so different, we might doubt that these judgments "are *about the same thing*."[56] She does not mean that they might be about different faces; the concern is that the diverse judgments might not be attribut-

---

[54] Foot's terminology in "Moral Relativism" can at least appear to suggest an alternative relativist line, which would allow that the assertions genuinely contradict one another, but would ascribe to each of them not truth but only "local truth," truth-by-the-appraisers'-standards. This would allow genuine disagreements while keeping the relativist from endorsing contradictions. However, this proposal creates enormous logical difficulties; and it fails in any case to accommodate Foot's clear view (p. 161) that those who make the first-order assertions, using no truth-predicate, are claiming only local truth for their views, and so not contradicting one another. Thus, I take her talk of "local truth" or "relative truth" to be shorthand for talk of the *truth* of local or relativized propositions, as explained in the text.

[55] Foot, "Morality and Art," p. 15.

[56] Foot, "Moral Relativism," p. 154; emphasis in original.

ing/denying the same property to the faces. The interesting surprise here is that she should regard this concern as a problem *for relativism*, even conceding that we would not count as "certainly relativistic" diverse judgments in any area that could not be shown to have a common subject matter. This is a surprise because, if relativism is the view that these apparently conflicting judgments are both true, the relativist should *want* to say that the judgments are not about the same thing, that each expresses only a relativized or local proposition fixed in part by the standards or reactions of the appraisers. It is the opponents of relativism who deny this; and Foot's remarks on this point seem a clear concession to those opponents.

I believe that it is not her only such concession. Consider her argument that I alluded to above, that her appraiser relativism leads to a limited form of what I am calling agent relativism. Her claim is that a relativist and a nonrelativist will have to judge differently the actions of a third party doing what they both, on their own principles, regard as wrong, but which they realize is in no way contrary to the principles of the agent. To keep our same example, suppose that our two appraisers, one a relativist and the other not, are opponents of abortion, and that our agent is obtaining one.[57] The nonrelativist, according to Foot, can regard the agent as acting badly, even though following her conscience, because the truth that her abortion is wrong is there to be discovered, and because she did not care enough about the truth to discover it. Her fault is thus a kind of negligence about moral truth.[58] But the relativist cannot see the agent as acting badly in this way, Foot says. For the relativist does not believe that this truth, that the abortion is wrong, is there for the agent to discover; there is no such truth.[59] Notice, however, that Foot's appeal in the last step of this argument seems not really to relativism at all, but

---

[57] Strictly, to fit Foot's schema, the agent should believe herself morally required to have the abortion. But this makes no difference to Foot's point or to my comment on it.

[58] Foot here cites Thomas Aquinas, *Summa Theologiae*, 1a, 2ae, Q6, A8, and Q19, A6, apparently with approval, agreeing that on a nonrelativist view the moral truth "is there to be seen by anyone who wants to see it" and that ignorance of it is therefore always culpable ("Moral Relativism," p. 160). This is surprising. At the end of the same essay, she turns to the question of whether persistent moral disagreements might in fact prove settleable, and argues that a negative answer is premature. She believes that we might make progress on many of them if we knew more of the nonmoral facts of human life than any of us now does, and had better philosophical theories than any now available on such key topics as value and happiness (*ibid.*, pp. 164–66). But it seems clear that if *that* is what it would take to settle some disputed moral issue, then it certainly does not follow, about anyone who is mistaken about it, that his error is culpable, a simple neglect of "what is there to be seen." And I believe that Foot is right the second time about how difficult settling a moral issue can be. People can be as obtuse or as willfully blind about morality as about anything else, but there are many other ways to go wrong.

[59] Foot, "Moral Relativism," pp. 159–60. Foot does not say why a *relativist* is required to agree that no one acts badly in following her conscience unless she should have known that her action was wrong. Perhaps this is supposed to be one of those objective principles to which relativism does not apply.

to nihilism. According to relativism, as Foot explains it, the appraiser's judgment about the agent, "Her abortion is wrong," claims only truth by local standards, and it may well be right. If it is, then this truth will be one that it is not too hard for anyone, including the agent, to discover, for it can be settled just by determining what the appraiser's standards for wrongness are and by seeing whether they are satisfied. Any appraiser, therefore, who knows that the agent's act is, by his standards, wrong, but who thinks nevertheless, "There's no fact of the matter, that her abortion is wrong, for her to discover," seems to be thinking something *inconsistent* with relativism. This is, instead, nihilism. But nihilism, as I have emphasized, differs from relativism in preserving the intuition that the appraiser, in thinking the agent's abortion wrong, and the agent, in thinking it not wrong, really disagree; what the nihilist adds is that, since this genuine disagreement is unsettleable, neither judgment is correct. Here again, Foot's appeal appears to be to the univocality intuition, and to a conclusion that would follow only if it were true.

Consider just one more example, in which another defender of relativism ascribes to the doctrine consequences that would seem to follow only if deep moral disagreements are genuine. David Wong writes about meta-ethical relativism (his term for appraiser relativism) that if it is true,

> even if only with respect to a limited set of moral conflicts such as abortion, then our moral condition is immeasurably complicated. We must strive to find what will be for us the right or best thing to do, and also deal with the feelings of unease caused by the recognition that there is no single right or best thing to do.[60]

But, to begin with, relativism does not imply "that there is no single right or best thing to do." If relativism is a correct account of our judgments then the reference of "right" or "best" for any appraiser is determined partly by some feature of the appraiser (such as his standards), and the resulting reference may well be unique. Other appraisers, according to relativism, speak truly in applying the same *words* to other things, but that is because the words are ambiguous; only momentary forgetfulness about this point, I surmise, could let one see them as attributing to actions the same property as do one's own judgments, thus forcing upward one's count of the right things to do.[61] And, more generally, if one is clear

---

[60] Wong, "Relativism," p. 449.

[61] Appraiser relativists sometimes compare moral terms to indexicals like "here" and "now" (Foot, "Morality and Art," p. 19; Wong, *Moral Relativity*, pp. 44–45). Imagine telling someone who has declared "I've decided to live here for a while" that this project will be immeasurably complicated by the fact that "here" is an indexical, so that there is no one place that is here. Precisely because it *does* function as an indexical, "here" in our agent's declaration picks out a single place, within the usual limits of vagueness, and there is typically no difficulty in settling what the place is. The implications of relativism for someone determined to do the right thing for a while, or for a lifetime, will be similar.

about these doctrines' differing positions on univocality, relativism surely looks more like a source of reassurance than of unease. Realism and nihilism agree that those other competent people with very different values are actually disagreeing with you, that their views are thus a challenge to yours and the fact that they are held a potential reason for doubt. Relativism, by contrast, denies that the disagreements are genuine, and so denies that they provide any challenge or any reason for doubting your own views. It assures you, in fact, that so long as your moral judgments fit whatever is said to be the appropriate feature of yourself (in Wong's version, your standards for applying the expression, "adequate moral system"), then your judgments are correct no matter what others may think. When any relativist describes her view as a *troubling* one, therefore, it seems again a reasonable surmise that she has lost sight of the relativist position on univocality: further testimony, I think, to the plausibility of the opposing intuition on that question.[62]

IV. A Relativist Proposal

The widely held intuition of univocality is not, then, simply a problem foisted on relativism by its opponents. As Bernard Williams summarizes the issue, to explain away a conflict relativism "has to say why there is no conflict and also why it looked as if there were one"; a problem is that "the more convincing it is to claim that the statements are really [compatible], the more puzzling it is that people should have thought there was a conflict."[63] But they have certainly thought this.

It appears to be because he regards this problem as insoluble that Williams, looking for an appropriate response to "nonobjectivity" in ethics, attaches the name "relativism" to a doctrine very different from any we have considered. This is his "relativism of distance," which depends on

[62] Wong's views on this issue are more interesting than this one (uncharacteristic) passage suggests. A fuller consideration of his reasons for thinking relativism a complication to our moral lives would have to examine his detailed argument (*Moral Relativity*, pp. 179–90) that, because of contingent features of our moral outlook, relativism speaks for tolerance by us of those who do not share it. As he explicitly notes (p. 189), his argument can *appear* to make the slip I have attributed to Foot, of appealing to nihilism in a way that is actually inconsistent with relativism. On his own understanding the argument appeals instead to an explanation of how moral disagreements between parties with very different standards can appear genuine. His explanation is that although there is no semantic disagreement in such cases, there is nevertheless a *pragmatic* one, in that different people who correctly attach a moral term to conflicting actions will then see reason to act in conflicting ways (pp. 44–45, 64). But I do not see in Wong's position adequate support for the postulated connection between moral judgments and reasons for actions. His account of moral judgments is, as he notes, externalist (p. 15; "On Moral Realism without Foundations," p. 112), as it appears it must be. Perhaps further explanation would fill this gap.

[63] Williams, *Ethics and the Limits of Philosophy*, pp. 156–57. Williams actually speaks only of "relational" relativism in the second sentence quoted, but he clearly doubts that any form of appraiser relativism escapes this difficulty.

a distinction between those divergent outlooks that are real options for someone, in that he could "go over" to them without engaging in extensive self-deception or losing his grip on reality, and the others that are not. Applied to ethics, this doctrine says that it is appropriate for him to use "the language of appraisal"—talk of what is good, bad, right, wrong, true, false—only of real options, not in what Williams calls merely "notional confrontations" with those outlooks so distant that he could not adopt them while retaining his hold on reality.[64] But this doctrine appears to have little to be said for it. It does not capture what seems the deepest relativist intuition, that there is something equally *correct* about the opposing views, even as it is applied to distant options, much less to real ones. It conflicts in a different direction with what I would suppose the more natural view, that if one has any confidence in one's own outlook, then one will more easily call false those conflicting outlooks to which one could not convert without losing one's sanity than those one could adopt far more easily. And, in any case, Williams himself does not take this doctrine very seriously. He explicitly calls attention to his unwillingness to apply it to judgments of social justice.[65] He does not point out that it also conflicts with one of his more striking doctrines, his ascription of ethical knowledge to a "hypertraditional society." The hypertraditionals make their way through life applying "thick" ethical concepts about which they never reflect critically. They surely provide a paradigm of a life none of us could turn to without losing our hold on reality and engaging in extensive self-deception. But Williams argues that their ethical judgments constitute knowledge, and he accepts the usual view that knowledge requires truth.[66] So he certainly holds that we may apply the language of appraisal to options that are not real for us.

If Williams's alternative proposal is a dead end, perhaps we ought to ask again whether the univocality problem for appraiser relativism is as hopeless as he appears to assume. Is there no way of explaining how it could be a surprising discovery, contrary to deeply held intuition, and yet a convincing one, that people are systematically talking past one another in the way relativists claim? As I have indicated, there does seem to me one suggestion a relativist can make here. It is modeled on the more interesting of the two arguments Harman gives for his agent relativism;

[64] *Ibid.*, pp. 160–62. Compare Williams, "The Truth in Relativism," pp. 137–42.

[65] Williams, *Ethics and the Limits of Philosophy*, pp. 220 (n. 3 to ch. 9), 165–67. In "The Truth in Relativism," Williams had endorsed this form of ethical relativism without qualification. As Samuel Scheffler points out, Williams's exception for judgments of social justice is not due to his thinking those judgments *objective*; see Scheffler, "Morality Through Thick and Thin," *Philosophical Review*, vol. 96 (1987), p. 428.

[66] Williams, *Ethics and the Limits of Philosophy*, pp. 142–48. If the unreflectiveness does not by itself disqualify the hypertraditionals' outlook as a real option, note that no limit is placed on the content of their "thick" concepts: so we may imagine their values to be as different from ours as we please.

indeed, Harman may mean to put forward something like it on behalf of appraiser relativism.[67] This suggestion has the advantage of addressing together both questions I raised at the outset: the question of why unsettleable disagreements should drive us to relativism rather than just to nihilism, and the question of what relativists should say about the intuition of univocality in these disagreements. It is also, I believe, a plausible response on behalf of relativism about at least some topics, such as judgments of taste.

The suggestion comes in three parts. (1) First, it concedes that many moral appraisers are not relativists. Some explicitly reject relativism: they believe that many of the deep moral disagreements on which they take sides have unique, objective answers. Others, perhaps a larger group, are at least implicitly nonrelativist: for, whatever they may say (possibly nothing) on multiple-choice quizzes in meta-ethics, they are like the first group in thinking and arguing about concrete moral issues *as if* even the most deeply contested ones had objective answers. There is thus considerable basis, explicit or implicit, for attributing nonrelativized moral beliefs to these appraisers, beliefs that genuinely conflict. And on this understanding of their beliefs about deeply contested moral issues (which is, explicitly or implicitly, the appraisers' own understanding), moral nihilism is true. (2) Second, it argues that appraiser relativism describes a use of moral language that provides a natural and uniquely reasonable alternative, a fallback position, from the mistaken nonrelativist view. By a "fallback position" I do not mean just anything one might do with the terminology of a position abandoned as mistaken, but one that involves using it to say what look like many of the same things, though now meaning by them something true and defensible. Thus, if the relativism in question is a relativism of standards, the proposal would be that one start meaning by the claim that a certain sort of action is wrong no more than that it is wrong by one's own basic standards.

So far this does not look like an argument that relativism is true. It looks like a concession that nihilism is true about the thought of many moral appraisers toward unsettleable issues, coupled with a recommendation for a new way of talking, and of understanding our own talk, that would *make* relativism true if everyone came to adopt it. (Call this way of talking and thinking a relativist *stance*.) But there is a third part to the suggestion. (3) With an eye to recent influential discussions of reference, and

---

[67] See notes 49 and 50. It is unclear to me whether Harman thinks the problem he addresses in "What is Moral Relativism?" pp. 159-60—the problem of genuinely conflicting judgments both taken to be true by the relativist—can arise on his own agent-relative theory. It is hard to see how it could, except (possibly) in the rather special case in which an agent accepts conflicting demands; for no matter how different the moralities accepted by two appraisers, they cannot on Harman's view make a true judgment about an agent except relative to the moral demands accepted by the *agent* (p. 158). So Harman may be offering his suggestion *simply* on behalf of appraiser relativism.

to plausible analogues in the history of science, the relativist may argue that this is a case in which the truth-conditions for the assertions of even nonrelativist appraisers depend on factors outside the appraisers' heads,[68] and are correctly captured by a relativist theory. Just as we take Lavoisier's claims about acids to refer to proton-donors, even though that could not have been his conception of an acid, with the result that his remarks turn out true or false in ways he could not have foreseen; so, the relativist will argue, the remarks of even nonrelativist appraisers can appropriately be evaluated as true or false by relativist standards. Something about what is in the heads of those appraisers does matter to the argument. It matters that if they became aware that many important moral issues, as they had been conceiving of them, have no answers — that is, that point (1) is correct — then they would themselves find reasonable the transition to the proposed relativist stance — that is, point (2) is correct. Indeed, according to this argument, it probably matters that they then would be inclined to apply this relativist reconstrual to their own past thought, just as we suppose that a better-informed Lavoisier would accept our construal of his.[69] Exactly why the transition to the relativist stance is put forward as reasonable may vary in detail with the variety of

---

[68] Hilary Putnam, "The Meaning of 'Meaning'," *Philosophical Papers* (Cambridge, UK: Cambridge University Press, 1975), vol. 2, pp. 215–71, and other essays in that volume; Saul Kripke, *Naming and Necessity* (Cambridge, MA: Harvard University Press, 1980); Richard Boyd, "Metaphor and Theory Change," in A. Ortony, ed., *Metaphor and Thought* (Cambridge, UK: Cambridge University Press, 1979), pp. 356–408. Putnam's article is the source of the claim that meanings "ain't in the *head*" (p. 227); he means, as the history of science examples are intended to illustrate, that the truth-conditions for a speaker's statement may be set by factors the speaker would not, and perhaps could not, recognize as playing this role. This is the suggestion I am supposing a relativist might want to exploit. Of course, the relativist will nominate for this role factors that, in another sense, certainly *are* in the speaker's head: namely, certain of his response-states or other subjective reactions.

A relativist who takes this line might see herself as turning the tables on recent moral realists, who have taken "externalist" or "causal" accounts of reference of this sort to be crucial to the defense of their own view. See, in addition to the works cited in note 51, Robert M. Adams, "Divine Command Metaethics Modified Again," in *The Virtue of Faith* (New York: Oxford University Press, 1987), esp. pp. 133–43; and Nicholas L. Sturgeon, "Moral Explanations," in David Copp and David Zimmerman, eds., *Morality, Reason, and Truth* (Totowa, NJ: Rowman and Allenheld, 1985), pp. 49–78.

[69] Strictly, and for the record: I doubt that counterfactuals like these must be true of every speaker whose remarks we are entitled to evaluate for truth by our own (as we think) improved standards. (For a writer who appears to think that they must apply, see Miller, "Ways of Moral Learning," p. 516.) It may be enough that there is a sequence of positions intervening between that of the speaker we are interpreting (Lavoisier, say) and our own, which looks to us like a series of successive improvements, and such that a better-informed Lavoisier would have accepted the reconstrual provided by the first, a better-informed proponent of the first would have accepted the reconstrual of her view provided by the second . . . and a better-informed proponent of the last would have accepted our reconstrual. The same would apply to any reconstrual of moral assertions. This complication makes no difference to my argument in this essay, however, for in any sequence of reconstruals that begins with a nonrelativist moral understanding and ends with a relativist one, there must be one that makes the transition from nonrelativism to relativism, and the argument that follows in the text will apply to that step. I am grateful to Geoffrey Sayre-McCord for pressing me on this point.

relativism, but not, I believe, by much. A standards-relativist will say that the transition preserves much of the structure of the appraisers' moral thinking, by having them continue to rely on their standards as they have all along; and she can add that the reconstrual takes as the truth-maker for their views the only factor in the world that has *actually* been regulating their judgments on unsettleable issues, namely these same standards, rather than any moral facts independent of the standards. Ideal-observer theories, though as different in their motivation as I explained above, are nevertheless typically defended by claiming that the test they propose is implicit in our actual standards; and in that case the argument on this issue will be the same.

Attribution of content to beliefs is notoriously context-sensitive, and if a story this complex is correct, it would not be plausible to say that the relativist reconstrual captures for every purpose what moral appraisers who do not accept relativism are claiming. It would probably be better just to say that there is one natural perspective, comparable to the one we often take toward Lavoisier, from which it does capture this—but to add that any overall interpretation of their views must tell a story at least as complex as this three-step one.[70] Despite this concession, most philosophers would regard this story, if it were true, as a vindication of relativism. And its complexity is an advantage, not a weakness. For it certainly makes clear why defenders of relativism would, and should, retain a sense that the disagreements to which they apply their doctrine are in a way genuine, and that relativism is a response to the discovery that these genuine disagreements are unsettleable. It thus makes sense of Foot's restricting relativism to differences that are, on their initial understanding, about the same thing, however they may look on a relativist reconstrual; and it removes the inconsistency from her supposing that a relativist can recognize, about a moral claim true by his own standards, a natural understanding of it on which it instead states no truth that is available to be discovered. The question of whether moral relativism should occasion unease seems to me more complicated, and I shall come back to it in Section VI. But the complex relativist story I have just sketched is nihilist about the issues in intractable moral disagreements when those issues are understood as the participants themselves understand them; and that can provide a disquieting piece of news even when accompanied by the suggestion that a reasonable fallback position is available.

This way of approaching relativism also helps to bring out something distinctive, but easily overlooked, about the fallback stance the relativist

---

[70] Harman ("What is Moral Relativism?" pp. 159–60) relies on the nonrelativist construal in determining whether appraisers disagree, but the relativist one in assessing truth, and thus gets the striking result that appraisers who genuinely disagree can both be right. But, of course, on the construal on which they disagree, the relativist will say neither is right, and on the construal on which both are right, they don't disagree.

proposes as reasonable. It differs from an alternative fallback stance that I shall call "simple disambiguation." Suppose that I and another novice in biology have been debating whether some simple organism is a plant or not, and that we then discover (a) that there are two ways of drawing this line that are equal-best scientifically, and (b) that I have been using one of them and am right by that standard, and my friend has been using the other and is right by her standard. In some ways this resembles what relativists think happens in ethics. We thought our disagreement was univocal, and on that understanding of it, it had no answer. Noticing in retrospect that it was not univocal, moreover, we can each see a way in which we were both right. There the resemblance ends, however. For we can *also* both see in retrospect a way, exactly equally important, in which we were both *mistaken*. And precisely for this reason it would strike us both as perverse, and not at all a reasonable fallback stance, for us now to use language as the relativist would recommend: that is, each keeping the world "plant," for example, and continuing to apply it only by whichever standard we had been employing in the course of our disagreement. Instead, we would now each have *two* terms in our vocabularies, each associated with a different standard, and both standards would have become ours.

Unrecognized ambiguities can occur in moral debate as anywhere else and need to be diagnosed. Recognition of them can complicate our moral lives.[71] But their existence does not establish relativism. The relativist has to insist in addition on the rational superiority of a quite distinctive response to them, one that evaluates each appraiser's views for truth *only* by her own standards, even though other standards are acknowledged to be equally good. This seems to be the truth in the suggestion that relativism treats key moral terms as implicitly and ineliminably indexical: [72] it is as if "That's wrong" meant (on a relativism of standards), "That's contrary to my (or 'our') standards."

V. Problems for Relativism: Theory

For purposes of my discussion the three-step relativist story I have sketched breaks naturally into two parts. The first claims that there are pervasive unsettleable moral disagreements about which nihilism is (in a way) true. This much I continue to allow for the sake of argument.

---

[71] By analogy, notice the complication to my practical life if the borderline organism of my example is edible and I am a vegetarian; I will need somehow to refine my practical commitment. And notice that there would *not* be this complication if my use of the term "plant" *merely* referred to what fit my own standards for planthood, as relativism would suggest, for in that case my determination to eat only plants had and has a determinate reference, and discovery that there are other equally good ways of drawing the line would not be troubling. See note 61.

[72] See note 61.

The second part recommends a revised relativist stance in thinking and talking, in response to the first point, and appeals to the unique reasonableness of this fallback stance as a reason for applying relativist truth-conditions even to the moral views of nonrelativists. I believe that there are severe difficulties with this second part for every version of appraiser moral relativism. The fallback stance is not reasonable, if it is even available. I shall offer three objections, the first directed at any moral relativism of standards, the second partly dependent on the first but directed at moral-ideal-observer relativisms, the third an independent criticism that depends on a feature of Foot's and Wong's theories.

I should emphasize that my objections are not to this general strategy for assigning truth-conditions to beliefs that rest partly on mistaken assumptions. This strategy yields plausible results in other applications; and something like it seems required for anyone who wishes, as I do, to defend a naturalistic semantics for moral discourse while conceding (for example) that for many appraisers moral claims are barely distinguishable from theological ones. It would be reasonable for a moral relativist to hope, therefore, that it might help in defense of her doctrine. But it turns out to be no help.

1. Here is a problem for any relativism of standards, in particular for the view that the reasonable stance to fall back to from nihilism, about an issue discovered to be unsettleable, is to begin meaning by one's claims about the issue only that the claims are true by one's own basic standards. I have done enough stage-setting that the objection can be put briefly. It is intended to capture the intuition that there is something self-defeating about trying to save one's doubtful views by (as it were) relativizing them to the fact of one's holding them. The central difficulty is that if nihilism is the appropriate response to the discovery that an issue, as one has been conceiving of it, is unsettleable, then that provisional nihilism must extend not just to views one has held directly on that issue but also to whatever features of one's standards required those views. If there is no truth about an issue, then one cannot regard as true any standards one has held that require one view rather than another about it. As a consequence, the starting point for the proposed transition to relativism will be one in which one *has* no standards bearing on the disputed issue. A relativistic stance is offered as a reasonable way of filling that vacuum, but there is no way it can. Adopting that stance involves counting as true whatever one's basic standards dictate about the issue, and no more. But one has abandoned one's old nonrelativist standards, as they bear on it, so they dictate nothing about it, and this new relativist standard will of course dictate nothing by itself. Before it can do that, it requires that one have other basic standards for it to endorse. So, contrary to what was promised, a transition to a relativistic stance will not preserve the structure of one's moral thought, keeping one relying on the same old standards. Those standards have been abandoned, and a rela-

tivistic stance can do nothing to retrieve them. Thus, it is not really a fall-back position at all, much less a reasonable one, for it leaves one essentially where one began.

Contrast this with a case of simple disambiguation. Here too we may react to unsettleability with a provisional nihilism: to the question, "Is this a plant or not?" as we had been understanding it, neither of our answers is correct. But there is no difficulty falling back to a more reasonable con-strual of the question (or questions), because there are two standards that are equally good objectively and we disambiguate by accepting them both. There is no requirement, as there is in the proposed transition to a relativistic stance, that one adopt either standard on the ground that it is *one's own*.

Someone may now object that it is artificial to think of moving to a rel-ativistic stance by way of nihilism. It strikes me, on the contrary, as the most natural way to think of it. And, in any case, I have shown that defenders of relativism regularly appeal to nihilist construals of moral assertions, as opposed to strictly relativist construals, particularly in acknowledging the force of their opponents' intuition that unsettleable moral disagreements are genuine. My story about how to become a rel-ativist is an attempt to make sense of this duality of vision; and without it, relativism is again vulnerable to the objection that it must deny the genuineness of many disagreements that everyone, including the relativ-ist, does regard in this way.[73]

What I am here endorsing will be recognized as a version of the famil-iar claim, often denied by relativists, that relativism undermines convic-tion. It gets you into nihilism, and then lacks the resources to get you out. It is of course a criticism of relativists that they fail to see this. But I do not suggest that undermining conviction is always a bad thing. As I have indicated, I believe that a reasonable moral realism must allow that there are moral questions which, as they are framed, lack determinate answers. Insofar as lacking conviction involves refusing to pretend that there are determinate answers where there aren't, it is of course the right way to think about these issues, not the wrong one.

2. Foot notices that many arguments against moral relativism seem to prove too much. For they would apply equally against relativism about

[73] There may also be a temptation to play with the formulation of relativism. My objec-tion could be avoided if relativism took the truth-conditions for an appraiser's views to be fixed, not necessarily by her current standards, but by the most recent standards she has held bearing determinately on the issue. There is an air of ad hoc desperation about such a suggestion, however. This is not what relativists have in general meant to say about appraisers whose standards are in transition. Even if basic standards are not objective, rel-ativists allow that they may change. So imagine someone who has always held standards by which abortion is wrong, but who is now quite uncertain about this issue, and whose standards have adjusted to cohere with this uncertainty. No appraiser relativist wants to say that, when she contemplates her former confident view that abortion is wrong, this appraiser's thought still counts as true because of what she *used* to think.

judgments of taste, but relativism about some judgments of taste seems quite plausible.[74] The argument I have just given is certainly general: it would apply to a relativism of standards about any topic, not just morality. So have I proven too much?

I believe that the answer is one I suggested above, that Foot's relativism about the good-tasting and good-looking is easily construed as an ideal-observer relativism, not a relativism of standards. And it is a plausible ideal-observer relativism. There is a standard involved, to be sure, to the effect that these predicates apply to what we would have certain responses (Foot says "reactions") to under somewhat idealized conditions. Our idea of the relevant conditions is undoubtedly vague, but that is no difficulty if our thoughts about the good-tasting and good-looking are vague in the same way. But we treat this standard not just as *ours* but as objective: we rely on it, in fact, in deciding whether to construe the judgments of distant cultures as being about *this* topic. But when it appears that different appraisers would react differently even with those conditions in place, we accept an appraiser relativism.

A natural question, then, is whether an ideal-observer relativism might also be available for morality. I believe not. As I have explained, there are two cases to consider. If the ideal-observer theory is a response theory, then the difficulty derives from an important difference between the response-states that are appropriate to taste and looks, on the one hand, and moral emotions such as resentment and approval, on the other: a difference that makes my objection to a relativism of standards relevant also to moral-ideal-observer theories. This difference is that moral emotions are irrational unless based on corresponding moral beliefs. They can *exist* without the beliefs.[75] People sometimes feel guilty without really believing that they have done anything wrong. But guilt under those circumstances is irrational, as is moral approval felt toward what one does not really think of as morally good. This view of these emotions is widely held, and although it can be challenged it remains enormously plausible. But it implies that there is a serious difficulty for anyone attempting to fall back from a provisional nihilism about unsettleable moral issues to a relativism of this sort. He proposes now to understand the truth of his views on those issues to be settled by what he would (for example) approve of on those issues under the right conditions. But since he now has no moral beliefs about them, any approval he feels will be irrational and unjustified. Relativists have not wanted to advertise their doctrine as one that could apply to appraisers only in virtue of such lapses in rationality.

The contrast between moral emotions and such responses as being pleased by a taste or a look, or such as color sensations, is interesting. All are what I called response-states, naturally thought of as functioning as

---

[74] Foot, "Moral Relativism," pp. 153–55, 161.
[75] As Roderick Firth notes, in "Ethical Absolutism and the Ideal Observer," p. 328.

responses to some kind of independent fact. But there is nothing irrational about being pleased by a taste or a look if one has no views about the good-tasting or good-looking, or in having sensations of yellow even if one doubts that there is anything yellow before one. That is what makes it possible for an ideal-observer account of the good-tasting or good-looking, or for a dispositional secondary-quality account of color to undermine, at least partly, the naive conception of these responses, by making their presence under the right conditions constitutive of the truth of the corresponding judgments. And it is also what makes it possible for us to fall back, without the paradox or irrationality we find in the moral case, to a relativistic understanding of these judgments, if it turns out that there are fundamental differences in the responses of different individuals or communities. Roderick Firth took the aim of a moral-ideal-observer theory to be to find some response of ours that stands to being morally right, as sensations of yellow stand to being yellow.[76] It is a problem for such theories, but especially for relativistic versions, that nothing comes very close to meeting that condition.

What about the other case, what I called reaction theories? I find these interesting partly because they seem framed with an eye to the very difficulty I have been insisting on: namely, that other forms of appraiser moral relativism ask appraisers to base their moral judgments on responses (their standards, their moral emotions) that *ought not to be there* in a rational appraiser confronted with a moral issue recognized as unsettleable. But precisely because they cannot appeal to any of these factors, and because of the limits on the idealizations they can appeal to, the truth-conditions these theories suggest seem highly arbitrary. Richard Brandt, my primary example, suggests that in calling an action wrong I might mean that I would after cognitive psychotherapy be motivated to support a moral code that prohibited it.[77] This is offered as an account of what I might mean in calling others' actions wrong, not just my own, and I am supposed to adopt it even in full knowledge that my own motivational reaction after cognitive psychotherapy would be different from theirs. Nor is it a noncognitivist proposal, according to which I should call others' actions wrong in order to express my motivational opposition without describing it. It suggests instead that I regard my own motivational idiosyncrasy as making it *true* that certain actions by others are wrong. No one could believe this. It would have some plausibility if it were proposed instead as a test for what agents should do, rather than for how appraisers should judge: for it might then look like a version of the view that people ought to follow their own rational natures, coupled

[76] *Ibid.*, p. 327.
[77] Brandt, *A Theory of the Good and the Right*, p. 194. In reporting this proposal I correct for an obvious misprint ("permitted" for "prohibited") and ignore the even less plausible suggestion that it might be "your" reactions—that is, those of my audience—that make my judgments true or false.

with Brandt's distinctive theory of practical rationality and with the observation that this might require different things of different people. But that would take it beyond the range of my discussion.[78]

3. I take the preceding arguments to pose a very serious challenge for any form of appraiser moral relativism. But there is an additional difficulty in seeing either Foot's or Wong's relativism as a reasonable alternative to nihilism about irresolvable issues. This difficulty arises from their both regarding at least some moral claims as entirely objective. Wong thinks it likely that Hitler's moral depravity constitutes an objective moral fact, and Foot also cites the "Nazi treatment of the Jews" as an indisputable example of immorality.[79] But both believe that on many other moral issues there may be, or is, no fact of the matter. My question is whether, starting from this mixed assessment—realism about some issues, nihilism about many others—we would really find it natural or appropriate to move to talking in the same objective-sounding, truth-claiming way about both sorts of issues. I mentioned above that this does not seem a very attractive alternative when the indeterminate issues are few, but I add now that it does not look much better when they are many. It will yield a strikingly nonunified semantics for moral assertions, some of them made true or false by the nature of morality, the rest merely by the fact that the appraisers employ certain standards. Foot herself was once inclined to charge a kind of fraud in moral language that marked no difference between these cases, and I suspect many would agree.[80] Wong says that "we cannot rest content" with silence about indeterminate issues if they are pervasive,[81] but the choice need not be between using moral language as before and saying nothing. There is the option of keeping to more subjective language instead, saying what one wants or cherishes or fears, and why. I am more optimistic than either of these relativist views about how much determinate objective truth there may

---

[78] Would this be agent *relativism*? It fits Harman's definition, though we know that his is too broad; it escapes my initial proposal, but, as I have conceded, mine is too narrow. Perhaps it is an indeterminate case.

[79] Wong, "On Moral Realism without Foundations," p. 106; Foot, "Moral Relativism," p. 163.

[80] Foot, "Morality and Art," pp. 15–16:

> My suspicion is that the existing use of "true" and "false," and the choice of an objective form of expression ("It is right") does have a role but a rather disreputable role. When we say that something "just is" right or wrong we want to give the *impression* of some kind of fact or authority standing behind our words, though by hypothesis both are here ruled out, maintaining the trappings of objectivity though the substance is not there.

Note, in a similar vein, that the discovery that one's standards are the only feature of the world that has been regulating one's judgments is likely under even the best of circumstances to undermine confidence in the judgments, not to convince one that it is the standards that are making them true. It will *certainly* have this effect if only *some* of one's moral judgments receive this subjectivist explanation.

[81] Wong, "On Moral Realism without Foundations," p. 109.

be about morality; but, as I have emphasized, I see no virtue in pretending that there are determinate truths where there are not.

Falling back to a relativist stance looks problematic on Foot's or Wong's assumptions because doing so would blur a distinction both recognize between the truly objective issues and the rest. One could not raise this same objection to a relativist who recognized *no* objective issues in ethics, though I believe Foot and Wong would agree that this change would not be worth the cost in overall plausibility. But this point suggests a possible additional answer to Foot's question of why relativism should seem plausible about judgments of taste but not about (part of) morality. We do not seem to have theories of the nature of the tasty or the handsome, as Foot and Wong both think we do of the nature of morality, to mark off the deeply objective judgments of taste from the others; nor is it commonly supposed that any are very deeply objective. As a result, we run no danger, as we might in morality on their view of it, of contributing to a misleading assimilation of the less to the more objective, if we push objective ways of talking about taste as far as our shared responses will bear.

VI. Problems for Relativism: Practice

Finally, I want to make a point about one implication of relativism for practice that is not always noticed, and that could easily trouble someone not yet certain that relativism is correct. Of course, a doctrine with troubling implications for practice could nevertheless turn out to be true, so what I offer here is not a further argument that relativism is false. However, I believe that it does show why many people, if they fully understood the doctrine, would hesitate to embrace it unless presented with quite compelling arguments in its favor; and my discussion so far shows why, for moral relativism, they are unlikely to confront such arguments.[82]

I shall begin by returning to the question of whether moral relativism itself is a doctrine agents should find troubling. I have made this a more difficult question to address by making it harder to know what a relativist will believe, for I have raised serious objections to every version I have considered. Fortunately, however, my criticism applies no matter which version a relativist holds.

What I first suggested was that relativism should seem reassuring rather than troubling. It tells you how to insure that your own moral views are correct, and it assures you that people who appear to be in deep moral disagreement with you are not. As I then pointed out, how-

---

[82] For relativism about taste, on the other hand, there may be such arguments. Even on this topic, I regard the point I make here as highlighting a reason for retreating to relativism only as a last resort.

ever, that is too quick a verdict if relativism can incorporate, as a relativist should want it to, nihilism about those same disagreements, construed nonrelativistically; for on that understanding the disagreements are genuine and your views (as you may once have understood them) are not correct. But I believe that there is one significant truth in that initial verdict that still applies even when relativism is given a more sophisticated formulation. It concerns our reasons for thinking that we need to *learn* anything from those who appear to disagree with us. Popular impressions of relativism can be quite mistaken. It continues to appeal to many as a tolerant doctrine, for example, even though any connection between relativism and even a limited endorsement of tolerance is, at best, highly indirect. But one popular view about the implications of relativism nevertheless seems to me basically right. Among those to whom the doctrine has appealed, historically, have been critics seeking a platform from which to object to the widespread assumption in our own society that other peoples have a great deal to learn from our superior moral insights. Though I have sympathy for parts of this critical project, it will be no surprise that I have little for the attempt to base it on relativism. That is not, however, because the critics are wrong in this instance about what relativism implies. I think that they have been right to understand it as saying, about any disagreement within its orbit, that the people on the other side do not need to learn anything from us. The problem is that it also implies, for just the same reasons, that we need learn nothing from them.

On the simpler understanding of relativism, the case for this claim is straightforward, and will help me make clear what I mean by it. Disagreement is a challenge to our views and a stimulus to inquiry, for we care that our views be correct and in a genuine disagreement we cannot both be right. To be sure, we are not equally challenged by disagreement with just anyone: we are intellectually most disconcerted when challenged by people who seem competent, thoughtful, knowledgeable in ways relevant to the issue, and so on. But, of course, our adversaries in the moral disagreements to which relativists apply their doctrine will tend to include people with such qualifications: if that were not so, the disagreements would have little chance of looking unsettleable to us. To be told that these disagreements are not genuine, therefore, and that we and the other parties are merely talking past one another, is to be deprived of an important motive for trying to understand the opposing viewpoint, seek common intellectual ground, and in other ways learn from one another. Of course, we might find other motives for doing some of these things, but then again we might not. The point is that a standard concern to deal with challenges to our views will no longer provide one.

This strikes me as posing the risk of a significant loss to moral life in a pluralistic society, one not to be accepted lightly. Listening carefully to opposing views, regarding them as a challenge to one's own and attempting to appropriate their insights is, among other things, a mark of mutual respect that can provide a bond even across considerable disagreement. Of course, there *can* be cases of real miscommunication. People do sometimes talk past one another, and when they do it is best to recognize this fact. But it seems that this diagnosis, about disputes that seem genuine to all involved, should be a last resort. And here it is worth recalling a point I have emphasized: that even staunch defenders of relativism seem unable to lose the sense that the disagreements to which they apply their doctrine are genuine.

My case turns more complex when relativism does. Since I am pressing a complaint against relativism in particular, it is not enough to say, about a relativism that manages to incorporate nihilism, that nihilism, too, can discourage discussion and inquiry. It can: why pursue a question, one might wonder, with no correct answer? But that point will apply not only to this subtler relativism but also to the positions I am contrasting it with, not just global nihilism but also, as I insisted, any sensible realism, which will have to admit at least local indeterminacies. What I need to say instead, and what I believe is true, is that a nihilist view of an issue we disagree about *need not* discourage discussion and mutual learning at all. My very simple example from biology illustrates why. Even if my friend and I suspect that our question as initially framed has no uniquely correct answer, we learn in discussing it. One of the most important things that we learn is how to reframe the question, and in my example we learn that partly from one another. (In an example with experts rather than self-acknowledged novices, the latter feature would become essential.) This seems to me to happen all the time with more complex questions in almost all disciplines. We debate and discuss disagreements, fully anticipating that one result will be refinement or replacement of the initial question, in the light of distinctions the disagreeing parties force on one another's attention. I have called this "falling back" from an initial understanding of a question, and although the expression is in general apt, it misleads if it suggests that the process is merely a reverse or retreat. For it is a standard mode of cooperative intellectual progress.

Thus, disagreement remains a perfectly good stimulus to learning from one another, local nihilism notwithstanding, so long as we expect to need help from competing perspectives in figuring out what new, better, and (we hope) shared understanding of an issue to fall back to. Moral realists will think that we are often in this position in ethics. Relativists, however, will not. For the fallback stance recommended by relativism is not an understanding that tries somehow to incorporate what is right in all the competing perspectives. What it recommends instead is *simply* a retreat to reliance on one's own standards (if, at this point, they can be found) or on one's own reactions. For that project, no help from the competing perspectives is required.

Now, it is possible that relativism appeals to some people, about some issues, precisely because it promises to insulate their views in this way from challenge and criticism.[83] But I suspect that, especially outside academic philosophy, most people who profess moral relativism are also among those most sympathetic to the idea that representatives of competing moral perspectives, precisely because of their disagreements, have a great deal to learn from one another. If so, they need a better understanding of the doctrine they are advocating.[84]

VII. CONCLUSION

I have simplified my discussion by relying on several assumptions that I have tried to make explicit, and to motivate, but have not fully defended here: for example, that noncognitivism can be put to one side, and that these criticisms of individual appraiser relativism can be extended to social versions. Within the constraints of these assumptions, however, I believe that I have made a strong case that no form of moral relativism provides either a plausible or an attractive response to the problem of moral disagreement. The unattractiveness, at least to anyone troubled by the implication that we need not learn from those with whom we deeply disagree, I have just explained. The case for its implausibility has occupied more of my discussion, and has run briefly as follows. The only form of relativism that could actually be a response to the unsettleability of moral disagreements is appraiser relativism. But appraiser relativism needs some way to accommodate the strong intuition that these unsettleable disagreements are univocal. It can do this, I suggested, only by granting that at one level nihilism is correct about these disagreements, in that neither side is right; and then by proposing relativism as a reasonable fallback stance toward the same issues. This maneuver may save relativism about some topics, such as judgments of taste. But it fails in the moral case, I argued, for one of two reasons. Either the relativistic stance requires the presence of responses which, in a reasonable appraiser, should have disappeared as soon as the appraiser became a nihilist about the issues in question; or else that stance ties moral judgments to reac-

---

[83] See Robert Nozick, *Philosophical Explanations* (Cambridge, MA: Harvard University Press, 1981), pp. 626–27n. —though I would suspect that the culprits were more broadly scattered across political and other spectra than he suggests.

[84] The fault is not all theirs. Academic philosophers could also do a better job of comparing the implications of the competing positions. In their introduction to *Relativism*, pp. 1–3, Krausz and Meiland distinguish three possible responses to deep moral disagreements, especially between societies. One is relativism; a second is skepticism, defined to include nihilism; and the third, which must be intended to do duty for objectivism or realism, is to think that our views are "advanced" or "civilized" and the others' "backward." Realists *can* think such things: about slavery, one of the authors' examples, the result would not be such an extravagant conjecture. But one would have thought there were other alternatives: for example, thinking that *they* are more advanced and our view the backward one, or else simply thinking that, if competent people disagree this deeply, we must have something to learn from one another. A realist can also think either of these latter two things; a relativist, it should be noted, cannot.

tions which survive the nihilism, all right, but which for that very reason will seem highly arbitrary to any reflective appraiser as indicators of moral truth. Thus, no relativist stance is available as a reasonable fallback position; and relativism is left without resources to explain the intuition, widely shared by relativists and nonrelativists alike, that many deep moral disagreements remain genuine even when unsettleable.

Philosophy, Cornell University

MORAL RELATIVISM, COGNITIVISM, AND DEFEASIBLE RULES*

By Ernest Sosa

Naturalism rejects a sui generis and fundamental realm of the evaluative or normative. Thought and talk about the good and the right must hence be understood without appeal to any such evaluative or normative concepts or properties. In Sections I and II, we see noncognitivism step forward with its account of evaluative and normative language as fundamentally optative (that is, expressive of wishes or desires) or prescriptive.[1] Prescriptivism falls afoul of several problems. Prominent among them below is the "problem of prima facie reasons": the problem, namely, that prescriptions do not properly capture the character of defeasibility, of the prima facie, featured by nearly all our moral convictions. We find in Section II that, ironically, emotivism, with its emphasis on optative rather than prescriptive language, though historically more primitive, is yet better attuned to that crucial prima facie aspect of the normative and the evaluative. But even emotivism still faces serious difficulties that beset noncognitivism generally, such as the problem of embedding in subordinate clauses, and the problem of normative fallibility. That takes us up to Section III.

Relativism then steps into the breach with an alternative account of what one ought to do. This is now to be understood by reference to a presupposed or contextually indicated moral code. Sections III and IV consider relativist proposals. And Section V is a closing statement.

I. Prescriptivism and Its Problems

Normative disciplines such as ethics and epistemology are notoriously subject to disagreement even by expert practitioners, and even on fundamental questions about the very nature and point of the discipline. One main divide separates practical from theoretical conceptions. On a practical conception the discipline aims to arrive at rules, maxims, or guide-

---

* For philosophical comments and discussion, my warm thanks to James Dreier, Gilbert Harman, and David Sosa; and for editorial help, to Ellen Frankel Paul and her staff.

[1] *Noncognitivism* in ethics has taken two main forms: according to *prescriptivism*, "One ought to keep one's promises" is tantamount to "Let's all keep our promises!" or some such prescription; according to *emotivism*, it amounts rather to "Would that people kept their promises!" or the like.

lines that can aid choice or conduct. On a theoretical conception the aim is rather to formulate principles that will explain in general terms what it is that in the pertinent area makes choice or conduct appropriate or right or justified or apt.[2]

Each normative discipline comes with its own key concepts: axiology with concepts of the good and the valuable; ethics with concepts of right choice or action, and of what one, morally, ought to do; epistemology with concepts of epistemically justified or apt belief.[3]

For the noncognitivist such concepts or terms do not represent any mind- or language-independent constituent or aspect of reality. Their significance is rather only functional: like that of the imperative mood or the exclamation mark.

Because such functional devices do not embed well in subordinate clauses, noncognitivists have difficulty recognizing any theoretical conception of a normative discipline.[4] They have trouble grasping the objective someone might have of trying to understand in general terms what makes action or belief right or apt or justified. "What makes promise-keeping right?" Here is a question that comes easily to the cognitivist, who can view it as a request for explanation, like "What causes the rotation of the Earth?" Given a well-defined sort of action such as promise-keeping, and given our belief that rightness applies to it, a cognitivist might well wonder what explains why it does so. And his curiosity is rather like the curiosity in wondering why rotation applies to our planet as it does. By contrast, the noncognitivist seems unable to understand any such curiosity. For the prescriptivist, for example, to try to wonder why it should be that promise-keeping is right would be rather like trying to wonder why it should be that: Let us keep our promises!

Of course we *can* easily wonder about either of the following:

Why we should accept that promise-keeping is right.

Why we do accept that promise-keeping is right.

And these questions—one "epistemological," one psychological—the noncognitivist can assimilate as follows:

Why we should accept or endorse: Let us keep our promises!

Why we do accept or endorse: Let us keep our promises!

---

[2] "Conduct" here should be interpreted in the broadest possible way so that even believing something in certain circumstances can be viewed as a sort of "conduct."

[3] If seriously ill, one may have good prudential reasons for believing one will recover, while still lacking the hard evidence required for *epistemic* justification.

[4] Thus, e.g., "Hurray!" does not embed grammatically in antecedents of conditionals: "If Hurray! then . . ."

But can't we also wonder as follows:

Why is it that promise-keeping *is* right?

This question is *normative*, in the sense that even raising it presupposes a normative commitment. To wonder about this normative question is to wonder what makes it the case that promise-keeping is right, to wonder in virtue of what it is that promise-keeping is right. However, such questions seem beyond the noncognitivist.

Some would say that our normative questions do not admit of any very interesting answer, since what makes it right to keep a promise is simply that it is the keeping of a promise. But, even granted this, the cognitivist can still make his point vivid by moving to more specific and determinate levels, distinguishing as follows:

Why *should we accept* that he acts rightly to arrive by noon?

Why *do we accept* that he acts rightly to arrive by noon?

Why *does* he act rightly to arrive by noon?

A good answer to this last, more specific, normative question might be: "Because he promised." Barring overriding or conflicting reasons, this would seem a sufficient answer and explanation.

The noncognitivist insists that since there is no real property of rightness that might attach to a sort of action (promise-keeping) or to a particular action (his arriving by noon), there is no possible object of curiosity constituted by that property's attaching to an action type or token; and the cognitivist is hence said to labor under an illusion. The noncognitivist might then provide surrogates for the cognitivist's demands for explanation. For example, the question "Why is promise-keeping right?" might be taken as just a request for a deeper principle on which "Let us keep our promises!" can rest. Such proposed deeper answers might include: "Because you should treat others as ends, not just as means," or "Because you should treat others as you would have them treat you," or "Because you should always opt for a best alternative, than which none other will cause more happiness." The cognitivist might give the same answers, of course, but he would treat them as deeper facts. The noncognitivist, by contrast, will treat each such answer as the promulgation of a deeper, more general, prescriptive principle—a principle from which, given collateral information, one can draw as a conclusion the prescription "Let us keep our promises!"

Very well, suppose we conceive of ethical inquiry in the way proposed: requests for explanation are hence just requests for "deeper" principles. And suppose we reach a point where an "inquirer" hits bedrock with a principle P and is totally unable or unwilling to go further; and suppose, finally, that a second "inquirer" similarly hits bedrock, this time with a principle P' incompatible with P, in the sense that, relative to logic, or a law of nature, or mere fact, P and P' cannot be satisfied together. What might possibly distinguish P from P' apart from the obvious differences of content and apart from such empirical differences as who accepts either principle and the actual consequences of such acceptance?

One inquirer or agent may thus hold obedience to his Maximum Leader fundamental, while another takes the welfare of humanity as his basic value. Is there any problem in understanding the possibility of such divergence? As we survey the length and breadth of human history and cultures, don't we find plenty of it?

So far there appears nothing here radically surprising or unacceptable to the noncognitivist. True, we must say that unconditional followers of the Maximum Leader are *fundamentally* at odds with our own basic principles. But that does not preclude condemning them, opposing them, struggling against them, and even fighting them to the death. And indeed what do we add of any great significance when we call our own principles "valid" or "right" or "true," or when we say that human welfare is fundamentally valuable whereas obeying the Maximum Leader is not? What do we add beyond what is already present in our fundamental adherence to human welfare and our readiness to oppose the Leader and his followers?

Such questions may lead us in either or both of two main directions: (a) to the "semantics" of the normative, and (b) to the "epistemology" of the normative. Since we are still exploring consequences of noncognitivism, our main concern is the "semantics" and "epistemology" of prescriptive or optative language or thought. Our questions are hence such as the following: Is there a "semantic" value akin to truth or falsity that applies to prescriptions like "Follow the dictates of the Maximum Leader!"? Can we view such a prescription as *invalid*? Is there an "epistemic" value akin to "justification" that applies to such prescriptions? Can we view the prescription to obey the Maximum Leader as one that his followers are not *justified* in accepting? Yes, the noncognitivist can allow all this, but since the concepts involved — validity and justification — are themselves normative or evaluative, the most coherent prescriptivism would understand even these concepts in prescriptivist terms.[5] Saying that a certain prescription is invalid or unjustified, therefore, is tantamount to actually prescribing the opposite. With this the noncognitivist has no quarrel.

It should be clear, then, that the noncognitivist prescriptivist is not forced to grant the equal validity of normative views opposed to his own. He is not even forced to countenance only a relative validity such that

---

[5] Calling an attitude "valid" or "justified" would thus amount to *endorsing* the adoption of such an attitude in such circumstances, or the like.

opposing prescriptions can be valid each relative to its own surrounding system. For he can take refuge in a prescriptivism of validity itself, such that to call one's own view "valid" is to prescribe it at a meta-level, and to call an opposing view "invalid" is again a meta-level route to represcribing one's own favored view. (And he can treat justification analogously.)

II. Emotivism Redux

Noncognitivism has yet to face further problems, however. Perhaps the most famous is a more general form of one already discussed: namely, that of how to make room for evaluative or normative language in subordinate clauses generally, such as the antecedents of conditionals. If the vocabulary of the 'good' and the 'right' is just used to commend or to prescribe, then it is hard to understand how it could figure in such subordinate clauses where no commending or prescribing is involved. Noncognitivists have long been well aware of this difficulty and have made many attempts to meet it, some of which are still under discussion in the literature.[6]

There are, moreover, two further difficulties for noncognitivism, and each seems serious and so far unmet: the problem of normative fallibility, and the problem of prima facie reasons.

I deal first with the problem of normative fallibility. Suppose at the deepest level some noncognitivist upholds end E. Can he then be humble enough to wonder whether he is right to do so, whether his commitment to E is valid or legitimate? So long as, *ex hypothesi*, he does uphold E, he would seem incoherent to wonder whether he is right to do so, whether his commitment is valid. For to hold his commitment valid is just to express his commitment; to uphold the validity of his commitment is just to uphold his commitment.

But that does not yet constitute a special difficulty for the noncognitivist prescriptivist, since surely even a cognitivist realist would be in the same boat: even someone who believes in a real property of *validity* would have to grant that so long as one seriously upholds end E one is committed in coherence to upholding the validity of one's doing so. Still, the cognitivist can make room for something that the noncognitivist cannot countenance. The cognitivist can allow that he *might* be wrong even

---

[6] See especially the writings of Richard Hare, Simon Blackburn, and Allan Gibbard: e.g., Hare, *The Language of Morals* (Oxford: Oxford University Press, 1952), and *Moral Thinking: Its Levels, Method, and Point* (Oxford: Oxford University Press, 1981); Blackburn, *Spreading the Word* (Oxford: Oxford University Press, 1984); and Gibbard, *Wise Choices, Apt Feelings* (Cambridge, MA: Harvard University Press, 1990). The problem was first raised by Peter Geach in "Ascriptivism," *Philosophical Review*, vol. 69 (1960), pp. 121–25, and then in "Assertion," *Philosophical Review*, vol. 74 (1965), pp. 449–65. See also John Searle, *Speech Acts* (Cambridge, UK: Cambridge University Press, 1969).

with regard to his most basic ends such as E, that it *might* be *invalid* to uphold these ends. The difficulty here is again closely allied to the fact that prescriptions do not embed smoothly in subordinate clauses. Thus, it makes no sense to say "It might be that let us not always keep our promises," or "Possibly, let us not always keep our promises."

A closely related point applies against redundancy accounts of truth. We need the conceptual resources for the humility to grant that our own opinions *might* be wrong, might be false. Yet this seems not to be allowed by the view that the vocabulary of truth has just a redundant function of emphasis. If so, then so long as, *ex hypothesi*, one does believe B, one cannot coherently wonder whether one is right to do so, whether one's belief is true. For to call one's belief true is just to emphatically reaffirm one's belief; to uphold the truth of one's belief is just to uphold one's belief.

But here again, in the case of truth and belief, we have not quite pinpointed the problem for the noncognitivist, since even a realist cognitivist would be in the same boat. Even someone who believes in a substantial property of *truth* would have to grant that, so long as one seriously believes something, one is committed in coherence to believing in the truth of one's belief. Still, the realist cognitivist about truth can make room for something that his opponent cannot countenance. The realist cognitivist can allow that he *might* be wrong even with regard to something he firmly believes, that something he believes *might* still be false. It is hard to see how the redundancy theorist could admit this.

I turn now to the second problem, the problem of prima facie reasons. This derives from the fact that much of our most secure knowledge or opinion in matters normative takes the form of judgments of prima facie reason. Not all lies are wrong, but we take the fact that to ϕ would be to lie as a point against ϕ-ing. Lying is prima facie wrong. Not all inflictions of pain are on the whole wrong, but we take the fact that to ϕ would be to inflict pain as a point against ϕ-ing. Inflicting pain is prima facie wrong. How is the noncognitivist to handle this? How can the noncognitivist understand judgments of the form:

X is prima facie right (wrong).

This is prima facie a problem for noncognitivism, one that so far as I know has not been seriously faced, much less met. Let us pause over this.

Some, or most, or perhaps even all of our most secure convictions on practical matters are about prima facie reasons. Most of us are not certain that every lie is wrong but only that lies are prima facie wrong or, to put it another way, that if to do a certain thing would be to lie then that is a reason against it. The fact that to ϕ would be to lie is a reason against ϕ-ing.

A similar phenomenon is familiar with regard to evaluation. A thick and well-marbled steak may be desirable in the respect that it is delicious, but undesirable in the respect that it is unhealthy. More schematically: X may be desirable in the respect that it is F, but undesirable in the respect that it is G.

At a higher level of abstraction, we may speak of entities of whatever sort — be they individuals, events, actions, or states of affairs — as being subject to "pluses" or "minuses," or as having "advantages" or "disadvantages," or "points in favor" and "points against." Thus, it is a point against acting in a certain way in certain circumstances that to so act then would be to lie, but so acting may at the same time have a point in its favor: for example, that it would also save an innocent life. Similarly, it is a point in favor of a juicy, marbled steak that it is delicious, but a point against it that it is unhealthy.

Perhaps all forms of evaluation could be reduced to one basic form. Perhaps the evaluation of an action reduces to the evaluation of a state of affairs of that action's being performed, or perhaps, on the contrary, the evaluation of objects and states of affairs reduces to the evaluation of actions of bringing them about, or "consuming" them, or the like. But here we need not enter that controversy. Regardless of how it is to be resolved, the fact remains that the following form of statement or thought is extremely important to evaluation and deliberation generally:

> It is a point in favor of ϕ-ing that it would be to ψ.

And the question remains: How is noncognitivism to express the content of such a claim? Obviously, it would not do to propose:

> ϕ-ing would be to ψ; and do always ψ!

or to propose:

> ϕ-ing would be to ψ; and do ψ by ϕ-ing now!

Its being a point against ϕ-ing that it would be to lie does not preclude more weighty considerations *in favor* of ϕ-ing constituted by the fact that ϕ-ing would be not only to lie but also to save a life.

Here is a response on behalf of the prescriptivist: "In fact, many prescriptions have only a prima facie character, including many ordinary prescriptions which we all assume have a naturalistic explication. 'Don't count your chickens before they are hatched' should not be taken as an exceptionless rule, nor even should 'Look before you leap' (else 'He who hesitates is lost' would be false). 'If you reply to an invitation written in the third person, use the third person to answer' is a prescription of etiquette, but has exceptions (for royalty, maybe). 'Do not allow your queen to be exchanged for a rook' is not intended to advise chess players to pass up a chance to win the game with a brilliant queen sacrifice. So it is with the prescriptions that lie underneath the surface grammar of moral language. We now ask the imperative logician for some general account, and adopt it." So far the prescriptivist response.

Well, the standard "semantic" value used in the logic of imperatives is that of "satisfaction," where "Let it be the case that such and such!" is satisfied by the truth of "It is the case that such and such." Then, just as validity in indicative logic is necessary preservation of truth, so validity in imperative logic is (roughly) necessary preservation of satisfaction.

The key question is then: What satisfies the prima facie rule "Don't lie!" when addressed to S? Is it S's *never* lying? Then we have the problem that moral codes are hardly ever in a position to issue rules of such generality. Is it S's almost never lying? Rarely lying? Less-often-than-not lying? None of these is at all plausible. Moral codes are not in a position to speak even with *such* generality absent information about the circumstances that S will face at various junctures. The question remains: What satisfies the prescription "Don't lie!" understood as a prima facie or *pro tanto* rule? [7]

For the reasons canvassed, including the importance of the prima facie to the normative and evaluative generally, as well as prescriptivism's apparent inability to accommodate the prima facie, I will assume that prescriptivism is not acceptable. Whatever exactly may be the functions of normative or evaluative language, they must go beyond prescribing.

Ironically, an earlier version of noncognitivism may have a significant advantage, on the present score, over the later, more sophisticated prescriptivism. For emotivism, evaluative and normative language has a primary function of expressing emotions or attitudes. So, if one opposes lying one might, at a primitive level, say "Boo for lying!" or in more sophisticated language, but to similar effect: "Lying is wrong!" Yet to oppose lying is not to oppose anything and everything that ever amounts to lying. If in a particular situation one can save a life, but only by lying, then one may have divided loyalties: one may hate and regret having to lie, but one may be relieved nevertheless at being able to save the life. One opposes one's acting as one does to the extent that it is to lie, or under the aspect of its being a lie, but it does not follow that one opposes (flat out) one's so acting. In any case, it is precisely in this sort of "opposition under an aspect" that noncognitivism may find a basis for the claims of prima facie rightness or wrongness constitutive of ordinary morality. According to such a return to emotivism, in saying that lying is prima facie wrong one expresses one's attitude of opposition to lying. This attitude is, moreover, sophisticated enough not to imply absolute and unconditional abhorrence of lying. Thus, when applied to known particular instances of lying, it would imply only an attitude of "opposition under the aspect of being a lie."

---

[7] We shall return to this general issue below, when we consider whether relativism is in a better position to resolve it.

The problem of the prima facie may force noncognitivism to beat a tactical retreat to an earlier position of emotivism or something close to that. Even so, noncognitivism would still face the problem of embedded clauses, and, especially, the problem of normative fallibility. Let us, then, explore an alternative response to the failure of prescriptivism.

III. RELATIVISM

Relativism offers to take up prescriptivism's failed mission: to provide a perspicuous account of normative and evaluative concepts within the confines of a broad naturalism.[8] Given our recent reflections, it would seem that such an account needs to be cognitivist. Let us now consider the prospects for cognitivist, naturalist relativism.

What is rude and what is illegal may be defined by reference to codes of conduct such as etiquette and the law of the land. But what is rude relative to one set of rules may not be so relative to another; and one and the same type of action may be an infraction relative to one system of law but not an infraction relative to another. Rudeness and illegality are clearly relative in that sense.

Many if not all societies will have a third sort of code of conduct in addition to rules of etiquette and a legal system: namely, a morality or moral code. Hence, a third sort of wrongdoing will be definable in addition to violations of etiquette or of the law, namely, *moral wrongdoing* defined as violations of the society's moral code. And *this* sort of immorality is also clearly relative, since moral codes differ from society to society, as do rules of etiquette and legal systems.

It seems uncontroversial that there is such relativistic wrongdoing. The more interesting question is whether there is any concept of moral wrongdoing that is *not* thus relativistic but is instead "absolute."

There can be many different sorts of relativity. Relativity can be (a) of content or of context, (b) to an issuer group (to a group of which the issuer is a member, including, as a limiting case, just the issuer alone), (c) to an addressee group, and (d) to a subject group. (An issuer, I, may address an addressee A with a moral claim, about subject S, of the form "S ought to ϕ," or more explicitly, "S ought *morally* to ϕ.")

Relativity of content is explicit relativity, as in "Relative to Christian morality, it is right to turn the other cheek," a claim that is absolutely true, given the content of Christian morality. Relativity of context is not necessarily flagged explicitly in the judgment itself. Thus, the judgment "It is right to turn the other cheek" may be true in the context of a Sun-

---

[8] For "naturalism" as an approach to ethics, and a contrast with "autonomous ethics," see Gilbert Harman, "Is There a Single True Morality?" in *Relativism: Interpretation and Confrontation*, ed. M. Krausz (Notre Dame: University of Notre Dame Press, 1989), pp. 363–87.

day school class, with its relativity to Christian morality, but false in the quite different context of a Supremacist Party meeting.

Gilbert Harman's relativism of inner judgments is contextualist in approximately our sense, and amounts to this:

> "Ought (A, D, C, M)" means roughly that, given that A has motivating attitudes M and given C, D is the course of action for A that is supported by the best reasons.[9]

For Harman adds that in "judgments using this sense of 'ought,' C and M are often not explicitly mentioned but are indicated by the context of utterance. Normally, when that happens, C will be 'all things considered' and M will be attitudes that are shared by the speaker and audience."

As an objection to this view of the moral ought, one might cite the horrified moral condemnation directed by missionaries and colonizers against what they regard as cruel and unusual practices. Bernard Williams, for example, cites the outrage of Cortez against the Aztec sacrifice of the vanquished.[10] One might try to defend Harman's account of inner judgments by arguing that Cortez's outrage could not correctly take the form of a judgment that the Aztecs ought not to treat their prisoners that way, but must rather find expression in a claim that the Aztecs and their practices are "evil," or the like. But it is not easy to perceive the fine nuances that this requires, nor is it easily credible that people observe them in their usage. Besides, a satisfactory naturalism would require accounts of what is "evil" and of what "ought to be" in addition to the inner-judgments account of the "ought to do."

Finally, Harman faces a further difficulty. One main advantage of his inner-judgments account is that it helps explain in a satisfying way the otherwise puzzling distinction which we draw between the moral prohibition against harming and the moral injunction to help. Thus, even though by drawing five healthy organs from an innocent victim we could save five terminally ill patients, we would regard it as morally outrageous for a doctor to proceed accordingly. The explanation, argues Harman, is that morality requires consensus, and all will consent to the prohibition against harming, whereas the rich and strong will not accept any general injunction to help. However, this argument in favor of the inner-judgments account of moral ought-to-do judgments supports only *one aspect* of that account, one that it shares with other forms of relativism: namely, the aspect that requires relativity to a consensually accepted moral code. But the argument does not support the *subject-relativity* of the inner-judgments account.

---

[9] Gilbert Harman, "Moral Relativism Defended," in *Relativism*, ed. J. Meiland and M. Krausz (Notre Dame: University of Notre Dame Press, 1982), p. 195.

[10] Bernard Williams, *Morality: An Introduction to Ethics* (New York: Harper, 1972).

We may well conclude, therefore, that Harman's reasoning is most successful in defending contextual relativity of moral ought-to-do judgments to some consensual moral code, and less successful in showing that they are also subject-relative in the sense that, for it to be true that S ought (morally) to ϕ, it is required that S already have a motivating reason to ϕ. The broader relativism that we have reached might be put as follows:

(H) "S ought (morally) to ϕ" issued by issuer I to addressee A (where I and A may be the same or different) in context C, is true if and only if $\langle I, C, A \rangle$ determines a moral code M such that S's ϕ-ing would be F, and M implies that F actions are to be done.

Let us say that such relativism is *radical* if and only if there is no restriction on the content of M. So far as its context is concerned, what makes a code M a moral code has to do merely with its being a comprehensive code for the regulation of conduct regarded by the group as vitally affecting the interests of its members. Other than that, it is required only that certain conditions be satisfied regarding how the code attains its status as operative and how it is sustained in that status. Thus, a legal code may overlap importantly with a moral code, but requires the formal backing of the polity and perhaps the threat of formal sanctions for infractions. A moral code's sanctions are more implicit and less formal. And so on.

Philippa Foot has argued frequently (in effect) that such radical relativism must be wrong, since

> the thought of moral goodness and badness cannot be held steady through any and every change in the codes of behavior taught, and in their grounds. From this it follows that not everything that anyone might want to call a 'moral code' should properly be so described. And this shows, incidentally, that hypotheses about 'cultural relativism' are not totally independent of moral theory. Even if an anthropologist is inclined to call a certain code a moral code, and to go on to talk about a morality radically different from our own, it does not follow that we should accept this way of describing the phenomenon. An anthropologist may be as confused or prejudiced as anyone else in applying words such as 'morality' to the teaching of an alien culture.[11]

However, this position, so defended, only invites the response "Why be moral?" Suppose what makes a code moral includes not only facts about its role in the group involved, but also some specific content, such as a prohibition against killing the innocent. And suppose we are told on that basis that killing the innocent could not possibly be *moral*, and that this

---

[11] Philippa Foot, "Moral Relativism," in Meiland and Krausz, eds., *Relativism*, p. 162.

is not just something relative, but an absolute moral truth. Would this not be like saying that moving the rooks diagonally (as well as vertically and horizontally) could not possibly be *chess*, and that this is not just something relative (to a particular version of chess), but an absolute truth of eternal and essential chess? Anyone who already knows that it is definitely "chess" he wishes to play must pay attention, then, and not allow the rooks to be moved diagonally. Similarly, then, anyone who already knows that it is definitely a "moral" code she wishes to observe must pay attention and avoid the killing of the innocent.

The analogy is not compelling, however. Morality seems unlike a game or practice in the relevant respects. It is not that "morality" by definition requires a certain sort of content no matter how minimal, and that because it is "morally" we wish to act, we therefore must abide at a minimum by that minimal content, as with the playing of chess. Our allegiance to the rules and principles constitutive of morality seems otherwise. Sparing the innocent is perhaps essentially, by definition, constitutive of a practice called "morality" in which we want to participate. But it is not just because it is constitutive of "morality," by definition, and we happen to want to participate in that practice, that we adopt that rule or principle. If that is the best we can do in favor of the prohibition against killing the innocent, morality is in a way trivialized and we invite the question "Why be moral?" For what we say then amounts to nothing more than the claim that any code C that includes a permission to kill the innocent is by definition not a "moral" code. But if this is all it amounts to, why should we care much whether or not our conduct abides by such codes, by codes that satisfy the requirements for being "moral" in that sense? This leaves us wondering why it is entirely up to one whether one opts for chess (rather than, say, bridge) whereas it is not thus optional whether one chooses morality.[12]

Foot's defense of absolute morality has been charged with trivializing our deepest moral commitments by making them a matter of definition. We do not opt for morality the way we opt for chess. The rules of chess have no important claim on us individually and independently from their place in the game. In this respect the analogy between chess and the law (much of it, in any case) is better. Driving on the right has no intrinsic claim on us in America independently of the fact that it is the law, just as moving the bishops only diagonally has no intrinsic claim on us independently of the fact that it is the rule in chess.

Chess, systems of law, and moral codes all contain rules. But the rules of chess and many of the rules contained in a system of law have no independent claim on our agreement. We are bound to abide by them only contingently on the fact that they are rules with the appropriate standing

---

[12] It might be replied that the peremptoriness of morality derives precisely from the fact that it is *morality* (and not any game). This will be considered some pages hence, in connection with position (F).

within the practice or game. Thus, we abide by the prohibition against driving on the left only because this follows from the law of the land. And we abide by the prohibition against moving the bishops horizontally only because this follows from the chess rules (and it is chess we wish to play).

Initially at least, morality seems quite different. It is morally wrong to murder, we agree, but not just because our moral code says so. Here the explanation goes the other way around. Our moral code includes the prohibition against murder because it is wrong to murder. It is this that seems so unlike chess or the law. The chess rulebook includes the rule that bishops move only diagonally, but *not* because it would somehow independently be wrong for bishops to move otherwise. Our traffic laws in America include a prohibition against driving (normally) on the left, but not because it would be in itself wrong to do so.

The comparison may well be thought unfair, however, since plenty of laws prohibit actions regarded as independently and intrinsically wrong: murder, for a start. Besides, requirements of a moral code may come to seem arbitrary: witness our recent changes in gender-based requirements and in sexual mores.

Of course, just as the very fact that it is the law offers an excellent — though defeasible — reason for driving on the right, so the very fact that it is a requirement of a moral code may give a reason — again defeasible — against strolling nude in public, and even against topless dining, especially for women.

The point remains, nevertheless, that something required by the law or by our moral code may have a claim on us that goes beyond its being so required. Our obligation not to kill people for sport is a case in point.

Fortunately, Foot goes beyond her definitional argument for absolute moral truths, when she argues as follows:

> Granted that it is wrong to assume identity of aim between peoples of different cultures; nevertheless there is a great deal that all men have in common. All need affection, the cooperation of others, a place in the community, and help in trouble. . . . We are not, therefore, simply expressing values that we happen to have if we think of some moral systems as good moral systems and others as bad. Communities as well as individuals can live wisely or unwisely, and this is largely the result of their values and the codes of behavior that they teach. . . . These things have different harvests and unmistakably different connexions with human good.[13]

In his discussions of moral relativism, David Wong also relies substantially on the assessment of moral systems: in his favored terms, a system can be either "adequate" or "inadequate." Thus, quoting Wong:

[13] Foot, "Moral Relativism," p. 164.

(W) . . . I conceive of "A ought to do D," very roughly as holding that D is required by the adequate system or systems of moral rules. Whether there is more than one true morality comes down to the question of whether the extension of 'adequate moral system' does vary over different communities of moral language users. I have argued [in *Moral Relativity* (Berkeley: University of California Press, 1984)] that the criteria determining the extension can be different enough across different communities so that the extension indeed does vary.[14]

Wong holds that there is a "limited plurality of true moralities," a plurality limited by constraints such as that an adequate moral system must provide for an effective and relatively stable resolution or regulation of interpersonal conflicts of interest. And, in keeping with such a requirement, "an adequate moral system must require people to be able to set aside some of their most pressing interests in favor of others or for the sake of some larger goal."[15] This means, in turn, that an adequate moral system needs to instill and foster certain virtues of character. These, it is argued finally, require recognition of the special duties involved in kinship and friendship, etc.

Certain virtues and duties gain their moral status, then, through the fact that they require a place in any adequate moral system—in any moral system that, among other things, would provide for acceptable ways to deal with interpersonal conflicts. But what is the basis of the goals or criteria by which the adequacy of a moral system is determined? What is the basis of the desideratum of having an effective and relatively stable resolution or regulation of interpersonal conflicts? Is this supposed to be more fundamental than the moral prohibition against taking innocent lives just for fun? Does the latter gain its moral or normative status simply from the fact that it must be part of any moral system that is adequate in, among other things, dealing with conflicts of interest?

Quibbles aside, a quasi-absolute ought can clearly be defined in the way (W) does so. It is a kind of "rule-utilitarian ought" with allowance for some degree of relativity in the sort of adequacy required. And it is an "ought" that enables discussion of the advantages and disadvantages of moral rules while sticking to evaluation of particular actions that might fall under such rules.

At the same time it is by no means ruled out that occasionally, or more often, or even *most* often, we employ a sort of moral ought much closer to that defined by our relativistic (H), according to which the claim that S morally ought to φ is true if and only if the claim contextually deter-

[14] David Wong, "Commentary on Sayre-McCord's 'Being a Realist about Relativism'," *Philosophical Studies*, vol. 61 (1991), p. 182.
[15] *Ibid.*, p. 184.

mines a code according to which F actions are to be performed, where in the circumstances S's ϕ-ing would be an F action. Let us now consider this alternative, which has substantial advantages. The quasi-absolute ought defined by (W) seems rather limited in its scope: clearly, many different moral systems could be adequate for any given group G in circumstances C at a time T, and these would overlap only to a limited extent. We get some sense of this as we view the full variety of social arrangements to be found in viable societies or cultures as revealed by history and anthropology. Since quasi-absolute moral truth would be found at most within the overlap of *all* such systems, such truth is bound to have a very limited extent. Besides, how plausible is it that when we engage in solitary or dialogical deliberation, we are attempting to determine what would be found at least in such overlap?

Much is left indeterminate by the totality of quasi-absolute oughts as defined by (W). Suppose, then, that we consider a less elaborate conception—labeled (M) for G. E. Moore:

(M) S ought (morally) to ϕ if and only if ϕ-ing is, all things considered, the best of the options open to S.

As problems for this account I would suggest the following. First, are there not aspects of an action that might render it better than its alternatives without being moral aspects (and hence while having little or no relevance to the question of whether it is an action that the agent morally ought to perform)? Second, given the great diversity and incommensurability of goods, will it not be rare for a particular action to attain the status of *summum bonum* among its class of alternatives, *all things considered*? And if so, will it not be rare for there to be an action that one morally ought to do? [16]

In any case, it seems plausible that most often, or at least *very* often, what we try to determine in moral debate or deliberation, is what one's individual or collective moral code requires at a certain juncture, given the information available. Why not understand the ought involved in such ordinary deliberation as "ought given my (our) moral code"?

---

[16] I do not argue that there is no important truth captured by (M) (or something close: compare "what one ought morally to do" with "the thing to do"). I argue rather that there are important senses of "ought" and, especially, "ought morally" that are *not* captured by (M). Moreover, as Harman has pointed out to me in correspondence,

> our morality itself allows nonmoral considerations to override moral considerations sometimes. If I promise someone to meet them at such and such a time and it then emerges that I will collect a large sum of money if I instead go to the lottery office, and I am unable to reach the party I have promised to meet, then morality says it is OK for me to inconvenience the other party, despite my promise, even though in this case we would not say that I ought morally to go to the lottery office. (We do say I am not morally wrong to do so.)

Surely, it may be urged, that does not mean anything goes; it is not implied that nothing is intrinsically ruled out, that now it all depends on the arbitrary contingency of what happens to be included in one's moral code. For, with Foot, we may believe that some types of conduct will be prohibited in every moral code; and that these prohibitions hence lie beyond mere arbitrary contingency. Note well that Foot's move here, though urged by her as an argument *against* moral relativism, might actually be co-opted by the relativist and turned to his own ends. For the relativist might now use the notion of universal presence in moral codes in order to explain the special status of murder by contrast with bishops moving horizontally and with driving on the left. What gives murder the special status of being, in a sense, *absolutely* wrong is that any *moral* code worthy of the title would prohibit it, and nothing like this holds true of the lesser sexual mores or traffic laws.

Leaving aside the earlier doubts about Foot's position, can it be co-opted successfully by the relativist? Is Footian relativism a sufficient response to our questions about intrinsic wrongness? Is a requirement rendered in the relevant sense intrinsic or absolute through being thus universally required? Here we must consider *why* all moral codes include the requirement in question. If what makes a prohibition part of a community's moral code is just that it is one regarded as vitally important by that community, and hence attended by sanctions of commensurate severity, that seems insufficient to yield a wrongness in the relevant sense absolute. Thus, if human beings had been affected by a mutation that produced an overpowering desire to see themselves and others absolutely bald, this might have led to a universal prohibition against hirsuteness, one to be found in every human moral code. So in one sense regular shaving would have been an "absolute" moral requirement, except for the blessed few who were naturally bald. Yet this seems importantly different from the universal injunction against murder or theft or lying.

Unimpressed by our thought experiment, someone might respond with a thought experiment of his own: "Suppose we were constructed so differently that none of us cared at all whether we lived to see the morrow. Wouldn't murder lose its wrongness?" But what if when the morrow does come around we always enjoy it enormously and accomplish great things? "Well, suppose then that none of this happens and that instead we all continue indefinitely to suffer the privations and tortures of the damned. What then?" Point taken. But then is even deliberate killing something we take to be more than prima facie wrong? Euthanasia is of course now controversial, but many, and even whole countries, are convinced that there are times when it is appropriate.

The point remains, however: to target someone innocent who would otherwise fare well and who wants to live, and to kill him just for sport seems altogether different from strolling unshaven and with a full head of hair among those who abhor hair. And this would remain so even if we all suffered willy-nilly from such abhorrence.[17]

Foot's point seems in any case rather different, and stronger. It imports some sort of modal status into her "absolute" moral injunctions. It is supposed that the very concept of morality rules out the possibility that a truly "moral" code could permit murder.

Might the relativist now co-opt Foot's point? Can he accept the notion that murder is not only prohibited in every actual moral code but *would* always be prohibited by any code that was truly *moral*? And does this enable him to explain the special moral status of murder, a special status evidently missing from the lesser sexual mores, from driving on the right, and so on? Can he now say that the prohibition against murder is morally special only in the sense that it must always be present in any code that is truly moral?

At this point in the argument, it is important to recall that the relativist of interest to us is one who takes over from the prescriptivist noncognitivist the mission of providing a plausible and perspicuous account of moral concepts within the confines of naturalism. Our relativist hence aims to explicate concepts like those of moral wrongness and of the moral ought in a way that will be cognitivist and will allow the corresponding terms — 'morally wrong', 'morally right', etc. — a place in subordinate clauses, etc., without abandoning naturalism for primitive moral concepts or properties.

Now our relativist has been moved to accept the following Footian concept:

(F) X is absolutely morally wrong if and only if X would be prohibited by any code that was truly moral.

But here we have moral terminology — 'absolutely morally wrong' — explicated in terms of a sort of terminology — 'moral code' — itself in some relevant sense moral, or in any case normative. So the question remains: How is *this* concept of a truly moral code to be explicated so that it remains cognitivist yet naturalist?

IV. RELATIVISM AND THE PRIMA FACIE

There is an intriguing analogy between relativist naturalism on the normative, and instrumentalism and other forms of antirealism on the micro-

---

[17] An alternative reply seems also in the end unpromising, but I will not be able to go into it much here: namely, to relativize to human societies and codes as they are throughout history in the *actual* world. (For one quick thing: there seem to be intrinsically and absolutely wrong actions *not* prohibited in every *actual* code.)

theoretical, on the mental, on the mathematical, etc. The antirealist may be loath to accept individuals or properties in a certain domain as truly real, but may also resist abandoning ordinary talk in that domain. A favored response would be to hold the following, for any claim that *Fa* in the domain in question:

> The claim *Fa* is equivalent to the claim *It is true that Fa*, where what is required for such "truth" is "being contained in the relevant body of accepted doctrine," or "being a useful thing to believe in the pertinent area, in virtue of helping us to control or predict better," or the like.

It is important for this strategy, however, that it explain what it is to *believe* that *Fa*, and that it do so while avoiding commitment to any real property of *F*-ness or to any real individual *a*. So it is not enough just to give a proposed definition of truth without appeal to "correspondence." Whatever we admit as the subject of truth must also be unburdened of any realist baggage of properties or individuals in the relevant domain.

And there is an analogous requirement for the relativist naturalist. In securing cognitivist moral concepts, the relativist appeals to moral codes. But it will not do to suppose these are constituted by moral propositions like the proposition that it is wrong to murder, where the wrongness in question is allowed unreduced, as a sui generis and fundamental moral concept. No, a large part of the attraction of relativism resides precisely in its ability to claim much of the advantage of prescriptivism while making room for perspicuous, naturalist and cognitivist conceptions of the wrong, the obligatory, etc. All this it can manage, however, only so long as what *constitutes* moral codes will include only elements acceptable to naturalism, like prescriptions but *unlike* moral propositions composed of any property of primitive moral wrongness or the like.

We turn now to a further question for relativism. How do we understand the "ought"s used *within* a moral code? If the code includes the principle that when in condition C one ought to ϕ, for example, how do we understand the concept of "ought" involved *within* this principle? And isn't the relevance and importance of the ordinary "ought," when relativized to my (our) moral code, based on the assumption that my (our) code is itself correct? And if so are we not committed to the correctness of some "ought" principle or statement whose correctness cannot be understood in the relativist manner under consideration now?

So we are back to an ought that cannot plausibly be understood as relative to one's moral code, since it is *constitutive* of one's moral code; an ought, moreover, that cannot plausibly be understood as "best, all things considered," since otherwise "One ought not to lie" would make an incredibly strong claim that it would always be best, all things considered, not to lie. Nor, finally, can this constitutive ought be understood in any absolutist fashion akin to (W): too few of our ordinary ought principles in our moral codes could survive such an interpretation.

Now the problem of the prima facie finds purchase not only against the prescriptivist, as before, but also against his successor ally, the naturalist relativist. For recall: the problem resides in the fact that nearly all our moral convictions take the form not of absolutely general injunctions — such as "Always act in such and such a way when in so-and-so circumstances!" Rarely if ever is a code in a position to commit with such finality and generality: much more frequent, if not universal, is the prima facie generalization. "Never lie!" is just too unrealistic, by contrast with "Lying is prima facie wrong," or "That to act a certain way would be to lie is always a reason against so acting." On this conception, ordinary principles in our individual or collective moral codes specify moral reasons for or against courses of action, but few if any indefeasible requirements or prohibitions. The application of such a code would then require a practical judgment that balances considerations for and against and reaches an all-things-considered, all-in verdict. That being so, it is not entirely clear just how relativism can represent a real advance. For the moral codes relative to which relativism defines its concept of relative wrongness are now seen to be *constituted* by propositions that contain unreduced moral content such as being prima facie wrong, or being a reason against. And *these* cannot be eliminated in turn by relativistic appeal to moral codes, on pain of vicious circularity.

Besides, there remains in addition the following special problem. Relativism explains what one ought to do as what the relevant moral code requires or implies that one is to do. This is fine so long as moral codes are understood as constituted explicitly or implicitly by general prescriptions. For when a general prescription — "Do A when in C!" — is combined with information about the circumstances — that you are now in C — we can derive the implication: "Do A now!" And in that sense the code requires or implies that you are now to do A, and we can thus conclude that by the relativist account you now *ought* to do A. But we have reason to believe that moral codes cannot plausibly be viewed as constituted by general prescriptions, but must contain instead prima facie rules of the form "Being in C is a prima facie reason for doing A." And there is simply no implication from such a rule to the conclusion that one is now to do A, even relative to the assumption that one is now in condition C. Accordingly, there remains for relativism the special problem of explaining the sense in which a moral code can require or imply anything.

We have emphasized a difficult and quite general problem, that of how to understand this phenomenon of the prima facie.[18] But there is for rel-

---

[18] And an analogous problem arises with regard to the generalizations we believe in common sense and in many scientific disciplines — generalizations which seem to hold true only *ceteris paribus*.

ativism a very special and especially nasty problem here. For recall: relativism had hoped to supply a perfectly cognitivist but naturalistically acceptable concept of what one ought, morally, to do, by appeal to a relevant (and, probably, a contextually indicated) moral code and what this moral code implies. And this was just fine and promising, so long as the moral code could be viewed as constituted by the naturalistically acceptable prescriptions dear to prescriptivism. For there is a clear enough sense in which general prescriptions have relevant implications. Once we see the apparent need to replace general prescriptions with prima facie rules, *two* problems arise for relativism: (1) how to understand the prima facie rules themselves in a naturalistically acceptable way, without allowing a primitive sort of ought claim; and (2) how to understand any idea of such prima facie rules implying what one is to do in given circumstances. A return to the optative language of emotivism offers an attractive response to (1). But relativism is still left with problem (2). And what makes this especially troublesome is that, lacking some such appropriate implication, relativism is deprived of its main point and contribution, namely the very definition of a concept of what one ought, morally, to do.

But the relativist has a reply: "According to my view," he may explain, "moral judgments have a content relative to a moral system, M, picked out in the context of utterance (perhaps largely by the moral commitments of the speaker). M may contain some absolute rules. But it may also contain some weighted rules. Weighted rules can be outweighed. And when they are, M prescribes (by definition) that they be broken. Weighted rules are what are represented in judgments of prima facie wrongness."

The reply continues: "A collection of weighted rules together can now be said to imply a definite moral prescription in a particular case when the rules are summed and their resultant vector computed, so to speak — when all the weights are balanced and the weightiest considerations are given their due force. Admittedly, we are often able to make a judgment of prima facie wrongness without being able to say much of anything about the assignment of weights, as, for example, when we judge with some confidence that lying is prima facie wrong. But the specific weights are lurking below the surface. They emerge only upon extensive rational reflection. They are determined by an idealization from our actual conative state. It is consonant with this view that we should often be able to say with confidence that ϕ-ing is prima facie wrong (that is, that according to the relevant code M there will be some rule with some positive weight that lying will generally violate) without being able to say exactly what the weight of the grounding principle is. In fact, the phenomenon may be said to be a feature of our ignorance." So far the relativist reply.

But a problem remains: How do we understand these "weightings" or "degrees of strength"? In the proposal above, the key element in "weightings" of rules seems to be comparative. The nonabsolute rules in a code are, in effect, supposed to come with an elaborate and comprehensive ranking (if only implicitly) such that when one or more prohibitions conflict with one or more positive injunctions, relative to given circumstances, the code always delivers a verdict that decides the issue. But this seems insufficient to capture the *full* measure of tentativeness contained in a prima facie or *pro tanto* rule. Such rules are not simply tentative in a "close-ended" way, as suggested by the proposal above. They are not simply tentative vis-à-vis possible conflicts with other rules *already part of the code*. On the contrary, a sane and realistic code must recognize its own fallibility and openness to improvement, and this would be reflected in the *open-ended* tentativeness of its rules. This may well be a function of our obvious ignorance in the face of the complexities we normally encounter, or at least might well or might conceivably encounter. Because of this, we are reasonably reluctant to commit with full finality and generality, even when we add, implicitly or explicitly, numerous and varied exceptions. For these are just the exceptions we have thought of so far. Bitter experience has taught us repeatedly that we can expect additional exceptions in due course. It is this awareness of our limits that lies behind the tentativeness of the prima facie, one not removable just by piling on more abstract rules. Within the foreseeable future, the cure evidently lies not in a more complex set of abstractions, but in the concreteness and delicacy of the particular practical judgment, one that takes adequately into account all the relevant complexities of the actual circumstances.

"Is the problem distinctively about prima facie principles?"[19] Well, no, not strictly, since even a relativist whose moral code contains only absolute and general rules may hesitate to press the notion that his code has already made proper allowance for all contingencies that might conceivably have moral relevance. However, the advantages of a prima facie principle is that it commits us only to the "vectorial character" of a morally relevant consideration vis-à-vis some way of acting: only to its being a pro or a con, though of course it might be overridden. Prima facie rules hence cater to our tentativeness through the weakness of their content. But relativism loses that advantage when it views its moral code as a set of prescriptions, and tries to accommodate the prima facie character of ordinary rules by means of an intra-code ranking that helps decide all conflicts. For the full code then retains, after all, the all-or-nothing peremptoriness of ordinary prescriptions. The weakness (tentativeness) of individual prima facie rules is restricted to possible conflicts with other rules already part of the code. And since the code is now supposed to break all such conflicts, the full code will have no such weakness.

Again, the problem for relativism is not that it must uphold its code fervently, in the way of a "true believer." No, a code of absolute, peremptory principles may be held quite tentatively — there is no incoherence in

---

[19] A question I owe to Harman.

that. But our ordinary moral rules are *not* held thus tentatively: in at least some cases we can feel very confident indeed. And in at least some cases our confidence is commensurate with the modesty of our rule's content. "Lying is prima facie wrong" is thus more modest than "Don't lie!" The problem is that even when we add lots of exceptions — "Don't lie, except when $E1$ or $E2$ or $E3$!" — we still fall short of a rule that inspires the confidence of "Lying is prima facie wrong." Thus, we are still owed a way of understanding such prima facie rules within the confines of a relativism based on a code of prescriptions, without losing the peculiar weakness that suits such rules to match so well the special "tentativeness" of our general moral commitments.

V. CONCLUSION

Noncognitivism is an attractive way for the naturalist to make room for the evaluative and the normative. We began by reviewing problems for noncognitivism, and found a surprising and important advantage in favor of the earlier emotivism by comparison with the later prescriptivism. However, even emotivism still has to face the problem of embedding in subordinate clauses and the problem of normative fallibility. So we turned to a different strategy that beckons to the failed noncognitivist: namely, to adopt a relativist account of normative and evaluative terms and concepts.

Our discussion next turned up problems for moral relativism. First, there is the problem of the attribution of moral status to a moral code said to be *moral*. Second, moral codes seem constituted mostly or wholly by claims or rules attributing a rightness or wrongness that is only prima facie, a sort of status not easily explicable in the all-or-nothing terms of prescriptions for or against.

At this juncture, relativism seemed required to join the return to earlier, more emotivist and less prescriptivist, forms of noncognitivism. Relativism, after all, needs some account of the components of a moral code. As we have seen, these cannot plausibly be regarded as ordinary prescriptions. And the most attractive fallback position seems to be that sketched earlier as one beckoning to failed prescriptivism: namely, to conceive of the prima facie as expressive of moral opposition (or favoring) under an aspect. However, it remains to be seen whether this reborn emotivism is more viable than the old-time emotivism dead and buried these many years.

Suppose relativism indeed falls back on that much emotivism, and accepts its share of the burden of adequately explicating and defending it. Still there remains a further special problem for relativism in particular. The problem issues as follows from the prima facie character of the "rules" constitutive of our moral codes, however this character is to be understood. Relativism, such as that stated by account (H) above, speaks of a moral code "implying" that a certain action is to be done. According to relativism, an action ought to be done if and only if the relevant code thus "implies" that it is to be done. But it is not clear what such "implication" can amount to when the source of it is limited to prima facie "rules." That lying is prima facie wrong does not "imply," for any particular set of circumstances, that in them one must not lie. Nor does it seem plausible that any realistic moral code will have any such "implications." Thus, relativism seems to be pushed back to square one: How are we to understand what we say when in a particular situation we conclude that the agent *ought not* to lie?

Philosophy, Brown University

MORAL CHANGE AND SOCIAL RELATIVISM*

By Joseph Raz

I. The Structure of the Argument

A. Multiculturalism, moral knowledge, and relativism

I could not write the essay I hoped to write. I hoped to write about cultural pluralism and moral epistemology by assuming that the first is the case and exploring what implications this may have for the second. But I soon realized that I do not know what cultural pluralism is. I do not mean that I have just belatedly discovered that the phrase "cultural pluralism" is used in different ways on different occasions. I mean that I realized that I myself did not know in what sense the phrase may be used which makes it relevant to the inquiry suggested by the general topic of this volume. So the following reflections are based on one assumption: *The fact of multiculturalism cannot have much bearing on moral epistemology unless it bears on moral truths.* [1]

One can, for example, imagine that membership in a cultural group is either essential or helpful to knowledge of certain moral matters. If so, then multiculturalism creates a rupture in moral knowledge in multicultural societies, with members of different cultural groups having partial moral knowledge, some of it never, or much less frequently, reached by members of other groups.

That something like this is indeed the case would not surprise me. I doubt whether the rupture is absolute, but it is not surprising if the moral significance of certain modes of conduct, individual or institutional, is easily perceived by members of cultural groups which are morally directly affected by it, whereas the access of most other people to it is rather like that of a blind person to the colors of objects in his immediate vicinity. Those who are not members of directly affected groups, or those who are not familiar with their life and problems at close quarters, may be unable to perceive the moral significance of the conduct I have in mind, but they may come to learn how to tell what it is by indirect signs, or by the testimony of others who are directly affected by it.

* I am grateful to Andrei Marmor, John Hyman, and Carl Wellman for challenging and helpful comments on an earlier draft.
[1] In this essay I am proceeding on the assumption—not to be examined here—that at least some types of moral statements bear truth values.

For multiculturalism to have such significance for moral knowledge it is not enough to establish that members of different cultural groups differ in their moral opinions regarding the same phenomena. We are not interested in the phenomenology of moral error, but in differential access to moral truths. So the epistemic implications of multiculturalism presuppose that members of different cultural groups find that ease of access to at least some moral truths varies with one's cultural group. One – though not the only – plausible explanation of such differential access is that membership in cultural groups has moral implications – that is, that the moral significance of actions, attitudes, and their like differs in different cultural communities. There is a sense in which this is trivially true. We need only think of the fact that the same form of address may be polite in one cultural group, and rude in another. The question is: Is there a more interesting way in which the moral significance of acts or facts depends on the cultural groups in which they take place?

I should hasten to say that the supposition that close familiarity with a cultural group gives one easy access to some moral knowledge does not require that the variability of moral meaning of acts and attitudes be philosophically deep or interesting. Even simple moral/cultural variation gives rise to some epistemic consequences. However, if multiculturalism has more profound implications for moral truths, its epistemic implications are correspondingly more far-reaching.

The question we face is whether social/cultural practices affect morality. The stumbling block in coming to grips with the question is that we seem to lack an adequate model for a plausible explanation of such dependence. In this essay I will explore one oft-refuted, oft-revived explanation – social relativism. The verdict will be a mixed one. Radical social relativism, I will follow many in arguing, fails. But constrained social relativism is plausible.

Social relativism is, though not among philosophers, a popular view. Belief in the possibility of moral change is, on the other hand, rarer. Yet the two seem to be analogous, the one seeming to be the temporal reflection, even consequence, of the other. Can we learn any lessons from the analogy? Or is it merely deceptive? This will be the route followed in this essay. I will explore the limits of the possibility of moral change, and explore the analogy between it and the limits on plausible versions of social relativism. To begin with, some preliminary ground clearing and terminological clarification is offered, followed by a brief argument to show that social relativism presupposes the possibility of moral change. Section II explains the meaning of "moral change" and argues that if radical moral change is possible it must remain unintelligible. Section III contains a brief argument to the effect that morality is inherently intelligible. It follows that radical moral change is impossible. Does it also follow that there are eternal moral verities? This is the question undertaken in Section IV. Its tentative conclusion is that it is likely that there are no eternal moral verities. Rather, morality should be thought of as evolving toward greater abstractedness and comprehensiveness, as human history evolves. This means, of course, that morality is in a significant way conditioned by social practices. My argument for that depends on the assumption that social conditions set limits to the possibilities of human understanding. However, in the final section, Section V, I argue that this degree of social dependence is not sufficient to vindicate the social relativism identified at the outset, which is social relativism as popularly conceived. That form of the social relativism of morality stands refuted by the argument about the impossibility of a radical moral change in Section II.

B. Defining social relativism and moral change

By "social relativism" I mean the view that

(A) the morality (the moral doctrines and principles) which is binding or valid for a person is a function of the moral practices[2] of his society.

The simplest form of social relativism holds that

(A1) each person is morally subject to (and only to) the morality practiced in his society.

The truth of social relativism, if it is true, is not relativistic in any sense. That is, it is presented as a thesis which is true for all people at all times. Presumably, it is also a thesis whose truth is, in principle, available, i.e., discoverable, by all people at all times.[3] This makes it difficult to espouse social relativism as a moral principle. If (A) is a moral principle, then it can be true only if

(C) the practices of all societies (past, present, and future) are such that given the correct function by which their practices determine the moral principles which are binding or valid on their members, (A) is a valid principle in their societies.

---

[2] When referring to "the moral practices" of a society, I wish to imply neither that members of that society never fail to conform to the standards generally endorsed in that society, nor that mere lip service paid to a standard which is systematically disregarded in action is enough to make that standard part of the practice of the society. Rather, the phrase refers, as it commonly does, to a general but unspecified degree of endorsement coupled with a similarly general and unspecified degree of compliance in action.

When referring to morality being a function of moral practices, I mean "function" in its natural signification — i.e., a thing that depends on and varies with something else — which includes the idea that morality is a function sensitive to variations in moral practices. Functions which yield the same morality for all societies regardless of variations in their moral practices are excluded.

[3] This condition will be examined below.

If the function is identity and the correct version of social relativism is (A1), then (A) — and (A1) — is true only if

> (C1) the practices of all societies require all people to be guided by (and only by) the practices of their society.

If this condition is met, then (A) is a self-verifying moral principle. That it is self-verifying does not of course show that it is true. Conflicting principles can be self-verifying. But the fact that it is self-verifying, if it is a fact, may be thought to give it some weight. If, however, the condition is not met, then (A) is false by its own terms. That is, given — as (A) says — that every person is morally subject to the practices of his society and to them alone, it follows that it is not the case that all are morally bound by the practices of their own society, unless the practices of their society say so.

We know that if this is how (A) is to be understood, i.e., if it is to be seen as a moral principle, and therefore subject to condition (C), then it is false. Many of us live in societies whose practices do not support such a conclusion, and we all know of such societies. It is true that the practices of most societies require their own members to abide by the practices of their own societies. There are ways of understanding this statement which render it tautological (and by most other interpretations it is probably false).[4] Not many societies, however, recognize that the same holds for members of other societies regarding their practices. They tend to judge others by the standards by which they judge themselves.

This refutes (A1) as a moral principle. Similar considerations tell against (A) in all its forms. It is difficult to present them in anything like a conclusive form with complete generality. Broadly speaking, they consist in pointing out that the morality practiced in various societies does not take any notice of the moral practices of other societies when judging some actions of their members.[5]

There is another, independent, reason for rejecting (A), or at least (A1),[6] if it is taken as a moral principle. It imposes a conventionalist interpretation on morality. According to it, one's rights and duties are those one enjoys by the practices of one's society. The principle makes this coincidence necessary. This poses a problem to anyone who accepts (A1) when facing questions about the justification of having a duty or a

---

[4] It is tautological if it is read as saying: "The moral rules practiced in this society which apply to its members, apply to its members"; i.e., the rules require conformity from those they apply to. It is false if it means: "The moral rules practiced in this society stipulate that the fact that they are practiced is a reason for members of the society in which they are practiced to follow them."

[5] Though quite often we invoke the practices of other societies to excuse or mitigate our judgment of actions of their members.

[6] I do not know whether the argument applies to other, yet to be specified, versions of (A). The following remarks constitute a prima facie case for thinking that it does.

right, or regarding the justification of any other aspect of morality. Of course, the practices of his society will include principles and considerations which can be adduced as a justification of the rights or duties he is concerned to justify. But he has to face the question of whether (A1) itself is irrelevant to such justification. Since it is assumed to be a moral principle, and since it directly bears on the question of what rights and duties people have, it is difficult to avoid regarding it as (at least one) justification for them. That justification, however, turns all morality into a matter of convention: this is how one ought to behave because this is how people generally behave, and how they think they ought to behave, and so on.

It hardly needs arguing that thoroughgoing justificatory conventionalism is a travesty of morality. While people may sometimes appeal to what everyone believes, and to how people act, as evidence for accepting that their views are correct, only in special cases do they regard such facts as (nonepistemic) justificatory reasons. As a moral principle, (A) must be rejected.

But (A) can be understood not as a moral principle but as something else. I will consider the possibility that it is a result of the meaning, or essence, of morality. Whatever moral principles are valid, they will be of a different order from an explanation of what morality is. Such an explanation may include claims like "Moral statements are statements about one person's duties to his fellow beings." These need not be statements of moral principle to be true. They can include a thesis like (A). This would be a statement that, of the different rules which apply to a person, the moral rules which apply to him are those which are practiced in his society. This "meta-ethical" statement is not a piece of verbal legislation. It is a thesis about what morality really is. But it is not a moral view about what moral duties people have. It is a "meta-ethical" view, on a par with the thesis that, of the duties which a person is subject to, his duties to others are his moral duties. On this understanding, the primary import of the social relativistic thesis is not to argue which rights, duties, etc. people have but to classify and clarify the nature of rights and duties, etc., which people do have.

This understanding of the social relativistic thesis is compatible with the possibility that the thesis bears on the question "Which rights and duties do people have?" as well. No independence or priority of the theory of morality relative to morality, or vice versa, is assumed. This may raise some people's eyebrows regarding the very distinction between morality and the theory of morality. But such suspicions are misplaced. The distinction is present in our common reflections on morality and the concepts we employ in it. It is not meant to do much heavy duty. It is pointless to try a general characterization. For present purposes, suffice it to emphasize that moral principles are reason-giving or explanatory. That means that a principle of the form "If C, then one has a right to A" states more than a juxtaposition of C and a right to A. It states that C is (at least a part of) a reason for, or an explanation or justification of, such a right. It follows that not all statements of this form are statements of moral principles. Some of them may be true theoretical statements about morality.

While I have treated "social relativism" as a term of art, "moral change" is meant to be understood in its ordinary meaning—except that usually when we think of moral change we think of a person or a society changing their moral views or practices. The moral change we will be concerned with is that of morality itself. Can morality change? In a minimal sense, morality changes when a moral statement which is true at one point is no longer true. It is necessary, however, to distinguish between a change in the rights, duties, etc., which are the consequences of applying (possibly an unchanged) morality to changing circumstances, and a change in morality itself. As a partial first step in that direction,[7] let me say that a moral change occurs when a moral statement which does not refer to any particular individual is true at one time and false at another. Thus, that JR now has a duty he did not have yesterday is not sufficient to establish that a moral change has occurred (though a change in JR's duties may be due to a moral change). But that it was true yesterday and is no longer true that those who promise have a duty to do as they promised does establish, if true, the occurrence of a moral change.

C. Social relativism presupposes moral change

Social relativism can be sustained only if moral change is possible. We know that social practices can (and do) change. If, as social relativism claims, morality is a function of social practices, then morality can (and does) change as well. To assume that it is a function of social practices which is indifferent to changes in such practices would be to run against the very idea of social relativism. It is true, e.g., that by pegging the function to some primordial stage of development, even an unvarying function can preserve something of the intuitions behind social relativism, namely that members of different societies are subject to different moral principles (members of each society being subject to a morality fixed once and for all for members of that society as a function of their social condition at a specified time). But this is achieved at the cost of abandoning the other, and central, intuition which makes social relativism attractive, i.e., that the moral principles which apply to a person reflect his social environment (this may be thought, e.g., necessary to show that it is possible for people to come to know the moral principles which apply to them—or, according to other views, to show that they can always be motivated by those principles, that such a motivation is available to them).

---

[7] The distinction is discussed again in the next section. No final and comprehensive criteria for drawing it are needed for the purposes of this essay.

This suggests a simple refutation of social relativism: Since social relativism presupposes the possibility of moral change, and since moral change is impossible, social relativism is false. This is the argument to be explored below. We need to inquire into the possibility of moral change and into the reasons for rejecting it in order to establish that the moral change social relativism presupposes is in fact impossible. The conclusions will be far less clear-cut than the argument assumes. Some moral change is possible. Therefore, so far as this argument goes there is room for some forms of social relativism. Whether the constrained social relativism one ends up with satisfies the intuitions of real hard-boiled social relativists is a question I will only be able to touch on in concluding this essay.

II. The Intelligibility of Moral Change

A. Narrowing the issue

A common view has it that there can be no moral change. Morality (i.e., all true moral propositions) is, according to this view, universal and, in some sense, necessary. Hence, it cannot be contingent on facts which may change over time. But why should this be so? Moreover, can this view be consistently sustained? It seems impossible to deny that some moral change occurs. For example, the duties of charity depend on the political situation in one's country. The introduction of a just tax law, and of adequate and efficient welfare services radically changes one's duty to give to charity. The nature of the change depends on the circumstances before and after the change. But the following, e.g., may be true of some hypothetical situation: until the change in the law, one had a duty to give one-tenth of one's income to charity, but after that the duty is to give only half as much.

Some may say that this is not really moral change. It is merely a change in the application of a moral principle at a fairly low level of generalization. Notice though that the change can occur at any level of generality. According to common rule-utilitarian moralities, all moral principles barring one—that is, barring the principle of utility itself—are subject to change. Why must the principle of utility itself be an exception? It seems that the underlying idea is that there cannot be a complete moral change; not everything can change, at least not at once. Belief in the impossibility of total moral change is, however, but a special case of the underlying thesis that any change must be an application of an unchanging principle to changing circumstances. The only moral change which is impossible is one which does not presuppose this combination of unchanging principle and changing circumstances.

B. The basic argument

Why must all moral change presuppose an unchanging moral background? It is not as if a presupposed unchanging moral background is necessary for us to be able to distinguish between continuity and change. All we need for this is the ability to distinguish between different moral principles, and to be able to establish whether they are true or not. If we can tell that proposition P expresses a moral principle, and that it was true at t_0 and false at t_1, we know that a moral change has occurred.

There is, however, a powerful argument against the possibility of moral change. While conceding that moral change can be detected even when it is not merely a change in the application of the same principle to changing circumstances, the argument claims that if such change is possible it is bound to remain unintelligible. The reason, according to the argument, is that to explain any moral change we need a backdrop of an unchanging principle. Here is one way of spelling out the argument: Suppose that the moral change we have in mind entails that from today I may not do something which I was allowed to do until now. If I inquire why I may not do it, the answer is that it is prohibited by a principle. If so, why was it permissible until now? Because, the answer goes, the principle is a new one. But this is puzzling. What could explain how a principle which was not valid until now has become a binding moral principle? Perhaps things have changed, and this explains its becoming binding. In that case there is a complete statement of the change, call it P, such that there is a valid universal principle which has not changed on the relevant occasion:

(D) If P, then acts of the relevant kind are forbidden.

The consequent of (D) ("acts of the relevant kind are forbidden") is the new principle. (D) itself, however, is an unchanging principle, and one which explains the validity of the new principle.

This, you may say, is cheating. Conditionals such as (D) are not really moral principles. Rather, they are statements that the antecedent brings about a moral change. What else could count as a moral change? That is, the objection goes, when people say that morality cannot change, they say that something which is imaginable (moral change) cannot happen. But if (D) counts as a moral principle, then there is nothing which could be imagined as a moral change, for it follows from the supervenience of the moral on the nonmoral[8] that there cannot be any moral change without a change describable in nonmoral terms.[9] There are problems here which cannot be fully explored now. Surely some universal statements

---

[8] "The supervenience of the moral on the nonmoral" refers to a familiar philosophical doctrine according to which two things can vary in their moral properties only if they vary in their nonmoral properties.

[9] Can it be otherwise? Perhaps if the moral change is not merely in one principle, but if the whole of morality valid at one point is replaced by a different morality at a later time.

with nonmoral antecedents and moral consequents are statements of moral principles. Take, for example,

(D1) When you knowingly cause another person to rely on you to act in a certain way, and when, because of his reliance, failing to so act will be to his detriment, you have an obligation to act in that way.

We need, therefore, an account of when statements like (D) state a principle and when they state the conditions which will bring about the coming into force of the principle stated in the consequent. Whatever it may be (and I will give a partial elucidation of the distinction below), let us agree that such an account can be given. Is it possible that some nonmoral change will make a moral change intelligible? But what change could explain a change in the validity of a moral principle?

Suppose that the alleged new principle is that women should have the same employment opportunities as men. What sort of change can explain the principle's newly acquired validity? Perhaps the change is in the domestic technologies which mean that housekeeping and child-rearing are no longer a full-time job (clothes and bread and the like are bought rather than made at home; cleaning, washing, and cooking are easier with the new implements available; and if only there were child-minding facilities, neither parent would need to spend a whole day at home). But why should these changes make a moral difference? Why should the fact that housekeeping and child-rearing are a full-time job mean that women need not have equal job opportunities? Should it not be their choice which parent stays at home and which one goes on the job market? The story is familiar. Any factual narrative either will require moral assumptions to explain why it leads to a change of moral principle or will itself incorporate moral factors (which have not changed) which will explain how the moral change has come about. Either way, a moral change cannot be intelligible except through an unchanging moral background which explains why changing circumstances brought it about.

We can now better see when conditionals such as (D) state moral principles and when they do not. The requirement that moral predicates supervene on nonmoral ones implies no more than that some such conditional is true whenever a new moral principle, i.e., the one stated by the consequent, becomes valid. But it does not imply that these conditionals are themselves moral principles. It is satisfied, e.g., by

(D2) If a star has collapsed, smoking is wrong.

Perhaps then the new morality can still supervene on the same nonmoral facts, only in a different configuration. But if such a change were to happen, its occurrence would surely be unintelligible.

The possibility of moral change through conceptual change will be separately considered below.

This is not a moral principle, for the fact that a star has collapsed is not a reason why smoking is prohibited. That smoking damages the health of those who inhale tobacco smoke is — perhaps — a reason why smoking, or smoking in public, is wrong. But if so, then the statement

> (D3) If inhaling tobacco smoke damages one's health, then smoking in public is wrong

is a statement of moral principle. Conditionals of the (D) form in which the antecedent specifies the reason for the validity of the consequent are statements of moral principles. But if so, it follows that the coming into effect of a new moral principle is explicable only if there is another (D)-type principle specifying the reasons for it and thus explaining why it came into effect. If there is no such explanatory principle already in force, then the coming into effect of the new principle is unintelligible.

The question of the boundary of morality may pose another difficulty here. Is it unintelligible for evaluative/normative principles which are not moral ones to explain a moral change? Must it be made explicable by reference to other specifically moral considerations? I do not mean to suggest that it must. The argument is really about the conditions for the intelligibility of change of normative/evaluative principles of any kind, be they moral or not. It claims that for such change to be intelligible there must be an unchanging evaluative/normative principle, whether classified as moral or not, which explains the change. I will continue to discuss the problem in terms of the relations between moral principles. But everything I say should be understood as subject to this explanation.

C. À propos *supervenience*

The basic argument took us into a consideration of supervenience and justifies a brief detour to comment on the relation between the requirement of supervenience and that of moral intelligibility. They show that supervenience does not guarantee intelligibility. It can be satisfied by the truth of propositions such as (D2) which leave the moral principle concerned entirely unintelligible. I believe that the requirement of supervenience owes its appeal to the thought that without it morality is unintelligible. If so, then it may be tempting to react to the above by saying that supervenience is a necessary but not a sufficient condition for the intelligibility of morality. But the condition of intelligibility we were exploring — that is, that there be a background normative/evaluative principle which states a reason for the principle to be explained, even if it is only a sufficient and not a necessary condition of intelligibility (and I wish to express no opinion on this point) — does not itself presuppose supervenience. It can be satisfied by an antecedent which includes reference to other evaluative/normative considerations. Intelligibility, in other words, can be achieved through a series of ultimately circular explanations. This does not mean that morality can be made intelligible without any reference to nonmoral facts. But it does mean that if there are reasons for accepting the requirement of supervenience, then they must be independent of the claim that without it morality cannot be intelligible.

D. The case of conceptual change

We can now return to our main topic. Moral change can be intelligible only if we assume a currently unchanging principle which states the reasons for the change. This view may be too simplistic. Possibly, radical moral change, i.e., that which does not presuppose a continuing background, requires conceptual change. Our moral concepts are not constant. See, for example, the vying for central-stage position of the concepts 'happiness', 'eudaimonia', 'well-being', 'individual welfare', and 'flourishing'. They all aim at roughly the same role in moral thought, and while being similar they clearly differ. Similarly, it makes a difference whether souls, human beings, rational beings, persons, or members of some other category are thought to be the primary moral subjects. "Treat every soul as an end in itself" differs from "Treat every rational being as an end in itself." These are examples of rival concepts which are part of our conceptual armory. We are aware, however, that over the years moral principles have "changed their meaning" through conceptual changes in which similar but not identical concepts succeeded each other in the moral principles in which they are embedded. Imagine such a change in a fundamental principle. Imagine a change which may happen through a subtle change which is not even echoed in a terminological change: the principle may be stated using the same words, but the meaning of the words may have shifted, so that they now state a different, and therefore new, principle. Is it not true that these cases exemplify moral changes which are intelligible, but do not presuppose a continuing moral principle to make them intelligible?

These cases are far from clear. When it is possible for people to realize that a conceptual change has occurred, they are likely to be aware that it accompanied a change of their moral views. In that case they may well regard the previous, unmodified principle as inferior to the new one, i.e., as having been mistaken. If so, then there is no evidence here that morality has changed; so far as we know, only people's views on morality have changed. Alternatively, it may be a case of a moral change subsumed under and explained by some unchanging principle. These are the only ways in which the situation can be viewed. Suppose, however, that people cannot establish that a conceptual change has occurred. It may be in principle imperceptible from the new vantage point. Would that warrant saying that there has been a moral change (through the change in the meaning of the principle embodying the concept which changed its meaning) which need not be subsumed under any unchanging principle to be intelligible? I do not believe so. The people whose concept it is do not believe that there was a moral change, since they are unaware of the conceptual shift which led to it. So far as they are concerned, the principle they now believe to be valid has always been valid, and any principle inconsistent with it — as we assume the old one to be — was always, in their eyes, invalid. For anyone who is aware of the change, and who regards it as a moral change rather than as a change in people's moral views, it will not be intelligible unless it can be accounted for in the ordinary way, i.e., as an application of an unchanging principle. So this is not an example of the intelligibility of radical moral change.

III. Must Morality Be Intelligible?

Accepting that to be intelligible a moral change must assume an unchanging moral principle(s) which explains how changing circumstances brought into effect a new moral principle, or led to the lapse of an old one, the question remains: Must morality be intelligible? Can we not say that the fact that an action is morally required or morally prohibited, or that a character trait is virtuous or evil, is a matter of how the world is, and there is no a priori reason to believe that the world must be intelligible? It is what it is. We may or may not find out how it is, and we are lucky if we ever understand why it is as it is.

An over-simple, yet fundamentally correct, answer to this question is that morality *is* intelligible, for its role is to enable people to comprehend themselves and their world. This answer may be disputed in various ways. First, it is true that we explain how people ought to behave, and also how they actually conduct themselves and society, by reference to moral facts (e.g., the broadening of the scope of moral sensitivity led to a decline in the spirit of community, and to a growth in selfishness, which itself accounts for the decline in the fortunes of elderly people). But this does not mean that morality must be intelligible through and through. It may explain what it explains insofar as it is itself intelligible, and not beyond. Second, it is wrong, some may say, to suggest that it is "the role" of morality to make things intelligible. To say so is to suggest that it is the nature of morality to be instrumental to some purpose external to it. In fact, morality is, to repeat the previous point, simply part of the world. Moral principles just happen to be valid in this world. This is just how the world is. Like other facts about the world, morality helps explain people and society to the extent that it is itself understood. But we cannot assume that it is altogether intelligible any more than we can assume this about other aspects of the world. Moreover, morality must be conceived in this way, for it could not explain anything if it were not an aspect of reality. Whatever it explains, it explains by reference to this aspect of the world. How else could it explain either how people should behave or how they do?

The second objection is beside the point. No one is denying (nor is it affirmed) that moral discourse is about an aspect of the world. All that is asserted is that moral statements are essentially explicable, intelligible. It is not consistent with our idea of morality, with the nature of our moral discourse, that what is morally permissible or forbidden, etc., is so for no reason or for mysterious reasons. If moral discourse is about a part of reality, then it is an inherently intelligible part of reality. That is all. Herein lies one of the differences between morality and taboo, magical instructions, etc.: that the former is necessarily intelligible, whereas the latter are not necessarily so. Moral facts are in order, but they are not like facts about the weather. Besides reasons for believing that something is morally so and so, there are reasons which justify its being so and so, and they are noncontingently related to what they are reasons for.[10] Likewise, moral facts are noncontingently related to the conclusions they support, including conclusions about the appropriateness of certain actions or evaluations.

Part of the opposition to the thought that morality is inherently intelligible results from an incorrect understanding of the implications of that thought. For example, the claim that morality is intelligible may be thought to assign morality an excessively rationalistic character. But this is not so. There is no implication here that people who make moral statements must fully understand their implication or be fully cognizant of their justification, or that they are at fault to some degree if this is not so. With moral as with other knowledge, possessing it does not presuppose full understanding of its grounds and justification.[11] Nor should we think of intelligibility as involving a rationalistic view. It is intelligible to people that hunger makes concentration difficult, and slows down mental processes. There is nothing rationalistic about this. To be intelligible, such connections require appropriate experience, or learning from (or about) those who have such experience. Finally, to repeat the obvious, intelligibility does not depend on showing that morality serves a purpose external to itself.[12] Intelligibility may consist in explaining the point of a rule or a goal rather than its external purpose.

But, another objector may say, is a moral change less intelligible than its absence? Do we not need an explanation for why moral changes do

---

[10] The justifying reasons may also be one's epistemic reasons. But one may have other epistemic reasons, e.g., reliable advice.

[11] A closely related point is discussed in some detail in the appendix to Joseph Raz, *Practical Reason and Norms*, 2d ed. (Princeton: Princeton University Press, 1990), as well as by Samuel Scheffler in *Human Morality* (New York: Oxford University Press, 1992).

[12] The view that it does is a legacy of the instrumental conception of reason. Unfortunately, many who reject it do accept instrumental rationality as the clearest and safest form of practical rationality. See, however, Jean Hampton, "Rethinking Reason," *American Philosophical Quarterly*, vol. 29, no. 3 (July 1992), pp. 219–36, for arguments that, far from being so instrumental, rationality presupposes noninstrumental practical rationality. Arguments to the same effect were pressed by Warren Quinn, and will be included in the collection of his essays to be published by Oxford University Press in 1993.

not occur? That is a misunderstanding. We explain why morality is as it is by giving reasons for the moral doctrines and principles which are valid. This explains why they are as they are, i.e., why they are not different, why they do not change. It is change that, to be intelligible, requires additional explanation, not its absence. Nor can one object that it is impossible on pain of infinite regress to explain why morality is as it is. Every "why" question can receive an answer. Infinite regress or (wide) circles are no objection to intelligibility. What is intelligible is a self-supporting whole (including its potential for infinite expansion).

These comments are meant to remove objections to the claim that morality is inherently intelligible. The argument for the claim proceeds from the basic features of moral discourse and its presuppositions. That discourse is explanatory and clarifying, or it assumes that all moral statements can be justified, and their justification can be understood. Hence the claim about the essential intelligibility of morality. This way of proceeding from discourse to aspects of the world will strike some as odd. But I believe that it is sound and not unique to morality. To the extent that our discourse clarifies aspects of the world, we can learn from the nature of the discourse which aspects of the world it is about. It is possible that the discourse as a whole is incoherent. But barring that possibility it follows that the world has aspects which display the attributes ascribed to them by the essential features of that discourse. In other words, assuming that the discourse is not incoherent as a whole, its essential features are reflected in reality. Any assumption of a stronger independence of thought and reality is itself incoherent.

IV. ARE THERE ETERNAL MORAL VERITIES?

A. An argument for timeless moral verities

Does the argument advanced above show that there are timeless valid moral[13] principles? The issue is far from clear. On its face it only shows that no change is intelligible except against the background of a (then) unchanging principle, which may itself have come into force, or which may lose validity, at some time or another—a change which will itself become intelligible because of yet another principle. One may think that this leaves the door open to the possibility that all moral principles are valid only for a limited time.[14]

---

[13] Or at least timeless normative/evaluative principles?

[14] It may be that morality itself makes sense or is in force only under certain conditions, e.g., only while moral agents exist. The discussion of the temporal boundaries of moral principles is not meant to reflect this fact but to assume it. That is, the question under consideration is whether there must be one or more moral principles which must be valid for as long as morality is in force or makes sense, or whether this is not so and it is possible that no single moral principle is valid throughout the period during which morality is in force.

The requirement of intelligibility seems, however, to be the basis of a stronger conclusion. It means not only that a moral change is intelligible when it occurs but that it remains intelligible. If the only principles which explain the change at the time are then superseded, the change they explained is no longer explicable.

In some cases, the explaining principles (i.e., the ones explaining the original change) are not the only ones to explain that change. Commonly, there may be more abstract principles which explain the explaining principles. These more abstract principles will explain the conditions under which the explaining principles may themselves change, but they also — perhaps indirectly — explain the original change. In that case, there is no difficulty in imagining that the explaining principles themselves change at some later date. But their change is possible only because of the persistence of more abstract principles which remain unchanged.

The process here envisaged is one of continuing ascent toward more abstract and more permanent principles. We can readily imagine that more and more abstract principles emerge with time. As history unfolds we are continuously forced to conclude that principles which appeared immutable are in fact valid only under specific social, economic, or cultural conditions. As those conditions change, the principles lose their validity. But the realization that this is so is made possible by the emergence of those more abstract principles we talked about which explain that change. The more abstract principles are taken to apply to the old as well as to the new conditions. They can explain the change because they span the periods, old and new, and provide the background continuity necessary for the intelligibility of moral change. This is why their emergence is itself a discovery of principles which were valid all along, rather than an emergence of new principles. Were they new, they would not be able to explain why the old explaining principles lapsed.

This story is schematic and "cleansed" of any suggestion that previous generations were in part mistaken in their moral beliefs. Typically, as the conditions of life change we come to discover new, more abstract principles which explain the limited durability of moral verities hitherto believed to be eternal, and, at the same time, we come to believe that the previous generations were in part mistaken about morality, and that what we now see as the lapsed principles were not exactly as people then believed them to be.

B. A counterargument

If I am right so far, morality does contain unchanging principles. But there is a powerful objection to this line of argument. Why should the fact that the explaining principle lapses make the change that it explained inexplicable? It remains intelligible by reference to the lapsed principle which was valid at the time. The fact that the principle is no longer valid does not matter to the intelligibility of a moral change which it explained and justified when it was in force. In this respect, the case of moral change is like that of any action or anything else subject to moral judgment on the basis of the now-lapsed, but at the time valid, principle. Action taken at the time the principle was in force, which the principle showed to be right, remains right even though the principle lapsed. It does not lapse retroactively. Its moral significance at the time it was valid is not annulled.

How convincing is the counterargument? It is surely sound in its implications for the assessment of actions, emotions, character, institutions, and other subjects of moral evaluation. But does it also apply to the assessment of morality itself? This seems to me far from clear. One may hold that if the counterargument succeeds then it may be the case that our morality, i.e., the morality which is currently in force, contains no explanation for the past change in moral principle. This, one may hold, is impossible. It is, of course, true that we know today of a moral explanation for the moral change, i.e., its explanation by the then-valid, now-lapsed principle. But since we do not now hold that explaining principle to be valid, our current morality does not contain an explanation for the change.

This attempted rebuttal depends on a subtle distinction: the distinction between (1) an explanation provided by the morality currently in force, and (2) an explanation which relies on principles no longer in force, but an explanation which is still true today. The rebuttal claims that morality must be intelligible and that it is intelligible only if, for any given time t, a moral change which occurred at any time is intelligible only if a moral explanation of it is available in terms of principles valid at t.

The claim does not seem implausible, but I can think of no argument to support it. Even if we grant it, we are still short of an argument for the existence of timeless moral truths. There can be more than one explanation of a single moral change. It may be possible for a moral change to be explicable by reference to one explaining principle at the time that it occurred, and to become additionally explicable in terms of another principle which comes into force at a later time. If so, then if the first, original explaining principle lapses some time after the new explanation becomes available, the condition of intelligibility stated in the attempted rebuttal is met, and yet there may be no timeless moral truths.

To succeed, the rebuttal has to be reinforced by another claim. One way of doing so is to claim that to be good an explanation of a moral change has to be available at the time of the change. An explanation cannot be retroactive, relying on principles which were not valid at the time the change occurred. If morality has to be intelligible, and if moral change is intelligible only if it is explicable in terms of principles valid both at the time of the change and at the time of the explanation, then there are timeless moral truths.

C. Moral progress toward unchanging principles

The second condition for the success of the rebuttal seems more intu-itively obvious than the first. How can a change be explained by a prin-ciple not valid at the time it occurred? Nevertheless it admits of an exception. Admittedly, the exception I have in mind is not only of lim-ited scope, but is also not out of sympathy with the spirit of the require-ment that the principle explaining a change be valid at the time of the change.

A simple case will illustrate how an exception can be sympathetic. Imagine that a law is replaced with another law similar in its general char-acter but correcting certain anomalies due to over-generalized application of the original law. The old law is no longer in force, and the new one was not in force until now. But we could still admit that a legal change explicable at the time by an aspect of the old law which has not changed, an aspect which remained unaffected by the difference between the old and the new law, is now explicable on the basis of the new law. Even though the new law was not valid at the time, its spirit—incorporated in the old law—was. Of course, this case is not directly relevant to moral-ity. The old law is replaced because it was defective all along. The case of moral change is not like that. Morality cannot be defective. Moral change, we are assuming, follows change in the circumstances of the life of the people to whom the morality applies. I mention the legal case only as an analogy. For I believe that it finds analogy in morality.

If the analogy can be sustained, then we have two rival views of how to understand a moral change which happens when a moral principle believed at the time to be ultimate and universal changes. Both views assume that while the lapsed principle was valid at the time, belief in its timeless validity was mistaken. One view discussed earlier assumes unchanging, universal moral principles which are discovered (often roughly at the time when some of the known principles lapse) as a result of changes in the circumstances of people's lives, and which explain the moral change.

The legal analogy suggests a different way of understanding roughly the same story. It too allows for a change in circumstances which leads to principles hitherto in force losing their point and validity. It too regards this change as explicable by more abstract principles which were not pre-viously accepted or known, and which vindicate the old principles as valid in the past, while explaining why they are valid no more.[15] But now we are invited to conceive of these more abstract principles, not as unchanging principles recently discovered, but as new principles which have recently emerged. Even though they are new—the legal analogy suggests—since they are in keeping with the spirit of the old principles

---

[15] Some changes are explained by principles which were known and understood all along. I am simply interested in the case where this is not so.

(as is witnessed by the fact that they vindicate their validity for their time, and that they are, broadly speaking, generalizations of the earlier principles which are now a special case of the new principles), they can explain why the old principles lapsed.

How are we to judge between the picture of morality as resting on eternal verities and the one which sees it as perpetually evolving toward more general principles? Oddly enough, the very argument—that morality is inherently intelligible—which I have used to set limits to the possibility of moral change provides a reason for preferring the view which allows for the possibility that some changes are made intelligible only through new emerging principles. For the intelligibility of morality requires that morality should be in principle accessible to the people to whom it applies. Again the argument for this thesis cannot be examined here. It turns once more on the point I have relied upon earlier, i.e., that morality has a role which it ought to play in people's lives, the role of making intelligible, giving meaning to, various aspects of their lives, and the possibilities open to them in life, and thus also providing guidance in their lives. The argument relies on the contention that principles which in principle cannot fulfill that role cannot be valid moral principles.

Arguably, moral principles can be conceived, understood, and believed only by people who either share a culture or know or could find out about a culture which makes the principles conceivable. Arguably, people who lived long before the rise of the great monotheistic religions and in conditions which made their rise impossible to envisage could not have understood moral notions and moral principles which those religions brought in their wake (such as the universal moral standing of all persons). If so—and the argument cannot be examined here—then there is substantive bite to the thesis that moral principles cannot be valid at a time when they cannot be conceived, or when it is impossible for people to come to know them.

For current purposes I will simply accept these contentions. In particular, I will accept the exception to the rule that a moral change is intelligible only by reference to principles valid both at the time the change occurred and at the time of the explanation. The exception allows that a change is intelligible if explained by principles which, though not valid at the time it occurred because at that time they were beyond people's grasp, vindicate the principles then valid. This exception disproves the claim that there must be timeless moral verities. There may be no timeless moral principles after all. Morality may be essentially temporal. This type of change, consisting as it does of ever-increasing generality of scope, is not disruptive change. It does not turn morality into disjointed temporal segments. At any given time, the whole of morality, past and present, is comprehensible in the light of currently valid moral principles. Morality may be pluralistic, but its pluralism does not comprise distinct and unconnected temporal segments. This view of the limits to moral change, while allowing that there may be no eternal moral verities, justifies the claim that morality continuously and endlessly develops toward unchanging moral principles, since every change is subsumed under a principle, old or new, which is of greater scope and generality.

V. From Change to Social Relativism

The impossibility of radical moral change, i.e., one which does not presuppose a continuing moral principle, does not establish that there cannot be any moral change. As we saw, it does not even establish that there is a moral principle which cannot change. Moreover, someone may say that everything but one principle can change all at once. This is in principle so, if one believes in a monolithic ethic. Not so for moral pluralists. For pluralists, the message is that many principles must persist through any moral change, however far-reaching. For present purposes, however, the main importance of the impossibility of radical moral change is that it provides strong reasons for suspecting that social relativism is untenable.

How so? The argument is simple. The very idea of social relativism implies that a change in social practice is sufficient for a change of moral principle; i.e., what is asserted is precisely that no continuing moral principle is necessary. If the function from social practices to moral principles presupposes some moral principles—that is, if it is a function from social practices and moral principles to moral principles—there would be no guarantee that social practices condition morality until some continuing principles were known, and by definition these could not be a function of social practices themselves.

Another way of arguing for the same conclusion is this: If the morality valid for a person is a function of the moral practices of that person's society, then it changes as the moral practices of that society change. Moral practices can change completely. Since morality in its entirety is supposed by social relativists to be a function of social practices, it follows that morality, too, must be capable of changing completely. Hence, again, the possibility of radical moral change is a consequence of social relativism. Since we have just seen that radical moral change is impossible, it follows that social relativism is untenable. Can the argument be avoided by assuming that social change is gradual? After all, if social change is gradual, every change in a social practice occurs against a backdrop of continuing social practices. That appears to satisfy the limit on change which our argument imposed, i.e., that while every moral principle may change, every change occurs against a backdrop of continuing moral principles. But this reconciliation is illusory. The argument against radical moral change establishes more than that every change happens against a backdrop of continuing principles, so that morality cannot change all at once. It establishes also that it cannot change completely. At any time, the principle which explains change is either one which has always been valid or one which embraces and explains principles which were valid prior to its emergence. Since morality cannot change completely and social practices can, social relativism is untenable.

I believe that one of the main attractions of social relativism is the thought that morality must be accessible to the people whom it binds. I have argued that that very thought derives from the fact that morality is inherently intelligible, and that the inherent intelligibility of morality is inconsistent with its being a function of the social practices of the society which it binds. The requirement of the intelligibility of morality means that morality is constrained by the culture of the people whom it binds. It cannot contain principles inaccessible to their understanding, and their culture sets boundaries to their understanding. But this constraint is satisfied by much which is unrelated to their own practices, and which history, travel, writing, or human imagination make comprehensible to them.

Some moral philosophers regard ethics as limited by tradition, with the conversation of the deaf being conducted across the boundaries of traditions. If so, and if the different cultures in a multicultural society stand for different traditions, then multiculturalism imports the existence of a moral chasm between the different traditions and communities in society. The argument of this essay suggests that this thought is incompatible with an understanding of the nature of morality. Multiculturalism gives rise to problems of communication and of comprehension. But there is something to communicate and something to comprehend. There is a morality which applies to all the traditions and all the cultures, a morality which bridges the divide between them.

We can now see that the impossibility of radical moral change is a stronger thesis than may appear at first sight. It denies the compartmentalization of morality into a changing and an unchanging part. In other words, morality cannot be partly universal and partly socially relative, unless the socially relative part is a mere application of the universal part. So it is not merely that every morality must contain a universal part, principles such as "Do not torture" and "Do not intentionally kill the innocent." Its universal part must explain why the contingent part is cogent, why it is as it is. This universal part explains how social practices and other circumstances can make a moral difference. This means that social relativism is untenable even in the modest form which says that part of morality is socially relative, and is not subsumed under (is not mere application of) non–socially relative moral principles.

Philosophy, Balliol College, Oxford University

THE EXPIRATION OF MORALITY*

By Wallace I. Matson

Religion blushing veils her sacred fires,
And unawares *Morality* expires.

The Dunciad, IV, 649f.

Has Alexander Pope's prediction,[1] made a quarter of a millennium ago (1742), come true in our own day?

No one who has lived through the last thirty years is unaware of the spectacular alterations of behavior norms that have occurred in most Western societies. It is not merely that everywhere incivility and crime are on the increase, that there are more and more violations of moral standards which nevertheless continue to be acknowledged. Rather, we witness the relaxation or disappearance of the standards themselves. What was bad becomes permissible or even a positive good.

At the same time, there has never been a greater volume of talk about what is moral and what immoral. Judging by words, one might suppose our era to be one of greatly heightened moral sensitivity. If morality is expiring, it is "unawares."

Pope's verses presuppose the theory that religion (viz., Christianity) is the foundation of morality both as authoritative formulation and as necessary motivation: implying that if Christianity, "blushing" in embarrassment at her inability to refute her rationalist critics, is obliged to "veil her sacred fires" (the poet's delicate imagery for de-emphasis of post-mortem punishments), then nothing can any longer restrain the wickedness of natural man and woman: "morality expires." This view, that morality stands and falls with Christianity (or Judeo-Christianity, or at any rate some supernaturalist belief structure), while no longer taken for granted almost universally as it was in Pope's day, is still widespread and influential, and is taken by many as providing the obvious explanation for the depravity of the times. Secular moralists, including most moral philosophers, hold on the other hand that the validity of moral norms is independent of religion, and that the furtherance of moral behavior is the province of social engineers. They regard the revaluations of the past gen-

* I am grateful to the editors of this volume, and to Paul Gomberg, Max Hocutt, Charles Jarrett, Michael Levin, David Schmidtz, and Bruce Vermazen, for helpful comments on an earlier draft.

[1] It *was* a prediction: the present tense is "vatic."

eration as a salutary overthrow of taboos and redirection of moral effort toward the righting of age-old wrongs.

This essay is neither a celebration nor a lamentation. It tries to explain, first, what the core of morality is, in terms of conditions of survival for gregarious animals; second, how morality came to be involved with and subordinated to religion; finally, why emancipation of morality from religion is a more complicated and difficult matter than it is commonly supposed to be.

I. COPING

Let us begin at the fundamentals of voluntary action, which is the universe of moral discourse.

An animal *copes* when it interacts with its environment so as to preserve its form, either of itself as an individual, or of other individuals in close genetic relationship.

The basic coping activities are muscular motions that (1) transfer the animal from a less favorable location to one where the probability of preserving its form is greater (because the new location is less dangerous, or is richer in nutrients, or affords opportunity for mating), or (2) alter the bodily posture to increase further the probability of self-preservation (e.g., grasping the food and conveying it into the mouth, mating, firing back at the posse from behind a boulder).

An animal must possess some means of discriminating between less and more favorable locations and postures. Energy from the environment impinges on the animal's integument in various forms, such as light rays, sound waves, pressures, chemical reactions. If the animal is to have much chance of surviving, it must possess means of inferring from these impingements — *sensings* — which portions of its environment are favorable and which unfavorable, and in what ways. The means is its faculty of *perception*, of sizing up the situation. Further, the animal must have the ability, given the information about its surroundings, to alter its stance to take advantage of favorable aspects of those surroundings and to guard against those that are unfavorable. This is its ability to initiate action, its *will* (for lack of a better term). In reflex action, sensing and willing are directly coupled; in instinctive behavior, the connection is hard-wired, as it were. But in animals of much complexity, not all actions will be reflexive or instinctive. More than one possible action may suggest itself as appropriate, and the animal must *choose*.

Perception results in *belief* on the part of the animal as to how things *are*. Subsequent action expresses the animal's *choice*: in light of the belief, this is what the animal *ought* to do. "Ought" is used here in the broadest sense: all things considered, this action will best promote coping.

Perceptually induced beliefs are *true* when the lay of things is as perceived, that is to say, when the animal's expectations are (or would be) borne out in the event, so that its effort to cope is not frustrated by mis-apprehension of the facts of the situation; otherwise such beliefs are *false*. Choices are *right* when the animal's action is more apt for coping than the alternatives; otherwise they are *wrong*.

All the beliefs of subhuman animals are perceptually induced, and nearly all of them are put to an experimental test in short order. If they fail the test, they cease to be beliefs. Consequently, nearly all of them are true. Let us call perceptually induced beliefs that have survived empiri-cal testing, *low beliefs*.

The true/false distinction is much sharper than the right/wrong. Since beliefs are less detailed than the states of affairs they purport to represent, and elements of approximation always enter, the relation of a true belief to its object is not one of strict correspondence. Nevertheless, a somewhat fuzzy "law of excluded middle" holds for perceptually induced beliefs; that is, it is possible to tell (at least after the fact) whether the belief was true or false. No such clarity reigns in the realm of right and wrong. Even if the action was successful, some other might have been better; and even if its result was calamitous, it still might have been the best that could be done. This means that in making our choices of the right thing to do we must rely on statistics, as it were; we judge by whether the proposed action conforms to a *rule* the observance of which has been shown by experience to lead, on the whole, to better results than contrary behav-ior probably would.

Reflexes and instincts are wired-in rules of this sort. Evolution does the wiring. Thus, reflexive and instinctive behavior is right far more often than it is wrong — practically always, if the circumstances are similar enough to those in which the instinct evolved.

Reflexes and instincts by themselves seem to be enough to keep ants and spiders going; but for coping with novel situations an ability to *learn how* is essential. Learning-how consists in progressive modification of the perception-to-will nexus in the light of *memories* of (i.e., stored beliefs about) previous similar situations. The outcome of successful learning is more-efficient coping, acquisition of facility in making right choices in a broad variety of situations: new *precepts* of action.

Few subhuman animals in the wild die of old age. Nevertheless, it is seldom that a beast does the wrong thing, acts contrary to what it ought to do. In the words of Robert Frost:

To err is human, not to, animal.

Evolution has honed instincts and perceptual and learning abilities to the point where the animal can be counted on to do its best in most situations that it is likely to encounter; that is to say, it is "adjusted." Collisions with comets, and the incursion of human beings with panoplies of guns, traps, and pesticides, are events that it cannot cope with, but that is not the beast's fault, nor evolution's either.

II. Gregarious Animals

Even solitary animals have to be able to differentiate between individuals that do, and that do not, belong to their own species. For what ought to be done to their congeners differs from right behavior with respect to others: some of the former, but not of the latter, can be mated with, and (usually) should not be killed and eaten. In many species this differentiation progresses to the point of gregariousness: there turn out to be evolutionary advantages to living permanently in proximity and sharing food-finding and defensive activities. A member of a herd, troop, tribe, gaggle, pride, or whatever we call the relevant *community*, must *cooperate* with its fellows in standing watch and giving the alarm, driving prey into reach of other members, flying in formation, caring for the young, and so on — all of which are activities that the animal does not engage in with animals of other species, nor, in general, of other communities within the same species. It is not fanciful to speak of the gregarious animal as having *duties*. This is the earliest appearance in the animal kingdom of the "moral ought." As we have noted, beasts usually act as they ought. However, in animal societies, conflicts sometimes arise: e.g., chimpanzee murder has been recorded.

For gregariousness to be an advantage, behavior within the community must be such that the probability is fairly high of an individual's being better off, i.e., coping better, in it than out of it. This means, first and foremost, that security must be enhanced by membership: the group must be more effective at warding off predators than the individuals separately would be; moreover, intra-communal aggression must be, if not eliminated, at any rate less on the whole than what the member would experience on its own. Peace must be kept. From this requirement a number of fairly definite characteristics of gregarious behavior follow:

(1) There will be a hierarchy (pecking order), for if there is not, if individuals do not know their places vis-à-vis the others, there will be constant bickering or worse. To be sure, the hierarchical order often gets established by violent competition; but that process must be kept within bounds (recognized "I give up" signals, etc.).

(2) The young must be nourished and protected.

(3) The members of the group will aid each other, offensively and defensively, to the extent feasible by animals of their kind.

(4) Surplus food will be shared; at least there will be some rule of precedence in feeding, and no individual, however high in the hierarchy, can monopolize the supply.

(5) Communal outrage will be felt toward members of the group believed to have transgressed these precepts. It may manifest itself in various hostile acts. This is the germ of justice and punishment.

These are some elements of *morality*, that is, the structure of biases on the behavioral choices that individual members of a gregarious animal species make in their dealings with fellow members of the species. Evolutionary processes will result in tendencies to behave in the right ways being built into the genes — "right" meaning "promoting species survival."[2]

These rules apply within the community, but not necessarily between communities. However, inasmuch as biological fitness requires exogamy, there will be a sort of "Geneva convention" between different communities of the same species, which will not, in general, indulge in no-holds-barred aggression toward one another as they do with prey species.

The individual animal, hungry but refraining from eating its den mate, may not experience its forbearance as a restraint, or, indeed, have any conception of itself as an individual, or any other conceptions for that matter. It is nevertheless the case that the animal's behavior, in the social context, is biased in the direction of furthering the group interest (as defined by survival). That is enough to constitute the behavior as proto-morality. It is of course in no way conventional.

III. Language

No doubt the proto-moral rules are more numerous and more complex for chimpanzee society than for (say) zebras. But the enormous divide between one (viz., our) species of gregarious animal, and all the others, is occasioned by the acquisition of language.

All social animals can communicate with each other to some extent; but only ability to manipulate symbols makes possible the notion of the future, and the conception of present action as having a bearing on what is to come. An offshoot of that notion is the *promise* and associated concepts such as trust and duty. A betrayed trust, a shirked duty, being socially disruptive, further moral rules come into being. These new rules can be and are explicitly taught: children can be told what is expected of them, rather than having to find it out by trial and error.

---

[2] I am not here either affirming or denying that evolution can produce a tendency to self-sacrifice in the phenotype.

Without language, it is difficult or impossible for one animal to get another to do some specific thing. With language, *orders* (and requests) become possible. This gives a new dimension to social activity, which now becomes *ordered* — on the basis, to be sure, of an already existing hierarchy. The virtues of obedience and loyalty, and the vices of insubordination and treason, come into being.

IV. Low Morality

The root principle of animal association is that internal peace must be established and kept: aggression between members of the group must not be allowed to proceed to annihilation of the losing party. Above we listed minimal conditions of this sort which must obtain in any successful group of gregarious animals: we called this the herd's morality. To the list we may add, for human beings:

(6) Truth-telling.

(7) Promise-keeping.

Let us call this set of internal constraints on the interpersonal behavior of human beings *low morality*. It is continuous with the morality of subhuman gregarious animals, and is basically the same for all human groups, being a specification of how "normal" people must habitually behave if a community is to be viable — though precisely how the requirements are to be realized will vary with the size, complexity, and capabilities of the particular group. For human self-sufficient communities at the current level of technology, experience seems to show that unless the following conditions are substantially met, intra-group dissatisfaction may rise to a dangerous level; i.e., there will be a widely shared perception that one would be better off living entirely on one's own — "in the state of nature," they would have said in the seventeenth century — than in the community.

(1) Who has control of whom and what — that is, power and property — must be known attributes of persons, and alterations in them must proceed in regular ways, recognized as in accord with perceptions of entitlement, including merit, not haphazardly and by sheer force. This is the chief element in the rule of law: people must be able to count on obtaining and retaining the status to which they are entitled.

(2) Although primary responsibility for care of the young will in general rest with their parents, the community will take over if necessary. Care will include not only nourishment and protection from attacks and other hazards, but education to a level appropriate to the child's status and potential.

(3) Members of the community must be liable, according to their abilities, to assist in communal defense, and to aid each other in calamities.

(4) Those unable to provide necessities for themselves must be cared for communally (a social safety net). Communal costs must be shared; those more able to pay must pay more — not, however, to the point of confiscation, which would be incompatible with requirement (1).

(5) Wrongdoers — perpetrators of *mala in se* (acts wrong in themselves), and of *mala prohibita* (acts which are made offenses by positive law) insofar as the prohibitions are socially necessary — must not be allowed to profit from their offenses, but must suffer socially imposed penalties expressing the community's disapproval and serving as deterrents.

(6) The things that people say must be closely correlated with what they believe. Otherwise, communication — a social necessity — becomes impossible.[3]

(7) One must be held morally delinquent who does not, in general, keep his or her promises. Human society is largely structured on the basis of trust.

The low morality, it should be noted, is concerned with the *right* (thing to do) and not with The Good, some shining ideal condition to the realization of which individual or social effort must be directed. The Good is essentially a religious or political concept, not a moral one. Low morality is not concerned with ultimate aims, as long as they are not incompatible with doing the right thing; and this leaves much leeway. As far as low morality goes, it is all right to pursue wealth, or learning, or political power, or pleasure, or stamp collecting, as long as the means employed are above board. The "moral ought" may be characterized as what is the right thing for an individual to do, as a member of a community, with respect to actions affecting the interests of other members of his or her community. These types of actions (and abstentions) may be spoken of as *duties*.[4]

---

[3] Of course, much fibbing is tolerated and even required in every community. I have in mind only Donald Davidson's (and Kant's) point that if lying becomes the rule rather than the exception, communication breaks down. Religious and political discourses present special problems in this regard.

[4] Moreover, the *rights* that any human being has just by being a member of a community are to be treated by others in ways that respect these necessary conditions for viable association. They are the only rights antecedent to establishment of the state, and include the "unalienable rights" of the Declaration of Independence. Possession of these rights is the respect in which "all men are created equal" — and the *only* respect; Jefferson subscribed to nothing so absurd as physical, mental, or moral egalitarianism. See Antony Flew, "Equal Value: Or Equal Rights to Equal Liberties?" *Cogito*, Spring 1990, p. 27.

The "natural" human social unit, the context of 99 percent or so of human evolution, is the hunter-gatherer group of forty people, more or less, which anthropologists call a *band*. Children in a band are taught the right things to do with respect to building shelters, making and shooting arrows, hunting—and dealing with their fellows. The social skills are skills like any other: they are learned by precept and example; some are better at them than others, but nearly all are pretty good; excellence is praised and delinquent performance criticized. A reflective, even philosophical tribesman would not be likely to see in them any mysterious quality setting them apart from other desirable accomplishments. Social obligations are not experienced as burdens imposed from outside, or as in need of justification. The question "Why be moral?"—if *per impossibile* it were raised—would seem as odd as "Why shoot straight?"

Nevertheless, that question would have an answer, though the tribesman would not know it. It would be: This kind of behavior is in fact a necessary condition of a viable community; consequently, will and aptitude to it have been built into your genes in the evolutionary process. It is part of your nature; you would, literally, not be a human being if you lacked it.[5]

Low morality persisted through the invention of language, augmented as, in consequence of that invention, social relations became more complex. Nevertheless, it remained universal, and does so to this day, for the necessary conditions for a viable society are everywhere the same. *There is no alternative to low morality.*

V. IMAGINATION

Although *low* morality is constant and transcends tribal boundaries, it is only the common core of actual comprehensive moralities, which of course exhibit much variety. The variable element I shall call *high* morality. To explain it, let us return to consideration of the anthropoid group that has just acquired language.

Language creates *imagination*, first in the basic and literal sense of ability to summon up images "in the mind's eye." With words, reference can be made to things not present where or when the utterance is made. When the narrator relates what has happened on the other side of the mountain, the auditor forms a "picture" of what it must have been like, without having actually been there. This is something that an animal without language cannot do, at least not on cue. A faculty of creating images of what is or was, immediately leads to imagination in the more usual sense, of "envisioning" what is not and was not, and perhaps never will be—that is to say, the contents of stories and lies.

---

[5] This is substantially the answer of Protagoras in Plato's dialogue of that name.

Belief is liberated from its former necessary connection to perception: one can believe what one is told, and if the belief is not of such a kind as to be shown up as false by immediate confrontation with experience, it may persist indefinitely, e.g., belief that some remnant of the individual consciousness migrates to another world after bodily death. Let us call such beliefs, that have not *in fact* been subjected to the risk of contradiction by experience, *high* beliefs.

Inasmuch as high beliefs originate in stories, and all stories are about people, their content will be built on analogies to human beings and their ordinary experiences. It is characteristic of us that when things go wrong, we impute *guilt* to persons whose actions are supposed to have brought about the mishaps. Imagination makes possible the envisaging of superhuman yet personal powers to which guilt can be ascribed for whatever is extraordinary, mysterious, and important for well-being — weather, famine, earthquakes, tempests, fertility, and all the host of things and events on which human existence is dependent but which are beyond the primitive human being's control. This assignment of guilt is the simplest kind of causal explanation.

VI. Religion

The idea is not long in coming that these powerful persons may be amenable to some of the influences that serve to modify behavior of one's fellows: threats, entreaties, flattery, promises of reward. Such stratagems will be tried, and sometimes they will "work": the virgins are thrown into the volcano, and the eruption stops; the happy outcome is taken as confirming the hypothesis. *Religion* gets established.[6] Religion is a fabric of high beliefs, and of actions predicated on those beliefs.

If this account is correct in outline, it is already clear that morality as such cannot be dependent on religion. Morality exists wherever there is a herd; but religion depends on imagination, which in turn depends on language, which itself presupposes society; so the institution of religion in even the most rudimentary form must postdate morality. Nor is it the case that only religion can provide motives for moral behavior, since rules of morality are (sometimes) followed by beings without language and therefore without religion.

This is not to say, however, that religion has nothing to do with morality.

Religious beliefs and other high beliefs have various functions, one of which is to make sense of the world. If the important uncontrollable things are thought of as manifesting the powers of supernatural hominids, that means they come within the ambit of the categories of human

---

[6] Magic also. The distinction is superficial, being merely that the priest entreats, the magician commands.

thought and desire, such as contrivance, love, fear, will to power; and to that extent their strangeness is mitigated and hope achieves a foothold. Earthquake and drought cannot be coped with, but perhaps Poseidon and Zeus can.

This imaginative view of things personalizes the world. It is misleading, however, to express this fact by saying that to the primitive religious mind the world is a "thou," or even a multitude of thous. True, the gods are objects of possible communication; but they are seldom thought of as members of the community. Typically, the things thought to need explaining are calamities; the forces controlling them, therefore, are modeled on "Them": they tend to be supernatural counterparts of the menacing hostile tribesmen lurking in the interior of the forest. These powers are often thought of as engaging in practices that would be grossly immoral if done by people, e.g., incest. This is just what should be expected, for religion is *essentially* concerned with the uncontrollable and antisocial forces that run things.

It becomes a high-priority community project, then, to placate these forces. The usual means for doing so is sacrifice—giving (or at least promising) precious things to the gods, as one would buy off hostile tribesmen. Now, in such transactions morality is not involved in any positive way, any more than it is in relations with alien tribes. Nor are the gods conceived as moral agents—to the contrary, the reason why it is so hard to deal with them is their perceived malice. As part of the process of coping with them, the strategy may be adopted of making them "honorary tribesmen," as it were—but if this is done, the aim is to put them in a position of sharing in the tribe's moral concerns. No one dreams of them as constituting the *sources* of morality.

Indeed, the dangerousness of the supernatural is likely to have a negative effect on morals, in that the need to appease the gods may *trump* ordinary moral values. Deliberate killing of a fellow is always forbidden by the low morality; nevertheless, it may be deemed necessary to kill someone—even someone important, as the Chief; or beloved, as the Chief's daughter—in order to placate the powers. "Teleological suspension of the ethical," to use Kierkegaard's euphemism,[7] is the rule rather than the exception in primitive religion. Practices intended to appease supernatural forces will be ritualized, i.e., will become standard and stereotyped; and ritual will take precedence over low moral duty.

VII. High Morality

Further, since the *modi operandi* of the gods, as well as their names, natures, sexes, and other attributes, are all products of imagination, the

---

[7] Søren A. Kierkegaard, *Fear and Trembling and The Sickness Unto Death*, trans. Walter Lowrie (Princeton: Princeton University Press, 1941), p. 64.

beliefs and rituals about them will vary more or less at random from tribe to tribe. That is to say, high beliefs and the practices based on them, unlike low beliefs and practices, will not be uniform; what is believed and done on this side of the mountain and on the other side will be "diverse." *We* want to say that this shows the rituals to be conventional. To the people in the actual situation, however—especially when, before the invention of writing, a practice can attain the status of having been what was done "from time immemorial" in a few generations—the rituals will be seen and felt as "the right thing to do" in just the same way as the right practices enjoined by the low morality. They may be distinguished as "piety," but the important thing is that one who does not conform to them is regarded as "bad," deficient in the qualities necessary for social living.

These new duties and obligations constitute the *high morality*. The actual morality at a given time and place, then, will be a compound of high and low. Hence, despite the common core of low morality shared with all the moralities of all the other tribes, a particular moral "code" considered as a whole will be perceived as quite different from that practiced elsewhere, and in consequence the natural view that strangers— "They"—are "immoral" will be reinforced. For actions (e.g., burning babies to death) that in themselves would be considered wrong according to the low morality may, if believed to be required by the gods, trump that low morality and thereby take their place within the high—and therefore in the total—morality.

The upshot is that the way is paved for confrontations like the famous sociological experiment performed at the court of Persia:

> Darius [the Great King of the Persians] called together the Greeks who were around and asked them what price they would demand for eating the bodies of their dead fathers. They said they would not do that for any amount. Then he summoned the Indians called Callatians, who eat their parents, and asked them—in the presence of the Greeks who knew through interpreters what was being said— how much they would want for burning their fathers' remains. Loudly shouting, they bade him not to talk about such things.[8]

Observations of this sort in turn lead to the belief that morals are "relative." In a way they are; but only in a way. What is really plural is religion (and the *high* morality derived from it), not the rules as to how it is necessary to behave if a society—any society—is to be viable (*low* morality).

---

[8] Herodotus III 38.

VIII. Commandments

> [I]t would be hard to estimate the amount of harm done by the
> assumption that moral (and legal) prescriptions have the character of
> commands.
>
> Robert Fogelin[9]

How gods are related to the peoples who acknowledge them, is a
theme with many variations. They may, as we have pointed out, be conceived as demanding or hostile, to be sated or appeased at enormous
expense (Baal, Huiztilopochtli, Homeric Apollo), or as helpful friends
exhibiting valued traits in ideal fashion (Athena, classical Apollo), or at
any intermediate position in a more than one-dimensional continuum.
Seldom, however, are they conceived as actual leaders of the people, or
as members of the community within which the low morality is operative.

With one big exception: among the Jews. Yahweh came to be thought
of as the generalissimo of the Jewish people, personally smiting their enemies. As leader, he demanded obedience and punished insubordination.
The novelty of this notion—that a god might tell you what to do, and it
would be sinful (immoral) not to do it—has not been sufficiently remarked.
It is virtually absent from Greek religion. The gods gave advice, and it
might be folly to ignore it (only "might be"—on numerous occasions the
gods engaged in deceit), but it was not sin or wickedness to do so.

In the Jewish literature, on the other hand, the first sin was disobedience—the flouting, moreover, of a quite arbitrary prohibition. (There is
nothing in low morality that makes it immoral to eat fruit.) In the book
of Exodus the doctrine is developed in such a way that both high and low
morality are construed as divine commandments. This is extraordinary.
It is inconceivable that even the benighted Egyptians were unaware of the
necessity, in any viable society, of discouraging murder, theft, adultery,
perjury, envy, and neglect of aged parents. But these rules, part of the
universal low morality, are made by Moses into the Second Table of Yahweh's commands; while the principal Jewish rituals and taboos, their
high morality, are codified in the First.

This episode marks also the birth of the very first moral theory. As in
the television game-show *Jeopardy!*, the answer comes before the question. The answer is: Yahweh has commanded his chosen people to
behave morally, and will punish disobedience. The question is: Why be
moral?

Pre-Exodus morality stood on its own feet, the way rules for adding
numbers or firing pots do: this is simply the *right way*. However often and
flagrantly the moral precepts might have been flouted, they were never-

⁹ Robert Fogelin, *Philosophical Interpretations* (New York: Oxford University Press, 1991),
p. 249.

theless recognized as carrying their own obligation. You shouldn't go around murdering and lying, because murder and mendacity are *wrong*. You will, further, suffer unpleasant consequences if caught murdering and lying; but that is not what makes murder and perjury wrong, they simply are. Or perhaps the Egyptian mother would rhetorically ask her errant son, "What if everybody did that?"

Moses changed all that. You were to abstain from murder and perjury from "fear of the Lord," fear that he would smite you, or even the whole people, if he were disobeyed. Thus, disobedience, for the Jews, became the only vice (sin), and avoidance of divine punishment the only moral motive.

Nietzsche[10] was partly right: the Jews did bring about a fundamental revolution in morality; but it was not the one he described. Rather, it was this assimilation of the very concept of morality to law, and of law, further, to divine command, with consequent debasement of moral motivation to mere prudence.

Of course, Moses did not do this in one fell swoop. Recalling our distinction between high and low moralities, it is evident that any high-moral precept is in effect a divine commandment, either directly and explicitly, or a priestly strategy for securing divine favor, which amounts to the same thing. In other words, the divine-command theory *is* true of what we have called "high morality." Moses' innovation was in conceiving the low morality (the Second Table) as having the same kind of status; and this would have been very natural for a tribe that already untypically held its sole god to be both commander and father of the people.

IX. Law, Morality, Command

But while low morality is a system of constraints on behavior that can be expressed (to some extent) in precepts and rules, it is not and cannot be a set of positive laws or commands.

Laws are not commands; however, we need not go into their differences here. For both laws and commands presuppose a conception foreign to low morality: that of an external authority capable of imposing a sanction for noncompliance. Commands (from individuals) and laws (from legislatures) are speech acts that are infelicitous unless the utterer is a person (natural or corporate) invested with competent authority to initiate punishment for disobedience. Further, commander and subordinate, lawgiver and subject, are distinct persons.

None of these features holds of the relation between morality and the moral person, unless metaphorically. The requirement of low morality is

---

[10] Friedrich Nietzsche, *Beyond Good and Evil*, Section 195; *On the Genealogy of Morals*, First Essay.

not experienced as imposed from without, much less as expressing the
will of an external authority. It is more analogous to aesthetic judgment.
Guilt or remorse does not feel like the consequence of having disobeyed
an authority or of having failed to carry out a command; it is, rather, self-
loathing for not living up to the model of humanity that one has put
before oneself. This at any rate is how Aristotle and Spinoza looked at the
matter, though not how Saint Paul and Saint Augustine saw it.

But not only does the concept of command involve these three notions —
authority, penalty, and externality — that are foreign to low morality; it is
also the case that command lacks the basic moral character of *normativity*.
Anything that it is possible to do can be commanded, and its being good,
bad, indifferent, virtuous or wicked has no effect on its status as command. To equate moral rules to commands is therefore to remove their
normative halo. It can then be put back only as Thomas Hobbes did, via
the implausible and ad hoc doctrine of "might makes right."

The Greeks envisaged morals as a system of rules, more like prescriptions for the successful practice of an art than like explicit and rigid rules
of a game, or of metrical composition. It was no sign of linguistic poverty
that one adjective, *kalos*, served the Greeks as the most general term of
both aesthetic and moral commendation.

Nothing is said in the *Nicomachean Ethics* about law other than human
law, and when this is spoken of, as in Book 5 on justice, it is in the context of making the point that observing the law of the state is characteristic of one who possesses the virtue of justice. Greek moral philosophy
is "practical," i.e., concerned primarily with the question of what is the
best way to live. One who has this knowledge and uses it is a virtuous
person. And virtue, for Aristotle (who here as elsewhere is typical) is "a
disposition concerned with choice, lying in a mean relative to us";[11] the
virtuous person follows a rule, but not a rigid or fixed one. Virtue is man-
ifested in the exercise of judgment. In hard cases, one is counseled to
imagine what the man of practical wisdom would do, and then to do it.
No notion of obedience to law is involved.[12]

All this was fundamentally changed by the triumph of Christianity, a
sect of Judaism inheriting its divine-command moral theory. Morality
henceforth meant obedience to the commandments of God (in reality, of
the priests), with conformity to rituals and — for the first time — conformity
in beliefs attaining equal importance with abstention from *mala in se*, the
prohibitions of low morality. Indeed, even greater importance: you would
be burnt for heresy, merely hanged for murder. The high still trumped
the low.

---

[11] Aristotle, *Nicomachean Ethics*, Book 2, ch. 6, 1106b36.
[12] Socrates' "I will obey the god, not you [Athenians]" (Plato, *Apology*, 29D) is no real
exception. The obedience in question was to a particular specific command, viz., "Pursue
your mission."

The true moral motive is inner: one does the right thing because it is the right thing. When morality is construed as commands, however, the motive for moral behavior becomes extrinsic, as it is in paradigmatic command/obedience situations: one must obey in order to reap the rewards of fealty and to escape the punishment for defiance. In Kantian terms, the Greeks recognized morality as autonomous, whereas Judaism and Christianity made it heteronomous.

X. FURTHER CONSEQUENCES

Christianity, despite continuing political influence in Ireland, the United States, and elsewhere, is now intellectually defunct—or at the least "blushing," as Pope put it.[13] But that does not mean things are back where they were before it took over. Two respects in which its influence is still pervasive are (1) the notion of moral law, and (2) the notion of the pervasiveness of morality: in particular, that all sorts of actions, and even beliefs, are subject to moral appraisal.

The persistence of Christian moral theory is very evident, e.g., in Kantianism, which finds the Moral Law Within to be of equal awesomeness with the Starry Heavens Above. Kant emancipated himself from Pietism and from theology, but he continued to take it for granted that what every rational being, however untutored, recognizes within is a *law* that *commands* him or her to do this and abstain from that. Kant analogized this law to the laws of nature (another unfortunate metaphor) and postulated reason as the legislator. There is truth behind this, namely, that the low morality is reasonable, i.e., its observance is necessary for the successful prosecution of human ends. But Kant's way of putting it casts reason in a dubious role as a commander. Moreover, if moral law is like (scientific) law of nature it must be exceptionless; hence, the model encourages the delusion that to be moral is to be unswervingly obedient to rigid prescriptions. This comes out clearly in Kant's disastrous casuistry: since the moral law forbids lying, one must not lie even to save an innocent person's life.

These awkwardnesses in Kantian moral theory are consequences of the incompatibility that we have noted at its core, between the concepts of law (construed as command) and autonomy. It was to no avail that Kant made the law in question one that the moral agent prescribed to himself.

But it was not only Kant who carried over the Judeo-Christian assimilation of law to command into philosophical theory. No book of moral philosophy could be more resolutely secular than Jeremy Bentham's *Principles of Morals and Legislation*—which, nevertheless, famously begins with a paragraph describing the *subjection* of mankind to the *governance* of the two *sovereign masters*, pleasure and pain, to whose *throne* the standard of

---

[13] Consider, e.g., the Pope's recent "pardon" of Galileo.

right and wrong are fastened. Thus, the notion of moral law infects the other main system of ethical theory too.

Indeed, so tenaciously (and unconsciously) do secular moral theorists hold to the command model, that, God and reason having been rejected, *society* is recruited to fill the role of commander (thus obliterating the distinction between morality and law); and when even this expedient proves inadequate (e.g, what does society command about abortion?), moral prescriptions are construed as commands issued on speculation, as it were, by the individual utterer hoping that someone will hear and obey. Thus, Charles Stevenson[14] analyzes "This is good [right]" as "I approve of this and I want you to do so as well," attributing imperial megalomania to the most diffident venturer of a moral judgment, as Sartrean existentialists also do. Things having come to this pass, perhaps it is time for the command theory to be retired.

XI. An Advantage of the Command Theory

But after all, even though grave theoretical difficulties can be discerned in the Jewish project of religion's swallowing up morals, it was—and still is—a stupendous practical success. Why?

From the evolutionary standpoint, low morality is a set of dispositions constituting a survival technique for a certain kind of gregarious and omnivorous animal that makes its living by hunting and gathering foodstuffs in a (usually nomadic) band rarely exceeding forty in number. Much of it can be summed up as "Love thy neighbor"; however, the neighbor in question is one among only thirty-nine people. Everybody else is "Them," members of other groups, rivals whom it would be folly to deal with in the same considerate manner.

A numerical limit on the scope of morality presented a problem only when, about five hundred generations ago, agriculture was invented. The resultant civilization necessitated tremendously larger social units. The problem was, how to make communities of them? The solution was the invention of *government*: a development of the "natural" marauding party of the hunter-gatherer tribe into a permanent concentration of force under central direction, which would keep the intra-communal peace according to more or less formally promulgated *laws*.

To exert force effectively, the governmental body must be united and hierarchically organized; and this order cannot itself be maintained by force. Further, it needs to be perceived by the governed as legitimate, as something more than a band of ruffians. Both ends were encompassed through *high beliefs*, a sanctifying mythology, a state church.

As high beliefs are insulated from the experience of coping, there is no evolutionary sorting of the true from the false among them, and in fact virtually all of them are false. This does not mean, however, that it is a

---

[14] Charles L. Stevenson, *Ethics and Language* (New Haven: Yale University Press, 1944), pp. 24, 97, and *passim.*

matter of chance which high beliefs are adopted in a community and which are rejected. Some high beliefs are *edifying*: they make believers feel better or more vigorous or enhance communal solidarity. Bands whose high beliefs are edifying will have an evolutionary advantage over those whose high beliefs are not.

Religious beliefs — imagination of superhuman powers — are high beliefs. Furthermore, any group sharing high beliefs forms a community, to that extent. High beliefs are social glue. They were already there when the need arose for them to bond hunter-gatherer bands into agricultural (and subsequently urban) societies with governments.

Thus, from the beginning of civilization down to the close of the eighteenth century, church (high beliefs and high morality) and state (guarantor of intra-communal order, based on low morality) were inseparable allies.

The extraordinary power of survival exhibited by the Jews is, then, to be explained in large part by the strength of their attachment to a codified, definite, and all-encompassing set of high beliefs. The divine-command theory meant that in Jewish thought *all* morality was dependent on the will of Yahweh; consequently, severance from him would mean the collapse of literally all that made social living feasible. "If X did not exist, everything would be permitted" is ridiculous for X = Zeus; but with "Yahweh" as the value of the variable, it is a truism, within the system.

This feature of Judaism carried over into Christianity, and was a cause of its triumph, as well as of its persistence through periods when it had to stand on its own, unsupported by governmental authority.

XII. HIGH BELIEFS IN JEOPARDY

The social arrangement we have been describing is one in which morality — the recognized norms of what is right for people to do — has two components: *low*, the precepts whose general observance is necessary for any viable community; and *high*, the rituals and taboos enjoined by the high beliefs the sharing of which defines the community. Deviations are kept in check by the government, which itself derives its authority from the high belief in its divine provenance.

Although this state of things is an innovation, compared to the genetically programmed morality of the hunter-gatherer band, it is traditional enough to be regarded as "natural" for human societies based on agriculture. It is stable; in China and India it persisted without essential change for millennia. Presumably, its Western forms would have shown equivalent staying power had it not been for the Greeks and their invention of science. The scientific world-view is an integration and extension of *low* beliefs. Like religion, it is an enterprise requiring imagination; but unlike religion, the scientific imagination remains connected to the facts of experienced reality by the bond of logical inference — logic itself being a set of low beliefs. The picture of things revealed by science turns out to be self-sufficient; that is, nature can be understood in its own terms without supplementation by supernatural agencies. In the process some high beliefs are directly confuted; others succumb to Ockham's razor.

XIII. Now

This epic struggle is far from being over; witness the current resurgence of fundamentalism. Science shows high beliefs to be irrational from the standpoint of epistemology. But it is also a finding of science that high beliefs are socially useful, perhaps indispensable, and that we tend instinctively to hang on to them at almost any cost. Nevertheless, the history of the past four centuries is one of inexorable scientific advance, while religion has more and more veiled her sacred fires. Where does this leave morality?

Where it *should* leave us, from the logical point of view, is back at square one. That is, it should leave us with the low morality intact, minus the high morality, the rituals and taboos which are the actions that are the right things to do given (counterfactually) the validity of the high beliefs. Science, the true view of how things are, can only confirm, never call into question, the low morality, which comprises the necessary conditions of human communal living. (There is such a thing as moral knowledge; it consists of this fact, which is as independent of "cultural determination" as the Pythagorean theorem.) And perhaps the demise of various religious taboos is not altogether regrettable.

This is congruent to the aim of the more thoroughgoing *philosophes* such as Diderot and d'Holbach, which was to abolish all high beliefs and the high morality based on them. They supposed that the low morality, which could be said to be precepts of reason, would then be left to extend its gentle sway over all mankind. For reason is universal. Rational people, confronted with the same evidence, come to the same impersonal conclusions, both theoretical and practical. Kant's "Kingdom of Ends" would cover the earth. This vision continues to inspire philosophers down to John Rawls.

If the argument of this essay is correct, one reason why this vision remains visionary is that decline in religious belief entails concomitant fading of sense of community. After family, the church is, to its believers, the institution generating the strongest sentiments of communion. Within the community, morality, by and large, can be counted on to take care of itself. But the boundaries of community are marked by high beliefs.

The historical function of a universal church such as original Christianity was to expand the emotional scope of community to the point where geography became almost irrelevant. It has failed, not on account of specific weaknesses that might be absent from some other system of high beliefs, but because the very idea of a system of high beliefs has fallen into disrepute. The great irony of the high belief is that it can do its (sometimes) beneficial work only as long as the fact that it *is* a high belief — a (mere) imaginative construction — escapes the notice of its believers.

To be specific: Expiration of high (Christian) morality would involve changes in attitude from disapproval to indifference or approval of most of the following: divorce, birth control, extra-marital sex, abortion, illegitimacy, homosexuality, nudity, pornography, blasphemy. It is clear that shifts of attitude toward these things have occurred on a broad scale, not just among the intelligentsia but all down the line, so that they are often even reflected in legislation. Save for divorce and birth control, the changes have taken place almost entirely in the last thirty years.

If low morality were to go, people would be indifferent, or even sympathetic, to promise-breaking, theft, assault, murder, destruction of property, perjury (and lying in general), gross incivility, draft dodging, contempt of authority of all kinds. Common experience and, no doubt, statistical studies bear out increases in all these behavioral categories in recent years. On the whole, however, and except for the last two, it does not seem that these activities enjoy any significant amount of overt approval, although they are often *excused* when perpetrated by members of one community against those of another, if the first community is (really or allegedly) being oppressed by the second. An this is what is predicted by the hypothesis that low morality is built into everyone's genes but is felt as applying only within one's community, whereas high morality imposes obligations only on people who share a set of high beliefs.

XIV. Recapitulation

1. Animals, to cope, acquire information about their environment through their senses. Relying on this information, they act in such ways as to maintain themselves and their species. Some actions are not instinctive or reflexive but involve choice. Evolutionary pressures tend to minimize propensities to make lethally wrong choices.

2. Gregarious animals cannot act habitually in ways incompatible with maintenance and efficacy of the group. Hence, they are biased to within-group choices that favor establishment and recognition of hierarchy, limitation of intra-group violence and rivalry, nurturing of the young, cooperation in obtaining and distributing food. These biases against disruptive activities we call *low morality*. They are basically the same for all gregarious animals, though they are more developed in species capable of more varied activities.

3. The low morality is most elaborated in human beings, because language makes possible kinds of cooperation (especially the giving and following of commands) that are beyond the capabilities of mute beasts. Language also makes possible imagination, hence stories, and beliefs not immediately associated with perception. We call these *high beliefs*. Among them are beliefs in the existence of powerful person-like agents responsible for uncontrollable and catastrophic natural occurrences. It is deemed

possible and transcendently important to get on the good side of these agents by propitiatory sacrifices. Making these sacrifices may entail actions deemed indifferent by the low morality, or even contrary to it; but service to the gods takes precedence. Its obligatoriness is the high morality.

4. This was the situation generally in the ancient world: Each community had a morality consisting of low and high components. The low component was the same for all. The high varied according to the local conception of the gods and their demands. No question of why it was right to follow the low morality ("Why be moral?") arose.

5. Among one people, the Jews, an innovation occurred. They recognized only one god, whom they conceptualized as their leader. Not only did he demand certain rituals, as all gods do, but the low morality was supposed to be obligatory because he had commanded it. Being moral, then, meant being obedient to the supernatural leader, and immorality was disobedience. He was further thought to reward and punish accordingly; at first, with earthly prosperity or misery; later, post-mortem. Taken up into Christianity, this command theory of morals became universal in the Western world. Utilitarian and Kantian efforts to rebuild morality on secular foundations fail because both still conceive of morality as a system of imperatives, which are unintelligible without commanders.

6. Hence, it was taken as obvious that religion and morals stand and fall together: morality must "expire" when or if religion does.

7. The rise of science affords a world-view dispensing with high beliefs, hence with religion. Christianity consequently suffers from terminal intellectual anemia. The question of whether morality must go down with it thus becomes pressing. It is patent that the specifically Christian (high) elements of morality are in fact disappearing. Low morality is not in so perilous a state, but it is endangered indirectly by the loosening of the bonds of community consequent on religious failure.

XV. Non-Conclusion

This essay has been etiological and diagnostic. On another occasion we may consider whether the prognosis is still as bleak as Pope made it out to be:

> Lo! thy dread Empire, Chaos! is restored;
> Light dies before thy uncreating word;
> Thy hand, great Anarch! lets the curtain fall,
> And universal Darkness buries All.

Philosophy, University of California, Berkeley

COMMON SENSE AND FIRST PRINCIPLES
IN SIDGWICK'S *METHODS**

By David O. Brink

What role, if any, should our moral intuitions play in moral epistemology? We make, or are prepared to make, moral judgments about a variety of actual and hypothetical situations. Some of these moral judgments are more informed, reflective, and stable than others (call these our *considered* moral judgments); some we make more confidently than others; and some, though not all, are judgments about which there is substantial consensus. What bearing do our moral judgments have on philosophical ethics and the search for first principles in ethics? Should these judgments constrain, or be constrained by, philosophical theorizing about morality? On the one hand, we might expect first principles to conform to our moral intuitions or at least to our considered moral judgments. After all, we begin the reflection that may lead to first principles from particular moral convictions. And some of our moral intuitions (e.g., that genocide is wrong) are more fixed and compelling than any putative first principle. If so, we might expect common moral beliefs to have an important evidential role in the construction and assessment of first principles. On the other hand, common moral beliefs often rest on poor information, reflect bias, or are otherwise mistaken. We often appeal to moral principles to justify our particular moral convictions or to resolve our disagreements. Insofar as this is true, we may expect first principles to provide a foundation on the basis of which to test common moral beliefs and, where necessary, form new moral convictions.

This ambivalence about the probative value of common moral beliefs is nicely illustrated in Sidgwick's moral epistemology and his claims about the relationship between utilitarianism and the precepts of common-sense morality. In Book IV of *The Methods of Ethics*, Sidgwick claims that the precepts of common-sense morality are "inchoately and imperfectly Utilitarian" (*ME*, 427).[1] Let us refer to this thesis as *common-sense utilitarianism*. Common-sense utilitarianism seems to imply interesting things about both common-sense morality and utilitarianism. On the one hand, Sidg-

* I am indebted to David Estlund, Gerald Gaus, Terry Irwin, Jerome Schneewind, Alan Sidelle, Ernest Sosa, an audience at Brown University, the other contributors to this volume, and its editors, for helpful discussion of issues in this essay.

[1] Henry Sidgwick, *The Methods of Ethics*, 7th ed. (Chicago: University of Chicago Press, 1907); this work will be referred to hereafter as *ME*, and page references will be given parenthetically in the text.

wick seems to think that common-sense utilitarianism confers respectability upon common-sense morality by showing it to be more systematic and principled than it would otherwise be, and motivates sensible revisions and improvements in the details of common-sense morality. On the other hand, he also seems to think that common-sense utilitarianism confers respectability on utilitarianism by showing its ability to sustain and explain well-established precepts of common-sense morality. I am not so much interested in whether common-sense utilitarianism is true; indeed, it is simpler, for my purposes, to assume that it is true. Instead, I am interested in the nature and significance of this *dialectical* relationship Sidgwick sees between common sense and first principles in ethics. Utilitarianism happens to be the principle that Sidgwick believes stands in this relationship to common-sense morality. Because it is the relationship and its significance that interests me, much of my discussion has wider application, not restricted to utilitarian reconstructions of common-sense morality. Though I believe recognition of this dialectical relationship is a virtue of Sidgwick's view, it is in tension with his foundationalist epistemology; and this tension raises important philosophical and interpretive puzzles that deserve our attention.

I. Common-Sense Utilitarianism

It is worth quoting at length Sidgwick's most comprehensive statement of the relation between utilitarianism and common-sense morality:

> [T]he Utilitarian argument cannot be fairly judged unless we take fully into account the cumulative force which it derives from the complex character of the coincidence between Utilitarianism and Common Sense. It may be shown, I think, that the Utilitarian estimate of consequences not only supports broadly the current moral rules, but also sustains their generally received limitations and qualifications: that, again, it explains anomalies in the Morality of Common Sense, which from any other point of view must seem unsatisfactory to the reflective intellect; and moreover, where the current formula is not sufficiently precise for the guidance of conduct, while at the same time difficulties and perplexities arise in the attempt to give it additional precision, the Utilitarian method resolves these difficulties and perplexities in general accordance with the vague instincts of Common Sense, and it is naturally appealed to for such solution in ordinary moral discussions. It may be shown further, that it not only supports the generally received view of the relative importance of different duties, but is also naturally called in as arbiter, where rules commonly regarded as co-ordinate come into conflict. . . . (*ME*, 425–26)

Common-sense morality is not consciously or explicitly utilitarian, because it consists of moral rules or maxims that classify types of actions as right or wrong independently of the (full) consequences of the actions in question (*ME*, 200, 337–38). So these maxims do not function in ordinary moral reasoning as rules of thumb in a utilitarian calculation about the probable effects of different kinds of actions. Indeed, common-sense morality recognizes various special obligations and concern for those to whom one stands in special relationships and does not accept the sort of disinterested and impartial benevolence that utilitarianism would seem to require.

But the sensible utilitarian will herself typically reason by appeal to various moral maxims, rather than the utilitarian principle. Appeal to a moral rule, rather than application of the utilitarian principle, is justified on utilitarian grounds, according to Sidgwick, if (a) acceptance of the rule generally, but not always, produces optimal acts, and (b) the suboptimal acts that adherence to the rule produces cannot reliably and efficiently be identified in advance. There are a number of advantages to operating with fairly coarse-grained rules, even though adherence to them will produce some suboptimal acts. We may mistakenly identify cases in which adherence to the rule produces suboptimal results, and so our deviations from the rule may be suboptimal; even when we get the calculations right, case-by-case calculation is itself costly; and a simpler, more coarse-grained rule will be easier to internalize and less subject to various forms of bias and self-deception in its application than extremely complex rules or case-by-case evaluation.

This explains Sidgwick's regular insistence on the need for motives and rules that function in our practical reasoning in lieu of direct appeals to the utilitarian first principle:

> Finally, the doctrine that Universal Happiness is the ultimate *standard* must not be understood to imply that Universal Benevolence is the only right or always the best *motive* of action. For, as we have before observed, it is not necessary that the end which gives the criterion of rightness should always be the end at which we consciously aim: and if experience shows that the general happiness will be more satisfactorily attained if men frequently act from other motives than pure universal philanthropy, it is obvious that these other motives are reasonably to be preferred on Utilitarian principles. (*ME*, 413)

When conditions (a) and (b) are met, the associated moral rule should be appealed to and applied automatically in most cases and should be set aside in favor of direct appeal to the utilitarian principle only in very unusual circumstances (e.g., where it is obvious that adherence to the rule would have disastrous consequences) and in cases of conflicts among moral rules each of which has a utilitarian justification.[2]

---

[2] Sidgwick's utilitarian reliance on such "secondary principles" closely resembles Mill's view; see David O. Brink, "Mill's Deliberative Utilitarianism," *Philosophy & Public Affairs*,

This explains the way in which Sidgwick wants to claim that common-sense morality is utilitarian. In particular, he thinks that recognition of special obligations and a differentially greater concern for those to whom one stands in close relationships is in general optimal because we derive more pleasure from interactions with intimates, we often have better knowledge about how to benefit intimates, and we are often better situated causally to confer benefits on intimates (*ME*, 431–39). He believes that the acceptance value of the rules and motives of common-sense morality imperfectly approximates optimality (*ME*, 422, 425, 453, 463, 467, 475).

II. DIALECTICAL FIT AND EXPLANATORY DEPENDENCE

We might distinguish two interpretations of common-sense utilitarianism.[3] According to the first interpretation, there is a *dialectical fit* between utilitarianism and the precepts of common-sense morality. On this view, utilitarianism is the theory that best systematizes the precepts of common-sense morality, even if it requires some revisions in those precepts. According to the other interpretation, common-sense morality is *explanatorily dependent* on utilitarianism in the sense that the making of common moral judgments is guided by an implicit grasp of utilitarianism. People's adherence to and reliance on common moral precepts is, in the relevant way, regulated by the felicific tendencies of adherence to and reliance on those precepts; moral judgments not so regulated are to be viewed as performance errors made by someone with an underlying utilitarian competence.

Once we distinguish them, we may wonder whether Sidgwick is concerned with dialectical fit, explanatory dependence, or both. Most of Sidgwick's explicit remarks about common-sense utilitarianism endorse only dialectical fit (cf. *ME*, 422, 425, 454, 461, 475), and it is this claim and its epistemological relevance that raise the most interesting philosophical issues about his position. Nonetheless, a brief discussion of the explanatory thesis and its relation to the dialectical one is in order.

It may seem artificial to distinguish the two theses. Wouldn't evidence for one be evidence for the other? If we think that common-sense morality reflects an implicit and imperfect grasp and application of utilitarianism, then we should expect utilitarianism to be the result of a philosophical

---

vol. 21 (1992), pp. 92–93. Moreover, it should be noted, this reliance on moral rules and motives is compatible with *act* utilitarianism. Acting on the best rules or motives will result in some wrong acts; but because these acts will be part of an optimal pattern of behavior, an act utilitarian can represent them as cases of *blameless* wrongdoing. If so, Sidgwick's reliance on rules and motives does not imply rule utilitarianism or motive utilitarianism

[3] Cf. A. John Simmons, "Utilitarianism and Unconscious Utilitarianism," in *The Limits of Utilitarianism*, ed. H. Miller and W. Williams (Minneapolis: University of Minnesota Press, 1982).

reconstruction of common-sense morality, and so we should expect to see the dialectical fit of utilitarianism and common-sense morality. But it might also seem that there could be no dialectical fit unless common-sense morality is implicitly and imperfectly guided by utilitarianism; systematic fit seems to be evidence of explanatory dependence.

But this last inference is problematic. There are different ways of understanding the dialectical fit of common-sense morality with utilitarianism or any other method of ethics, not all of which license the inference from dialectical fit to explanatory dependence.

We introduce a moral principle in order to systematize our considered moral convictions, especially those about particular cases and kinds of case; moral principles purport to explain why the various acts that we judge to be right are right by appeal to some common factors as right-making factors. We examine candidate principles, in part, by drawing out their implications for real or imagined cases and comparing their implications with our own existing or reflective assessments of those cases. If a principle has counterintuitive implications, this counts against it. If the counterintuitive implications of the principle are fairly common, this is reason to abandon or modify the principle. But if this counterintuitive implication is isolated and the principle explains our views, especially our common moral views, better than alternative principles, then this is reason to revise the particular judgment or precept that conflicted with the principle. Ideally, we make tradeoffs among our principles, considered moral judgments, and other views in response to conflicts, making adjustments here at one point and there at another, as coherence seems to require, until our ethical views are in dialectical equilibrium. This, in essence, is the sort of dialectical fit Sidgwick claims to have found between utilitarianism and common-sense morality (*ME*, 373–74, 422, 497).[4]

But a principle might be in *narrow* or *broad* dialectical equilibrium. A narrow equilibrium seeks a dialectical accommodation between candidate principles and common moral beliefs; it relies on nonmoral beliefs only in order to determine the implications for particular cases of more general moral principles and rules (that is, it treats these nonmoral beliefs as minor premises in practical syllogisms). A broad equilibrium seeks dialectical accommodation among a much wider range of claims. It takes as input not simply common moral beliefs, candidate principles, and initial conditions, but also background philosophical and social theories about such things as the way in which common beliefs may be biased and subject to distortion, the social role of moral and political theories, an ideal of the person, the nature of personal identity, freedom of the will, and

---

[4] Compare Rawls's description of the process of "reflective equilibrium"; see John Rawls, *A Theory of Justice* (Cambridge, MA: Harvard University Press, 1971), pp. 19–21, 46–53, 579–81. Rawls claims a Sidgwickian pedigree for his view in *A Theory of Justice*, p. 51n.

the existence and nature of a divine being. A broad dialectical equilibrium seeks a fit between moral theories and common-sense morality, but the fit may be very imperfect. A theory in broad dialectical equilibrium will draw support from common-sense morality in the sense that common-sense morality is among the inputs to broad equilibrium, but the theory may revise common-sense morality in significant ways. If the revisions are driven by enough social and philosophical theory and are drastic enough, the resulting fit between the theory and common-sense morality may not support the explanatory dependence of the actual precepts of common-sense morality (that is, prior to their revision) on people's implicit grasp of the theory. At some point, as we increasingly count common judgments as the performance errors of someone with an underlying utilitarian competence, we begin to discredit ascription to people of a utilitarian competence. Conversely, a theory that does explanatorily regulate our moral sensibilities may therefore be in narrow equilibrium but need not be in broad equilibrium.

Because Sidgwick's main claims about the relation between common-sense morality and the various methods are confined to dialectical fit, whether he is committed to the explanatory thesis seems to depend upon whether the dialectical fit he seeks is narrow or broad.

III. DIALECTICAL BREADTH

One would expect Sidgwick to look for as broad a dialectical fit as possible. In assessing moral theories and other moral beliefs, we ought, in principle, to examine any other beliefs on which their plausibility depends. Sidgwick's own views about appropriate dialectical breadth are hard to pin down, but insofar as he sympathizes with dialectical inquiry, I think he implicitly seeks a fairly broad dialectical equilibrium. I say this because, as a general matter, he recognizes a variety of ways in which ethical principles depend for their plausibility on auxiliary moral and nonmoral views.

First, in discussing the dualism of practical reason, Sidgwick recognizes that the convergence of happiness and duty, and so of egoism and utilitarianism, would be complete if we could posit a divine being who ensured that performance of duty was rewarded and breach of duty was punished in this or some other world (ME, 503–9). Whether the existence of such a divine sanction is settled by moral reasoning determines

> the very important question whether ethical science can be constructed on an independent basis; or whether it is forced to borrow a fundamental and indispensable premiss from Theology or some other source. (ME, 507)

Because Sidgwick finds no moral intuition of this sanction (ME, 507), he must conclude that ethical science does depend upon claims from other special sciences.

Second, Sidgwick thinks utilitarianism might be motivated by an analogy between intrapersonal and interpersonal distribution (*ME*, 381–82). Just as egoism requires temporal-neutrality in the distribution of goods and harms across different temporal stages within a single life, so too utilitarianism requires person-neutrality in the distribution of goods and harms across different lives. Whereas utilitarianism is fully neutral, egoism is a hybrid; it is temporally neutral, but person relative. As Sidgwick notes, this hybrid character may seem arbitrary:

> From the point of view, indeed, of abstract philosophy, I do not see why the axiom of Prudence should not be questioned, when it conflicts with present inclination, on a ground similar to that on which Egoists refuse to admit the axiom of Rational Benevolence. If the Utilitarian has to answer the question, 'Why should I sacrifice my own happiness for the greater happiness of another?' it must surely be admissible to ask the Egoist, 'Why should I sacrifice a present pleasure for a greater one in the future? Why should I concern myself about my own future feelings any more than about the feelings of other persons?' (*ME*, 418)

If the interpersonal sacrifice that utilitarianism demands is problematic, perhaps the intrapersonal sacrifice that egoism demands is as well. Sidgwick goes on to suggest that the rationality of intrapersonal sacrifice may depend upon our views of personal identity; the passage continues as follows:

> It undoubtedly seems to Common Sense paradoxical to ask for a reason why one should seek one's own happiness on the whole; but I do not see how the demand can be repudiated as absurd by those who adopt the views of the extreme empirical school of psychologists. . . . Grant that the Ego is merely a system of coherent phenomena, that the permanent identical 'I' is not a fact but a fiction, as Hume and his followers maintain; why, then, should one part of the series of feelings into which the Ego is resolved be concerned with another part of the same series, any more than with any other series? (*ME*, 418–19)

Unfortunately, Sidgwick allows the egoist to defend himself simply by claiming that the Humean view of personal identity is contrary to common sense (*ME*, 498).[5] But the significant point, for our purposes, is that Sidgwick does recognize that the plausibility of rational egoism depends upon certain metaphysical claims about the nature of personal identity through time.

---

[5] Elsewhere, I have argued that the egoist rationale is metaphysically robust; see David O. Brink, "Sidgwick and the Rationale for Rational Egoism," in *Essays on Henry Sidgwick*, ed. B. Schultz (New York: Cambridge University Press, 1991).

Third, Sidgwick maintains that ethical theory need not enter into the free will controversy (*ME*, bk. i, ch. 5). This may look like a rejection of the sort of systematic connections that a broad equilibrium seeks, but the appearance is misleading. Sidgwick believes that the external perspective on an agent's action in which we understand or predict an agent's behavior in light of regularities in her conduct is compatible with libertarianism as well as determinism, and that the internal perspective in which an agent sees herself as free to act on the result of her deliberations is compatible with determinism as well as libertarianism (*ME*, 70). Sidgwick does seem to think that backward-looking justifications of punishment and ascriptions of responsibility presuppose freedom of the will and, in particular, libertarianism; however, this does not require deciding between competing views about free will, Sidgwick thinks, because forward-looking justifications are the only defensible ones (*ME*, 71–72). Sidgwick's discussion may strike us as superficial in compensating ways. On the one hand, if we treat compatibilism as a serious view (as Sidgwick seems not to), we may think that the backward-looking accounts of punishment and responsibility do not presuppose libertarianism and so are metaphysically more robust than Sidgwick thinks. On the other hand, we may think that backward-looking accounts are morally more robust than Sidgwick thinks and that, as a result, it becomes more important to know whether incompatibilism and determinism are both true. The important point, for present purposes, is neither how much Sidgwick thinks ethics is affected by metaphysics nor which package of metaphysical and ethical views he thinks is right, but rather that he thinks that one's ethics must be shown to square with one's metaphysics.

Finally, we might consider Sidgwick's discussion of the possibility of an "esoteric morality" (*ME*, 489–90). Common-sense utilitarianism claims that the acceptance value of the precepts of common-sense morality approximates optimality. This leads Sidgwick to consider the possibility that in some circumstances utilitarianism should be an esoteric doctrine, known only to an enlightened few, with the bulk of society treating the precepts of common-sense morality as exceptionless and nonderivatively justified. But this would offend against publicity. It seems important that people understand and be able to affirm to themselves and others the justification of their actions and institutions. It may seem that Sidgwick ignores the way in which true moral theories are supposed to play this sort of public educational and justificatory role and so ignores auxiliary expectations we have for ethical theories. Sidgwick may not take these auxiliary beliefs seriously enough, but he is not unaware of them or their bearing on utilitarianism. Moreover, in rejecting any nonderivative role for publicity, Sidgwick implicitly appeals to the distinction between a theory's truth and the value of accepting it. In doing so, he rests his case for utilitarianism in part upon a cognitivist or realist meta-ethics and so recognizes the possibility of systematic connections between first principles of normative ethics and meta-ethics.

Thus, even if we disagree with the elements and connections in Sidgwick's own broad equilibrium, insofar as he seeks a dialectical fit, it seems to be a broad one. If so, Sidgwick's dialectical thesis need not be committed to the explanatory thesis. The dialectical thesis may be true, but whether the explanatory thesis is true depends upon how broad and revisionary is the fit between utilitarianism and common-sense morality.

IV. DIALECTICAL FIT AND PHILOSOPHICAL INTUITIONISM

Sidgwick thinks that utilitarianism is in some kind of dialectical fit with our considered moral judgments. What, if anything, is the epistemological significance of this? In particular, is a principle's ability to sustain and explain common moral precepts reason for thinking the principle is true? If so, Sidgwick seems to have a problem, for his official epistemological position — *philosophical intuitionism* — seems to preclude his assigning any probative value or evidential role to common-sense morality.

Intuitionism, of course, is one of Sidgwick's three methods of ethics, along with egoism and utilitarianism.[6] In its broadest sense, intuitionism is a form of epistemological foundationalism; it claims that our moral knowledge consists in or rests upon noninferentially justified or self-evident moral beliefs (*ME*, 98, 200–201). Sidgwick defends the need for some moral intuitions by appeal to the familiar idea that there is a logical gap between *is* and *ought* and a familiar regress argument (cf. *ME*, 98).[7] His argument has something like the following form:

(1) No moral statement can be derived from purely nonmoral statements.
(2) Hence, if a moral statement is to be derived from further claims, these claims must contain moral statements.
(3) Hence, if a moral belief is to be inferentially justified, its justification must appeal to other moral beliefs.
(4) But, on pain of infinite regress or circularity, the process of inferential justification must come to a stop somewhere.
(5) Hence, there must be some self-evident moral beliefs.

Further, Sidgwick claims that self-evident moral beliefs must satisfy four conditions: (a) their content must be clear and precise, (b) their truth must

---

[6] Sidgwick thinks that there is something right or defensible about each of his three methods. Intuitionism is defensible when it is understood as a foundationalist epistemological view, whereas egoism and utilitarianism are substantive normative views. Sidgwick concludes that egoist and utilitarian first principles each rest on a fundamental intuition; it is this fact that constitutes the dualism of practical reason.

[7] See also Henry Sidgwick, "The Establishment of Ethical First Principles," *Mind*, vol. 4 (1879), pp. 107–8; the essay will be referred to hereafter as "First Principles," and page references will be given parenthetically in the text.

be evident upon reflection, (c) they must be mutually consistent, and (d) they must be capable of sustaining consensus (*ME*, 338–42).

Different versions of intuitionism correspond to different views about the level of generality of these foundational intuitions. Sidgwick distinguishes among three different levels of generality in our moral claims: particular moral judgments concern specific actions or action tokens; moral rules concern classes of action or action types; and moral principles or first principles apply to many or all action types and purport to systematize and explain particular moral judgments and moral rules. *Perceptual* intuitionism locates moral intuitions at the level of particular moral judgments; *dogmatic* intuitionism locates them at the level of moral rules; and *philosophical* intuitionism locates them at the level of first principles (*ME*, 97–102). In defense of perceptual or dogmatic intuitionism, Sidgwick points out that many particular moral judgments (e.g., that this act of genocide is wrong) or moral rules (e.g., that genocide is wrong) are much more certain and much less dubitable than any abstract philosophical first principle (e.g., utilitarianism) (*ME*, 98–99, 101). Nonetheless, Sidgwick believes that justification in ethics has a certain structure that supports philosophical intuitionism; there are various reasons for *justificatory ascent* to first principles.

There is a *practical* need to ascend from considered judgments to moral rules. A list of discrete judgments about particular actions will typically prove inadequate. First, sometimes one has no moral intuition about a new case; here nothing is evident upon reflection (*ME*, 100). If so, condition (b) is not satisfied. Particular judgments about other cases do not help; one needs a general view about a class of cases under which the present case falls. Second, sometimes one notices differences in one's judgments about similar cases (*ME*, 100). By themselves, different particular judgments are not inconsistent, but they do make for inconsistency if we also believe that the cases are relevantly similar and that there can be no moral difference between two cases unless they are relevantly different in nonmoral ways. Here condition (c) is violated. Appeal to moral rules specifying right-making factors would identify which differences are morally relevant and how, and so would either remove the appearance of inconsistency or indicate how the agent should revise her moral judgments so as to avoid a genuine inconsistency. Third, intrapersonally consistent judgments may be interpersonally inconsistent; different people often reach different judgments about the same cases (*ME*, 100). If so, condition (d) is violated. We may hope to get leverage on our disagreement by ascending to shared moral rules; they could be used to show that one of us must be misapplying the rule to the particular case.

But even if none of these practical problems arises or becomes apparent, there is an *intellectual* need to make the ascent, because there will remain an *explanatory* problem for a system consisting only of considered moral judgments. Even if all my moral judgments are true, there is still the question of *why* they are all true (cf. *ME*, 102). What makes various cases of promise-keeping or truth-telling obligatory? We answer these questions by finding a right-making factor that is common to the various cases. There is an *asymmetrical dependence* between particular and general here. An action token that is obligatory is obligatory in virtue of possessing a right-making property F, that is, in virtue of a certain moral rule being true. However, it is not true that F is a right-making property in virtue of the action token that is F being obligatory; because the action token has many other properties as well, the fact that it is obligatory cannot explain why F is a right-making property.[8] This is why we say that the action token is obligatory *insofar* as it possesses the right-making property F. And this metaphysical asymmetry seems to have epistemological significance. Because the particular truth depends on the more general truth, one's reasons for accepting the particular claim ought to refer to the more general truth.[9]

Similar reasoning motivates an ascent from moral rules to first principles. First, I may have no moral beliefs about a particular type of action; appeal to my acceptance of other moral rules will by itself be of no help. However, a more general principle that subsumes the moral rules I do accept may have implications for the type of action about which I do not yet have moral beliefs. Second, I may recognize conflicts among different moral rules that I accept (e.g., truth-telling and nonmaleficence);

[8] This metaphysical dependence of moral truths about action tokens on truths about right-making properties asserts of *each* token that it has the moral properties it does by virtue of certain properties, which that token possesses, being right-making properties. As such, this kind of metaphysical dependence is compatible with a wide variety of metaphysical views about the nature of properties and their relations to particulars.

[9] Someone might wonder whether this metaphysical dependence of particular truths on general truths requires the epistemic dependence of particular beliefs on general beliefs. There are properties on which the gender of particular chicks depends and in virtue of which chicken-sexers sort particular chicks by sex. But we may nonetheless be inclined to ascribe knowledge to the reliable but inarticulate chicken-sexer who cannot cite these properties that justify his practice. This externalist view about knowledge may seem to undermine the inference from metaphysical dependence to epistemic dependence. But I am not sure about this. General beliefs, like any others, need not be articulate to play a role in justification or knowledge. We ascribe tacit or implicit beliefs when they are needed to explain regularities in a person's behavior. If the chicken-sexer's reliability is counterfactually stable in the relevant way, then there is a regularity whose explanation requires ascribing to the chicken-sexer implicit recognition of those properties that make the sex of a chick detectable. If the chicken-sexer's reliability is not counterfactually stable in the relevant way, then we are less inclined to ascribe knowledge to him, though we may attribute a certain knack to him.

A different worry is that the relata in metaphysical dependence are different from those in epistemic dependence. With metaphysical dependence, the fact that x is F depends upon the fact that x is G and on the fact that G is an F-making feature. But with epistemic dependence, it may seem, the justification of my particular belief that x is F depends upon some general belief — not about G being an F-making feature, but about the reliability of the cognitive process by which I formed my belief that x is F, for example, the belief that I am a reliable detector of F. However, it seems reasonable to suppose that the justification for this belief rests upon my being able to detect G and my belief that G is an F-making feature. If so, metaphysical dependence must eventually be represented in the content of one's justified beliefs.

appealing to more general principles that rank different right-making features may help to resolve these conflicts. Third, the moral rules I accept may not be the same as those you accept; we might try to exert leverage on our dispute by finding shared general principles and seeing which moral rules the principles subsume and explain. Finally, whether or not we experience these difficulties, there is an explanatory problem for a moral code consisting only of moral rules. Even if we accept all and only true moral rules, as Sidgwick says, "still the resulting code seems an accidental aggregate of precepts, which stands in need of rational synthesis" (*ME*, 102). We need to know what more general property it is in virtue of which these disparate right-making features are all right-making features. We make this explanatory demand because we recognize a further asymmetrical dependence of moral rules on first principles.

The result of this justificatory ascent is philosophical intuitionism (*ME*, 98–100, 200–201, 338–42, 379–87). It takes our moral beliefs about action tokens to be inferentially justifiable on the basis of moral beliefs about action types, and it takes these moral rules to be inferentially justifiable on the basis of first principles. Because of the asymmetrical dependence of the particular on the more general, these first principles cannot be justified by their relation to anything less general, and, *ex hypothesi*, there is nothing more general than first principles in terms of which they might be justified. Hence, it is at the level of first principles that we should look for self-evident moral beliefs.[10]

Thus, Sidgwick is a friend of intuitionism in the broad sense, because he accepts philosophical intuitionism. But he rejects intuitionism in a narrow sense, which he associates with dogmatic intuitionism, that takes the

[10] There is an interesting difference in the apparent plausibility of locating the foundations at the level of general principle in the moral domain (philosophical intuitionism) and the nonmoral domain (philosophical foundationalism). Whereas Sidgwick argues that philosophical intuitionism is the most plausible form of intuitionism, philosophical foundationalism has not seemed especially plausible; instead, it has seemed more plausible to locate the foundations at the level of particular beliefs in the nonmoral domain (particular foundationalism).

This difference can, I think, be explained. Classical foundationalism treats as self-evident beliefs reporting (occurrent) sense data (e.g., the belief that I now see a reddish patch on my visual field). These beliefs concern *private* objects and, as a result, might seem to be infallible; they are beliefs whose private content is such that it is not clear how one could mistakenly hold a belief with that content. By contrast, particular moral beliefs (e.g., the belief that this act is wrong) concern *common* objects; as such, they seem eminently fallible.

Whereas classical foundationalism has seemed the most plausible form of foundationalism for the nonmoral domain, for familiar reasons, I do not think that it is. Classical foundationalism can hope to rest our knowledge on infallible foundations only by restricting these foundational beliefs to private objects. But this threatens to commit us to skepticism, because it seems we cannot move from beliefs exclusively about private objects to beliefs about common objects by deductive or abductive inference. Moreover, it is doubtful that infallible beliefs are self-justifying. Their justification would seem to depend upon recognition of their infallible character, and this will involve recognition of how beliefs with a certain kind of content could not be held mistakenly. But then a particular infallible belief will depend for its justification on general beliefs whose truth explains why the particular belief is true.

precepts of common-sense morality to be fundamental intuitions. Sidg-wick does not rest content with the arguments we have just reviewed against dogmatic intuitionism. He also claims that the precepts of com-mon-sense morality, in particular, do not qualify as fundamental intu-itions, because, on closer examination, they prove to be either false (e.g., always keep your promises) or uninformative (e.g., keep your promises unless it violates some stronger obligation) (*ME*, 342, 360–61). In the pro-cess of revising common-sense precepts so as to avoid these errors, Sidg-wick believes that we are led to those axioms—justice, self-love, and benevolence—that do meet the tests of self-evidence (*ME*, 379–83, 386–87). And this explains the way in which Sidgwick finds truth in each of the three methods of ethics; egoist and utilitarian first principles each rest on a fundamental intuition.[11]

V. THE TENSION BETWEEN INTUITIONISM AND DIALECTICAL INQUIRY

We can now see the problem Sidgwick faces if he takes the (alleged) fit between utilitarianism and common-sense morality to be evidence for the truth of utilitarianism. As a philosophical intuitionist, Sidgwick must claim that belief in utilitarianism, when justified, is self-justified or non-inferentially justified. As such, its justification apparently cannot consist in the fact (if it is a fact) that utilitarianism sustains and explains various precepts of common-sense morality. How then can Sidgwick understand the significance of the (alleged) dialectical fit between utilitarianism and common-sense morality, and why should a dialectical examination of common-sense morality be helpful or important to reaching first princi-ples if these principles are self-evident? Why not simply isolate candidate first principles and assess their plausibility without any examination of common-sense morality? Several strategies for reconciling Sidgwick's dia-lectical and intuitionist commitments are worth exploring.

First, it might be denied that there is any real tension between Sidg-wick's dialectical and intuitionist commitments. First principles might be self-evident, yet they might receive *further* justification from their ability to sustain and explain common moral beliefs; part of their total justifica-tion may be nondiscursive, but another part may be discursive. If so,

---

[11] On a familiar internalist reading of Sidgwick's views about the relationship between morality and rationality, he faces a problem reconciling the "dualism of practical reason" with his own philosophical intuitionism. For the dualism of practical reason consists in the fact that egoism and utilitarianism each rest on a fundamental intuition. But, on this inter-nalist reading, egoism and utilitarianism are competing theories about morality and ratio-nal conduct. Yet if, as Sidgwick claims, fundamental intuitions must be mutually consistent (condition [c]), then it is not true that both egoism and utilitarianism can rest on fundamen-tal intuitions. I argue that this is one reason, among others, to favor an externalist reading of the dualism of practical reason, according to which egoism is the correct theory of ratio-nality, whereas utilitarianism is the correct theory of morality; see my "Sidgwick and the Rationale for Rational Egoism" (*supra* n. 5), section 2.

Sidgwick's intuitionist commitments do not prevent him from assigning probative value to dialectical reasoning from common-sense morality.

However, I think that Sidgwick's epistemological tension is not so easily resolved. For one thing, Sidgwick motivates intuitionism at least in part by the regress argument (Section IV above). But that argument has as one of its premises the claim that circular reasoning confers no justification. But dialectical reasoning is circular; particular common moral beliefs are justified by appeal to moral principles that subsume and explain them, and these principles are justified by their ability to subsume and explain common moral beliefs. But if circular reasoning confers no justification, then it is hard to see how dialectical reasoning could confer even partial justification.[12]

Moreover, in expressing his dialectical commitments, Sidgwick appears to claim that the discursive justification of first principles exhausts their justification:

> If systematic reflection upon the Morality of Common Sense thus exhibits the Utilitarian principle as that to which Common Sense naturally appeals for the further development of its system which this same reflection shows to be necessary, the proof of Utilitarianism seems as complete as it can be made. (*ME*, 422)

If "proof" means justification, then discursive (dialectical) reasoning establishes justification that is as complete as possible; this would leave no room for nondiscursive justification.[13]

Alternatively, someone might try to reconcile Sidgwick's dialectical and intuitionist commitments by appeal to his third and fourth conditions on self-evidence. They require that self-evident beliefs be mutually consistent and capable of supporting a consensus. In this way, Sidgwick may

---

[12] It is sometimes held that dialectical reasoning has probative value only if one's initial beliefs are credible independently of their inferential connections. Cf. C. I. Lewis, *An Analysis of Knowledge and Valuation* (La Salle: Open Court, 1946), p. 339. But this is not the view that the present interpretation ascribes to Sidgwick. For the starting points of dialectical method are common moral beliefs; what Sidgwick (in some moods) takes to be self-evident are first principles, not common moral beliefs.

[13] This passage is a problem for philosophical intuitionism as long as "proof" is understood as justification. The passage presents no problem for intuitionism, under this strategy for reconciling intuitionism and dialectical inquiry, if "proof" is understood to refer only to discursive demonstration or reasoning. Sidgwick clearly denies that "proof" here refers to discursive demonstration (*ME*, 419–20). At one point in this context, he seems to equate proof with dialectical reasoning (*ME*, 420). But then the passage would make the puzzling assertion that the dialectical support for utilitarianism makes the dialectical justification of utilitarianism as complete as possible. So I think it is unclear exactly how Sidgwick does want to understand proof in this passage. For this reason, I would not want to resist the first reconciliation strategy solely on the basis of this passage. The difficulty in squaring this reconciliation strategy with Sidgwick's reliance on the regress argument seems to be sufficient reason to resist this strategy.

seem to make conformity with common-sense moral beliefs part of the conditions of a first principle qualifying as self-evident.

But the third condition could not be any real help reconciling the probative value of common-sense moral precepts and the self-evidence of first principles, because the third condition requires that beliefs that otherwise qualify as self-evident must also be mutually consistent. But, as we have seen (in Section IV), Sidgwick does not think that the precepts of common-sense morality qualify as self-evident; when stated clearly and precisely, they are not evident, and they depend for what justification they have on more general principles. So consistency among intuitions does not require that we compare first principles with common moral precepts, because, according to Sidgwick, whereas true first principles are objects of intuition, common moral precepts are not. By contrast, the fourth condition does promise to secure an evidential role for common-sense moral beliefs. A principle that has significant counterintuitive implications seems unlikely to be able to sustain a consensus. But this condition does not resolve the tension between intuitionist and dialectical commitments; it locates it within philosophical intuitionism itself. Precisely because the fourth condition makes the justification of first principles depend upon their implications for other beliefs we hold, it means that first principles, when justified, are discursively justified, rather than self-evident.

A different reconciliation strategy appeals to Sidgwick's first two conditions on self-evidence. In reflecting upon the plausibility of a claim, we need to make sure we understand the content of the claim (condition [a]) before giving our reflective assent to it (condition [b]). If so, it might be claimed that we need to identify the implications of a first principle if it is to be sufficiently clear and precise for us to consider its plausibility independently of its inferential connections. If this is all Sidgwick's examination of common-sense morality involved, then we would have a legitimate role for it within philosophical intuitionism. But Sidgwick not only identifies the implications of putative first principles for particular cases, he *compares* their implications with the requirements of common-sense morality as a test for the plausibility of the principles. Sidgwick allows common-sense morality to test and drive revisions in moral principles. The constraints on deviations from common-sense morality

> are firmly, though indefinitely fixed: the truth of a philosopher's premises will always be tested by the acceptability of his conclusions: if in any important point he be found in flagrant conflict with common opinion, his method is likely to be declared invalid. (*ME*, 373)

This is just to point out what we have already seen, that Sidgwick does assign probative value to common-sense morality.

This will be a problem for any reconciliation strategy that attempts to resolve the tension between Sidgwick's intuitionist and dialectical commitments by denying that he gives an evidential role to common-sense morality. So this problem will afflict the reconciliation strategy that treats the dialectical examination as part of "the psychology of discovery," rather than the "logic of justification." On this view, the dialectical examination of common-sense morality serves to *identify* candidate first principles whose truth must then be intuited, that is, whose truth must be evident independently of its conformity with the judgments of common-sense morality.[14] This reading may seem to fit the structure of Sidgwick's inquiry: he concludes that the precepts of common-sense morality cannot be fundamental intuitions but that the dialectical examination of common-sense morality identifies axioms of justice, prudence, and benevolence that do meet the tests of self-evidence.

> I have tried to show how in the principles of Justice, Prudence, and Benevolence as commonly recognized there is at least a self-evident element, immediately cognisable by abstract intuition. . . . I regard the apprehension, with more or less distinctness, of these abstract truths, as the permanent basis of the common conviction that the fundamental precepts of morality are essentially reasonable. (*ME*, 382–83)

Dialectical reasoning, on this interpretation, plays a heuristic, rather than an evidential, role.

Like the previous interpretation, this one fails to account for the fact that Sidgwick does assign an evidential role to common-sense morality (*ME*, 373 [quoted above], 389, 422 [quoted above], 425–26, 497). Moreover, there is the further difficulty that this interpretation does not explain why the examination of common-sense morality is necessary to the identification of first principles. Consider Sidgwick's so-called "proof" of utilitarianism. Prudence rests on the allegedly self-evident requirement of temporal-neutrality that one ought to be neutral about the temporal location of benefits and harms within one's own life (*ME*, 381). Utilitarianism rests on the requirement of person-neutrality that one ought to be neutral about the distribution of benefits and harms across different lives.

> [J]ust as this notion [the Good on the Whole of a single individual] is constructed by comparison and integration of different goods that succeed one another in the series of our conscious states, so we have

---

[14] Cf. Peter Singer, "Sidgwick and Reflective Equilibrium," *The Monist*, vol. 57 (1974), pp. 490–517; Jerome Schneewind, *Sidgwick's Ethics and Victorian Moral Philosophy* (Oxford: Clarendon Press, 1977), chs. 9–10; and T. H. Irwin, "Aristotle's Methods of Ethics," in *Studies in Aristotle*, ed. D. O'Meara (Washington, DC: Catholic University of America Press, 1981), p. 203.

formed the notion of Universal Good by comparison and integration of the goods of all individual human — or sentient — existences. And here, again, just as in the former case, by considering the relation of the integrant parts to the whole and each other, I obtain the self-evident principle that the good of any one individual is of no more importance, from the point of view (if I may say so) of the Universe, than the good of any other. . . . And it is evident to me that as a rational being I am bound to aim at good generally, so far as this is attainable by my efforts, not merely at a particular part of it. (*ME*, 382)

Here Sidgwick exploits an analogy between intertemporal (but intrapersonal) and interpersonal distribution of benefits and harms. He finds temporal-neutrality self-evident, and the analogy leads him to accept person-neutrality. We may wonder whether this argument shows that utilitarianism is the object of a fundamental intuition, because its constituent axiom — person-neutrality — seems really to be a theorem derived from the axiom (if that's what it is) of temporal-neutrality together with an analogy between intertemporal and interpersonal distribution. But whatever its merits, this line of argumentation can apparently be understood and assessed without an examination of common-sense morality. So it remains unclear how the examination of common-sense morality plays an essential heuristic role.

Sidgwick is not entirely unaware of this tension between his intuitionist and dialectical commitments. In "The Establishment of Ethical First Principles" (1879), he addresses a more general epistemological dilemma of which the present problem is just a special case.[15] On the one hand, it would seem that genuine first principles must not depend for their justification on other moral claims; on the other hand, it seems appropriate, in the face of disagreement over first principles, to be able to offer reasons why one should accept the first principle one does, rather than another ("First Principles," 106). Our problem is a special case of this, because a particular principle's dialectical conformity with common-sense morality is one way of supplying reasons for accepting the principle. Sidgwick attempts to resolve the more general problem by appeal to Aristotle's distinction between that which is "naturally prior" and that which is "prior for us":[16]

To find a way out of this difficulty we require, I think, to take Aristotle's distinction between logical or natural priority in cognition and priority in the knowledge of any particular mind. We are thus ena-

---

[15] "First Principles" (*supra* n. 7) was published two years after the second edition of *The Methods of Ethics*.

[16] See Aristotle, *Posterior Analytics*, 72a1–5, and *Metaphysics*, 1029b3–12.

bled to see that a proposition may be self-evident, i.e., may be properly cognisable without being viewed in connexion with any other
propositions; though in order that its truth may be apparent to some
particular mind, there is still required some rational process connect-
ing it with propositions previously accepted by that mind. ("First
Principles," 106)

According to this suggestion, whereas a first principle such as utilitarianism may be self-evident, it can be evident to individual cognizers only by
virtue of its dialectical fit with common-sense morality.

This solution differs from the one that assigns a heuristic role to the
examination of common-sense morality, insofar as it concedes that dialectical reasoning provides individual cognizers with their justification for
accepting first principles. But it is not clear that this solution leaves any
room for philosophical intuitionism. Sidgwick treats natural priority as a
kind of priority in knowledge or justification which is not represented in
the knowledge or justification that particular cognizers possess. But
knowledge or justification seems precisely something that cognizers have
(or lack); a cognizer's beliefs are justified or count as knowledge if they
meet certain conditions. It is hard to understand what is being asserted
if it is claimed that certain propositions are known (or justified) but by (or
for) no one.

There is a more natural interpretation of the relevance of Aristotle's distinction between natural priority and priority for us, which takes natural
priority to be a metaphysical relation and priority for us to be an epistemological relation. Recall our discussion of Sidgwick's motivation for philosophical intuitionism. Philosophical intuitionism reflects recognition of
the asymmetrical dependence of particular moral truths on general moral
truths; true first principles explain in virtue of what properties right acts
are right, rather than the other way around (cf. *ME*, 98–100). This is a
kind of metaphysical asymmetry or priority in nature. But what epistemological significance, if any, does asymmetrical metaphysical dependence have? As I argued earlier, the philosophical intuitionist plausibly
concludes from the metaphysical dependence of the particular on the
general that the particular moral beliefs must be dependent for their justification on more general moral beliefs. The important question is
whether epistemic dependence must be asymmetrical as metaphysical
dependence is.

The problem, on this interpretation, is that Sidgwick seems simply to
be of two minds here. On the one hand, he thinks dialectical reasoning
about first principles and their relation to common moral precepts is part
of justifying those principles; on the other hand, this seems to him to
compromise their status as genuine first principles:

[I]t seems undeniable that first principles cannot stand in need of
what is strictly to be called proof: they would obviously cease to be

first principles if they were exhibited as dependent for their certainty on the acceptance by the mind of certain other truths. ("First Principles," 106; cf. *ME*, 419)

But this reasoning confuses metaphysical and epistemic dependence. What is clear is that particular moral truths are asymmetrically metaphysically dependent upon the more general moral truths stated in first principles; this is what we signal when we call them *first* principles. But asymmetrical metaphysical dependence does not itself imply asymmetrical epistemic dependence. A first principle identifies the ultimate (or an ultimate) right-making factor (e.g., F). It makes no sense to ask of a first principle that we take to be true, "In virtue of what (further) property is F an ultimate right-making property?" But we can quite sensibly ask about some first principle, "Is that first principle true?" or "Is F an ultimate right-making factor?" And the answer to these questions may appeal to the principle's ability to sustain and explain moral judgments we find independently plausible. The metaphysical priority of first principles does not show that our evidence for what first principle is true cannot include our (defeasible) beliefs about what acts are right.

Indeed, it is hard to make sense of the idea that moral claims could be *self*-evident; asymmetrical epistemic dependence seems very troublesome. What is puzzling about philosophical intuitionism is that it reasonably insists that we can and should seek an inferential justification of moral beliefs about action tokens and types, even when they are indubitable or nearly so, but claims that the more abstract and more dubitable principles we produce as justifications do not admit of justification in terms of anything else. But how can a more abstract and more dubitable proposition be self-evident if a less dubitable one is not? Given that we permit the demand for explanation and justification in the first place, as Sidgwick allows we must if ethics is to contain debate and dialogue at all, philosophical intuitionism seems to limit the demand in an arbitrary and perverse way. In fact, moral philosophy, past and present, does assume that first principles are discursively justified; we challenge and defend moral theories by comparing their implications about particular cases with our independent moral beliefs about those cases.[17] And this, we have seen, is Sidgwick's other view about the justification of first principles; they are to be justified by showing that they are in dialectical equilibrium with beliefs that take common-sense morality as input.

Thus, whereas I do think that this interpretation of Aristotle's distinction allows us to reconcile asymmetrical metaphysical dependence with symmetrical epistemic dependence, it does not help Sidgwick resolve his dilemma, because it does not allow us to reconcile asymmetrical and sym-

---

[17] And this is not simply a development of contemporary moral and political theory. Consider, for example, Aristotle's dialectical reasoning from common or respected opinions at various points in the *Nicomachean Ethics* or John Stuart Mill's defense of utilitarianism's implications in chs. 2 and 5 of *Utilitarianism*.

metrical aspects of epistemic dependence. Sidgwick's epistemological views are not fully consistent; he must choose between his intuitionist and dialectical accounts of the justification of first principles.[18] And I have tried to suggest reasons why the dialectical account is more promising than the intuitionist one.

VI. THE DIALECTICAL JUSTIFICATION OF FIRST PRINCIPLES

Even if the philosophical intuitionist limits our demands for justification in an arbitrary way and the dialectical account of the justification of first principles fits our philosophical practice, the dialectical account requires further development. If a dialectical process that takes common or considered moral judgments as a significant part of the input is to have moral knowledge as output, then there ought to be reason to think that the judgments of common-sense morality are sufficiently close to the truth. Dialectical inquiry can identify and correct various sorts of errors, even very significant and far-reaching errors, but it is unable to identify or correct systematic error, because the grounds and direction for correction must emerge from reflection on the beliefs with which cognizers start. Do we have any reason to think that the considered moral convictions of common-sense morality are generally reliable or at least not systematically seriously mistaken?

Though Sidgwick does not address this problem for dialectical inquiry directly, a promising defense of dialectical inquiry draws on resources Sidgwick does discuss. We can defend dialectical inquiry if we can explain why ordinary people should be fairly good detectors of moral properties. We can explain this if we can explain why people would tend to recognize, apply, and attach importance to the categories and properties of actions that common-sense morality treats as morally relevant.[19]

In discussing the relation between duty and happiness, Sidgwick argues that there is a substantial but imperfect coincidence between an agent's moral obligations and her own self-interest (*ME*, bk. ii, ch. 5). Because of the interest that each person takes in her own happiness, the (imperfect) coincidence of happiness and duty assures us that it is no accident that people are fairly reliable detectors of moral properties if those properties are roughly the ones common-sense morality recognizes.

---

[18] So, unlike Singer, Schneewind, and Irwin, I do not think one can provide consistent intuitionist readings of Sidgwick's various claims.

[19] We can explain how it is that we are generally reliable only by assuming (defeasibly) that our general moral outlook is roughly right. For according to dialectical methods, the credentials of a particular belief or theory are normally assessed in the context of other beliefs that are not themselves in question. If we demand that all of these beliefs be justified at once, then according to dialectical methods, their justification can only be a matter of their mutual support. See David O. Brink, *Moral Realism and the Foundations of Ethics* (New York: Cambridge University Press, 1989), pp. 122–25.

The basic story is familiar enough.[20] Common-sense morality is concerned with, among other things, the appropriate terms for personal and social interaction and sometimes requires people to restrain their pursuit of their own aims and interests and accept a fair division of goods and resources. It recognizes duties of cooperation (including duties of promise-keeping and fair play), forbearance, and mutual aid. Each individual has an interest in the fruits of interaction conducted according to these norms. Though it might be desirable from a self-interested point of view to reap the benefits of others' compliance with norms of forbearance and cooperation without incurring the burdens of one's own, the opportunities to do this are infrequent. Noncompliance is generally detectable, and others will not be forbearing and cooperative toward agents who are known to be noncompliant. If so, compliance arguably secures greater long-term benefits than noncompliance.

Moreover, because of the generally beneficial character of cooperative and restrained behavior, together with the cognitive and affective advantages of acting from fairly coarse-grained dispositions, people will have reason to develop and act on social sentiments and other-regarding attitudes. These attitudes will also receive external support. Because each has an interest in others' cooperation and restraint, communities will tend to reinforce compliant behavior and discourage noncompliant behavior. Community pressure, therefore, will also foster the development of fairly coarse-grained compliant dispositions.

Thus, the individual and collective benefits of regulating our interactions by norms like those of common-sense morality ensure that such norms will be culturally transmitted and internalized; if such a moral capacity is adaptive, it could have been selected for by evolution. It is no accident, therefore, that people will have the moral sentiments and other-regarding attitudes prescribed by common-sense morality.[21] If so, we have a sketch of a plausible explanation of why, if morality is roughly what we think it is, it is to be expected that, at least under favorable conditions (where our judgments are not subject to excessive interference or distortion), we are fairly good detectors of moral properties.[22]

And dialectical inquiry requires no more than this; in particular, it does not require that everyone (or even anyone) be morally infallible. This is

---

[20] Protagoras offers just such a story to explain to Socrates why moral knowledge is distributed more widely than other forms of craft knowledge; see Plato's *Protagoras*, 323a, 324d–325a.

[21] Whereas some may wish to derive the content of morality from strategic egoism or evolution, I have no such reductive ambitions. My claim is that, if the moral facts are roughly what common-sense morality says they are, then strategic and evolutionary considerations help explain why these facts are ones that we reliably recognize and attach importance to.

[22] It is a defect of my discussion in *Moral Realism and the Foundations of Ethics*, ch. 5, that it omits this explanation of the reliability of considered moral judgments. Whereas that discussion aims primarily to explain why our considered moral beliefs are likely to be true, this discussion aims primarily to explain why true moral beliefs are likely to be commonly held.

important to understand, because moral disagreement may seem to threaten dialectical methods. The fact that we can explain why it is no accident that most of us accept some elementary moral requirements ensures some modest moral agreement, but is compatible with significant moral disagreement. Because dialectical methods begin from people's moral beliefs, which then affect the choice of first principles, and because these initial beliefs can differ significantly, dialectical methods may seem unable to resolve disagreements over first principles.

A satisfactory treatment of moral disagreement is not possible here, but we can outline the resources that dialectical methods possess for resolving disagreement.[23] Whereas dialectical reasoning takes people's pre-theoretical moral beliefs as input, these beliefs will be revised in the process of reaching dialectical equilibrium. Indeed, there is no guarantee that any of the beliefs with which one begins the dialectical process will be preserved unmodified. And, as Sidgwick recognizes, a proper dialectical equilibrium should be broad (see Section III above). But a broad dialectical equilibrium can be even more revisionary than a simple narrow equilibrium, provided that it is driven by enough philosophical and social theory (see Section II above). Given the dependence of many of our moral beliefs on complex empirical and philosophical issues, there is every reason to expect any broad dialectical fit to be revisionary. Because a broad dialectical fit is an intellectual aim that we can at best hope to approximate, the existence of pre-theoretical and even reflective moral disagreement is no sign that moral disagreement is in principle unresolvable. Indeed, the claim that moral disagreements are in principle unresolvable by dialectical methods is just one claim about what the results of a systematic dialectical inquiry among different interlocutors would be and enjoys no privileged a priori position in relation to its nonskeptical competitors. This means that, whereas there is in the nature of things no guarantee that disputes are resolvable in principle, this provides no reason to doubt that they are, or that dialectical methods are our route to moral knowledge.

VII. CONCLUSION

Common-sense utilitarianism invites us to find a dialectical fit between first principles and the precepts of common-sense morality. Sidgwick is instructively ambivalent about the probative value of such dialectical reasoning. On the one hand, he sees reason to deny dialectical inquiry any probative value. He recognizes the asymmetrical metaphysical dependence of particular moral truths on more general ones; this fact demonstrates the need for first principles and explains why particular moral

---

[23] A more satisfactory treatment can be found in my *Moral Realism and the Foundations of Ethics*, pp. 197–209.

beliefs must be epistemically dependent upon beliefs about first principles. Sidgwick infers that this epistemic dependence must also be asymmetrical; this is why he accepts philosophical intuitionism and concludes
that the dialectical fit of first principles with common-sense morality can
be of heuristic but not evidential value. But this reasoning conflates metaphysical and epistemic dependence; whereas particular moral truths are
asymmetrically dependent on true first principles, epistemic dependence
between first principles and particular moral beliefs can be bi-directional.
Our justification for accepting a particular judgment consists in its being
subsumed and explained by a suitable first principle, and what makes
a first principle suitable is, in part, its ability to subsume and explain
various particular judgments, including that one. This sort of dialectical
reasoning describes the way we do defend first principles, as Sidgwick
himself often recognizes. We can defend this practice by explaining the
general reliability of common-sense precepts, and we can do this in part
by appealing to Sidgwick's remarks about the general coincidence of duty
and self-interest.

Philosophy, Massachusetts Institute of Technology

ON WHY HUME'S "GENERAL POINT OF VIEW" ISN'T IDEAL—AND SHOULDN'T BE*

By Geoffrey Sayre-McCord

I. Introduction

It is tempting and not at all uncommon to find the striking—even noble—visage of an Ideal Observer staring out from the center of Hume's moral theory.[1] When Hume claims, for instance, that virtue is *"whatever mental action or quality gives to a spectator the pleasing sentiment of approbation,"* it is only natural to think that he must have in mind not just any spectator but a spectator who is fully informed and unsullied by prejudice.[2] And when Hume writes that "the true standard of taste and beauty" is set by those who exhibit "[s]trong sense, united to delicate sentiment, improved by practice, perfected by comparison, and cleared of all prejudice," he appears to describe a character no ordinary human could

---

* This paper was presented at a conference on Cultural Pluralism and Moral Knowledge at Bowling Green State University, as well as Santa Clara University's Conference on David Hume's Philosophy, the 1993 Pacific Division Meetings of the American Philosophical Association, the Research Triangle Ethics Circle, and the Nineteenth Hume Conference at the Université De Nantes, France. The audiences on each occasion proved to be both useful and agreeable, even on the many occasions when they did not agree. I have benefited considerably too from comments by and discussions with Annette Baier, Simon Blackburn, Charlotte Brown, Rachel Cohon, David Cummiskey, Richard Dean, Harry Dolan, Don Garrett, Patricia Greenspan, Paul Hurley, Roderick Long, Kurt Norlin, Gerald Postema, Elizabeth Radcliffe, and Christopher Williams.

[1] Among the many who have given in to the temptation are John Rawls in *A Theory of Justice* (Cambridge, MA: Harvard University Press, 1971), pp. 185–88; Roderick Firth in "Ethical Absolutism and the Ideal Observer," *Philosophy and Phenomenological Research*, 1952, pp. 336–41; Jonathan Harrison in *Hume's Moral Epistemology* (Oxford: Oxford University Press, 1976), p. 114; and Ronald Glossop in "The Nature of Hume's Ethics," *Philosophy and Phenomenological Research*, 1967, pp. 527–36. When Ideal Observer theories are discussed, Hume is almost always cited as an early advocate of the view.

[2] Hume, *Enquiry concerning the Principles of Morals*, p. 286. Likewise, when he holds that "everything, which gives uneasiness in human actions, upon the general survey, is call'd Vice, and whatever produces satisfaction, in the same manner, is denominated Virtue . . ." (*Treatise*, p. 499), the survey that matters, one might think, is that taken by a suitably qualified judge. See also p. 591 of Hume, *A Treatise of Human Nature*, ed. L. A. Selby-Bigge, 2d ed. with revisions and notes by P. H. Nidditch (Oxford: Oxford University Press, 1978). A number of passages from the *Enquiry* also suggest this interpretation, usually in the context of emphasizing the proper role of reason in moral judgment. See, for example, pp. 173 and 290–91 of David Hume, *Enquiries concerning Human Understanding and concerning the Principles of Morals*, ed. L. A. Selby-Bigge, 3d ed. with revisions and notes by P. H. Nidditch (Oxford: Oxford University Press, 1975). References in the body of the essay for the *Treatise* will appear parenthetically as (T.), while those for the *Enquiry concerning the Principles of Morals* will appear as (E.).

actually possess.[3] Indeed, Hume's frequent appeals to the moral sentiments of spectators, his insistence that those sentiments depend upon
taking "the general survey," and his persistent invocation of the general
point of view (and the corrections it requires), together make the temptation almost irresistible.

Moreover, the Ideal Observer interpretation has the advantage of combining nicely a Humean recognition of the importance of sentiment with
the promise of a single stable standard that could serve to adjudicate
among the heartfelt, though often conflicting, attitudes and commitments
one finds across people, times, and cultures. Fully informed, free from
prejudice, proportionately sympathetic to all humanity, the Ideal Observer might seem the perfect standard to use in measuring the adequacy
of our own moral responses.

Yet, I will argue, it is not a standard Hume advocates, and for good reason. Hume does identify and defend a standard of moral judgment—
fixed by the attitudes of one taking the general point of view—that
controls for ignorance, adjusts for the distortions of perspective, and
leaves to one side self-interest. But his standard supposes neither an
impossible omniscience nor an angelic equi-sympathetic engagement with
all of humanity. Hume's is a standard both more human in scope and
more accessible in practice than any set by an Ideal Observer. And its
very accessibility, according to Hume, is crucial to its playing the distinctive role in practical life that gives point to its introduction and adoption.
Tempting as it is to see Hume as an Ideal Observer theorist, a cure for the
temptation is found, I believe, in appreciating the place of the general
point of view in Hume's moral theory.

Significantly, Hume has two separate but, as it turns out, related ambitions for his moral theory. He attempts, first of all and most explicitly, to
give an *explanation* of morality, one that offers an account of morality's origins, an articulation of its principles, and a picture of its contribution to
both personal and social life. At the same time, though, he hopes his theory succeeds not just in explaining moral thought but also in *justifying* it,
by showing that our moral practice has a point, that it serves a purpose.
Far from alienating us, reflection on the nature of morality will, Hume
thinks, bring it closer to our hearts. In fact, he is convinced, the sense of
morals "must certainly acquire new force, when reflecting on itself, it
approves of those principles, from whence it is deriv'd, and finds nothing but what is great and good in its rise and origin."[4]

---

[3] David Hume, "Of the Standard of Taste," in his *Essays: Moral, Political, and Literary*, ed.
Eugene F. Miller (Indianapolis: LibertyClassics, 1985), p. 241. References in the body of the
essay for "Of the Standard of Taste" will appear parenthetically as ("Taste").

[4] Hume, *Treatise*, p. 619. Combining the explanatory and justificatory projects, of course,
carries significant risks. An explanation of any fairly predominant moral view will likely be
an explanation of a view many of us think is inadequate in some important way. If the theory offered is to be remotely plausible as a normative theory, the principles advanced must

The two ambitions come into play throughout Hume's moral theory. In places, they encourage him to stretch, bend, or otherwise construe the facts so as to have them support an appealing account.[5] In other places, they lead him to find attractive, when he shouldn't, an actual practice seemingly only because he is well able to explain its existence.[6] Nonetheless, and to a surprising extent, Hume combines the two ambitions admirably, coming up with plausible explanations of our practices and producing a picture of virtue, and of moral thought more generally, that does represent "her genuine and most engaging charms, and make[s] us approach her with ease, familiarity, affection."[7]

The dual ambitions work together strikingly when it comes to Hume's invocation of the general point of view. This point of view, as he would have it, sets the standard we do and should use to correct and regulate our moral judgments. By introducing it, Hume improves mightily his ability to explain why we make the moral judgments we do. At the same time, he advances compelling and underexplored reasons for the practice he describes.

I will try, in what follows, to identify and keep separate—in a way Hume does not—both the reasons Hume has for introducing the general point of view into his explanation of moral judgment and the reasons we have, according to Hume, for embracing that point of view as setting the standard for our judgments. In the process, I hope to make clear why the general point of view, as Hume conceived of it, is not and should not be an Ideal Observer's. Throughout, the contrast I draw will be between Hume's theory and a theory according to which the standard we either do or should appeal to is set by an Ideal Observer—an observer who enjoys, and responds equi-sympathetically in light of, full information about the actual effects on everyone of what is being evaluated (someone's character, an action, an institutional practice, etc.).[8]

---

give us a purchase on actual practice that allows critical evaluation of what happens to be in place. Even so, there must be some explanation of why we hold the views we do see as justified, so the explanatory and justificatory projects cannot diverge completely (at least when the views being explained are our own). And the hope is that what explains our particular moral views and our practice of forming such views might simultaneously serve as a justification in our own eyes of both the views and the practice.

Christine Korsgaard does a nice job of articulating Hume's conception of normativity as reflective endorsement in the second lecture of her 1992 Tanner Lectures, "The Sources of Normativity" (manuscript).

[5] I am thinking here, for instance, of his tendency to see human nature as extraordinarily and conveniently uniform.

[6] His account of the artificial virtues, for instance, seems to tempt him in this direction (justice's silence concerning the weak, and modesty's especially strong claim on women, come to mind here).

[7] Hume, *Enquiry*, p. 279.

[8] Thus, the idealizations involved are at least (i) the requirement of *full* knowledge, (ii) the *complete* impartiality of the responses, and (iii) the inclusion of the effects on *everyone*.

II. The Basic Framework

Famously, Hume traces the origins of morality not to reason, but to sentiment.[9] As he sees things, "the approbation of moral qualities most certainly is not derived from reason . . . but proceeds entirely from a moral taste, and from certain sentiments of pleasure or disgust, which arise upon the contemplation and view of particular qualities or characters" (T. 581). But which sentiment and why? With a collection of lovely arguments, Hume maintains that self-love is not the relevant sentiment. "Avarice, ambition, vanity, and all passions vulgarly . . . comprised under the denomination of self-love, are here excluded from our theory concerning the origin of morals," Hume writes, "not because they are too weak, but because they have not a proper direction for that purpose" (E. 271). Only a sentiment that is commonly shared, comprehensive in scope, and more or less unified in its deliverances, he maintains, can explain both why we expect others to concur in our judgments and why we judge not simply those around us but people in distant lands and ages. Only our humanity, our ability to be moved by sympathy with others, meets these requirements.[10] "One man's ambition is not another's ambition, nor will the same event or object satisfy both; but the humanity of one man is the humanity of every one, and the same object touches this passion in all human creatures" (E. 273), and this is true "however remote the person" (E. 274).

Sympathy's distinctive role becomes clear when Hume collects together first virtues and then vices, and tries "to discover the circumstances on both sides, which are common to these qualities; to observe that particular in which the estimable qualities agree on the one hand, and the blamable on the other; and thence to reach the foundation of ethics. . . ."[11] He discovers . . .

Even more, or more specific, idealizations might be imposed. Roderick Firth, for instance, characterizes the Ideal Observer as not only omniscient with respect to nonethical facts, but as omnipercipient, disinterested, dispassionate, and consistent. Others, taking a lead from Richard Brandt, might suggest that an appropriate observer must have undergone cognitive psychotherapy. See Richard Brandt, *A Theory of the Good and the Right* (Oxford: Oxford University Press, 1979), where the condition is advanced as part of an account of what sets the standard for an individual's good. The contrast I will be pressing would only be heightened by adding some or all of these other idealizations. See also Peter Railton, "Moral Realism," *Philosophical Review*, vol. 95 (1986).

[9] "Morals," he observes, "excite passions, and produce or prevent actions. Reason of itself is utterly impotent in this particular. The rules of morality, therefore, are not conclusions of our reason" (*Treatise*, p. 457). This argument is just the first in a salvo Hume fires at attempts to found morality on reason. I will not here either rehearse or endorse the whole collection.

[10] Hume's argument is set out nicely on p. 272 of the *Enquiry*.

[11] Hume, *Enquiry*, p. 174; see also pp. 173 and 312. In the *Treatise*, Hume takes on the same project, asking what "distinguishes moral good and evil, *From what principles is it derived, and whence does it arise in the human mind?*" (p. 473). Interestingly, Hume is concerned

First, as he puts it in the *Enquiry*, that virtue is *"whatever mental action or quality gives to a spectator the pleasing sentiment of approbation;* and vice the contrary" (E. 289) — or, as he puts it in the *Treatise*, that "whatever mental quality in ourselves or others gives us a satisfaction, by the survey or reflexion, is of course virtuous; as every thing of this nature, that gives uneasiness, is vicious."[12] This leads naturally to the question, "which qualities have this effect?" And he discovers, . . .

Second, that everything we count as a virtue (because we approve of it in the relevant way) falls into one of four categories: either it is useful to others, or to the possessor, or it is immediately agreeable to others, or to the possessor.[13] This, in turn, leads naturally to the question, "why do these qualities have this effect?" And he discovers, . . .

Third, that the mechanism of sympathy (or our humanity or general benevolence)[14] explains why we approve of those traits we count as virtues. We approve of the character traits we do in the way we do, Hume says, because they present "the lively idea of pleasure" (T. 580), an idea which in turn engages our approbation, regardless of our connection to the person, thanks to the workings of sympathy.[15]

Putting the three together: The virtues secure our approbation because, on the one hand, virtues are traits that are either useful or agreeable to someone or other, and, on the other hand, we are moved by sympathy to take pleasure in our idea of others' benefit without regard to their connection to us. It is our ability to be engaged by our idea of others' benefit, through the workings of sympathy, that explains why traits that are

---

primarily to establish the principles that govern our judgments of virtue, not to explain the origin of our idea of virtue. This contrasts intriguingly both with Hume's own discussion of causation and with Francis Hutcheson, who seems especially concerned to show that our idea of virtue arises from a moral sense. See Francis Hutcheson, *Inquiry into the Original of Our Ideas of Beauty and Virtue*, selections of which can be found in *Moral Philosophy from Montaigne to Kant*, vol. 2, ed. J. B. Schneewind (Cambridge, UK: Cambridge University Press, 1990).

[12] Hume, *Treatise*, pp. 574–75; the same view is advanced on pp. 296, 471, and 499, as well as on p. 261 of the *Enquiry*.

[13] Combining the first claim with the second, Hume writes:

> Every quality of the mind is denominated virtuous, which gives pleasure by the mere survey; as every quality, which produces pain, is call'd vicious. This pleasure and this pain may arise from four different sources. For we reap a pleasure from the view of a character, which is naturally fitted to be useful to others, or to the person himself, or which is agreeable to others, or to the person himself. (*Treatise*, p. 591)

[14] In a footnote in the *Enquiry*, Hume distinguishes two kinds of benevolence, general and particular. He does this in a way that, on the one hand, distinguishes both from the universal benevolence he ridicules (as nonexistent) in the *Treatise* (p. 481) and, on the other hand, treats as pretty much equivalent general benevolence, humanity, and sympathy (*Enquiry*, p. 298n.). In this essay I will treat sympathy and humanity as interchangeable. There are, I think, some subtle and important differences, but not differences that matter to the issues I am exploring here.

[15] See also, for instance, Hume, *Enquiry*, p. 267.

either useful or agreeable (to others or the possessor) secure our moral approbation and are thus denominated "virtues." The story, in mirror image, goes for vices as well.

III. Problems on Two Fronts

As Hume recognizes, and even emphasizes, this account (as it stands) can neither explain nor justify the way we actually make moral judgments. On the one hand, it hasn't the resources needed to explain the pattern our moral judgments in fact exhibit. On the other hand, it fails to identify any standard whatsoever that we might willingly embrace for criticizing the views people happen to hold.

The explanatory problems arise because our sympathetic responses vary in ways that are not reflected in our moral judgments. It is true that sympathy's effect does require abstracting away from, or at least ignoring, one's personal interest; to that extent, the account is able to model our normal discounting of our own interests. Nonetheless, sympathy remains parochial and variable in ways moral judgment is not. Hume (in both the *Treatise* and the *Enquiry*) calls attention specifically to two aspects of sympathy that seemingly make it ill-suited to explaining why we make the moral judgments we do.

First, sympathy's effect is variable according to contiguity and vividness of presentation, so that we are more engaged by a character brought nearer, either "by our acquaintance or connexion with the persons, or even by an eloquent recital of the case" (E. 230). Yet we hold that two people with the same character are equally virtuous regardless of their connection to us, even as we are more engaged by one than the other.[16] "A statesman or patriot, who serves our own country in our own time," Hume points out, "has always a more passionate regard paid to him, than one whose beneficial influence operated on distant ages or remote nations," because the latter "affects us with a less lively sympathy." Still, Hume acknowledges, "[w]e may own the merit to be equally great, though our sentiments are not raised to an equal height, in both cases" (E. 227). Similarly, "[o]ur servant, if diligent and faithful, may excite stronger sentiments of love and kindness than *Marcus Brutus*, as represented in history; but we say not upon that account, that the former character is more laudable than the latter" (T. 582).

---

[16] See Hume, *Treatise*, p. 582. As Hume emphasizes, all sentiments "whence-ever they are deriv'd, must vary according to the distance or contiguity of the objects . . . ," so the first is a problem not just for the appeal to sympathy: "if the variation of the sentiment, without a variation of the esteem, be an objection, it must have equal force against every other system, as against that of sympathy"—assuming, as Hume does, that "[t]he approbation of moral qualities most certainly is not deriv'd from reason, or any comparison of ideas" (*ibid.*, p. 581).

Second, sympathy's influence is sensitive to the actual effects of some-one's character, so that we are more engaged by a character that actually does benefit people.[17] Yet we hold that two people with the same char-acter are equally virtuous regardless of whether they actually contribute to the welfare of others, even as we are more engaged by one than the other. "Where a person is possess'd of a character, that in its natural ten-dency is beneficial to society, we esteem him virtuous, . . . even tho' par-ticular accidents prevent its operation and incapacitate him from being serviceable to his friends and country."[18] We praise equally, for instance, the character of people equally honest, despite knowing that the honesty of one actually benefits people while the honesty of the other does not. In the first case, Hume admits, when "a good disposition is attended with good fortune . . . it gives a stronger pleasure to the spectator, and is attended with a more lively sympathy. We are more affected by it; and yet," he emphasizes, "we do not say that it is more virtuous, or that we esteem it more" (T. 585).

In short, when it comes to explanation, the fickleness of sympathy (and indeed any sentiment) runs afoul of the stability of moral judgment. *If our moral judgments were simply a reflection of sympathy, they would fluctuate along the same dimensions in the same way* — but they don't.

As Hume also recognizes, when it comes to justification, the account fails to provide a picture of morality that can enlist our hearts and com-mand our allegiance. It provides no "rule of right" (E. 272) and so con-flicts straight away with our conviction that in morality not everyone's view is equally valid. And, in the face of disagreement, the theory (as it stands) allows no nonarbitrary way to distinguish "a *right* or a *wrong* taste in morals" (T. 547). It provides no good grounds for criticizing either the monkish virtues of celibacy, fasting, penance, mortification, self-denial, humility, silence, and solitude that are "everywhere rejected by men of sense" or the acts of "treachery, inhumanity, cruelty, revenge, bigotry" that do in fact (according to Hume) secure the praise of those who are admirers and followers of the Alcoran.[19]

---

[17] This is because sympathy interests us in the welfare of others and "[t]he goodness of an end can bestow a merit on such means alone as are compleat, and actually produce the end." This means that "when the cause is compleat, and a good disposition is attended with good fortune, which renders it really beneficial to society, it gives a stronger pleasure to the spectator, and is attended with a more lively sympathy" (Hume, *Treatise*, pp. 584–85; see also the footnote in Hume, *Enquiry*, p. 228).

[18] The same point is made in Hume, *Enquiry*, p. 228:

> [T]he tendencies of actions and characters, not their real accidental consequences, are alone regarded in our moral determinations or general judgements; though in our real feeling or sentiment, we cannot help paying greater regard to one whose station, joined to virtue, renders him really useful to society, than to one, who exerts the social vir-tues only in good intentions and benevolent affections.

[19] Hume, "Of the Standard of Taste," p. 229. The great uniformity in the *general* senti-ments of mankind regarding the value of virtues might seem to reduce the importance of being able to distinguish a right taste from a wrong one. However, as Hume rightly points

"It is natural," Hume recognizes, "for us to seek a *Standard of Taste*; a rule by which the various sentiments of men may be reconciled; at least a decision afforded confirming one sentiment, and condemning another" ("Taste," 229). Yet this natural desire might well seem hopeless on a sentimentalist view. After all, while the determinations of the understanding answer to and can be measured against matters of fact, the deliverances of sentiment have a reference to nothing beyond themselves, represent nothing in the object, and only mark (as Hume puts it) "a certain conformity or relation between the object and the organs or faculties of the mind." If, as Hume thinks, morality is grounded in sentiment, it seems only reasonable that "every individual ought to acquiesce in his own sentiment, without pretending to regulate those of others."[20]

Hume's single solution to these explanatory and justificatory problems lies not with rejecting sentiment's role, but with identifying the nonarbitrary way we regulate sentiment's influence. He argues both that *we do*, and that *we have good reason to*, adjust the deliverances of sympathy according to a "steady rule of right" that simultaneously explains the relative stability (and intersubjectivity) of moral judgment and serves to characterize "a just sentiment of morals" ("Taste," 229). Our moral judgments, Hume holds, are usually, and are appropriately, guided not by how we individually feel at any given time, but instead by how we all would feel were we to take up a general point of view.[21] And, it turns out, the general point of view he relies upon and advocates is not, I'll argue, one taken by an Ideal Observer.

IV. EXPLAINING OUR PRACTICE

The distinctively *moral* sentiments that call for correction come in the first place, Hume says, "only when a character is considered in general, without reference to our particular interest" (T. 472; see also 517). That is, those sentiments arise at all only if we take (what he calls) the "general survey," by leaving aside our particular interest, and allowing sympathy its influence.[22] To take the general survey, however, is not yet to adopt

---

out, once we turn to particulars, dramatic differences emerge and loom large. The almost universal consensus concerning the value of the virtues masks deep differences concerning which particular character traits constitute the specific virtues. What one person counts as bravery, another sees as foolhardiness.

[20] Hume, "Of the Standard of Taste," p. 230. This goes a bit far, I think, since in the absence of any standard there seems no particular reason to refrain from regulating the sentiments of others to the extent one can.

[21] Hume's appeals to "points of view," not just in ethics but elsewhere, suggest that he sees a point of view primarily as a way of seeing or thinking of something, and not as the occupying of a particular position in the viewing of something. See, for instance, his appeal to the idea in Hume, *Treatise*, pp. 169, 220, 356, 389, and 440. See also Hume, "Of the Standard of Taste," p. 239.

[22] Hume's particular account of (uncorrected) moral sentiments, as having a distinctive qualitative feel and being the product only of sympathy is, I believe, quite implausible. But

the general point of view. Recognizing that it is not is important to seeing how Hume is able to mark the difference between merely having
moral sentiments and having the correct ones. Moreover, simply abstracting from our particular interest does not sufficiently eliminate variation
in our view. For even as we limit our responses to those prompted by
sympathy, we find ourselves differentially affected in a way that we are
not in our moral judgments. The moral sentiments we feel as a result of
sympathy upon the general survey will vary in intensity as our perspectives change. In fact, Hume observes not only that "all sentiments of blame
or praise are variable, according to our situation of nearness or remote-
ness, with regard to the person blam'd or prais'd," but also that they are
variable "according to the present disposition of our mind" (T. 582).

To explain why it is that our judgments do not vary along with these
sentiments, Hume notes that we control for the effects of distance, vividness, and fortune, on sympathy and thus on our moral sentiments of
approbation and disapprobation, even after we have abstracted from our
self-interest. In doing this, we in effect privilege a point of view that both
holds constant the distance from, and fixes attention on, the disposition
(rather than the actual effects) of the character being judged. And we
"confine our view to that narrow circle, in which any person moves, in
order to form a judgment of his moral character. When the natural tendency of his passions leads him to be serviceable and useful within his
sphere, we approve of his character . . ." (T. 602).[23] Our moral judgments
(as opposed to our sentiments) do not fluctuate with changing perspective and differences in the actual effects of the people judged, because the
standard we rely on is insensitive to these differences.

The process, of course, sometimes fails to have a fully effective influence on what we actually feel. So when it comes to what we *say*, when
it comes to the pronouncements and admonishments we make, we also
abstract from how we happen to feel even after our attempts to correct
for distortion.[24] "The passions," Hume recognizes, "do not always fol-

---

it plays an important role in his sentimentalist theory of morality, since any such theory must
have an account of which sentiments come into play and which do not. In "A Humean Theory of Moral Judgment" (manuscript), I argue that a Humean, even if not Hume, can provide
such an account. Relying on Hume's account of the indirect passions, the suggestion there
is that a Humean can make sense of the relevant sentiments as responses-for-reasons (e.g.,
being angry-because-he-hurt-you) where the cognitive features of the reactions are not at
the start moralized, but become so as those responses are themselves approved of by a judge
properly situated.

[23] We confine our view in this way, according to Hume, in response to, and in recognition of, the limits nature has placed on the scope of human affections (Hume, *Treatise*,
p. 602, and *Enquiry*, p. 225n.). The role played here by Hume's appeal to the "narrow circle" is in other places played by an appeal to those "who have a connexion" with the person judged (Hume, *Treatise*, pp. 591 and 602). Which group comes within our view depends
on the context and character of the person judged.

[24] Hume, I should add, is extraordinarily (and uncharacteristically) careful about respecting the difference between what we feel and what we say. (See Hume, *Treatise*, pp. 582 and

low our corrections; but these corrections serve sufficiently to regulate our abstract notions, and are alone regarded, when we pronounce in general concerning the degrees of vice and virtue" (T. 585). By making this last correction and guiding our moral judgments by *what we would feel from a certain mutually accessible point of view*, we establish a stable and common ground for evaluation.

The situation is, on Hume's view, perfectly analogous to all the others where we judge of things discovered by sense—e.g., taste, smell, beauty, color, size, shape, etc.[25] In each case, we draw the distinction between how things seem and how they are, by appeal to how they would seem from a certain point of view. And we find that our senses (of taste, smell, beauty, color, size, morality) are all subject to variations not "authorized" by, nor reflected in, our judgments. So, for instance, what color something appears as having depends on the ambient lighting as well as our own condition, whereas our judgments of color do not vary in the same way, and our standard of correctness is found in how things would appear to a normal observer in daylight. "[T]he appearance of objects in day-light, to the eye of a man in health, is denominated their true and real color, even while color is allowed to be merely a phantasm of the senses" ("Taste," 234). Certainly, we cannot without changing the conditions change how the thing appears, but we can and do, in judging the color of things, "correct" the momentary appearances.

The same holds for features not commonly allowed to be merely a phantasm of the senses: what shape a coin on the table appears to have depends on the angle from which we are viewing it, yet our judgments concerning its shape do not similarly vary, and our standard of correctness is found in how the coin would look to a normal observer from straight-on and not too far away.[26] Again, we cannot without changing the conditions change how the coin appears, but we can and do, in judg-

---

603.) His point is not that people are sometimes hypocrites, but that our moral judgments, though grounded in sentiment, are not a mere reflection of how we happen to feel. His account thus allows some slip between occurrent sentiments and occurrent judgments. This distinction raises some interesting complications when it comes to interpreting Hume's arguments against the rationalists. Elizabeth Radcliffe presses these difficulties in "Hume on Motivating Sentiments and Moral Reflection" (manuscript). I try to address them in "Practical Morality and Inert Reason" (manuscript).

[25] See Hume, *Treatise*, p. 603:

> The case is here the same as in our judgments concerning external bodies. All objects seem to diminish by their distance: But tho' the appearance of objects to our senses be the original standard, by which we judge of them, yet we do not say, that they actually diminish by the distance; but correcting the appearance by reflexion, arrive at a more constant and establish'd judgment concerning them.

Hume makes the same point, with the same example, in the *Enquiry*, pp. 227–28.

[26] It is worth emphasizing that the analogy is not just with "secondary properties," but with all properties "discovered" by sense. See Simon Blackburn's discussion of the dangers of stressing an analogy between secondary properties and moral properties in interpreting Hume in "Hume on the Mezzanine Level," *Hume Studies*, vol. 14 (November 1993).

ing the shape of things, "correct" the momentary appearance to take into account the effects of perspective.

When it comes to morality, there is one important difference. Because we can change our position in the relevant way through reflection, we can come to have the appropriate sentiments without having to change our external circumstances. This allows moral reflection to affect how things appear to us and makes it (frequently) practically efficacious. Nonetheless, when reflection fails to have that effect, we can and do, in judging of people's characters, "correct" the momentary appearance to take into account the effects of perspective.

Importantly, these "corrections" are not imposed because the momentary appearances are false or inaccurate. Things do, after all, actually cause the sensations or sentiments they do, under the given circumstances. What is subject to evaluation as true or false, correct or incorrect, are the judgments we make based on these experiences. And such evaluations make sense, Hume maintains, only after a standard has been introduced and adopted.

In all these cases, we define a set of standard conditions occupied by a standard observer and then take her reactions (her sense perceptions or sentiments) as setting the standard for ours. This then gives us the resources we use to distinguish, at least in principle, between how things seem and how they are—they are as they would seem to a suitably qualified person under appropriate conditions. Who counts as qualified, and under what conditions, depends of course on what is being judged. The emergence of some particular standard will reflect both the nature of what is judged and the needs and circumstances of those doing the judging.[27]

When it comes to morality, Hume holds that virtually all of us are qualified to judge, so long as we take into account only our sympathetic responses to people's characters, control for distortions of perspective, and focus on the tendencies rather than the actual effects of the characters judged on those in the "narrow circle." In taking up that point of view, we need know neither all the actual effects of the person's character nor the usual effects on all. So while an Ideal Observer, being fully informed, and equi-sympathetic, responds to all the actual effects on all, a person taking up the general point of view leaves out of account both those who bear no connection to the person and the actual (as opposed to usual) effects on those who do bear a connection. Extra information (about the actual consequences for all affected by the person) is not only

---

[27] That we have settled, in making ordinary color judgments, on normally sighted human observers in daylight conditions, is no accident, though presumably it could have been otherwise. Were we to evolve so as to be visually sensitive to ultraviolet light, or were we to establish prevailing lighting conditions that allowed (with relative ease) a more articulate range of discriminations, we might well shift the standard we use in regulating our color judgments.

of no help, it is actively put to one side in judging the person's character.[28]

That we do in fact regulate our moral judgments according to how we would feel were we to take up the general point of view explains why those judgments do not vary directly with our occurrent sentiments. And it explains why we approve of particular people's characters without regard to their actual effect. Moreover, it allows Hume to explain how we mark a difference between appearance and reality and thus enables him to construct an account of moral *judgment* that sees those judgments as distinct from, but built upon, moral sentiment.

These all count as the explanatory advantages Hume secures by introducing the general point of view into his sentimentalist account of morality. According to Hume, though, the specific features of the general point of view answer also to the reasons we have for establishing and respecting it, and, in the process, they work to meet Hume's justificatory goals as well.

V. Justifying Our Practice

If Hume is right, if we have good reason to regulate our moral judgments according to how we would feel were we to take up the general point of view, we will be well positioned to justify our approving of the characters we do (assuming we approve of them in the way Hume says we do). At the same time, it would mean we have a *nonarbitrary* rule of right that we might properly endorse as a standard of taste in moral matters.

Of course, for anyone advancing an account like Hume's, the justification for adopting particular conditions and responses as standard cannot be that those conditions are conducive to veridical perception. In the absence of the standard, there is no sense to be given to the claim that the perceptions are veridical. There must, therefore, be some other reason(s) for adopting the particular conditions and responses as standard.

What reasons are there for adopting the general point of view Hume describes as the standard for moral judgment? At the core of Hume's answer is his conviction that adopting the general point of view solves a problem we share. The problem that threatens is nicely captured in the children's story *The Phantom Tollbooth*. Milo, the young hero of the story, comes upon a grand vista only to find himself face to foot with a small boy about his own age who is standing in midair:

---

[28] "We know, that an alteration of fortune may render the benevolent disposition entirely impotent," but this reduces not at all our regard for the benevolent person, since "we separate, as much as possible, the fortune from the disposition" in reflecting on the value of the benevolent character (Hume, *Treatise*, p. 585).

"How do you manage to stand up there?" asked Milo, for this was the subject which most interested him.

"I was about to ask you a similar question," answered the boy, "for you must be much older than you look to be standing on the ground."

"What do you mean?" Milo asked.

"Well," said the boy, "in my family everyone is born in the air, with his head at exactly the height it's going to be when he's an adult, and then we all grow toward the ground. When we're fully grown up or, as you can see, grown down, our feet finally touch. Of course, there are a few of us whose feet never reach the ground no matter how old we get, but I suppose it's the same in every family. . . . You certainly must be very old to have reached the ground already."

"Oh, no," said Milo seriously. "In my family we all start on the ground and grow up, and we never know how far until we actually get there."

"What a silly system." The boy laughed. "Then your head keeps changing its height and you always see things in a different way? Why, when you're fifteen things won't look at all the way they did when you were ten, and at twenty everything will change again."

"I suppose so," replied Milo, for he had never really thought about the matter.[29]

Hume, in contrast, has clearly thought about the matter, although his concern is as much with all the variations we might find among people as with the variations we might each face within ourselves as our perspectives change. "Besides, that we ourselves often change our situation . . . ," he writes, "we every day often meet with persons, who are in a different situation from ourselves, and who cou'd never converse with us on any reasonable terms, were we to remain constantly in that situation and point of view, which is peculiar to us."[30] Hume worries, in effect, that if we each judged of others without taking into account the effects of perspective, we would be faced constantly by the frustrations that would come of each speaking from her own point of view. As Hume sets out the problem, two distinct considerations emerge, one having to do with our ability even to communicate with one another, the other having to do with our communicating in a way that might resolve conflict.

Hume emphasizes that we need some fixed standard or other simply to be able to talk intelligibly to one another about our evaluations:

---

[29] Norton Juster, *The Phantom Tollbooth* (New York: Random House, 1961), pp. 104–5.

[30] Hume, *Treatise*, p. 603. Virtually the same sentence occurs in Hume, *Enquiry*, p. 228.

" '[T]were impossible we cou'd ever make use of language, or communi-cate our sentiments to one another, did we not correct the momentary appearances of things, and overlook our present situation" (T. 582; see also E. 228). We cannot get a public language without a shared standard of some sort.[31] So to the extent we need to communicate about our moral sentiments, we need to establish some standard that we might share.

This point about the need for a shared standard, however, holds for talk about self-interest, and pain, no less than it does for color, shape, and morality. As a result, reflecting on our need to communicate does not yet tell us what particular point of view we ought to privilege as standard, and it certainly does not justify the really quite specific general point of view which Hume thinks regulates our moral thought. Any number of standards would be sufficient to make us intelligible to each other—even one that allowed us simply to talk the language of idiosyncratic and vari-able sympathy. Such a standard would parallel, in its sensitivity to the peculiar situation of the speaker, the standard we use to make talk of self-interest intelligible to one another. And there is clearly an intelligible lan-guage of self-interest—a language we can and do use to describe the tendency of people's characters to our own benefit. Thus, the concern for intelligibility alone will not be sufficient to justify adoption of a *general* point of view that abstracts away from, or controls for, our particular sit-uations.

We need to ask: What, over and above the need to speak intelligibly to one another, would justify our adopting the particular standard set by the general point of view? Why should we abstract from our own interests and our particular situations, focus on the tendencies of a person's char-acter rather than its actual effects, and limit our view to those with whom the person has some connection? Hume's answer turns on recognizing the purposes that motivate the introduction of moral thinking in the first place.

As Hume would have it, introducing moral thought and the general point of view that goes with it, is absolutely crucial to a harmonious social

---

[31] Even to communicate concerning how things seem, we need a shared standard for distinguishing how things seem from how they are. For instance, for me to understand your report that a box looks red, I need to know what it is for something to look red. And to do this, we need to have picked out a class of things we together denominate "red" and to have privileged certain conditions as setting the standard. We can then (but only then) under-stand what it is to look red as looking the way these things do to an appropriate observer under those standard conditions. The same shared practice allows us to communicate suc-cessfully under nonstandard conditions and without knowing the particular situation we each face as long as we both can figure out how the things we do see would look under stan-dard conditions. We introduce a standard for distinguishing how things are from how they seem, and then "correct" how they seem in making judgments about how they are, in order to communicate effectively. And it is against that background that we can say that a box that is red will look brown under certain light, or that a coin that is circular will look elliptical when viewed from a certain angle.

life. Without it, he says, we would be faced constantly by those "contradictions" that come of each speaking from her own point of view. "In order, therefore, to prevent those continual *contradictions*, and arrive at a more *stable* judgment of things," Hume suggests, "we fix on some *steady* and *general* points of view; and always, in our thoughts, place ourselves in them, whatever may be our present situation."[32] Hume thinks that "[w]e are quickly oblig'd to forget our own interest in our judgments of this kind, by reason of the perpetual contradictions, we meet with in society and conversation, from persons that are not plac'd in the same situation, and have not the same interest with ourselves."[33] The right point of view, whatever it is, must be one that works to eliminate or at least mitigate effectively the continual contradictions that come from each speaking, acting, and agitating from her own point of view (as when she speaks either the language of self-interest or the language of uncorrected sympathy).

The contradictions that threaten, of course, are not propositional contradictions.[34] There is obviously no (literal) contradiction in your saying, for instance, that you like someone, and my saying that I don't, or in your denominating my ally your enemy. Still, although our sentences do not contradict, our attitudes conflict. And it is such conflict Hume is focusing on when he highlights the threat of continual contradictions that come from each living and leading her life from her own point of view.

Exactly why these conflicts in attitude are a threat, however, is unclear. Why do they raise a *problem*? We can and do, after all, live with conflicts or at least differences in attitude all the time, and we sometimes benefit from them — as when your preference for white meat complements my own for dark. But, then, there are other circumstances and contexts in

[32] Hume, *Treatise*, pp. 581–82. Hume talks of general points of view here, rather than of the general point of view, because the problem he is pointing to is not unique to morality but arises "with regard both to persons and things." In different areas, different points of view will be relied upon to resolve the "contradictions" that inevitably emerge. In any case, "[w]hen we form our judgments of persons, merely from the tendency of their characters to our own benefit, or to that of our friends, we find so many contradictions to our sentiments in society and conversation, and such an uncertainty from the incessant changes of our situation, that we seek some other standard of merit and demerit, which may not admit of so great variation" (Hume, *Treatise*, p. 583; see also pp. 228 and 272 of the *Enquiry*).

[33] Hume, *Treatise*, p. 602. Hume observes that "every particular person's pleasure and interest being different, 'tis impossible men cou'd ever agree in their sentiments and judgments, unless they chose some common point of view, from which they might survey their object, and which might cause it to appear the same to all of them" (*ibid.*, p. 591). Hume makes the same point on p. 272 of the *Enquiry*.

[34] At least not at this point. Propositional contradictions will arise from each speaking from her own point of view once a regimented moral language is introduced — for then when you say someone is virtuous and I say she is not, we will be contradicting each other. But the regimentation that makes sense of the propositional contradictions comes only with the introduction of the general point of view, so the threat of such contradictions cannot be the grounds we have for introducing the regimentation.

which the differences are patently not complementary. In these cases, depending on the strength and "direction" of the attitudes, the conflicts can be serious and unmistakably problematic. Hume's sense of what is problematic and why is found, I think, in recognizing that our approbation and disapprobation for people's characters play a distinctive and profound role not simply in how we treat them (when we have the opportunity) but also in shaping the lives we try, and try to get others, to live. Because our sentiments of approval and disapproval take within their scope not simply isolated actions, but "durable principles of the mind," they are tied quite directly and reliably to characteristics that shape in fundamental ways how people live their lives (T. 575). To the extent these sentiments prove unstable, unpredictable, and idiosyncratic, and to the extent they conflict, so too will the plans and projects we and others undertake at their prodding.

Hume's worry is basically a civilized version of Hobbes's more nightmarish vision of unregulated self-interest leading to destructive interaction.[35] The civilizing effect comes with the mollifications provided by sympathy's softening of self-interest. Yet the structure of conflict remains unless and until some method of adjudication, regulation, and coordination is put into place. It may be a kinder, gentler, conflict than Hobbes envisioned, but no less real, nor essentially different. Hobbes, of course, thought that only an absolute ruler, backed by absolute power, could eliminate the conflict he feared. Hume, in contrast, believes that a less draconian solution (to an admittedly less drastic problem) is ready to hand and is found in our ability to introduce, adopt, and pass on, a shared standard for regulating our evaluations.

To serve this purpose the standard, whatever its particular features, must not only be salient and mutually accessible, but must also somehow lead our sentiments to concur in their deliverances. Otherwise it could hardly regulate our thoughts and decisions in a way that stably coordinates choice. This means we have reason, first of all, to embrace a standard that engages our affective nature while it leaves to one side all those sentiments that are rare, or weak, or idiosyncratic in their recommendations. A number of sentiments are virtually universal and undoubtedly powerful in their influence. Ambition and avidity, for instance, both satisfy these requirements — yet each leads to strife, not conciliation, when deployed by different people. Sympathy alone holds the promise of being not only sufficiently widespread, and suitably strong, but also acceptably univocal in its conclusions.

Uncorrected sympathy, though, cannot deliver on the promise, since it varies in ways that introduce conflict. Our sympathetic responses, only a bit less than our self-interested ones, reflect our own peculiar situation

---

[35] See Thomas Hobbes, *Leviathan* (Harmondsworth: Penguin, 1968), esp. ch. 13.

and lead us to be at odds with one another.[36] This means we have reason, second of all, to embrace a standard that controls for sympathy's variations without losing sympathy's appeal. The only way to do this, Hume argues, is to introduce a mutually accessible and stable perspective, a general point of view, from which we can all evaluate the world.

It will not do to settle simply on the point of view of our sympathetic selves responding proportionately to the perceived actual effects on everyone, even though it would control for variations due to our focusing on different people. Although individually accessible, that point of view is neither sufficiently stable nor acceptably univocal in its deliverances. Our predictably variable and often conflicting perceptions will lead to a lack of concurrence. If we each left aside our own interests and focused on (what we took to be) the character's effects on everyone, we would go some way toward resolving some of our differences, but neither far enough nor as far as we might.

Controlling for the variations, and correcting the perceptions, by settling instead on the Ideal Observer's point of view, the point of view of an unbiased, equi-sympathetic person responding with full knowledge to the actual effects on everyone of some particular person's character, will not do, either. Although stable, and presumably univocal in its deliverances, that point of view is not sufficiently accessible. We have neither the psychological equipment nor the knowledge required. Our estimates of the Ideal Observer's view of the effects of someone's character will differ in exactly the way our judgments of the actual effects differ. As a result, an Ideal Observer sets an inappropriate standard, not simply because we cannot take up her position ourselves (though we cannot), but because we cannot begin to anticipate what her reactions might be. Ignorant as we all inevitably are of the actual, subtle, and long-term effects of each person's character on everyone who might be affected, even earnest attempts by all to determine how an Ideal Observer would respond would leave us without a common standard around which to coordinate our actions and evaluations. No longer each speaking from her own peculiar point of view, each would still be speaking from her own peculiar take on a point of view she could not possibly occupy. And this means an Ideal Observer cannot play the role that needs to be filled.

In order to establish a standard that is accessible, stable, and sufficiently univocal, we need a point of view that relies on information that is generally accessible to all. This is accomplished, in part, by focusing on a character's effects on those who fall within a salient and readily identifiable group: "[I]n judging of characters," Hume argues, "the only inter-

---

[36] My sympathetic engagement with my own child's welfare, for instance, may well lead me to object to your treatment of him, even as that treatment by you is prompted by your own sympathetic engagement with your child's welfare. The conflict that emerges, though it reflects our own peculiar positions, in no way depends upon either of us being moved in this instance by self-interest.

est or pleasure, which appears the same to every spectator, is that of the person himself, whose character is examin'd; or that of persons, who have a connexion with him."[37] In this way we eliminate not only the variations due to our own relative proximity to the person judged, but also those due to esoteric information about the effects (for instance) on distant lands or future people.

Even here, because people have differential access to the actual effects of a particular person's character on the "narrow circle," we need to focus on the effects the character in question would normally have on the relevant people, not on those effects it does have. Just as we correct for the distortions of perspective in order to reach a common ground, "[f]or a like reason," Hume suggests, "the tendencies of actions and characters, not their real accidental consequences, are alone regarded in our moral determinations . . ." (E. 228n.). In this way we eliminate the variations due to our having different information about the actual effects of particular people's characters.

Thus, at least according to Hume, "[t]he only point of view, in which our sentiments concur with those of others, is, when we consider the tendency of any passion to the advantage or harm of those, who have any immediate connexion or intercourse with the person possess'd of it" (T. 602–3). And because we have compelling reason to seek a common ground with our fellows, we have reason to adopt that particular point of view as setting the standard for our moral judgment. According to Hume, "reason requires such an impartial conduct," because reason informs us that we will be unable to achieve a suitable consensus in evaluation without establishing a shared standard at least for our judgments, and sentiment makes attractive the end of achieving such a consensus. Reason here plays a role as "a general calm determination of the passions, founded on some distant view or reflexion" (T. 583).

So to the question: Why should we, when evaluating a particular person, focus on the usual effects of a character like hers on those typically affected by people with such a character? — Hume answers: Because only then will we have found a standard of evaluation we can use to resolve the conflicts that would otherwise inevitably arise. And to the question: Why shouldn't we, when evaluating a particular person, adopt the point

---

[37] Hume, *Treatise*, p. 591. Which group is relevant will of course depend both on which type of character is being evaluated and on what information is mutually accessible. Hume notes, for instance, that the character traits of statesmen, given their role, must often be evaluated with an eye to the welfare of whole countries (though only their own), even as he emphasizes that the relevant group will usually be those within a "narrow circle" (Hume, *Enquiry*, p. 225n). Annette Baier suggests that the process of correction is one of selectively sympathizing either with those who are close (when we are distant) or with those who are distant (if we are close). I think, in contrast, that the object of our sympathy is supposed to be always the same group of people — "the person himself, whose character is examin'd" and those "who have a connexion with him" (Hume, *Treatise*, p. 591). See Annette Baier, *A Progress of Sentiments* (Cambridge, MA: Harvard University Press, 1991), pp. 181–82.

of view of an Ideal Observer as our standard? — Hume answers: Because adopting that standard would not resolve the conflicts.

VI. TAKING THE GENERAL POINT OF VIEW

The most detailed account Hume offers of a standard of taste occurs in the context of discussing the qualifications of a "true judge in the finer arts," not in morality. The distinctive concerns that shape aesthetic judgments (and their relative distance from practical affairs) do in various ways influence the particular features of the standard Hume describes, especially by putting a premium on (what he calls) delicacy of taste. To the extent the standards differ, the differences reflect the roles the standards are to play in social life. Nonetheless, the general point of view, as it describes a standard of taste in morals, parallels to an extraordinary degree the point of view of a qualified critic.

As Hume describes the qualifications that serve to set the standard of taste in fine arts, the first he emphasizes is that a qualified judge must possess a *delicate* taste. Such a judge must be able to discern those qualities that "are fitted by nature" to produce sentiments of beauty or deformity ("Taste," 235).

To make clear what he has in mind, Hume retells a story from *Don Quixote*. In the story, two brothers, asked to give their opinion of some wine, each compliment it, but with reservations. The first detects a small taste of leather, the second a taste of iron. Hume reports that they were ridiculed by others for their reservations until, at the bottom of the hogshead, was discovered "an old key with a leathern thong tied to it." The key confirmed their superior sensibility. Yet if the hogshead had never been emptied, and the key never discovered, their sensibility would still have been superior to that of their fellows. In aesthetics and morals as well, the general rules systematizing our (collective) taste under appropriately conducive conditions, play the role of the key, in being that to which a delicate taste is sensitive. "To produce these general rules or avowed patterns of composition, is like finding the key with the leathern thong. . . ." But even when the rules are not produced, "the different degrees of taste would still have subsisted, and the judgment of one man been preferable to that of another . . ." ("Taste," 235–36).

Although people differ naturally when it comes to their sensibilities, being a fine judge of beauty, or morals, depends upon more than a gift of nature. Practice makes a significant difference to one's ability to detect relevant features of what one is judging, as does experience in drawing comparisons between different kinds and degrees of beauty. "By comparison alone we fix the epithets of praise or blame, and learn how to assign the due degree of each" ("Taste," 238).

In addition, though, a judge, in order to be qualified, must be free from prejudice, and this entails being able to take up "a certain point of view" — that of the intended audience of the production. "A person influenced by prejudice complies not with this condition, but obstinately maintains his natural position, without placing himself in that point of view which the performance supposes" ("Taste," 239). In morals, on Hume's view, the performance is the character, and the intended audience is the person himself and those either within the "narrow circle" or who have a "connexion with him." And freedom from prejudice's influence is a matter of putting aside the concerns that reflect our natural position and focusing instead on those who bear a connection with the person judged.

Finally, a qualified judge is one who is concerned with and able to judge just how well-suited something is for serving its purpose. "Every work of art has also a certain end or purpose for which it is calculated; and is to be deemed more or less perfect, as it is more or less fitted to attain this end" ("Taste," 240). The same is true of the virtues, according to Hume, in that their value is to be judged not by their actual effects but by their tendencies, by whether they are well-suited to the serving of certain purposes. Justice, for instance, counts as a virtue because it is well-suited to solving the problems that arise in circumstances of moderate scarcity, limited benevolence, and insecure possession. Even when (mis)fortune intervenes to undermine, in particular cases, the usefulness of a just person's character, that person still earns our approbation. "Virtue in rags," Hume observes, "is still virtue; and the love, which it procures, attends a man into a dungeon or desart [sic], where the virtue can no longer be exerted in action, and is lost to all the world" (T. 584). Similarly, a person's vicious character is neither redeemed nor vindicated by its happening to have salutary effects. The value of a character turns not on whether it actually benefits the person himself or those with whom he has some connection, but on whether it would, under standard conditions, benefit them.[38]

A true judge in matters of taste, whether moral or aesthetic, is thus fairly described quite generally as one who enjoys "strong sense, united to delicate sentiment, improved by practice, perfected by comparison, and cleared of all prejudice . . ." ("Taste," 241). What is involved in having these qualities will of course vary according to what is being judged. A qualified judge of music may have no claim to a taste in food or sculpture, let alone in people. And a fine judge of character may lack the skills and experience required to evaluate art. Precisely who qualifies in any particular area is also, not surprisingly, often an issue. "Whether any particular person be endowed with good sense and a delicate imagination, free from prejudice, may often be the subject of dispute, and be liable to

---

[38] In "Hume and the Bauhaus Theory of Ethics" (manuscript), I argue that Hume's functionalist account of morality in general, and the virtues in particular, accommodates the importance of utility while setting him apart from utilitarians in a distinctive and fundamental way.

great discussion and inquiry" ("Taste," 242). While few have the qualifications, when it comes to fine art, the fact that someone has them is
often strikingly clear—those who have them "are easily to be distinguished in society by the soundness of their understanding, and the
superiority of their faculties above the rest of mankind" ("Taste," 243).
Perhaps less easy to distinguish, but also notably less rare, are the cases
when someone has the qualifications for judging in moral matters. Here
a rarefied delicacy in taste matters less than an effective ability to put
aside one's own interest and a capacity for imagining how the character
in question would normally affect the relevant group of people.

No doubt people differ in their sensitivity to the actual characters of
those they judge, and, as a result, may make mistakes. But these mistakes
of fact impugn only their judgment of the particular person, not their
judgment of the kind of character they suppose that person to have. Who
counts as a good judge of this person or that, will depend on the delicacy
of taste they show in determining the person's real character. Yet who
counts as a judge of whether one kind of trait or another is a virtue, will
be a matter of public discussion and not the special province of an elite.

No doubt, too, people differ both in their willingness, and in their ability, to put aside their own interests and imagine how the character in
question would normally affect those in the "narrow circle." But Hume
is convinced, reasonably, that most people, in most circumstances, have
the requisite abilities and also have reason to be willing to exercise them.

Hume is not, however, committed to holding that we always have reason actually to take up the general point of view, even as we have reason to use that point of view in regulating our moral responses. In some
cases, at least, remaining in one's position of partiality, say with respect
to one's family and friends or oneself, is appropriate and would itself
secure the approval of those who do occupy the general point of view.
It is no part of Hume's theory that we should always take up the general
point of view in facing the world; nor does he hold that we should always
act on those sentiments we would feel were we to take that point of view.
Nonetheless, it is central to his account that we often do, and in any case
should, act on those motives and with those sentiments that we would
approve of from the general point of view. And his argument for thinking that this point of view sets the appropriate standard relies on emphasizing the interests we each have in establishing and maintaining a
standard of moral judgment that is both stable and mutually accessible.

VII. PRESSING THE CASE FOR THE IDEAL OBSERVER

In obvious and unsurprising ways, Hume's argument for introducing
the general point of view, and for privileging a certain version of it, parallels the one he offers for introducing the rules of justice, especially in

its appeal to mutual interest.[39] The guiding idea is that, given our nature and circumstances, we each have reason to regulate our moral responses to the world by a mutually accessible and steady "rule of right" that might serve to settle the conflicts that otherwise would inevitably arise.

It is worth considering, if only briefly, two kinds of problems the resulting view faces. On the one hand, by appealing to the mutual interest of those who rely on the standard, the theory invites, and seems to countenance, an unacceptable chauvinism. On the other hand, by insisting that the standard reflect our nature and circumstances, the theory risks, and seems (in any case) unable to rule out, a repugnant relativism. In both cases, it might seem as if the general point of view (as Hume describes it) faces problems that can be adequately resolved only if we adopt instead an Ideal Observer's responses as the standard for our own. The suggestion will be that reflection on the general point of view should lead us to overthrow it in favor of the Ideal Observer's. I shall take the worries in order.

If the standard of moral judgment is motivated and limited by mutual interest, won't the result be a standard that reproduces the boundaries of those interests? Won't this kind of argument inappropriately endorse a standard that demands in the name of morality only what serves the interests of those who have adopted the standard? This seems an easy recipe for a morality that merely ratifies the power structures that are in place without proper regard for the interests and welfare of the disenfranchised.

In addressing this worry, it is important to recognize the difference between (for instance) the circumstances of justice, shaped as they are by our limited benevolence and selfish concerns, and the circumstances of morality (as we might call them), which are shaped by our sympathetic nature. While the argument for introducing the general point of view parallels that for introducing the rules of justice in its appeal to mutual interest, the interests at issue differ crucially. The rules of justice, on Hume's view, are meant to answer to our (relatively confined) self-interest, while the standard of moral judgment is meant to answer in no small part to

---

[39] See Hume, *Treatise*, pp. 477–513, and *Enquiry*, pp. 183–204, 303–11. J. L. Mackie argues that a proper appreciation of the parallels undermines Hume's distinction between the artificial and natural virtues. But I think this is a mistake. Within this account of morality, it is still possible and important to mark the difference between artificial and natural virtues in just the way Hume does—that is, by noticing the difference between those character traits that one can specify and approve of only within the context of a set of conventions (e.g., justice) and those that one can specify and approve of absent an appeal to convention (e.g., benevolence). The natural virtues naturally engage approbation in a way that artificial virtues do not, although the natural virtues no less than the artificial ones count, in the end, as virtues only because they are properly approved of within a conventional system of approbation. See J. L. Mackie, *Hume's Moral Theory* (London: Routledge & Kegan Paul, 1980), p. 123. For an account that is more sensitive than Mackie's to the sort of artifice involved in moral judgment, see Baier, *A Progress of Sentiments*.

those interests we have in the welfare of others (without regard to their relation to us) thanks to our sympathetic nature. Because we are capable of sympathy, and susceptible to its effects, we find ourselves with an interest not just in how well we do, but in what we ourselves and others do with themselves and to others. This difference brings to morality a breadth of scope and a generosity of concern not matched by, nor reflected in, the "cautious, jealous virtue of justice" (E. 184).

Nonetheless, the scope of morality will, on Hume's theory, remain bounded by the actual reach of our sympathetic responses. Exactly what that reach is, we might not be able to say, but that it falls short of engaging us equally in the welfare of all sentient beings is clear. And this, a defender of the Ideal Observer might argue, introduces an unacceptably arbitrary, blatantly chauvinistic, element into the standard Hume advocates. If, as Hume argues, we need to adopt some standard for our moral evaluations, isn't the only nonarbitrary standard the one set by an Ideal Observer who takes into account all equally without bias or myopia?

Hume never directly confronts this worry. Nevertheless, the structure of his theory recommends a response. It begins by noting that a standard is arbitrary only if it makes demands we have no reason to accept. So which standard is arbitrary, and which not, depends on what reasons we might have for adopting one or the other. We all do have good reason, Hume argues, to establish together a stable and mutually accessible standard we might appeal to in resolving our differences. The standard set by the general point of view will not, of course, successfully resolve all disagreements. Yet it will do better, Hume thinks, than any of its competitors[40] — largely because we can each, often enough, actually take up the point of view and be moved by the sentiments we then feel. To recommend instead a standard that is inaccessible, in the name of the interests of those we take no interest in, is to advance a standard that will seem arbitrary in its demands, a standard we will reasonably see no reason to adopt. Moreover, were we, for instance, completely unmoved by the plight of cows, a standard — even if accessible — that insisted on giving weight to their welfare, would be a standard that could win neither our hearts nor our allegiance.[41] What chauvinism remains will be, on

[40] Whether embracing the general point of view, and not the Ideal Observer's, as the standard really does offer the best available solution is, certainly, open to debate. The Ideal Observer's inaccessibility does not automatically settle the issue, since it is possible, at least, that each of us doing the best we can to estimate the Ideal Observer's response might in itself be enough to resolve our conflicts. Still, Hume is on reasonably solid ground, I think, since our different perceptions of the actual effects of someone's character on everyone are virtually certain to find an echo in our estimates of what the Ideal Observer would perceive.

[41] For someone already convinced of the value, say, of pleasure no matter whose, any standard for moral judgment that stops short of taking into account the pleasures and pains of all sentient beings will no doubt seem a standard we have reason to move beyond. The burden, though, falls on that person to explain the value of pleasure (or whatever). And Hume will press the issue. We are, as a matter of fact, concerned with the welfare of those

Hume's view, neither arbitrary nor surmountable. Whether it is nevertheless objectionable, is a question I shall address after raising the worries posed by the threat of relativism.

Relativism threatens in two ways. First, it seems that different people each taking up the general point of view might differ in their evaluations, either because they have different views of what the usual effects are on the "narrow circle," or because they simply differ in their affective natures.[42] This means we might be left with irreconcilable differences even at the point when people succeed in taking up the point of view that supposedly sets the standard for our judgments. Second, because human nature might have been other than it is, or our circumstances other than they are, Hume is committed to the possibility that his argument for the general point of view might instead (under those conditions) have recommended a different standard that would certify different and incompatible evaluations.

Which of the incompatible responses (in the first case) or standards (in the second case) is right? Hume apparently has no answer whatsoever — unless he allows an appeal to an Ideal Observer's responses at this point. Were we to accept the general point of view as setting the standard, what the threat of relativism shows is that a second level of conflict in evaluation could easily emerge. Those new conflicts would be resolvable, some might argue, only if we embraced the Ideal Observer as the final arbitrator.

We need not, here, rely on an Ideal Observer who responds to all the actual consequences of someone's character. Hoping to avoid the problems faced by such an inaccessible standard, we might instead appeal to an Ideal Observer who responds to character types rather than their specific instances.[43] Still, if the observer is, in responding to the various character types, supposed to respond equi-sympathetically to all affected by that type of character, the observer continues to suffer the problem of setting an inaccessible, and for that reason unacceptable, standard. We do not and cannot know, of a given character type, what its actual effects on everyone are, not least of all because, to know this, we would have to know what the actual effects are of each of its instances. Suppose, then, that the observer is instead understood as responding sympathetically

---

with whom we can sympathize, and we have reason to regulate our judgments by how we would feel from the general point of view, but what reason is there for us to care, in the absence of sympathy or some other sentiment, about those who fall beyond the pale?

[42] Or they might differ because they take as relevant different "narrow circles," though presumably this difference is fairly and easily handled within the theory as a case of the two not both succeeding in taking the general point of view.

[43] Simon Blackburn has pressed this suggestion in conversation. This would mark a significant divergence from standard Ideal Observer theories, since on those the proper standard is set by an observer *responding to all the actual consequences* of someone's character, rather than to that character type's consequences. Suppose, though, that the change is made in the name of avoiding unnecessary inaccessibility.

only to the standard effects of a character type on the "narrow circle." Such an observer might well serve as a mutually accessible and suitably stable standard. Yet *this* observer is just one occupying the general point of view that Hume recommends. And such an observer is in no interesting way Ideal, since she need possess neither extravagant epistemic powers nor a superhuman engagement with the affairs of all. Moreover, hers is a point of view that we all might, and often enough do, occupy.

In any case, we have ended up just where we started, with no reply yet to the threat of relativism. Impressed by the threat, a defender of the Ideal Observer might insist that the pressures of accessibility that bring the observer down to earth must in the end be resisted if we are to secure a single fixed standard we might use in responding to the threat. So let us turn back to that threat.

Hume does not take seriously the possibility that two people who *succeed* in taking the general point of view would differ in their responses in any significant way. Given the specific characterization of the general point of view, that possibility does not really pose a threat. It might be that one person's heart beats more warmly in the cause of virtue than another's, but as they leave aside their own interests, and control for the distortions of perspective, they will inevitably approve of the same characters to roughly the same degree. Because the conditions imposed by the general point of view both fix attention on a common object (the usual effect of a person's character on the "narrow circle") and limit the basis of our response to sympathy, to succeed in taking up that point of view is to leave aside everything that might cause a difference in response. Once we take up the general point of view, and focus on the tendency of the character in question, only our humanity comes into play, and that, Hume emphasizes, is the same in everyone.[44] As long as the distinctions are drawn in the same way, thanks to the workings of our shared capacity for sympathy, what differences there are in the strengths of the sentiments felt will not affect the judgments we make. Although one person, for instance, might feel a stronger sentiment of approbation toward benevolence than does another, they will both approve of benevolence over indifference over malice. And it is this common verdict, induced by our shared humanity when it is subject to the corrections imposed by the general point of view, that will serve as the standard for our judgments.

Hume does consider and take seriously, though, the possibility of "a creature, absolutely malicious and spiteful" who would actively disapprove of those whose characters had a tendency to the good of mankind.[45] Such a creature, because of his "inverted" sentiments and lack of

[44] "One man's ambition is not another's ambition: But the humanity of one man," Hume insists, "is the humanity of every one; and the same object touches this passion in all human creatures" (Hume, *Enquiry*, p. 273).

[45] Hume, *Enquiry*, p. 226. However, he thinks that "[a]bsolute, unprovoked, disinterested malice has never perhaps place in any human breast" (*ibid.*, p. 227). And he maintains that "none are so entirely indifferent to the interest of their fellow-creatures, as to perceive no distinctions of moral good and evil . . ." (*ibid.*, p. 225).

sympathy, would of course be unable to take up the general point of view. Yet we can imagine a group of such beings coming together and establishing for their use a standard of evaluation that reflects their malicious dispositions. It would not be the general point of view (since sympathy would not be the guiding sentiment), but it would be a point of view they might each have reason to adopt and maintain. They might even offer in its defense just the arguments Hume marshals for the general point of view. What grounds could Hume possibly have for endorsing the standard set by his general point of view as against theirs?

Hume has a straightforward answer. Which standard is better depends on whether the adoption of one rather than the other has a greater tendency to benefit those within the "narrow circle." It may be, of course, that one is better in some circumstances and another in others. Hume might then have no grounds for criticizing their adoption of the malicious standard — as long as its adoption by them, in their circumstances, does not have a tendency to hurt those "who have any immediate connexion or intercourse" with them (T. 602–3). It is conceivable, though only barely so, that in their circumstances, given their malicious nature, the standard that reflects their disposition would properly secure our approval. Their practice might, that is, be approvable from the general point of view. More likely, though, would be the discovery that their standard deserves our condemnation precisely because its adoption by them would tend to undermine the welfare of those affected. In any case, given our circumstances, and our nature, there is little question that regulating our judgments by appeal to the general point of view has a tendency to benefit us all. And it is this feature of the general point of view that makes it better than the alternatives — better than the malicious standard because its adoption has a tendency to help rather than hurt, and better than the standard set by the Ideal Observer, given our circumstances and limitations, because its adoption is more likely to help more.

Of course, our having adopted the standard set by the general point of view will not, in each and every case, prove beneficial either to the individual who relies on that standard or to others. In particular cases, we might well wish that the voice of conscience could be silenced (temporarily). And we might wish this not for selfish motives but out of regard for the welfare of those affected in the instance by scruples. Nonetheless, because the character of one who relies on the standard has a tendency to benefit both "the person himself" and "persons, who have a connexion with him" (T. 591), it will earn our approval despite our recognizing that sometimes fortune will frustrate its (usual) good effects. As Hume argues, "not only virtue must be approv'd of, but also the sense of virtue: And not only that sense, but also the principles from whence it is derived" (T. 619).

Hume can offer, in effect, the same answer to those who worry that his theory, and our practice, are objectionably chauvinistic. Here the concern is that the natural limits of our sympathy impose an unjustified boundary on the interests that are given weight in our moral reflections. Whether the boundary is unjustified turns, on Hume's view, on whether we would approve of extending it, were we to take up the general point of view. Reflection on what we would approve of from that point of view (were we to leave aside our selfish interests) might well succeed in leading us to give weight to the interests we otherwise ignore, but the shift involved will not (and indeed cannot) extend beyond the natural limits of our sympathy — for it will be sympathy itself that prompts the change. If, as Hume thinks, no standard less susceptible to the chauvinism of our sentiments could serve as well the purposes that motivate the introduction of a standard of moral judgment, then whatever chauvinism remains cannot be objectionable.

As Hume sees it, given our circumstances and nature, we have reason to regulate our moral evaluations, and to do this effectively we must recognize our limitations, leave to one side our own interests, and then appeal only to what we all can know — the tendency of characters of that kind to benefit or harm those "who have any immediate connexion or intercourse with the person possess'd of it." We must, that is, regulate our responses by how we would feel were we to take up the general point of view. Only then will we succeed in establishing a suitably stable standard *accessible to all of us*. "And tho' such interests and pleasures touch us more faintly than our own, yet being more constant and universal, they counter-ballance the latter even in practice and are alone admitted in speculation as the standard of virtue and morality" (T. 591). By adopting together this point of view as our shared standard, we will have formed "in a manner, the *party* of human-kind against vice or disorder, its common enemy" (E. 275). And that is a party we all have reason to join.

Philosophy, The University of North Carolina at Chapel Hill

EXPLAINING VALUE*

By Gilbert Harman

I am concerned with values in the descriptive rather than in the normative sense. I am interested in theories that seek to explain one or another aspect of people's moral psychology. Why do people value what they value? Why do they have other moral reactions? What accounts for their feelings, their motivations to act morally, and their opinions about obligation, duty, rights, justice, and what people ought to do?

A moral theory like (one or another version of) utilitarianism (or social-contract theory, natural-law theory, Kantianism, or whatever) may be put forward as offering the correct normative account of justice, or of the good, or of what people ought morally to do. The answers such a theory offers may be surprising in suggesting that what people ought to do is quite different from what they think they ought to do. I am not concerned with normative moral theories of this revisionary sort. Indeed, I am interested in less revisionary normative theories only to the extent that they can be reinterpreted as offering potential explanations of people's actual moral reactions.

I believe that philosophers can profitably join forces with social psychologists. To some extent, that has already happened. John Darley and Thomas Shultz and other social psychologists investigating ordinary reasoning about retributive justice "have found theoretical inspiration in philosophical analyses of morality or law" by John Austin, H. L. A. Hart, and others.[1] Philosophers have been influenced by psychological discussions of moral development by Jean Piaget, Lawrence Kohlberg, and Carol Gilligan.[2] And philosophers are among the many who have reacted to the claims of sociobiology.[3]

* The preparation of this essay was supported in part by a grant from the James S. McDonnell Foundation to Princeton University.

[1] John M. Darley and Thomas R. Shultz, "Moral Rules: Their Content and Acquisition," *Annual Review of Psychology*, vol. 41 (1990), pp. 525–56.

[2] Jean Piaget, *The Moral Judgment of the Child* (New York: Free Press, 1956); Lawrence Kohlberg, *Essays on Moral Development*, vol. 1, *The Philosophy of Moral Development: Moral Stages and the Idea of Justice* (San Francisco: Harper & Row, 1981); Carol Gilligan, *In a Different Voice: Psychological Theory and Women's Development* (Cambridge, MA: Harvard University Press, 1982). Philosophical reaction appears, for example, in John Rawls, *A Theory of Justice* (Cambridge, MA: Harvard University Press, 1971); Eva Feder Kittay and Diana T. Meyers, eds., *Women and Moral Theory* (Totowa, NJ: Rowman and Littlefield, 1987); and Owen Flanagan, *Varieties of Moral Personality* (Cambridge, MA: Harvard University Press, 1991).

[3] See, for example, the journal *Biology and Philosophy*.

I am particularly interested in how philosophical speculation might be useful for social psychology. Philosophical work is most useful, I want to suggest, both in uncovering data of a sort not often considered in social psychology and in the explanations of the data that it offers.

A good example of new data comes in philosophical discussion of the *trolley* problem. As a trolley speeds down the track, five people are spotted on the track ahead, with no way for them to get off the track in time. The brakes on the trolley fail, but it can be turned onto a side track where there is only one person. Most people believe it would be morally permissible to turn the trolley onto the side track. But in many other cases, most people think it would be seriously wrong to sacrifice one person to save five.

For example, in the *surgeon* case, five patients are dying, but can be saved by cutting up a sixth patient and distributing his organs to the others. Almost everyone believes it would *not* be morally permissible to cut up the sixth patient for this purpose. Again, most people believe that it would be morally impermissible to push a fat person onto the track in order to stop the trolley, even though this would still be sacrificing one in order to save five.

Several principles have been proposed to account for people's reactions to such cases, principles I will come back to later, including the Catholic principle of double effect, Philippa Foot's principle that negative duties are stricter than positive duties, and Judith Jarvis Thomson's deflection principle.[4]

The philosophical literature discusses at length whether these ordinary distinctions are really justified and asks what really is the right or wrong thing to do in these and other cases discussed in the literature.[5] As I have already said, I propose to ignore normative questions about what really is right or wrong in order to concentrate on finding explanations of people's reactions to these cases.

In saying that, I do not mean to rule out explanations that appeal to the actual rightness or wrongness of various courses of action, although I will not be discussing such explanations in this essay. I mean only that I am concerned with explaining people's reactions. This is what I mean by "explaining values." Explaining why something is of value is to be distinguished from explaining why people value something.[6]

---

[4] Philippa Foot, "Abortion and the Doctrine of Double Effect," in Foot, *Virtues and Vices, and Other Essays in Moral Philosophy* (Oxford: Basil Blackwell, 1978); Judith Jarvis Thomson, *Rights, Restitution, and Risk: Essays in Moral Theory*, ed. William Parent (Cambridge, MA: Harvard University Press, 1986), ch. 6, "Killing, Letting Die, and the Trolley Problem," and ch. 7, "The Trolley Problem."

[5] A good sample of this discussion is collected in John Martin Fischer and Mark Ravizza, eds., *Ethics Problems and Principles* (Fort Worth, TX: Holt, Rinehart, and Winston, 1992).

[6] There can be significant relations between these two kinds of explanation, including these: (1) Explaining why something is of value might help to explain why people value it. (2) Given an impartial-spectator theory of morality, to explain why people value something may be to explain why it is of value. (3) Certain explanations of why people value what they value may undermine the conviction that the things valued are of value.

I. METHOD

The enterprise of explaining values requires an adherence to somewhat stricter procedures than philosophers may be used to. First, it is important to indicate what data are to be explained and it is important to establish that the data really are data. Data have to be objective. The data in the trolley problem might be that certain subjects have expressed the opinion that it is morally permissible to turn the trolley. It would be relevant to ask a group of subjects for their opinions on this and other questions to see how many say that it is OK to turn the trolley but not to cut up the sixth patient. It might turn out that in a class of fifty students, forty-five thought it was OK to turn the trolley and five were unsure; forty-eight thought it was not OK to cut up the sixth patient and two were unsure. Here it is important to specify what it is that is to be explained. An explanation might be offered for all responses or, alternatively, only certain features of the responses might be accounted for.

Opinions expressed about one or another version of the trolley problem can depend on the way questions are posed, how issues have been discussed up to that point, what other opinions have been expressed, whether opinions are solicited in private or in public, etc. So, reports of data should make explicit exactly how the data have been obtained, what questions were asked, and what other things were told to subjects.

Second, when an explanation for certain data is proposed, the explanation should be as clear and explicit as possible. Of course, an explanation may be more or less ambitious. A relatively unambitious explanation might be of the sort that merely seeks to bring the data under a generalization like "Subjects will almost always think that it is not permissible to sacrifice one person to save five others, unless the five are saved by deflecting a threat to them onto a smaller number of people." A more ambitious explanation would try to say something about the processes that lead subjects to react as they do—saying, for example, such things as: "Subjects tend to look at situations from the point of view of the people involved. . . ." In that case, it is important to indicate how exactly the process is envisioned.

Third, it is necessary to see how the suggested explanation fits in with other plausible accounts, including general theories in psychology, sociology, economics, and biology. Is the proposed explanation plausible in the light of other views we have about people?

Finally, it is necessary to consider competing explanations to determine whether either the given explanation or one of its competitors has more going for it than the others. If not, there is no reason to accept one rather than another explanation.

Not all explanations compete. Some help to fill out others. An explanation of Jack's death as due to poisoning need not compete with an explanation of his death as due to lack of oxygen getting to the brain, if that's part of the way the poisoning might work. A sociobiological expla-

nation of certain moral attitudes may fit together with a more psychological explanation in terms of sympathy, if the sociobiological explanation
allows for the possibility that natural selection has brought about the
desired moral attitudes by encouraging sympathy.

II. Hume on Chastity and Sexual Promiscuity

In order to bring out some of the issues involved in explaining values,
consider Hume's account of the different attitudes taken toward chastity
and promiscuity in men and in women.[7] Hume observes that it is normally thought to be worse for a woman to be sexually promiscuous than
it is for a man to be sexually promiscuous. His explanation of the difference appeals to the fact that women rather than men bear children.

Hume's explanation is roughly this. Children need to be cared for and
people are more likely to care for children toward whom they feel love
and affection. People are more likely to feel love and affection for children
they believe to be their own than for other children. Now, because
women rather than men bear children, it is more certain who the mother
of a child is than who the father is. A key point is that a husband will
tend to believe that his wife's children are his children to the extent that
he believes his wife is chaste and not promiscuous. Therefore, permitting
promiscuity in women would have bad consequences that would not be
consequences of promiscuity in men. Hume says that this difference
explains why we have different attitudes toward chastity and promiscuity in men and women.

This explanation may seem straightforward enough and even plausible. But how does it fit in with our tests?

First, what exactly are the data to be explained? Do people accept the
explicit general view that it is worse for women to be promiscuous than
for men? We can test this by asking subjects whether they accept the general proposition. I think we will find that few people hold that general
view in America today. I am confident that there have been some changes
in attitude since Hume's day (especially since 1960). Whether this is one,
I am not sure. Maybe in Hume's time people had the general view. But
I don't think many do now.

Nevertheless, there are probably different reactions to men and women
believed to be promiscuous. We might investigate what subjects say in
particular cases about the character of individuals described as promiscuous. Even if subjects will not accept as a general claim that it shows worse
character in a woman to be promiscuous than it does in a man, they may
very well make more severe particular judgments about women they
believe to be promiscuous than about men they believe to be promiscuous.

---

[7] David Hume, *Treatise of Human Nature*, Book 3, part 2, section 12, "Of Chastity and
Modesty."

In other words, the data may show that subjects' judgments about people are affected by whether they take the people to be promiscuous, that subjects tend to rank promiscuous people lower than other people, and that subjects tend to give more negative weight to promiscuity in women than to promiscuity in men.

I do not know whether anyone has actually done relevant experiments, but I believe that data of the suggested sort will be obtained. Suppose we had such data. Let us compare Hume's explanation of that data with a competing explanation in terms of power relations. The idea behind the competing explanation is that men are taken to be in charge, so men are taken to have the right to act as they please; women are supposed to find men to serve. For a woman to act promiscuously is for her to act as if she had the rights of a man, and such behavior is therefore treated as a kind of sedition.

Hume's explanation involves two claims: (1) that a woman's having a reputation for promiscuity tends to have worse consequences than a man's having such a reputation, and (2) that this difference explains why we have different attitudes toward promiscuity in men and women. But how exactly does the explanation work? Is the idea that the condemnation of a particular woman's promiscuity is based on the inference that her promiscuity puts her children at risk? If so, Hume's hypothesis would predict that subjects will condemn promiscuity in women only where there is the possibility that there will be children, and will therefore not condemn promiscuity in women who are past the childbearing age, whereas the power-relations hypothesis predicts that this will not matter, since it is sedition whether or not children are involved. But Hume himself says that in fact people generally continue to condemn promiscuity in women past the childbearing age more than they condemn promiscuity in men of the same age. So, it may seem that Hume's own data favor a competing theory over his own.

But Hume does not intend his explanation to be such an intellectualistic explanation. That is, he is not proposing that different reactions to promiscuity in men and women derive from explicit conscious reasoning about the effects such promiscuity may have on children.

Hume's actual explanation goes more like this (in my own words): In some cases, a man refuses to take care of children because of his doubts as to whether he is the father, doubts that arise because of promiscuity on the part of the mother. Consequently, the children suffer and observers come to blame the mother for the child's suffering. Psychological generalization occurs, leading observers to condemn promiscuity in other women. Other people go along with this condemnation without necessarily understanding its basis.

On the other hand, there are no cases in which a woman refuses to take care of children because she doubts whether she is the mother because of promiscuity on the part of the father! So, men do not get blamed in the way that women do.

Why do observers blame the woman rather than the man with whom she was involved? Because normally only she is identifiable as one of the people responsible for the birth of the child unwanted by her husband. Not knowing who the actual father of the child is, observers are not able to blame any particular identifiable man.

This explanation appeals to certain psychological principles. One is that, if something happens that is bad for someone and an action of an identifiable person can be seen to be responsible for the badness, then that can lead an observer to think badly of the person responsible. Second, if an observer thinks badly of a person because of something the person did, that can lead the observer to think badly of others who do similar things. (This leaves unexplained what counts as doing "similar things"; that is, it leaves unexplained why the application of the generalization is limited in this case to other women rather than people in general.) Third, there can be a herd effect. If some people condemn behavior of a certain sort, other people are likely to think badly of it also.

Here then is a brief development of Hume's explanation. A similar development is needed for the power-relations hypothesis, but I will not try to work out the details. It remains to be seen which hypothesis looks best, all things considered.

The two hypotheses do seem to make different predictions for a situation in which power relations are reversed between men and women, so that women are socially and financially dominant over men. The power-relations hypothesis predicts that in such a situation it will be worse for a man to be thought promiscuous than for a woman to be thought promiscuous, whereas Hume's more biological explanation predicts the reverse. I do not know whether there is evidence that favors one or the other of these predictions.

Of course, it is possible that both factors play a role in explaining current attitudes. They might reinforce each other. It is even possible that Hume's more biological explanation somehow plays a role in the explanation of male dominance.

We have been considering how Hume tries to explain a very specific and particular aspect of ordinary moral views. Let us now consider an attempt to explain a much larger part of ordinary morality.

III. UTILITARIANISM AND SYMPATHETIC OBSERVERS

Utilitarianism holds that certain moral decisions rest entirely on the utility (or expected utility) of one or another option, where the utility of an option might be measured by the total net happiness that would result from that option, that is, by the amount of happiness the option would lead to, minus the amount of unhappiness that it would lead to.[8]

---

[8] Expected utility is measured by the sum of the utility of each potential consequence of an option multiplied by the probability that the option will lead to that consequence. I will suppress further mention of expected utility.

Versions of utilitarianism are usually discussed as normative views. I want to consider related explanatory hypotheses. For example, there is the somewhat implausible intellectualistic claim that people normally reach moral decisions by explicitly calculating the amount of utility that various options would involve in order to favor the option with maximum utility. A more plausible explanatory hypothesis would follow Hume's lead in his discussion of chastity and promiscuity, hypothesizing that people's moral reactions are sensitive to the extent to which pleasure is produced and pain is avoided, but allowing also for the influence of psychological generalization, the association of ideas, and the influence of custom.

Why might someone be sensitive to utility? Hume appeals to what he calls the "sympathy" that he thinks an observer will feel when considering people who might be affected by the options being considered. For Hume, sympathy is like the sympathetic vibration in a piano string when a note of similar frequency is sounding. When an observer becomes aware of another person's pleasure or pain, the observer tends to vibrate sympathetically, feeling pleasure at the other's pleasure and pain at the other's pain. According to Hume, the mere awareness of another's pain or pleasure is enough to set us vibrating in a similar way.

Hume offers an impartial-sympathetic-spectator account of moral judgments. He hypothesizes that such judgments purport to represent the reactions you have when you view matters impartially. The reactions you have when you adopt an impartial point of view derive from the sympathy you feel with people affected by a given option. In Hume's view, these reactions have a strong utilitarian component: you are happy with options that make others happy and diminish their unhappiness, and you are unhappy with options that do the opposite. But, as I have already indicated, Hume thinks that other factors will affect these reactions also: various associations, psychological generalization, habit, and custom.[9]

Adam Smith, who also accepts an impartial-sympathetic-spectator account of moral judgments, rejects Hume's account of sympathy. Smith observes that you might know very well that someone I'll call J is in pain, yet fail to sympathize with J if J's reaction is out of proportion to his or her injury. Hume cannot easily account for this aspect of sympathy, nor for the fact that the sympathy of others makes a sufferer feel better. Suppose J is unhappy and a spectator I'll call K, aware of J's unhappiness, vibrates sympathetically and so unhappily. If perception of K's sympathetic unhappiness leads J to vibrate sympathetically with K, the result should be even more unhappy vibrations. But in fact K's sympathy can make J feel better, contrary to what Hume's theory predicts.

In Smith's view, feeling sympathy toward someone else is not just sympathetically vibrating with that person's experience. It involves a

---

[9] Hume, *Treatise of Human Nature*, Book 2, part 1, section 11, "Of the Law of Fame," and part 2, section 7, "Of Compassion." See also Hume, *An Enquiry Concerning the Principles of Morals*, section 5, "Why Utility Pleases."

judgment of the appropriateness of the way the other person is reacting to his or her circumstances. To be sympathetic is to judge that the other person's reaction is appropriate. People want sympathy because they want approval.

According to Smith, observers judge appropriateness by considering how they would react in a similar situation. The observer K imagines what it would be like to be in J's position and how he or she would react. If K envisions reacting as J does, K is sympathetic. If J is reacting more extremely than K envisions reacting, K will not be sympathetic and will disapprove of J.

Observers favor muted reactions. An imagined injury, for example, does not hurt as much as a real injury. Wanting sympathy, agents are motivated toward muted reactions. So, Smith's impartial-spectator theory tends more toward stoicism than utilitarianism.[10]

Both Hume and Smith stress the importance of custom and convention in moral thinking. For Hume, there is a utilitarian element to this importance, since it is often useful to have customs and conventions regarding exactly what the rules of property are or what the rules of succession are. For Smith, customs are more directly connected to moral judgment. Given a customary way of acting, people will sympathize with behavior that fits in with that way of acting, because, at least in the first instance, people sympathize with behavior only when they imagine that they would behave in the same way in the same circumstances. If there is a custom, that is the way most people behave, so it is the way most people imagine themselves behaving, so it is the standard by which others are judged.

IV. MORAL DEVELOPMENT

Adam Smith offers an account of moral development that in some ways is quite like Freud's.[11] It goes something like this: How others react to what you do affects you. So you have an interest in anticipating how others will react to you. This requires trying to imagine how others see you. You will eventually acquire a habit of imagining this. This habit of viewing yourself from the viewpoint of others amounts to looking at your situation from a more impartial or moral perspective. Having such a habit is like having an internal critic. Your internal critic tends to get idealized. Your actions become influenced by a desire to please the internalized critic. (For a contemporary example, compare the way in which athletes

---

[10] Adam Smith, *The Theory of Moral Sentiments*, part 1, section 1, "Of the Sense of Propriety." I discuss Smith's view in more detail in Gilbert Harman, "Moral Agent and Impartial Spectator," The Lindley Lecture at the University of Kansas (1986), Lawrence, Kansas.

[11] Smith, *Theory of Moral Sentiments*, part 3, ch. 1. Smith's internal critic is Freud's superego. See Sigmund Freud, *Civilization and Its Discontents*, trans. Jean Riviere (New York: J. Cape & H. Smith, 1930), chs. 8 and 9.

talk to themselves in developing an internalized coach.) As a result you become capable of guilt and you acquire the ability to make moral judgments.

Such an account of moral development might explain those elements of morality that are explainable by an impartial-spectator theory. It might also help to explain aspects of moral motivation. According to Smith, moral motivation begins with a desire to avoid the displeasure of others. It becomes a desire to avoid the displeasure of your internalized critic. Of course, you are that critic, so it becomes a desire to avoid your own displeasure when you view your actions from a moral or impartial point of view.

In Smith's theory, therefore, viewing things from an impartial standpoint has two aspects. It provides a way of finding out what is right, fair, just, etc. It also is a way of acquiring moral motivation to do what is right and promote what is fair and just.

There are other accounts of moral development. Piaget hypothesized general stages of cognitive development, including moral development; Kohlberg and Gilligan have made proposals within this framework; and there has been considerable philosophical interest in these ideas.[12] However, psychology seems mostly to reject this sort of approach nowadays. The hypothesis of unified cognitive stages has not stood up well to experimental testing.[13]

Darley and Shultz[14] point out that the principles followed when a child thinks about a situation morally may not be the same as the principles expressed when the child defends one or another judgment. The principles the child actually uses in his own reasoning may not be easily accessible to him. The approach pursued by Piaget, Kohlberg, and Gilligan looks at the principles used to rationalize or defend decisions. But when other investigators have studied the principles children actually follow, they find children using fairly sophisticated moral reasoning at relatively young ages.

Darley and Shultz also point out that since Kohlberg discusses fairly complex situations, his results may have little to do with children's moral reasoning and more to do with their ability to report on the reasoning they do.

"Social constructionist" theories of learning are concerned with how children learn to respond to challenges by adults and peers. There is current research, for example, about the extent to which individual differ-

---

[12] For a sympathetic account of Piaget's theory and later developments, see James R. Rest, "Morality," in *Handbook of Child Psychology*, 4th ed., vol. 3, ed. Paul H. Mussen (New York: Wiley, 1983), pp. 556–629.

[13] Susan Carey, "Cognitive Development," in Daniel N. Osherson and Edward E. Smith, eds., *Thinking: An Invitation to Cognitive Science, Volume 3* (Cambridge, MA: MIT, 1990), pp. 146–72.

[14] Darley and Schultz, "Moral Rules."

ences are traceable to differences in parents' moral rules. Darley and Shultz cite the following example: people differ in "how they integrate the intent of a harm-doer with the degree of harm caused to arrive at a punishment," and "in a majority of cases children's integration schemes matched those of their mothers." [15]

V. Sociobiology

Moral sociobiology appeals to natural selection to explain aspects of morality. Natural selection is possible when three conditions are met: (1) characteristics have to be heritable; (2) differences in characteristics have to make a difference to reproduction; and (3) there has to be some random variation in characteristics despite heritability.

Parents' concern to take care of their children could have a source in natural selection. Such concern is likely to make a difference in whether children will survive to be able to have their own children and thus in whether parents' genes will be transmitted to later generations. Children whose parents want to take care of them are more likely to survive than children whose parents do not want to take care of them. If there is some random variation in parental concern of this sort, and if it is heritable, then natural selection will tend to favor the existence of people who inherit concern for their children over other people who do not. Siblings' concern for each other might be similarly based, since there is the same genetic connection between siblings as between parent and child. Any particular gene is acquired either from father or mother (barring mutation). Thus, there is something like a 50 percent connection between mother and child, and the same 50 percent connection between two siblings. [16]

Exactly how this works depends on exactly what sort of thing is heritable. There might be an inborn tendency to be more altruistic toward others the more they resembled oneself. Or people might inherit a disposition to be altruistic toward others unless there was some reason to think that the others would not reciprocate. [17]

Other aspects of morality possibly explained via sociobiology might include incest prohibitions, a willingness to abide by rules, and even a sense of justice.

How are such potential explanations to be evaluated? First, we need to be sure about the data. Second, we need to have a coherent explanation and we have to make sure we understand just what the explanation involves. Third, we need to consider what competing explanations there

[15] *Ibid.*, p. 544.

[16] W. D. Hamilton, "The Genetic Evolution of Social Behavior," *Journal of Theoretical Biology*, vol. 7 (1964), pp. 1–16.

[17] R. L. Trivers, "The Evolution of Reciprocal Altruism," *Quarterly Review of Biology*, vol. 46 (1971), pp. 35–57.

might be of the data. Fourth, we need to try to assess whether any of the competing explanations seems sufficiently better than the others to be acceptable. This may involve getting more data.

Consider the following (presumed) data about altruism: (1) Mothers have special concern for their children that leads them to sacrifice their own interests for those of the children. (2) Fathers do too, although perhaps not to the same extent. (3) People seem more concerned in general for members of their family than for others. (4) More generally, people seem more concerned for their friends and acquaintances than for others — and similarly for people from one's own school, or country.

A sociobiological explanation might appeal to a mixture of kin selection and reciprocal altruism. This explanation assumes for example (a) that whether a mother is specially concerned for her child has a biological basis (and similarly for other altruistic concerns); (b) that this is a heritable feature; and (c) that it arose in a context where it was adaptive.

There are various competing hypotheses: (1) Altruism arises from conditioning.[18] Unhappiness leads a child to cry. Classical conditioning leads the child to associate the sound of crying with being unhappy. So, in particular, hearing other children cry makes the child unhappy, so he or she is motivated to do things that will stop others from crying. (2) There is a straightforward egoistic advantage to reciprocal altruism. Tit for tat is an excellent strategy in repeated Prisoner's Dilemmas.[19] This is something children can learn. (3) One can have selfish reasons to be concerned that other people's lives go well, if the other people are potential benefactors. Such concern develops over a period of time into direct concern for others, just as a miser tends to come to love money for its own sake. (4) There is random variation with respect to altruism: some people have more of it, others have less. The advantages and disadvantages tend to cancel each other out.

At the moment, none of these explanations is clearly preferable to the others.

VI. Posner on Wealth Maximization

Where utilitarianism attempts to account for aspects of our moral judgments as resting on considerations of general happiness and unhappiness, Richard Posner puts forward the hypothesis that many aspects of our moral and legal views reflect judgments about whether options will increase or decrease society's net wealth.[20]

---

[18] Richard B. Brandt, "The Psychology of Benevolence and Its Implications for Philosophy," *Journal of Philosophy*, vol. 73 (1976).

[19] Robert Axelrod, *The Evolution of Cooperation* (New York: Basic Books, 1984).

[20] Richard A. Posner, *The Economics of Justice* (Cambridge, MA: Harvard University Press, 1981), pp. 60–115.

Wealth is measured economically; it is connected with market price, although it is not to be crudely identified with market price. The value of something, in Posner's account, is determined by the price for which the owner would be willing to sell it, apart from bargaining considerations, and supposing that the owner really is the rightful owner.

Suppose that A sells something to B. Then both A and B will normally gain in wealth. A values the money received more than the object sold; B values the object received more than the money given up. The net wealth of A and B increases by the difference between the minimum for which A was willing to sell the object and the higher minimum for which B is now willing to sell it.

Posner argues that the goal of maximizing wealth gives a better account of our judgments of social practices than the goal of maximizing happiness. In particular, it gives a better account of our views about the sort of right that amounts to a veto power. For example, if A owns something, then A has a right against other people using it.

Here is a sketch of Posner's analysis.

1. Suppose A wants to engage in an activity that B does not want A to engage in. Suppose B has veto power. And suppose that transaction costs between A and B are insignificant. If the activity is worth enough to A, A can reach a deal with B and pay B to allow A to engage in that activity.

2. Alternatively, if nothing prevents A from proceeding, and it is worth a lot to B not to have A proceed, B can pay A not to proceed.

So, whether or not B gets a veto power, the more valuable outcome will still ensue, if transaction costs can be ignored. Posner argues that the only reason to assign veto power or rights one way rather than another has to do with the costs of transactions (a kind of friction). Initial rights should be assigned to the party who cares more by this test, i.e., the one that would otherwise pay to get his or her way.

Theft is ruled out. Since a thief T is not normally willing to buy what T steals, T acquires something that is worth less to T than it is to the owner. Theft diminishes wealth, even when it may maximize utility! Indeed, Posner argues that the usual Calvinist virtues (keeping promises, telling the truth, etc.) are supported by the wealth-maximization principle, because they facilitate transactions.

A serious study of Posner's hypothesis must consider the standard issues: (1) What are the data? Are we sure about them? (2) How does the explanation go in detail? How does it fit in with psychology, biology, and what is known about social evolution? (3) What competing explanations are there? (Utilitarianism is one, of course.) (4) How do these competing explanations compare, and is any sufficiently better than the others that it can be believed?

With respect to (4), Posner argues that standard worries about utilitarianism are not problems for his hypothesis. (a) *Utility monsters* are people who get so much utility from resources that utilitarianism implies that all resources should go to them.[21] Wealth maximization has no such implication. (b) Utilitarianism implies that the happiness of *animals* should be counted as much as the happiness of people. Wealth maximization does not imply this. (c) Utilitarianism has a problem with population size. Classical utilitarianism implies that the population should be increased to the point at which any further increase fails to add to the total happiness. If instead we are to maximize average utility, then utilitarianism seems to imply we should kill off (or allow to die) people whose happiness is sufficiently below average that their existence drags the average down. Again, wealth maximization has neither implication.

With respect to (2) — how does the explanation fit in with other things we believe? — Ronald Dworkin objects that "it is unclear *why* social wealth is a worthy goal."[22] Posner agrees that wealth maximization is not a basic value but gives the following hypothetical case in reply. Suppose we discover the following pattern in the decisions of courts of appeal in the United States: the number of cases that are reversed is approximately equal to the square of the number of cases that are affirmed during any sufficiently long time period (e.g., one year or more). This would be an interesting result with real predictive and in some sense explanatory value, even though we did not know why the pattern held. Similarly, when we find that common-law decisions in courts fall under the pattern suggested by wealth maximization, that is an interesting result with real explanatory power, even if we do not have a deeper account of this pattern.

VII. Double Effect

Posner's proposal strikes many people as bizarre, because they have trouble understanding how wealth maximization could be a relevant principle. Here utilitarianism would seem to have an edge, because utilitarianism makes sense if explained, for example, by appeal to Humean sympathy.

But utilitarianism has its problems. In addition to the difficulties Posner mentions, utilitarianism notoriously has trouble accounting for ordinary judgments about the surgeon case in a way that is also compatible with ordinary judgments about the trolley case, and Posner's principle of wealth maximization would seem to have the same trouble. Since sacrificing one to save five would normally maximize both expected utility and social wealth, both hypotheses would seem to treat the surgeon and trolley cases in the same way, which conflicts with the judgments most people make about these cases.

---

[21] Robert Nozick, *Anarchy, State, and Utopia* (New York: Basic Books, 1974), p. 41.

[22] Ronald M. Dworkin, "Is Wealth a Value?" in Dworkin, *A Matter of Principle* (Cambridge, MA: Harvard University Press, 1985), p. 240.

Principles have been proposed to account for the different ways people think about these cases, principles like double effect, the relative strictness of negative as compared with positive duties, and Thomson's deflection principle. It is interesting that these principles are often defended in the way in which Posner defends wealth maximization, by indicating how the principles fit cases and without any attempt to explain why ordinary judgments might be sensitive to such principles.

According to the principle of double effect, while it is an objection to a proposed course of action that it will harm someone, the objection is considerably more weighty if the harm is intended, either as one's aim or as a means to achieving one's end, than if the harm is merely foreseen as a side effect of one's action. The difference between the surgeon case and the trolley case is that the harm to the patient, whose organs are to be distributed to the other five, is an intended means of saving those five, whereas the harm to the person on the side track that results from switching the trolley is not a means of saving the five on the main track but merely a side effect of action taken to save them. This proposed explanation of the difference between these cases is like Posner's; it brings the cases under a generalization without indicating why that generalization holds.

Various hypotheses are possible as to why double effect is as successful as it seems to be in accounting for cases. One clearly false hypothesis would be that the principle of double effect is consciously adopted by people and used in reaching moral conclusions. That hypothesis is ruled out by the fact that few people are aware of the principle and those who are aware of the principle dispute whether the principle is correct and what its correct formulation might be.

A weaker hypothesis is that the principle is tacitly accepted in something like the way in which, say, principles of grammar are tacitly accepted, or the principles by which one does simple arithmetic.[23] These principles might represent what is often called "procedural knowledge" rather than "declarative knowledge." The hypothesis would raise the question why one has such tacit principles. They *might* somehow be innate, in which case we might turn to sociobiology for an explanation. They might be learned, in which case we might turn to sociology and the theory of convention. Or there might be some other explanation of the sort Hume appeals to in his hypothesis concerning attitudes about chastity and promiscuity.

Similar possibilities arise for Posner's hypothesis. It is clear that people do not consciously reach moral conclusions using Posner's principle

---

[23] Noam Chomsky, *Language and Problems of Knowledge: The Managua Lectures* (Cambridge, MA: MIT, 1988); Kurt Van Lehn, "Problem Solving and Cognitive Skill Acquisition," in Michael Posner, ed., *Foundations of Cognitive Science* (Cambridge, MA: MIT, 1989), pp. 526–79.

of wealth maximization, so if the people accept the principle, they do so tacitly. Questions arise about how they come to accept it. There might be a Humean type of explanation. For example, when something happens that decreases wealth, people may notice and disapprove of that event and, if this sort of thing happens enough, their disapproval could generalize to other events of a similar sort.

VIII. Positive and Negative Duties

Foot rejects the double-effect hypothesis in favor of a distinction between positive duties, such as the duty to help other people, and negative duties, such as the duty not to harm other people. Foot's hypothesis is that we take negative duties to be stricter than positive duties. If the surgeon were to distribute the organs of one person to five others, he or she would violate a negative duty not to harm the one person in order to uphold a positive duty to help the other five, and the relative strength of the negative duty rules this out. On the other hand, the trolley driver would violate a negative duty not to harm people, no matter what he or she does, so in his case the trolley driver is allowed to minimize the damage. (We will not be concerned with further questions about how much stricter negative duties are supposed to be than positive duties. We will not consider, for example, whether in this or any other view the surgeon could cut up one person to save *millions* of other people.)

Foot's hypothesis and double effect make different predictions concerning certain cases. Foot considers a surgeon who can save five patients by manufacturing a special medicine using a machine that produces fumes that will kill a sixth patient in the room next door, where neither the machine nor the sixth patient can be moved. Double effect would not keep the surgeon from using the machine, since the harm to the sixth patient is not part of the surgeon's means of saving the other five patients but is merely a side effect. On the other hand, Foot's hypothesis implies that the surgeon cannot use the machine to save the five, because that would be a case of violating the negative duty not to harm people simply in order to avoid violating the positive duty to save people. In other words, Foot's hypothesis takes the serum-machine case to be like the original surgeon case, whereas double effect takes the serum-machine case to be like the original trolley case.

Remember that we are interpreting these hypotheses as offering explanations of people's ordinary moral judgments. Controlled experiments are needed to determine how people actually react to the serum-machine case. My own preliminary investigations of student reactions in classes suggests that most people do react as Foot's hypothesis predicts rather than as double effect predicts. (But I find that student judgments about cases do not always coincide with published claims about the cases.)

Again this leaves open the question why there should be this difference in strength. Is it that people consciously believe that negative duties are stronger than positive duties? That seems wrong. Students in my classes do not seem to have had a view about this before the issue explicitly comes up. In any event, it remains unclear what it is about the duties involved that makes people attach more weight to negative duties (if indeed they do).

IX. Sociological Explanations of Aspects of Morality

Some aspects of morality are conventional — for example, what counts as a binding agreement, what the detailed principles of property are, etc.

Different sorts of explanation are possible for conventional aspects of morality. For example, specific historical events may be involved. Or something about the "logic" of social interaction may play a role — or class conflict, etc.

Even things that are not conventional (because they are true of all moralities) might receive a sociological explanation of this sort. A sociological explanation appeals to certain general sociological principles, principles about how groups develop, function, and evolve. Marxist explanations might be of this sort. (However, I do not know any good Marxist explanations.)

Sociological explanations tend to have a logic like natural selection. They do not require that people are acting in concert with the explicit goal of reaching a particular result. Many economic explanations are of this sort — for example, explanations of why there are lines at gas stations during some oil shortages but not others, depending on whether price controls are in place.

Many sociobiological explanations have sociological competitors. For example, the facts to be explained by kin selection might alternatively be explained by selection for better social conventions, if groups in which parents take care of their young have done better than other groups in the struggle for social survival. Sociological selection does not yield a biological bias toward relatives, only a conventional bias. (And situations may change. Groups may emerge that do better by having children brought up in other ways.)

It is unclear what sort of evidence might be relevant to deciding between biological and social explanations. It is also unclear that one or the other explanation is preferable on grounds of parsimony.

I have elsewhere suggested a possible sociological explanation for the pattern that Foot claims to find, namely, that normally killing is considered worse than letting someone die, that the negative duty of not harming others is normally treated as considerably stronger than the positive duty of helping others. My hypothesis is that morality is a compromise between rich and poor. Everyone benefits from the negative prohibition against harm, but the poor are the main beneficiaries of any general positive requirement to help others. So, we expect a strong negative prohibition against harm and a weaker positive requirement to help those in need. An explanation of this sort relies on something like Hume's account of implicit convention: people adjust their behavior to conform to the behavior of others; there is pressure to conform; things work out better for each person involved if he or she conforms.[24]

What explanations compete with the sociological account? Is there a competing sociobiological explanation? There is at least one: this is random drift! The sociological explanation is a "better explanation" in some sense. It says the distinction is "no accident." But sometimes it is more likely that something is due to accident than that it is "no accident."[25]

X. History

Historical explanations seem clearly appropriate where there are aspects of law or morality that differ from one society to another. Various aspects of the United States Constitution for which historical explanation is appropriate would include the bicameral legislature; the division between the presidency and Congress, as compared with parliamentary systems in which the prime minister is chosen by the legislature; the specific terms (four years for president, six for the Senate, two for the House); certain rights, recognized in the Bill of Rights, especially the right to bear arms, which is not to be found in other constitutions.

It is interesting to consider whether there are aspects of contemporary morality, as opposed to law, that have historical explanations of this sort. Of course, people's beliefs have changed in various ways over the last two centuries, and we can try to explain those changes—for example, views about slavery, the relations between the sexes, and so on. But in these cases, at least, it is plausible that the changes are due to a general appreciation of certain disadvantaged people and their situation. Are there other cases in which aspects of contemporary views seem more "accidental"?

To mention one possible case, it is sometimes argued[26] that the usual distinction in the United States between acceptable recreational drugs and unacceptable recreational drugs is to be explained by appeal to historical accident. The upper classes used alcohol and did not use marijuana.

[24] Hume, *Treatise of Human Nature*, Book 3, part 2, section 2, "Of the Origin of Justice and Property"; Gilbert Harman, "Moral Relativism Defended," *Philosophical Review*, vol. 84 (1975) pp. 3–22.

[25] Elliott Sober, "Let's Razor Ockham's Razor," in *Explanation and Its Limits*, ed. D. Knowles (Cambridge, UK: Cambridge University Press, 1990).

[26] I heard a discussion about this on the radio one day, but do not have a more specific reference.

Might similar "accidental" events be responsible for some of the complexities in present-day opinions in the United States about freedom of speech and freedom of religion? Consider the legal situation. The First Amendment to the U.S. Constitution reads:

> Congress shall make no law respecting an establishment of religion, or prohibiting the free exercise thereof; or abridging the freedom of speech, or of the press; or the right of the people peaceably to assemble, and to petition the Government for a redress of grievances.

This seemingly strong statement is normally deemed compatible with various restrictions on speech. There are currently laws against libel and slander, false medical claims and other false advertising, invasions of privacy, revealing classified information, and child pornography. On the other hand, under current law there are limits to the extent that public figures can sue for libel; racial insults are constitutionally protected; and most pornography is constitutionally protected except where it involves children.

The laws in other countries differ from those in the United States especially with respect to pornography and libel.

It is possible that the best way to understand the current legal situation in the United States (and therefore a certain amount of moral opinion) is historically, explaining just how certain events led to the current legal situation. It is interesting to try to develop a Herculean rationale for current law,[27] but that is probably not the best way to *explain* current law.

XI. DEFLECTION

Thomson's deflection principle (interpreted as a hypothesis about ordinary moral judgments) competes with double effect and with Foot's claim that negative duties are stricter than positive duties. The deflection principle assumes that people normally will judge that an agent may not bring harm to one person in order to save several others, but allows an exception if the harm threatening several others can be deflected onto a smaller number of people; in that case, people may think it permissible to deflect the harm. But people will not normally approve of initiating a new process that will harm someone in order to prevent harm to others.

The deflection principle clearly makes the correct distinction between the original trolley case and the original surgeon case. It also agrees with Foot's hypothesis as regards the serum machine that produces noxious gases that will kill a patient who cannot be moved. But it disagrees with Foot's hypothesis about one of Thomson's versions of the trolley case, in

---

[27] Hercules is Ronald Dworkin's ideal judge, e.g., in Dworkin, *Law's Empire* (Cambridge, MA: Belknap Press, 1986).

which the trolley is turned by a bystander who happens to be near a switch in the track, rather than by the original driver. If the bystander B does not turn the trolley, B does not kill the five people in the main track, and so B does not violate a negative duty not to kill them. Instead B merely refrains from saving them and so violates a positive duty. If B turns the trolley, on the other hand, B does violate a negative duty not to kill someone merely for the sake of the positive duty to save those on the track ahead. So, Foot's hypothesis classifies this case with the original surgeon case. Thomson's deflection hypothesis classifies it with the original trolley case, since in both trolley cases a threat to five people is deflected to one person.

The two hypotheses therefore make different predictions about people's judgments about the bystander-at-the-switch version of the trolley case. A poll of students at Princeton suggests that the prediction made by Foot's hypothesis is falsified and the one made by Thomson's deflection principle is correct. But it would be useful to have data more rigorously collected.

If Thomson's deflection principle accounts well for other similar cases, it captures a pattern in our moral judgments, a pattern that may seem as puzzling as Posner's wealth-maximization pattern. Why exactly the deflection pattern should be found remains an interesting and relatively unexplored question.

XII. STRUCTURES

Almost all moral principles seem to have exceptions—for example, the usual principles about not lying, not stealing, not harming others. How are we to account for such complications?[28]

Principles like "Do not lie" and "Do not steal" are sometimes called "prima facie principles," and the corresponding duties not to lie and steal are sometimes called "prima facie duties." These are like principles that have elsewhere been called "default principles," which are studied as part of the general subject of nonmonotonic implication.[29]

Several principles may apply to a given situation, giving conflicting advice about what to do. In "production systems" developed in artificial intelligence, conflict is resolved, for example, by preferring a more specific rule to a more general rule.

A different idea is to take certain specific examples as paradigmatic and then choose that solution for the present case that fits the paradigm closest to the present case. This is the method used in constraint-satisfaction

---

[28] Robert Nozick, "Moral Complications and Moral Structures," *Natural Law Forum*, vol. 13 (1968), pp. 1–50.

[29] A type of implication is "nonmonotonic" if something implied by a proposition P is not necessarily implied by the conjunction of P with something else Q. See Matthew L. Ginsberg, *Readings in Nonmonotonic Reasoning* (San Mateo, CA: Morgan Kaufmann, 1987).

systems, including neural networks. (Is this what is meant by "existential ethics"?)

A somewhat different and more traditional idea in moral philosophy is to assign right- and wrong-making features to an act based on certain principles and then try to balance these against each other. One difficulty with this approach is arriving at relevant weights to assign. Furthermore, as Nozick observes, features that are relevant to what should be done are not always simply pro or con considerations. The obligation to keep a promise can be eliminated if it becomes impossible to keep it, if there is no point in keeping it, if the promise was extracted by force, or by fraud, etc.[30]

It would be useful to be able to reduce moral reasoning to a more general theory of practical reasoning, but this has not yet been accomplished.

XIII. Final Remarks

Moral philosophers might join forces with social psychologists in attempting to explain people's values. Classical British moral philosophers like Hume and Smith present accounts of moral attitudes that are easily interpreted as social psychology. Hume's account of different attitudes toward chastity in men and in women is one example. Hume's and Smith's contrasting discussions of sympathy are two others.

Recent philosophical discussions of so-called "trolley problems" can also be understood as concerned with explaining people's actual moral attitudes. These discussions benefit through the methodological discipline of having to be clearer about objective data. The discussions are also useful in suggesting empirical hypotheses to account for certain data about people's moral attitudes.

Philosophy, Princeton University

---

[30] Nozick, "Moral Complications."

THE CULTURE OF POVERTY

By Bernard Boxill

A society is culturally plural when it contains a variety of cultural groups. A common view is that just societies are likely to be culturally plural. This view assumes that human beings have rights to remain in the cultures in which they were born, or even to adopt whatever culture they choose. It is also widely believed that cultural pluralism tends to have good consequences. For example, many people suppose that the variety of cultures in a culturally plural society adds savor and interest to the lives of its inhabitants. This view evidently assumes that culture is a consumer good. Another view that cultural pluralism tends to have good consequences rests on the premise that each culture has claims to moral knowledge.[1]

There is much that can be said in favor of this view. Moral knowledge is not independent of experience; it grows and deepens as cultures evolve. Further, given the basic biological and psychological similarity among human beings, there is no general reason to believe that moral knowledge is likely to grow more quickly or luxuriantly in one culture than in another.

But the view that cultures are repositories of moral insight does not straight away justify cultural pluralism. Isaiah Berlin argues that "values can clash" and suggests that this is why "civilizations are incompatible."[2] If he is right, a culturally plural society may be doomed to ineliminable internal conflict. I have a different worry about the view: I am wary about its readiness to attribute moral insight to all cultures. My qualms are not stirred by the folly in every culture. The view does not deny this. My qualms are stirred by the possibility that the domination of one people by another subverts reason and corrupts the social sentiments, and consequently may prevent a people from fashioning mores and practices that are morally acceptable. I illustrate these claims by an examination of the culture of poverty.

I. History of the Concept of a Culture of Poverty

The term "culture of poverty" was introduced in 1959 by the American anthropologist Oscar Lewis in his book *Five Families: Mexican Case Stud-*

---

[1] I first came across this idea in W. E. B. Du Bois, "The Conservation of Races," in *The Seventh Son: The Thought and Writing of W. E. B. Du Bois*, vol. 1, ed. Julius Lester (New York: Vintage Books, 1971), pp. 176–87. Apparently the idea has a long history. See the discussion in Isaiah Berlin, *The Crooked Timber of Humanity* (New York: Vintage Books, 1992), pp. 8–12.

[2] *Ibid.*, p. 12.

ies in the Culture of Poverty.[3] Lewis argued that some poor people may be poor not because they lack opportunities, but because their culture — the "culture of poverty" — keeps them poor. He drew this conclusion on the basis of his studies in Latin America, but he was willing to generalize it to include some of the poor in the United States. His theory was denounced and fell into disrepute, but the emergence of the American underclass has given it new currency. The underclass displays many of the behavioral traits that Lewis said characterized those with a culture of poverty. This has led certain publicists and theorists to reconsider Lewis's theory, although many of them do so with a great show of reluctance and still avoid using the term "culture of poverty." For example, William Julius Wilson prefers the euphemism "ghetto-specific culture."[4] Others are more candid. Many of these — including Christopher Jencks, Lawrence M. Mead, Thomas Sowell, Glenn C. Loury, and Nicholas Lemann[5] — had never retreated from the view that some of the poor may have a specific culture that helps to keep them poor.

There have always been social theorists who believed that some of the poor were poor because of their values and attitudes. This idea is obvious in theories of the idle and undeserving poor formulated by those on the right.[6] Many theorists have also held that the laboring poor can be held back by their own shortcomings. Some of these theorists allow that these shortcomings are caused by the way the laboring poor are compelled to live. For example, John Locke argued that the understanding of poor laborers can be "but little instructed, when all their whole time and pains is laid out to still the croaking of their own bellies, or the cries of their children."[7] Still, the clear implication is that whatever its cause, the poor's lack of instruction is an important part of the reason why so few of them rise out of their class.

Locke would probably have allowed that the poor had a distinctive way of life, but interpretations of this way of life as a culture seem to be more

---

[3] Oscar Lewis, *Five Families: Mexican Case Studies in the Culture of Poverty* (New York: Basic Books, 1959).

[4] See William Julius Wilson, *The Truly Disadvantaged* (Chicago: University of Chicago Press, 1987).

[5] See Christopher Jencks, *Rethinking Social Policy* (Cambridge: Harvard University Press, 1992), ch. 4; Lawrence M. Mead, *The New Politics of Poverty* (New York: Harper Collins Publishers, 1992), ch. 7; Thomas Sowell, *Ethnic America* (New York: Basic Books, 1981), ch. 8; Glenn C. Loury, "The Moral Quandary of the Black Community," *The Public Interest*, vol. 79 (Spring 1985), pp. 11–26; and Nicholas Lemann, "The Origins of the Underclass," *The Atlantic*, part 1, June 1986, pp. 31–55, part 2, July 1986, pp. 54–68.

[6] For the right, see, for example, Mead, *The New Politics of Poverty*, or Mickey Kaus, "The Work Ethic State," *The New Republic*, July 1986.

[7] John Locke, *An Essay Concerning Human Understanding* (Oxford: Oxford University Press, 1975), Book 4, ch. 20, section 2, p. 707. See also his comment that "where the hand is used to the plough and the spade, the head is seldom elevated to sublime notions . . . ," in Locke, *The Reasonableness of Christianity* (Washington, DC: Regency Gateway, 1965), p. 193.

recent. The classic example in America is that of sociologist Allison Davis. Davis postulated the existence of a distinctive "slum culture" and tried to explain why it emerged and persisted. According to Davis,

> [b]ecause the slum individual usually is responding to a different physical, economic and cultural reality from that in which the middle-class individual is trained, the slum individual's habits and values must also be different if they are to be realistic. The behavior which we regard as "delinquent" or "shiftless" or "unmotivated" in slum groups is usually a perfectly realistic, adaptive, and — in slum life — respectable response to reality.

Moreover, Davis maintained that slum culture was passed on from generation to generation because "[i]f a child associates intimately with no one but slum adults and children, he will learn only slum culture."[8] Somewhat similarly, the American sociologist Walter B. Miller insisted on the existence of a specific "lower-class culture." "There is," Miller wrote, "a substantial segment of present-day American society whose way of life, values, and characteristic patterns of behavior are the product of a distinctive cultural system which may be termed 'lower class.'" Moreover, he emphasized that this culture "cannot be seen merely as a reverse function of middle class culture — as middle class standards 'turned upside down'; lower class culture is a distinctive tradition, many centuries old with an integrity of its own."[9]

So neither the idea that the poor have a distinctive way of life, nor the idea that this way of life is a culture, is new. However, the term "culture of poverty" was coined by Oscar Lewis in 1959, and it caught on and crowded out "slum culture" and "lower-class culture" when Michael Harrington used it extensively in his influential book *The Other America*.[10]

Theories of a "slum culture," "lower-class culture," and a "culture of poverty" identify a class of poor people and try to explain their behavior in terms of their way of life. Since this way of life is conceived to be a culture or a subculture, sociologists refer to these theories in general as the "cultural school." The cultural school became a center of controversy in the war against poverty when it came to be associated with the views expressed in a slim volume written by Daniel Patrick Moynihan and published in 1965.

This book, *The Negro Family: The Case for National Action*, is the famous

---

[8] Allison Davis, *Social Class Influence upon Learning* (Cambridge: Harvard University Press, 1952), pp. 10–11.

[9] Walter B. Miller, "Focal Concerns of Lower-Class Culture," in Louis A. Ferman et al., *Poverty in America* (Ann Arbor: University of Michigan Press, 1970), pp. 396, 405.

[10] Michael Harrington, *The Other America* (New York: MacMillan Press, 1962).

"Moynihan Report."[11] It began with a warning that the United States was approaching "a new crisis in race relations."[12] Black Americans were beginning to expect that equal opportunities for them as a group would produce roughly equal results, as compared with other groups; but they were going to be bitterly disappointed unless the nation took special action. Moynihan gave two reasons for this. First, racism persisted; second, the debilitating effects of the past harsh treatment of black Americans prevented them from competing successfully with other groups. The most important of these effects was the breakdown of the black family. Moynihan did not mean that all black families were in danger. He was clear that middle-class black families were relatively secure. He was referring to lower-class black families. Here he felt that the evidence, "not final, but powerfully persuasive," supported the conclusion that the black family was "crumbling."[13] Moynihan was convinced that this crumbling of the black ghetto family was "at the center" of the growing high school drop-out rate, and the delinquency and crime in the black ghetto.[14] But although he blamed "white America" for starting and perpetuating this "tangle of pathology," in his opinion it was "capable of perpetuating itself without assistance from the white world."[15]

Moynihan did not refer to Lewis's work in his book. He relied mainly on the research of black sociologist E. Franklin Frazier. In his book *The Negro Family in the United States*, published in 1939, as well as in other works,[16] Frazier espoused the "catastrophic" view of slavery. According to Frazier, "slavery was a cruel and barbaric system that annihilated the Negro as a person. . . ."[17] In particular, he argued that slavery had produced this evil result mainly through its destruction of the black family, and that the ensuing years of harsh treatment had compounded the problem. These ideas formed the foundation of Moynihan's book. As he acknowledged later, data on the black family collected after Frazier supported the compelling hypothesis that "Frazier had been right."[18]

Moynihan's invocation of Frazier, for decades the best-known black sociologist in America, did not save him from censure. The unkindest cut was that his book "blamed the victim." Critics also attacked the cultural

[11] Daniel P. Moynihan, *The Negro Family: The Case for National Action* (Washington, DC: U.S. Department of Labor, 1965); reprinted in *The Moynihan Report and the Politics of Controversy*, ed. Lee Rainwater and William L. Yancy (Cambridge: MIT Press, 1967).

[12] Rainwater and Yancy, eds., *Moynihan Report*, p. 43.

[13] *Ibid.*

[14] *Ibid.*, p. 76.

[15] *Ibid.*, p. 93.

[16] E. Franklin Frazier, *The Negro Family in the United States* (Chicago: University of Chicago Press, 1939), *The Black Bourgeoisie* (New York: Collier Books, 1962), and *The Negro in the United States* (Toronto: The Macmillan Company, 1957).

[17] Frazier, *Black Bourgeoisie*, p. 10.

[18] Daniel P. Moynihan, "The President and the Negro: The Moment Lost," *Commentary*, vol. 43 (1967), p. 35.

school for providing the theoretical background for the book. Lewis's work came under specially heavy fire. His account of a culture of poverty, especially his claim that this culture involved a high incidence of broken homes and female-headed households, bore obvious resemblances to the "tangle of pathology" Moynihan claimed to find in the black ghetto. Moreover, Lewis had himself suggested that "very low-income Negroes" were among the relatively few people in the United States who had a "culture of poverty."[19]

II. Analysis of the Concept of a Culture of Poverty

I will set out Lewis's account of the culture of poverty in nine main points.

1. The culture of poverty differs from poverty per se.[20] Poverty per se is having little money and meeting few of the material conditions the society considers necessary for a comfortable life. The culture of poverty is a "way of life" some poor people have.[21]

Lewis is not claiming merely that poor people live differently from well-to-do people. Such a claim would be almost tautological given the constraints that poverty places on the behavior of poor people. Lewis is making the substantive claim that some poor people have a way of life—the culture of poverty—that is not strictly forced on them by the constraints poverty places on their behavior. As he points out, there are poor people who do not live in a culture of poverty. As examples, he gives "the primitive or preliterate peoples studied by anthropologists,"[22] the lower castes in India, the Jews of Eastern Europe, and, more tentatively, the poorer classes in socialist countries.[23] Later he adds that in "highly developed capitalist societies with a welfare state, the culture of poverty tends to decline," noting that "although there is still a great deal of poverty in the United States . . . there is relatively little of what I would call the culture of poverty."[24]

If the culture of poverty is not poverty, or even the way of life poverty forces on people, what is its relation to poverty? Why call it the culture of poverty? Lewis evidently believes that the culture of poverty is related to poverty in two main ways: it is an adaptation to poverty, and it tends to perpetuate poverty. I expand on these points in items 2 and 7 below.

2. The culture of poverty only emerges among the poor people of a

---

[19] Oscar Lewis, *La Vida* (New York: Vintage Books, 1968), p. li.
[20] *Ibid.*, p. xliii.
[21] *Ibid.*
[22] *Ibid.*, p. xlviii.
[23] *Ibid.*, pp. xlviii, xlix.
[24] *Ibid.*, p. li.

larger society when the culture of that larger society includes "a set of values . . . which stresses the accumulation of wealth and property, the possibility of upward mobility and thrift, and explains low economic status as the result of personal inadequacy or inferiority."[25] The culture of poverty is an adaptation of that culture to poverty. In particular, it is the culture that develops among some poor people to enable them to cope with "the feelings of hopelessness and despair" they experience at the "realization of the improbability of achieving success in terms of the values and goals of the larger society."[26] Although Lewis describes the culture of poverty as an adaptation of another culture to poverty, he makes it clear that it is nevertheless a culture or subculture because it has "its own structure and rationale" and is a "way of life which is passed down from generation to generation along family lines."[27]

3. The way of life of the culture of poverty has four main aspects: (a) the relation between those with a culture of poverty and the larger society; (b) the nature of the slum community; (c) the nature of the family in the slum community; and (d) the distinctive values and attitudes of those with a culture of poverty.

(a) Those with a culture of poverty fail to participate in most of the major institutions of the society. The main point here is that they are chronically unemployed or underemployed. They participate in some of the institutions of the society like the jails and the public-relief system, but this helps to perpetuate the behavioral and personality traits of the culture of poverty.[28] (b) At the level of the slum community, the most striking characteristic of the culture of poverty is the almost complete absence of any stable organizations. According to Lewis, the "existence of neighborhood gangs which cut across slum settlements represents a considerable advance" over the zero point of organization of the culture of poverty.[29] (c) The major traits of family in the culture of poverty are "the absence of childhood as a specially prolonged and protected stage in the life cycle, early initiation into sex, free unions or consensual marriages, a relatively high incidence of the abandonment of wives and children, a trend toward female- or mother-centered families . . . and a strong predisposition to authoritarianism. . . ."[30] (d) Finally, the structures of the culture of poverty at the community and family levels support, and are supported by, the "attitudes, values and character structure" of the individuals in the culture of poverty.[31] These attitudes and values include, a "strong feel-

[25] *Ibid.*, p. xliv.
[26] *Ibid.*
[27] *Ibid.*, p. xliii.
[28] *Ibid.*, pp. xlv, xlvi.
[29] *Ibid.*, p. xlvii.
[30] *Ibid.*, p. xlviii.
[31] *Ibid.*, p. xlv.

ing of marginality, of helplessness, of dependence and of inferiority,"[32] a "lack of impulse control," a "strong present-time orientation with relatively little ability to defer gratification and to plan for the future," a "sense of resignation and fatalism," a "widespread belief in male superiority," and a "high tolerance for psychological pathology of all sorts." Lewis also believes that people with a culture of poverty "are provincial and locally oriented," "have very little sense of history," "know only their own troubles," and are "not class conscious."[33]

4. The fundamental aspect of the culture of poverty consists in the distinctive attitudes and values of the individuals in it. These tend to generate the other aspects of the culture of poverty. This follows from the way Lewis supports his claim that once the culture of poverty comes into existence, "it tends to perpetuate itself because of its effect on the children." According to Lewis, "[b]y the time slum children are age six or seven they have usually absorbed the basic values and attitudes of their subculture. . . ."[34] Since this only says that the values and attitudes of the culture of poverty are passed on to the children, the claim that the culture of poverty tends to perpetuate itself because of its effects on the children implies that the values and attitudes of the culture of poverty are likely to generate its other aspects under most conditions.

5. The culture of poverty is difficult to eliminate. Lewis draws attention to this implication of his theory, noting that eliminating the culture of poverty is "much more difficult" than eliminating poverty per se.[35] It follows from his observation, noted above, that by the age of six or seven, slum children have "absorbed the basic values and attitudes of their subculture," at least if we assume that it is difficult to prevent children from absorbing the basic values and attitudes of their subculture, and that once absorbed, these values and attitudes become durable parts of their personalities and characters.

6. The culture of poverty is self-perpetuating in the sense that it can survive the elimination of poverty. Lewis warns explicitly of this implication of his theory, observing that "the elimination of physical poverty per se may not be enough to eliminate the culture of poverty which is a whole way of life."[36] It follows directly from point 4 above if we assume that the durable parts of our personalities and characters can usually survive changes in our material conditions. Since we already have the assumption that the values and attitudes children absorb from their subculture become durable parts of their personalities and characters, it follows that the culture of poverty can survive the elimination of poverty.

[32] *Ibid.*, p. xlvii.
[33] *Ibid.*, p. clviii.
[34] *Ibid.*, p. xlv.
[35] *Ibid.*, p. li.
[36] *Ibid.*, p. lii.

7. The culture of poverty tends to perpetuate poverty. This is the second main way the culture is related to poverty. Lewis states this plainly: for example, after remarking on how early slum children absorb the values and attitudes of their subculture, he concludes that they are "not psychologically geared to take full advantage of changing conditions or increased opportunities which may occur in their lifetime."[37] This conclusion is supported by the attitudes he lists as characteristic of people in the culture of poverty. As we saw, this list includes strong feelings of "helplessness," "dependence," and "inferiority," a lack of "impulse control," a sense of "resignation" and "fatalism," and, most famously, "a strong present-time orientation with relatively little ability to defer gratification and to plan for the future."

Point 6 says that the culture of poverty can survive the elimination of poverty, and point 7 says that the culture of poverty tends to perpetuate poverty. The two are not inconsistent. The culture of poverty tends to perpetuate poverty because those who have that way of life would remain poor if left to their own devices, but this does not rule out the possibility that some agency could lift them from poverty. If this were to happen, however, point 6 says that they would remain in the culture of poverty, and would probably sink back into poverty unless the agency continued to keep them out of it.

8. The culture of poverty cannot be eliminated by providing opportunities, because its values discourage taking advantage of opportunities. There are, however, two main strategies for eliminating the culture of poverty. The first is to "slowly" raise the "level of living" of the poor, while at the same time using "psychiatric treatment" and "social work" to help "incorporate them into the middle class."[38] So although eliminating poverty may not be enough, by itself, to eliminate the culture of poverty, it may be part of a strategy that can eliminate it. That strategy is, however, only possible in developed countries. In underdeveloped countries there are not enough social workers to cope with the "great masses of people who live in the culture of poverty," and in any case, such countries are often too poor to eliminate poverty. This takes us to Lewis's second strategy, which he allows may be more suitable for underdeveloped countries. This is revolution. According to Lewis, even when revolutions do not succeed in abolishing poverty, they may succeed in abolishing the culture of poverty by "creating basic structural changes," "redistributing wealth," and "organizing the poor and giving them a sense of belonging, of power and of leadership."[39] He based this view on his admittedly "limited" observation of the changes in some slum dwellers in Cuba

---

[37] *Ibid.*, p. xlv.

[38] *Ibid.*, p. lii. To be at all reasonable, I expect that Lewis means "social work" rather than "psychiatric treatment."

[39] *Ibid.*

before and after the "Castro revolution." Before that revolution, Lewis found the slum dwellers to have the usual traits of the culture of poverty. After the revolution, he found that though they were still "desperately poor," they were "highly organized," and suffered much less from the "despair, apathy and hopelessness which are so diagnostic of the urban slums in the culture of poverty."[40]

9. A "poverty of culture" is "one of the crucial aspects of the culture of poverty."[41] This is Lewis's answer to the cultural relativist who protests that while there may be reason to try to eliminate poverty, there is no reason to try to eliminate the culture of poverty.

Lewis allows that the culture of poverty "provides some rewards without which the poor could hardly carry on."[42] Besides being an adaptation to the exigencies of poverty, for example, "the low aspiration level" it involves "helps to reduce frustration."[43] It also includes positive traits that give it an advantage over middle-class culture: for example, Lewis suggests that one of its most characteristic traits, "living in the present," "may develop a capacity for spontaneity and adventure, for the enjoyment of the sensual, the indulgence of impulse, which is often blunted in the middle-class, future-oriented man."[44] However, Lewis believes that on balance these advantages of the culture of poverty are outweighed by its disadvantages. The culture of poverty, he concludes, is on the whole "a relatively thin culture. There is a great deal of pathos, suffering and emptiness among those who live in the culture of poverty. It does not provide much support or long-range satisfaction and its encouragement of mistrust tends to magnify helplessness and isolation."[45]

Lewis's dissatisfaction with the culture of poverty is not simply that it keeps people poor. He gives many examples of people who are poorer in material terms than those with a culture of poverty, but who nevertheless often have an "integrated" and "satisfying" culture. This also shows that Lewis does not object to the culture of poverty merely because it differs from mainstream culture. Lewis objects to the culture of poverty because in his view it is a radically imperfect adaptation of mainstream culture to poverty.

III. THE CRITICS

Lewis's critics fall into two main groups, the situationalists and what I call, for want of a better name, the existentialists. Though the situation-

---

[40] *Ibid.*, p. xlix.
[41] *Ibid.*, p. lii.
[42] *Ibid.*, p. xliii.
[43] *Ibid.*, p. lii.
[44] *Ibid.*, p. li.
[45] *Ibid.*, p. lii.

alists and existentialists both reject the way Lewis or the culturalists understand "lower-class culture," they do so for different reasons.

The situationalists have several criticisms of the culturalists. The first concerns the status of the culture of poverty as a culture. The culturalists believe that the culture of poverty is a genuine culture with its own distinctive system of values. The situationalists deny this. They allow that the culture of poverty appears to be a genuine culture, but they maintain that it shares the mainstream's system of values, and that its distinctiveness lies wholly in its adaptations of mainstream institutions and practices. Thus, American sociologist Herbert Gans, a prominent situationalist, insists that despite appearances, the values of the culture of poverty are the same as the values of the mainstream, and that the "essence of lower-class culture" is simply the "alternative behavioral guides" those with a lower-class culture have devised to enable them to cope with their poverty.[46]

The second criticism the situationalists level against the culturalists concerns the culturalists' view that the culture of poverty is a radically imperfect adaptation of the way of life of the larger society to poverty. The situationalists believe that the culture of poverty is rational and functional.

Situationalists also object to the culturalists' claims about the persistence of the culture of poverty. They maintain that eliminating poverty will eliminate the culture of poverty. This follows from the situationalists' basic claims, given certain plausible assumptions. If people with a culture of poverty have the same values as the other people in their society, if their way of life is distinctive only because of their distinctive institutions and practices, and if people adapt to changing material conditions by changing their institutions and practices rather than by changing their values, then changing the material conditions of those with a culture of poverty — in particular, eliminating their poverty — will eliminate their distinctive way of life.

Finally, situationalists object to the culturalists' claims about the difficulty of eliminating poverty among people with a culture of poverty. They maintain that such people have the same values as others in the society and are poor simply because they lack opportunities. On the situationalists' account, poverty among those with a culture of poverty can be eliminated by providing them with opportunities.

Let us now consider the existentialists. The existentialists agree with the situationalists in opposing the culturalists' view that the culture of poverty is pathological, but existentialists disagree with situationalists insofar as the latter tend to see the culture of poverty as simply a product of poor people reacting, responding, and adapting to their situation. Existentialists believe that the culture of poverty is a free and creative

---

[46] Herbert Gans, *The Urban Villagers* (New York: The Free Press, 1982), p. 284.

reply of poor people to their situation. Herbert Gutman, a twentieth-century American historian whose research corrected several popular misconceptions about the black family during and after slavery, used this passage from Sartre to express his perspective: "The essential is not what 'one' has done to man, but what man does with what 'one' has done to him."[47]

The novelist Ralph Ellison gives a more impassioned statement of the existentialists' position in his review of Gunnar Myrdal's *An American Dilemma*.[48] Ellison spoke directly to the question of "Negro culture," but since critics of the culture of poverty often cite him as a champion, I shall — provisionally — take his remarks to apply to the issue of the culture of poverty. On that stipulation, Ellison specifically attacked Myrdal's apparent endorsement of the culturalists' interpretation of what came to be called the "culture of poverty"; for example, he rejected Myrdal's view of "Negro culture and personality . . . as the product of a social pathology."[49] But he also expressed profound dissatisfaction with the general tendency in sociological thinking to view poor people, especially poor blacks, as merely reacting to oppression. As he put it,

> can a people . . . live and develop for over three hundred years sim-ply by reacting? Are American Negroes simply the creation of white men, or have they at least helped to create themselves out of what they found around them? Men have made a way of life in caves and upon cliffs, why cannot Negroes have made a life upon the horns of the white man's dilemma?[50]

And Ellison went on to distance himself from the culturalists and situationalists, who both tend to interpret Negro culture as a kind of "reflection," even if distorted, of white culture. "It does not occur to Myrdal," Ellison wrote,

> that many of the Negro cultural manifestations which he considers merely reflective might also embody a *rejection* of what he considers "higher values." There is a dualism at work here. It is only partly true that Negroes turn away from white patterns because they are refused participation. There is nothing like distance to create ob-jectivity, and exclusion gives rise to counter values. Men, as Dos-toievsky says, cannot live in revolt. Nor can they live in a state of "reacting."[51]

---

[47] Herbert Gutman, "Labor History and the 'Sartre Question'," in Herbert Gutman, *Power and Culture* (New York: The New Press, 1987), p. 326.

[48] Ralph Ellison, "An American Dilemma: A Review," in Ralph Ellison, *Shadow and Act* (London: Secker and Warburg, 1967), pp. 303–17.

[49] *Ibid.*, p. 316.

[50] *Ibid.*, pp. 315, 316.

[51] *Ibid.*, p. 316; emphasis in original.

IV. Assessment of the Situationalists

I now turn to a critical assessment of the views of the situationalists and existentialists. I deal with the situationalists at far greater length, concluding that they romanticize the culture of poverty. My criticisms of the situationalists' views suggest that we should also be skeptical of the existentialists' position.

I begin with the situationalists' view that the values of the culture of poverty are the same as mainstream values. Situationalists say this because, as the American anthropologist Ulf Hannerz notes, there is "much verbalization of mainstream ideals in the ghetto, even from those who often act ghetto-specifically in direct contradiction to these ideals." [52] But the idea that people's values are what they say they are is naive. Oscar Lewis understands people better; according to Lewis, "[p]eople with a culture of poverty are aware of middle-class values, talk about them and even claim some of them as their own, but on the whole they do not live by them." [53] He meant that people with a culture of poverty often pay lip service to middle-class values, but that their real values are different. As he commented in regard to those with a culture of poverty, "it is important to distinguish what they say and what they do." [54]

Situationalists are equally naive when they claim that people with a culture of poverty teach their children only mainstream values. The basis of this claim is that people with a culture of poverty usually tell their children to follow the mainstream values.[55] But, the inference is mistaken. We do not teach only by *telling* people things; we also teach by what we do, by the example we set. We even teach by what we do — unintentionally — when we are not trying to set an example. Hannerz points out that "[t]he role modelling which is generally held to be an important part of the transmission of sex roles is an obvious example of a process of cultural sharing where the instruction is largely accidental." [56] Finally, if, as Hannerz informs us, those who preach mainstream values in the culture of poverty often act "ghetto-specifically in direct contradiction" to these values, one can probably safely assume that the values reflected in the "ghetto-specific" behavior will be better learned than the mainstream values that are preached.

The preceding discussion seems to rely on the assumption that a person's values are always faithfully reflected in his actions. This assumption is false. There is room for weakness of will and excusing conditions: a person may believe that he ought to do certain things, and yet fail to do these things because he lacks perseverance, or ability, or because he is

---

[52] Ulf Hannerz, *Soulside* (New York: Columbia University Press, 1969), p. 183.
[53] Lewis, *La Vida*, p. xlvi.
[54] *Ibid.*
[55] Hannerz, *Soulside*, p. 185.
[56] *Ibid.*

unlucky. Thus, situationalists may argue that they are right when they insist that people with a culture of poverty have mainstream values, even though such people often act in "direct contradiction" with those values. I will show, however, that this consideration better fits the culturalists' general view than the situationalists'.

"Values" may refer to at least two different kinds of things that should be distinguished from one another in this debate. First, "values" may refer to the activities, states, or plans of life that a particular culture validates or celebrates. For example, the favored plan of life in one society may be soldiering, in another moneymaking, and in yet another learning or athletic prowess. In the literature on the culture of poverty, these are referred to as aspirations or goals.[57] Second, "values" may refer to a society's moral rules commanding or forbidding certain kinds of behavior. These set limits on what people are permitted to do in pursuit of their goals. In the literature on the culture of poverty, these rules are referred to as behavioral norms.[58]

Now suppose that the situationalists are right, and that people with a culture of poverty have internalized the values, that is, the aspirations and behavioral norms, of the mainstream. And suppose too that they often act in "direct contradiction" with these values; that is, they fail to try to achieve the aspirations of the society and fail to live by its behavioral norms. In that case they are likely to experience a loss of self-esteem, and to feel despair, shame, and guilt. The culturalists generally endorse this view of the troubled mental state of those with a culture of poverty. As we have seen, Lewis emphasizes their "resignation and fatalism," and their feelings of hopelessness and despair when they realize the "improbability of achieving success in terms of the values and goals of the larger society."[59] But the situationalists deny all of this. They view people with a culture of poverty as pragmatic problem solvers who are not about to torture themselves for what they cannot do. As one situationalist put it, if the individual in the culture of poverty "cannot get the resources to play the game successfully and thus experiences constant failure at it, he is not 'conceptual boob' enough to continue knocking his head against a stone wall — he will try to find a new game to play, either one that is already existing and at hand, or one that he himself invents."[60]

Another situationalist suggestion appeals to the "ought implies can" principle. Suppose that a person cannot do the things his avowed values require him to do. In that case the "ought implies can" principle implies

[57] See for example, Herbert Gans, "Culture and Class in the Study of Poverty," in *On Understanding Poverty*, ed. Daniel P. Moynihan (New York: Basic Books, 1968), p. 208.

[58] *Ibid.*

[59] Lewis, *La Vida*, p. xliv. This suggests that Lewis's culture of poverty is different from the "slum" or "lower-class" concept of Davis and Miller; *supra* nn. 8 and 9.

[60] Lee Rainwater, "The Lower-Class Culture and Poverty-War Strategy," in *On Understanding Poverty*, p. 242.

that it is false that he ought to do these things, or that he should feel guilty because he does not do them. What he ought to do is the best he can in the circumstances, and if he does, it is invidious to suggest that his avowed values are not his real values. This is the kind of consideration underlying a view urged by Herbert Gans. Gans argues that because people with a culture of poverty are too poor to obtain the "standard package" of "American goods, services and ideas," they devise "alternative behavioral guides" to "enable them to cope with poverty." He admits that these "alternative behavioral guides" involve behavior that appears to contradict mainstream values. But he insists that the people who follow these guides are forced to do so, and that they still have mainstream values. According to Gans,

> many poor people aspire to plan ahead, just like everyone else, but are prevented from doing so both by low income and economic insecurity. These force them to live on a day-to-day basis, making saving or "planning for a rainy day" impossible. Likewise, most of the unemployed men who develop a street corner culture to pass the time, earn the respect of peers, and hold on to as much self-respect and dignity as possible, would prefer to work full-time; and poor mothers who have developed quasi-familial mutual-aid networks usually want to live in the proto-typical two-parent family, with wedding certificate in hand.[61]

But Gans overstates his case. The people he describes are not "forced" to live the way they do, and an alternative way of life is not "impossible" for them. The now disparaged "deserving" poor are as poor as people with the culture of poverty, but they marry, accept menial jobs, and try to save.

Earlier I accused the situationalists of mistakenly assuming that the values of the culture of poverty are the values the people with that culture preach. It may be objected that I am committing a similar mistake here, because I seem to be assuming that mainstream values are the values mainstream people preach. Mainstream people say that they believe in "family values" and the "work ethic." The objection is that these are not really their values; they may seem to hold these values only because they live in circumstances in which living as if one believed in "family values" and the "work ethic" is easy; if they became poor, they would behave exactly like people with a culture of poverty.

If these considerations are cogent, the correct conclusion to draw is not so much that people with a culture of poverty have mainstream values, but rather that people in the mainstream have the values of the culture

---

[61] Gans, *The Urban Villagers*, pp. 284, 285.

of poverty. But the considerations are not cogent. Consider first the claim that if mainstream people became poor, they would behave exactly like people with a culture of poverty. This claim suffers from a weakness common to most counterfactual claims. In particular, how do we know that people in the mainstream would act like people with a culture of poverty if they became poor? We cannot appeal to some general principle of human nature. Not all poor people behave like people with a culture of poverty. The "deserving" poor prove this. Why couldn't mainstream people behave like them if they became poor, rather than like those with a culture of poverty? Further, even if those in the mainstream would behave exactly like those in the culture of poverty if they became poor, it does not follow that their values are *now* the values of the culture of poverty. It is possible that becoming poor would lead them to adopt the values of the culture of poverty.

But what about the adulteries and the increasing number of divorces and single-parent families in the middle class? Don't they prove that the values of the middle class are really the same as the values of those with a culture of poverty? But this popular argument is fallacious. The middle class and the poor are in different material circumstances. In the relatively affluent circumstances of the middle class, it is possible that the nuclear family is no longer essential for caring for and raising children. Consequently, the breakdown of the nuclear family in the middle class need not imply that the middle class is as casual about its children as people in the culture of poverty.

If these arguments are sound, the situationalists have no good reason to keep insisting, as they do, that the values of the mainstream and the culture of poverty are the same. I now attack the second plank of their position, viz., that the adaptations of mainstream institutions and practices in the culture of poverty are the best that can be expected in the circumstances.

Situationalists sometimes write as if the adaptations of mainstream institutions in the culture of poverty must be the best that can be expected in the circumstances just because they are adaptations. Such a belief is, of course, absurd. An adaptation is a modification to meet new conditions; there is no general reason why it must be the best that can be expected in the circumstances.

Modern economists build models on the assumption that people are rational. This may tempt situationalists to suppose that the adaptations of mainstream institutions in the culture of poverty must therefore be rational. They should resist the temptation. The economists' assumption of human rationality may be useful for their peculiar purposes. It is not, however, generally true. If it were, and if it implied that human institutions and practices were always rational, all our institutions and practices would be beyond rational criticism. This is, of course, preposterous, and the situationalists know it. They are quite prepared to find fault with the institutions and practices of the larger society.

Besides human fallibility in general, there are particular reasons to suspect that the institutions and practices of the culture of poverty are highly imperfect adaptations of the institutions and practices of the larger society. This becomes clear if we consider how the adaptations come about. There are two main kinds of cases. In the first, the adaptations come about unintentionally as people avoid the painful and frustrating behavior mainstream institutions may require. In the second, the adaptations are intended and planned. Let us begin with the first.

When an institution or practice requires unusually painful or frustrating behavior, it may change if people avoid the painful or frustrating behavior it requires. I give two possible examples of this kind of adaptation.

Poor people who develop a culture of poverty usually have a hard time finding work. Either there are few jobs or they lack the skills for the jobs that do exist. Naturally, they find searching for work in these circumstances painful and frustrating, and so many of them give up searching. If not working and not trying to find work becomes part of their way of life, they have, probably unintentionally, adapted the mainstream practice of working or trying to find work.[62]

The second example of a possibly unintended adaptation concerns the family. In the mainstream a man is supposed to help support and raise his children. These, together with their mother, are his family. But many poor men do not earn enough to help support their families, and since trying to do so in their circumstances is painful and frustrating, many of them stop trying. This is made easier for them psychologically where poor women with children are eligible for relief such as AFDC payments in the United States; in such circumstances the men know that their children will not starve because they do not help to support them, and the women have less reason to insist that fathers help to support their children. Further, since it is demeaning for a man to be around the house and not contribute to the support of his family, some poor men leave the house, and consequently are not present to help raise the children. If it becomes part of the way of life of these poor people for women to support and raise the children and for men to do neither, they have, probably unintentionally, adapted the mainstream institution of the family to their conditions.

Adaptations of mainstream institutions and practices that arise in this way are not likely to be the best that can be expected in the circumstances. Suppose first that the institutions and practices they are adap-

---

[62] It may be said that they have rejected the mainstream institution of working or trying to find work. But this suggests a more deliberate response to the dearth of employment opportunities than need be the case.

tations of are likely to secure people's interests. For example, searching for work is probably rational when there are lots of jobs available. In such circumstances (and when other things are equal — for example, the agent is not sick or independently wealthy) searching for work pretty plainly better serves his interests than choosing to be idle. But the question is whether the adaptations are rational. To take the same example, the question is whether not searching for work is likely to better serve the agent's interests than searching for work. Situationalists cannot infer that it is, just because it emerges in circumstances where jobs are scarce, and consequently where searching for work is not plainly the best way for the agent to try to secure his interests. Remember we are not asking whether it is natural, or part of human nature, or understandable for people to want to give up trying to find work where jobs are scarce; to want to give up trying to find work in these circumstances is probably all of these things. We are asking whether it is *rational* to give up trying to find work in these circumstances. My point is that the situationalists cannot infer that it is; even if, in the circumstances, searching for work is not plainly the best way for the agent to try to secure his interests, it may still be the best way for the agent to try to secure his interests.

Someone may point out that not trying to find work serves the agent's interests because it protects him from the frustration of trying and failing to find work. I agree. But avoiding frustration is not the only thing in an agent's interests. If it were, trying where we are not assured of success would always be irrational, which is absurd. More particularly, although I grant that not searching for work serves the agent's immediate interest in avoiding the frustration of trying and failing to find work, I see no reason to grant that it best serves his larger, longer-term interests in self-respect, happiness, self-development, and so on.

Situationalists may object that it is a further conclusion that the adaptation probably fails to be rational, and that I have no right to draw it. Though some of them seem prepared to allow that adaptations of the kind under consideration may possibly be less than fully rational, they seem to believe that there are no general reasons to suspect that they are. I allow that close study of a particular adaptation of the kind under consideration may reveal that it best serves the interests of people with a culture of poverty. But I maintain that a justified presumption is that such cases are exceptional.

Remember that such adaptations involve unintended and unplanned changes in institutions and practices which experience strongly suggests people must follow if they are to secure their larger, longer-term interests. To suppose that an unintended, unplanned change in such institutions will secure people's interests is as bizarre as to suppose that an unintended, unplanned change in a finely tuned engine will help it to work better. It may be objected that this argument depends on the false premise that institutions and practices are like finely tuned engines. Although

I believe that there is a presumption in favor of this premise, the present argument can dispense with it. Is it likely that unintended, unplanned changes in a *badly* tuned engine will help it to work better? As an illustration of this argument, consider again the culture of poverty's adaptation of the mainstream's practice of working and searching for work. In this case those with a culture of poverty have unintentionally changed — perhaps it is better to say unintentionally abandoned — a practice that experience has shown to be among the best ways a person can secure his larger, longer-term interests. I admit that the change came about because the practice was unusually painful and frustrating among those who developed a culture of poverty, but to suppose that it is therefore likely to secure people's interests is as absurd as to suppose that it is rational for a person to abandon the practice of going to the dentist twice a year because he has sensitive teeth. In general, the practices we may adopt in order to avoid immediately impending pain or frustration do not automatically serve our larger, longer-term interests. Practices that do serve such interests have to be carefully planned and designed. They almost never happen by accident. Jon Elster suggests that people tend to "over-adapt," that is, to "overshoot in their choices and go to extremes not required by the situation."[63] My point is weaker but still, I think, decisive, viz., that institutions and practices that serve our larger, longer-term interests rarely happen by accident.

There is a final important consideration that situationalists never mention. What about the poor who do not embrace the culture of poverty, and who continue to search for work, accepting even menial labor when they can find it? They used to be called the "deserving" poor, but if the practices of the culture of poverty best serve their interests, perhaps a more accurate name for them is the "foolish" poor. But this name would be unjustified. A life of effort, even if it does not achieve its goals, is better than a life of surrender and despair.

The arguments that adaptations of the kind under consideration are unlikely to serve the agent's best interests suggest that the adaptations are equally unlikely to respect others' rights and interests. If the institutions and practices they are adaptations of are designed to respect others' rights and interests, then unintended changes in these institutions and practices caused by some people trying to avoid immediately impending pain or frustration are hardly likely to help the institutions and practices better respect others' rights and interests. And if the institutions and practices they are adaptations of are not carefully designed to respect others' rights and interests, it seems even less likely that unintended, unplanned changes in these institutions will lead to improvement.

As an illustration of this argument, consider the culture of poverty's adaptation of the mainstream institution of the family. This adaptation is

---

[63] Jon Elster, *Sour Grapes* (New York: Cambridge University Press, 1983), p. 110.

supposed to emerge as some poor men avoid the frustration of trying to support their families. The men avoid frustration and to that extent the adaptation is perhaps an improvement. But on the whole it is worse than the institution it is adapted from: it seems to provide less protection for their children's rights and for the rights of the mothers of their children. This argument does not assume that the mainstream institution of the family is perfect. Critics complain that it violates women's rights to autonomy and self-fulfillment. I do not have to challenge that criticism; my claim is that the culture of poverty's adaptation of that institution probably does even worse.

Let us turn now to the adaptations of mainstream institutions and practices that people with a culture of poverty bring about deliberately and intentionally. Although I suspect that most adaptations are likely to be unintended, many will be deliberately designed. People are imperfectly rational and imperfectly moral, but most can plan ahead to some degree, and most have some concern for others. Consequently, we should expect that some of the adaptations of mainstream institutions and practices will be deliberately designed to protect the future interests, as well as the immediate interests, of the people in the culture of poverty. This expectation is confirmed by the various adaptations of the mainstream's version of the family found in the culture of poverty. The first of these adaptations emerged unintentionally as men gave up trying to support their families, but it was followed by a second adaptation evidently deliberately designed to offset the evil consequences of the first, unintended adaptation. The contemporary American anthropologist Carol Stack has described how some poor black women have carefully contrived a system of extended families that to some extent makes up for not having husbands to help support and raise their children.[64]

I will argue, however, that there are general reasons to fear that even the deliberately designed adaptations of mainstream institutions and practices found in the culture of poverty are likely to be highly imperfect. I do not mean only that the adaptations will fail to protect the rights and interests of people in the culture of poverty. Human creations are always imperfect, and the straitened circumstances of people in the culture of poverty make it highly unlikely that their interests and rights will be adequately protected however they adapt mainstream institutions. I mean that the adaptations are likely to be *abnormally* imperfect in protecting the rights and interests of people in the culture of poverty.

The major premise of my argument is that institutions that respect people's rights and interests do not happen by accident, but are always deliberately adapted to do so. This may seem to follow easily from the plain fact that nature does not spontaneously produce and justly distribute the

---

[64] Carol Stack, *All Our Kin: Strategies for Survival in a Black Community* (New York: Harper and Row, 1974).

things that we want and need. But the inference is not as obvious as it may seem. Certain theorists allow that nature does not spontaneously produce and justly distribute the things we need and want, but deny that institutions that respect people's rights and interests are deliberately adapted. They maintain that such institutions are always or almost always the unintended result of the actions of people pursuing other ends. This view has long been associated with F. A. Hayek.

Hayek often pointed to the widespread mistake of supposing that where there is an order "there must also have been a personal orderer."[65] According to Hayek, besides the order that results when "somebody puts the parts of an intended whole in their appropriate places," there also exist "in society orders of another kind which have not been designed by men but have resulted from the actions of individuals without their intending to create such an order. . . ."[66] As this remark indicates, Hayek does not deny that there can be order in society that is "intended" and designed. What he wishes to emphasize is that there can also be orders in society that are not "designed," but the unintended result of people pursuing other ends. Hayek sometimes made the distinction between the orders found in society in a slightly different way. According to Hayek, the "rules of conduct which govern the behavior of the individual members of the group" must be distinguished from the "order or pattern of actions which results" from the first kind of order and which applies to "the group as a whole."[67] Hayek emphasized that he used the word "rule" in this passage to stand for "any regularity of the conduct of individuals," whether or not such a "rule is 'known' to the individuals in any other sense than that they normally act in accordance with it."[68] This suggests that the order found in groups as a whole, which Hayek evidently believes is always unintended and spontaneous, may result from an order among individuals that is also unintended and spontaneous. But it also allows that the order found in groups as a whole may result from an order among individuals that is intended and designed, though the resulting order in the groups will still be unintended and spontaneous. Hayek makes this point explicitly in the first volume of *Law, Legislation, and Liberty*: "[W]hile the rules on which a spontaneous order rests may also be of spontaneous origin, this need not always be the case. . . . [I]t is possible that an order which would still have to be described as spontaneous rests on rules that are entirely the

---

[65] F. A. Hayek, "Kinds of Order in Society," *The New Individualist Review*, vol. 3 (1964), p. 5. See also "Notes on the Evolution of Systems of Rules of Conduct," and "The Results of Human Action but not of Human Design," both in F. A. Hayek, *Studies in Philosophy, Politics, and Economics* (Chicago: University of Chicago Press, 1967).

[66] Hayek, "Kinds of Order in Society," p. 4.

[67] Hayek, "Notes on the Evolution of Systems of Rules of Conduct," p. 66.

[68] *Ibid.*, p. 67.

result of deliberate design."[69] And the same point is allowed in "Kinds of Order in Society," published nine years earlier, though in that essay the emphasis is on the spontaneous and unintended nature of the order in the social whole that results from deliberately designed rules: "Though the conduct of the individuals which produces the social order is guided in part by deliberately enforced rules, the order is still a spontaneous order. . . ."[70]

I have no quarrel with this view. Indeed, I think that it is plausible, interesting, important, and probably true. But Hayek allies it with a theory of cultural evolution patterned on the analogy of biological evolution. This has led him to consistently play down the role of reason in the evolution of culture, and to depreciate the value and even the possibility of deliberately designed or adapted practices. The following comment is typical: "Tradition is the product of a process of selection guided not by reason but by success. It changes but can rarely be deliberately changed. Cultural selection is not a rational process. . . ."[71] I have a quarrel with this view. It directly contradicts what I claimed to be the major premise of my argument in the present section.

As in the case of biological evolution, Hayek believes that the driving force of cultural evolution is competition. According to Hayek, "the present order of society has largely arisen, not by design, but by the prevalence of the more effective institutions in a process of competition."[72] Hayek is not guilty of the gross error that invests an institution with positive qualities just because it survives. He argues that a mechanism exists that makes it likely that institutions that "prevail" are likely to be "effective." According to Hayek, effective institutions prevail because of the "selection by imitation of successful institutions."[73] Now I am willing to concede that people are likely to imitate successful institutions, but in order to argue that institutions that persist are effective, Hayek must have some reason to believe that institutions that persist have in fact "prevailed" in a "competition" with other institutions. Hayek's argument here is that institutions are always in competition with other institutions because of a human tendency to break traditional rules and try new ones. According to Hayek, "steps in the evolution of culture were made possible by some individuals breaking some traditional rules and practicing new forms of conduct." However, this appeal to human innovation is not

[69] F. A. Hayek, *Law, Legislation, and Liberty*, vol. 1, *Rules and Order* (London: Routledge and Kegan Paul, 1973), pp. 45, 46.

[70] Hayek, "Kinds of Order in Society," p. 8.

[71] F. A. Hayek, *Law, Legislation, and Liberty*, vol. 3, *The Political Order of a Free People* (London: Routledge and Kegan Paul, 1979), p. 166.

[72] *Ibid.*, p. 154.

[73] F. A. Hayek, *The Constitution of Liberty* (Chicago: University of Chicago Press, 1960), p. 59.

a concession that rules are deliberately designed. He goes on to say that culture continued to evolve, not because the innovators understood the changes they introduced to "be better," but "because the groups which acted on them prospered more than others and grew."[74] I take this to mean that the innovators were not trying to design better rules, although if their innovations were widely adopted and conduced to prosperity and growth, the unintended result may have been a change and a bettering of traditional rules.

Hayek's determination to depreciate the role of deliberately designed rules in the evolution of culture is also suggested by the following passage:

> The structures formed by traditional human practices are neither natural in the sense of being genetically determined, nor artificial in the sense of being the product of intelligent design, but the result of a process of winnowing or sifting, directed by the differential advantages gained by groups from practices adopted for some unknown and perhaps purely accidental reasons.[75]

The claim that the practices are adopted "for some unknown and perhaps purely accidental reasons" strongly suggests that the practices are not adopted because they are thought to be better practices. The implication is that although people change their practices by changing their behavior, in changing their behavior they do not thereby intend to change their practices.

I do not deny that practices and rules often change in this unintended way. I have myself suggested that various adaptations of mainstream institutions in the culture of poverty follow that pattern. But Hayek consistently suggests that changes in rules and practices are always or almost always unintended. I see no reason why this must be so. Hayek must have been misled by the evolutionary process as it occurs in biology. In that process the differences that are winnowed and sifted are accidental: nature introduces them, and nature has no intentions. But there is no warrant for the supposition that the differences that arise in the evolution of cultures *must* be accidental in a similar sense. Nature has no intentions, but human beings do. And if human beings have intentions, they can intend to change their practices.

Hayek may argue that although people may intend to change their practices, all practices arise unintentionally. I do not have to challenge this argument. I made no claim about the origins of practices; I claimed that institutions and practices that respect people's rights and interests are deliberately adapted to do so. The argument that all practices arise unin-

---

[74] *Ibid.*, p. 161.
[75] Hayek, *Law, Legislation, and Liberty*, vol. 3, p. 155.

tentionally does not contradict that claim; all practices may arise unintentionally, but they may have to be deliberately adapted in order to respect
people's rights and interests.

This is true of at least some practices. Not all practices that persist
respect people's rights and interests. Human history is replete with sav-
age, brutal, and wasteful practices. So even if Hayek is right that people
tend to imitate practices that conduce to growth and prosperity, the persistence of immoral practices implies either that practices that conduce to
growth and prosperity may be immoral, or that people sometimes imitate
practices that are immoral even when these practices do not conduce to
growth and prosperity. Hayek is aware of these possibilities: he suggests
that people tend to imitate the practices of successful groups as a whole,
without distinguishing between what the various practices that they imitate do.[76] This seems to concede that human beings must use their reason to distinguish between moral and immoral practices, and to redesign
effective but otherwise wasteful and wicked practices and prune them of
their wastefulness and wickedness.

Hayek does not altogether deny this. Speaking of moral rules, he
writes that "we must constantly re-examine our rules and be prepared to
question every single one of them. . . ." If questioning moral rules can
lead to changing them, Hayek seems to be allowing that we can change
our moral rules, and presumably that we can adjust our practices to make
them consistent with the new rules. But this concession to reason is
grudging. Hayek completes the sentence quoted above as follows: "we
can always do so only in terms of their consistency or compatibility with
the rest of the system from the angle of their effectiveness in contributing to the formation of the same kind of overall order of actions which all
the other rules serve."

The trouble with this claim is that it is not clear what Hayek means by
the "overall order of actions." In a footnote, he quotes a passage from
Ludwig von Mises which suggests that the order in question is "social
cooperation."[77] But this only raises the question of what Hayek means
by "social cooperation." Though he allows that the von Mises passage
expresses an "essential idea," he complains that it is too "rationalistically
formulated" for him. This suggests that the order he has in mind is simply the order that exists in the society. If this is correct, no argument is
needed to justify the conclusion that his concession to moral reform is not
only minimal but perverse.

Now consider the general claim that all or almost all institutions and
practices that respect others' rights and interests are deliberately designed
or adapted to do so. There is no reason to expect that practices that arise
as the unintended result of people pursuing other ends are going to

[76] *Ibid.*, p. 204.
[77] *Ibid.*, pp. 204, 205.

respect others' rights and interests. Why expect that accident will respect rights and interests? Perhaps it will be argued that people get involved in practices because it is in their interests to do so. This may be so, but it does not follow that the practices respect their rights and interests. A weak people become involved in a practice of paying tribute to a strong people. It is in their interests to do so because otherwise they will be slaughtered. Does it follow that the practice respects their rights and interests?

In rejecting the excesses of Hayek's view, I do not mean to imply that any human being, or any group of human beings, could ever devise efficient and moral institutions and practices for a people *de novo*. Plato may have believed that this was possible. In the *Republic*, he argued that the philosopher-kings could discover the "model" for appraising and reforming cities without drawing on the actual practices of real cities.[78] He expressed his contempt for such practices when he claimed that before genuine reformers—his philosopher-kings—would deign to sketch a constitution for a city, they would take it as their "sketching plate" and "wipe it clean."[79] But no one can devise a good constitution for a people without drawing heavily on the practices that it has intentionally—and unintentionally—produced. This is so, not only because the people will fail to understand, and will almost certainly reject, practices and rules that are completely alien to them, but also, and more importantly, because their practices and rules may contain moral truths that cannot be ignored in any plan to reform them.

Such reform can proceed in two main ways. One is the "piecemeal social engineering" suggested by Karl Popper.[80] The other is the more holistic engineering—perhaps it would be better to say "conservation"—associated with Rousseau. According to Rousseau, an unspoiled people can be saved from the otherwise inevitable descent into corruption by a constitution drawn up by a wise legislator.[81]

[78] See Plato, *Republic*, trans. G. M. A. Grube, rev. C. D. C. Reeve (Indianapolis: Hackett Publishing Company, 1992), Book IX, 592B.

[79] *Ibid.*, 501A.

[80] Hayek says that his idea that we can "tinker" with tradition is the same as Popper's idea of piecemeal social engineering (*Law, Legislation, and Liberty*, vol. 3, p. 204n. 50). This seems unlikely, although this is not the place to discuss the point at length. According to Popper, the piecemeal engineer will "adopt the method of searching for, and fighting against, the greatest and most urgent evils of society, rather than searching for, and fighting for, its greatest ultimate good" (Karl Popper, *The Open Society and Its Enemies* [New York: Harper and Row, 1965], vol. 1, p. 158). This does not sound like "tinkering" with tradition. See *ibid.*, p. 285n. 4, for Popper's cautious discussion of the similarity of his views to Hayek's views on this point.

[81] See, for example, ch. 7, "The Legislator," in Book II of Jean Jacques Rousseau, *The Social Contract*. In an earlier version of this essay, I had associated Rousseau's views with Plato's. I now believe that this was a serious error. Although Rousseau was, of course, strongly influenced by Plato, he did not share Plato's dismissive attitude toward the culture a people happens to have. He made it clear that the legislator must respect and draw on that culture. See, for example, *The Social Contract*, Book II, ch. 9.

If people must design and adjust their institutions to make them moral and effective, it is also the case that these institutions may always fail to be moral and effective. This is so not simply because human beings are fallible. More importantly, it is because unfavorable circumstances may make designing moral and effective institutions and practices particularly difficult. I believe that people who acquire a culture of poverty are in such unfavorable circumstances. This will be clear if we consider the circumstances that favor the reform of institutions and practices. I list four suggested by Rousseau.

First, the reformers must be in a position to adjust the institutions and practices to one another. This circumstance favors the reform of institutions and practices because institutions and practices interact. Its importance is reflected in Rousseau's insistence on the importance of a good constitution.

The second favorable circumstance for reforming institutions and practices is stable material conditions. This favors reform because such reform must adjust institutions and practices to particular material circumstances. If material circumstances change rapidly and unpredictably, the adjustment may be difficult or impossible to find, even if it exists. This is one of the reasons, though not the only one, why Rousseau was wary of material progress.

The third favorable circumstance for reforming institutions and practices is cultural autonomy. People are always reluctant to accept reform. This is why, as Rousseau put it, the "fathers of nations" have always tended to "attribute their own wisdom to the Gods."[82] But even this strategy is likely to fail if it is continually being disrupted by outside cultural influences.

The fourth favorable circumstance for reforming institutions and practices is the presence in the society of some factor that prevents the reformers from overlooking, ignoring, or slighting the interests of any group in the society. This circumstance will hardly be necessary if the reformers are extraordinarily sensitive, wise, and moral. Since they usually are not, reform is generally successful only to the extent that all groups in the society can compel the reformers to take proper account of their interests. Rousseau tried to combine these four conditions favorable to successful reform when he argued that a legitimate society could be founded only on the blueprint of a legislator, which must then be ratified by the assembled population.

Except for the fourth, these circumstances are often found in autonomous societies. Such societies have considerable ability to control changes in their material conditions, and to exclude or at least limit disruptive for-

[82] Jean Jacques Rousseau, *On the Social Contract with Geneva Manuscript and Political Economy*, ed. Roger D. Masters, trans. Judith R. Masters (New York: St. Martin's Press, 1978), p. 69.

eign cultural influences. Since they usually also have considerable control over their institutions and practices, they are usually able to achieve a good fit between their material conditions and their institutions and practices. The institutions and practices of such societies are therefore often reasonably effective in the sense that they usually tend to serve the interests of those who have the greatest say in how they are designed. However, these institutions and practices are often unjust, because the fourth circumstance usually fails to obtain even in autonomous societies. Autonomous societies have harbored the institution of slavery, discriminatory laws, and the practice of racial discrimination because various groups within them lacked the power or influence to ensure that institutions protected, or at least did not violate, their rights. More controversial examples of possibly immoral institutions harbored by autonomous societies are capitalism, socialism, private property, and the male-dominated nuclear family.

But unjust and imperfect as the institutions and practices of an autonomous society may be, there are general reasons to believe that the adaptations of these institutions and practices in dominated and dependent societies are likely to be worse. Since people with a culture of poverty are a dominated and dependent society, this claim applies to the adaptations they make of mainstream institutions and practices. This is not because people with a culture of poverty are less able or moral than people in the mainstream; it is because they live in circumstances that subvert reason and the social sentiments and prevent them from designing good and effective institutions. They have little control over their material conditions—these change drastically and unpredictably as the larger society tries to control and stabilize its own material conditions. Neither have people with a culture of poverty much control over outside cultural influences—these descend willy-nilly from the larger society as it adjusts to its very different material conditions. Further, people with a culture of poverty cannot soften economic and cultural shocks by making adjustments in the main institutions and practices that set the contexts for their lives, such as the legal system they must respect or the educational system they must use. They have no control over these institutions and practices. They have limited control over only some of the institutions in their communities, such as the family. Finally, the inequalities that undermine the morality of institutions and practices in the mainstream are duplicated among those with a culture of poverty, though sometimes with a new twist. For example, if institutions are malformed in the mainstream because men are able to dominate women there, in the culture of poverty some institutions may be malformed because in that context women are able to dominate men.

The case I have in mind is the family, and the imbalance of power in question is partly caused by the mainstream. Among the poor black people Oscar Lewis thinks are most likely to have a culture of poverty in the

United States, men have small opportunities for well-paying jobs, but unmarried women with children are eligible for AFDC payments. As Carol Stack observes, the welfare system thus "collaborates in weakening the position of the black male."[83] This discourages both the men and the women from entering into the traditional two-parent family, and encourages instead the spread of the single-parent female-headed family.[84] But the single-parent female-headed family evidently fails to protect the rights of the children nearly as well as the traditional two-parent family. According to one recent study, there is "an accumulation of data showing that intact biological-parent families offer children very large advantages compared to any other family or non-family structure one can imagine." Further, according to this study, the advantages in question are not only "indisputable in economic terms, they are equally hard to contest where children's emotional development, behavior, health and school performance are concerned."[85]

It may be objected that welfare plays a small role in the decline of the two-parent family. Christopher Jencks, among many others, has urged this point.[86] Jencks may or may not be right; the issue is controversial. But it does not affect my general argument. I am not concerned to indict welfare, but to argue that people with a culture of poverty are trying to adapt institutions in peculiarly unfavorable circumstances. Jencks's own explanation of the decline of the two-parent family confirms this. According to Jencks, the real culprit is cultural influences from the mainstream. In the mainstream, single-parenthood became acceptable as "a byproduct of growing individualism and commitment to personal freedom."[87] This change in attitude spread to those with a culture of poverty, making it even more difficult for them to design a version of the family suitable to their circumstances. As Jencks notes, though the change "certainly improved the lives of the educated elite," it proved disastrous to the poor in their very different circumstances.[88]

Another objection to my argument appeals to the peculiar sentiments those with a culture of poverty are likely to experience. It may be argued that since people with a culture of poverty are especially vulnerable to misfortune, they are likely to be especially capable of sympathizing with the misfortunes of others, and consequently are likely to be moved to

---

[83] Stack, *All Our Kin* (*supra* n. 64), p. 113.

[84] The most famous argument for this claim is in Charles Murray, *Losing Ground* (New York: Basic Books, 1984), p. 157.

[85] Richard T. Gill, "For the Sake of the Children," *The Public Interest*, no. 108 (Summer 1992), p. 81. Apparently this is somewhat controversial, at least with respect to the emotional and social development of children. See, for example, Jencks, *Rethinking Social Policy* (*supra* n. 5), p. 130.

[86] See, for example, Jencks, *Rethinking Social Policy*, pp. 130, 131.

[87] *Ibid.*, p. 135.

[88] *Ibid.*, p. 134. For further examples of this phenomenon, see Cornel West, *Race Matters* (Boston: Beacon Press, 1993), p. 56.

adapt mainstream institutions so as to protect each other's rights as much as is possible in the circumstances. On this general ground, a critic may argue that I may be overlooking subtle ways in which the culture of poverty's version of the family nurtures and protects the children. But sympathy is not enough to appropriately adapt practices and institutions to protect rights and interests. One must be able to see what to do, and people in the culture of poverty are not in circumstances where it is easy to see what to do. There are subjective difficulties in addition to the objective ones already mentioned. The anxiety that poverty may foster does not encourage clear thinking, and the envy and despair poverty amidst plenty may breed can only discourage it further. Finally, vulnerability may have effects that are less desirable than the ones just lauded. If it can make us more capable of sympathy, it can also make us insecure, self-concerned, and selfish. This may have occurred in the example under consideration. However much we admire the strength of those women in the culture of poverty who shoulder unaided the burden of raising their children, their adaptation of the mainstream's version of the family is worse for their children than the institution they adapted it from. It is true that it enables them to claim their independence, and enables the men to save their dignity. But independence in their straitened circumstances is too slender to be worth the lost generations, and it is a false dignity that is saved by abandoning one's children.

V. Assessment of the Existentialists

I turn now to the existentialists. My exposition of their position was based on the assumption that Ralph Ellison's comments on Negro culture apply to the culture of poverty. I made this supposition, provisionally, because critics of the culture of poverty often cite Ellison as a champion. To complicate matters further, certain writers who want to prove that a distinctive Negro culture exists think they can make their case by showing that some blacks have a distinctive culture. But what they usually do is show that some blacks have something remarkably like a culture of poverty.[89] This argument is fallacious. There is nothing distinctively Negro about the culture of poverty. And if there is a Negro culture it is certainly not a culture of poverty. This is so for the obvious reason that most blacks are not in the circumstances that breed the culture of poverty. Many of them may be, and these may have a culture of poverty, but it is invidious to argue that their culture is "Negro culture."

Ellison himself raises questions that are less easy to dispose of, because even if Negro culture is not a culture of poverty, Ellison seems ready to

---

[89] See, for example, Charles Keil, *Urban Blues* (Chicago: University of Chicago Press, 1968), and the discussion in Charles Valentine, *Culture and Poverty* (Chicago: University of Chicago Press, 1968), pp. 84–87 and 123–25.

reject the culture-of-poverty idea for the same sort of reasons he rejects the idea that "Negro culture" is pathological. For example, Ellison strongly attacked the "Moynihan Report," which dealt with a culture of poverty among poor blacks, in terms similar to those in which he defended "Negro culture."[90] His comments on a passage from Richard Wright's autobiography, Black Boy, also suggest that he would reject the idea of a culture of poverty. In that passage, Wright wrote of the "strange absence of real kindness in Negroes," of the "cultural barrenness" of their lives, and of how they lacked "genuine passion," "great hope," "traditions," and the "sentiments that bind man, to man," and reported that he had come to see that what had been taken for Negroes' "emotional strength" was really their "negative confusions," "flights," "fears," and "frenzy under pressure." This list of traits is clearly reminiscent of the psychological traits Lewis claimed to be common in the culture of poverty, and Ellison reacts to it with evident distaste. He denies that he could "even raise such a question about any segment of humanity."[91] The enigma of Wright, he says, is that Wright "could be so wonderful an example of human possibility but could not for ideological reasons depict a Negro as intelligent, as creative or as dedicated as himself."[92]

But it all depends on what Ellison means by people being creative. If he means that even in the circumstances of the culture of poverty people are likely to reason originally and soundly — and that consequently there cannot be any such thing as the culture of poverty, as Lewis interprets it — then his views are even less plausible than those of the situationalists that I have already criticized. Ellison reminds us that people have made an acceptable way of life in caves and on cliffs. What he says is true but irrelevant. People living in caves and on cliffs are not in the circumstances that people with a culture of poverty are in. Domination by nature, however harsh, is never as morally destructive as domination by other human beings. Although people in caves and on cliffs may be poorer in material terms than people in the culture of poverty, as Lewis suggests in his discussion of "primitive" and "preliterate" people, they are nevertheless in circumstances that are more favorable to the development of an "integrated, satisfying and self-sufficient culture."[93]

On the other hand, if Ellison means that people are creative in the sense that they often have ideas that are not derived in any straightforward, pedestrian way from extant ideas and influences, then I freely allow that people in the circumstances of the culture of poverty can be creative. But being creative in this sense, is consistent with being dreadfully wrong. Further, creative thinking is likely to be peculiarly wrong-

[90] Ralph Ellison, "No Apologies," Harper's Magazine, July 1967, pp. 8–20.
[91] Ralph Ellison, "The World and the Jug," in his Shadow and Act (supra n. 48), p. 119.
[92] Ibid., p. 120.
[93] Lewis, La Vida (supra n. 19), p. xlviii.

headed when it takes place among the oppressed. As Jon Elster notes, oppressed people have a "tendency" to "invent" ideologies justifying their oppression.[94] Ellison's own criticisms of Wright illustrate this. Ellison says that Wright was wonderfully creative; but he also implies that Wright was badly mistaken. And the circumstances of the culture of poverty are a particularly harsh form of oppression. Certainly then, we can allow that human beings are creative, and still insist that their culture can be conspicuously flawed.

In sum, I am inclined to agree with Lewis that the culture of poverty is a poverty of culture. As I have often emphasized, this is not because people with a culture of poverty are less able than other people. It is because they live in conditions that prevent normal human beings from creating a moral and rational way of life. Their failure to create a moral and rational way of life does not mean that they are unaware of the requirements of morality and of their loss. The way they live may beat some of them into amorality, but others will retain their moral sense, and express anger and mortification at their failure, and indignation at the circumstances that contribute to it, sometimes in the form of art of a high order. In these ways they reveal their inextinguishable humanity. I maintain, however, that it is sheer romanticism to expect that their mores and practices will be models of how to live.

There is one last difficulty that must be considered. Someone will object that even if I am right about the culture of poverty, I cannot use it to weaken the presupposition that cultures in general are repositories of moral insight, because the culture of poverty is not a genuine culture. This objection is always possible because of the notorious ambiguity about what a culture is.[95] The objector can always define culture so that all "genuine" cultures are paradigms of moral insight. This procedure is obviously question-begging; those who indulge in it must be more careful about what they endorse as cultural pluralism.

VI. Eliminating the Culture of Poverty

How can the culture of poverty be eliminated? Here I disagree with the culturalists; indeed, I think their position is inconsistent. They argue that the culture of poverty cannot be eliminated by providing opportunities because its values encourage people to ignore opportunities. But their account of the culture of poverty suggests that this argument is too simple. Lewis claims that people with a culture of poverty feel despair because they cannot achieve success in terms of the values and goals of

---

[94] Elster, *Sour Grapes* (*supra* n. 63), pp. 115, 145.
[95] See the variety of definitions in A. L. Kroeber and Clyde Kluckholm, *Culture* (New York: Vintage Books, 1952).

the mainstream. But no one feels despair because he cannot achieve success in terms of values and goals he rejects. Consequently, Lewis's claim implies that people in the culture of poverty somehow still cherish the values of the mainstream. But the values of the mainstream presumably encourage people to take advantage of opportunities. Consequently, people with a culture of poverty may very well take advantage of opportunities.

But if people with a culture of poverty cherish mainstream values, they also have other, nonmainstream values. In a classic paper, American anthropologist Hyman Rodman describes how this comes to pass. According to Rodman,

> the lower-class person, without abandoning the general values of the society, develops an alternative set of values. Without abandoning the values placed upon success, such as high income and high educational attainment, he stretches the values so that lesser degrees of success also become desirable. Without abandoning the values of marriage and legitimate childbirth, he stretches these values so that a non-legal union and legally illegitimate children are also desirable. The result is that the members of the lower class, in many areas, have a wider range of values than others within the society.[96]

Rodman gives a twist to the fable of the fox and the grapes to illustrate his theory. In the fable, the fox "adapted" by declaring the unattainable grapes to be sour; but Rodman points out that his "adaptive lower-class" foxes acquire a "taste for sour grapes."[97] This illustration is suggestive, but it also shows that Rodman's account of the "value stretch" cannot be altogether correct. There is nothing inconsistent in having a taste for sweet grapes and a taste for sour grapes. One can have both comfortably. But there is something inconsistent about having a taste for the values of the mainstream and a taste for the values of the culture of poverty. One cannot have both tastes comfortably. The values of the mainstream imply that one should not have the values of the culture of poverty. So Rodman's value stretchers cannot be as composed as he implies. They are disturbed by their failure to live by mainstream values, and they *try* to get relief by adopting new values as Rodman suggests. But this strategy cannot give them relief, because the new values are inconsistent with the old ones, and human beings are distressed by having inconsistent values and try to eliminate such inconsistencies by changing their values.[98] Since

[96] Hyman Rodman, "The Lower-Class Value Stretch," *Social Forces*, December 1963, p. 209.

[97] *Ibid.*

[98] Leon Festinger, *A Theory of Dissonance* (Evanston: Row, Peterson and Co., 1956), pp. 3–7.

people with a culture of poverty are in circumstances that make it difficult for them to change either set of values, they lurch continually
between distress and despair. This may be the cause of their alleged
pathologies, but it is also reason to believe that the culture of poverty is
not durable, and will not outlast a favorable change in the circumstances
of the poor.

Philosophy, The University of North Carolina at Chapel Hill

INDEX